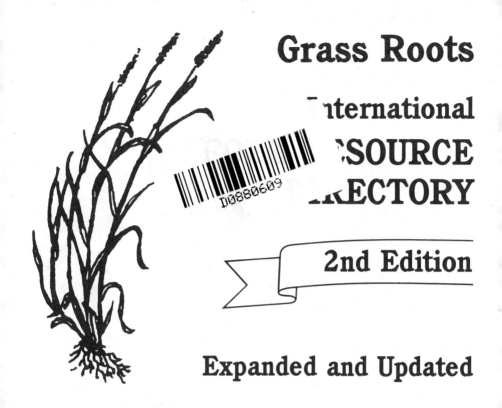

Grass Roots

International RESOURCE DIRECTORY

2nd Edition

Expanded and Updated

Edited by

Leslie Berman and Heather Wood

GRASS ROOTS PRODUCTIONS
NEW YORK•HOBOKEN•NEW LISBON

The cover photograph was taken by Emily Friedman at the Winnipeg Folk Festival (Canada).

Cover photo : (l to r) John Munro (Scotland/Australia), Eric Bogle (Australia), Larry Hanks (United States), Steve Goodman (United States), Richard Thompson (United Kingdom).

Many of the logos and symbols used in this book are the Trade Marks of the various companies listed.

The editors wish to express their heartfelt appreciation and thanks to the following persons and organizations, whose help in compiling this directory was inestimable:
Paula Ballan, Allison Berman, Sharon Davis, Roger Dietz, Richard Flohil, Emily Friedman, Dr. Nancy Groce, Sherry Hicks Glover, Niles Hokkanen, Tom Martin-Erickson, Mark Moss of SING OUT, Sonny Ochs, Tom Paley, Rik Palieri, Ken Roseman, Barry Smiler, Tracy Strann, Andy Wallace, Suzette Watkins, Thom Wolke, and all the people who took the trouble to return questionnaires and answer our telephone calls.
Special thanks to Richard Factor of Eventide, without whom the book would not exist.
Special thanks to Daniel Fisher, for maintaining calm in the face of hysteria.
Thanks to Andy Wallace who started Grass Roots Productions.

Data processed by an Osborne I computer, output via a Juki 6100 printer.

AB Graphics of New York City kindly allowed us to use their facilities for design and production. Thanks to Ron Schindlinger, David Blue, and John Guzik for typesetting assistance.

Printed by Braun Brumfield, Ann Arbor, Michigan.

GRASS ROOTS INTERNATIONAL FOLK RESOURCE DIRECTORY 1986/87

10 9 8 7 6 5 4 3 2 1

ISSN Number: 8755-6855

ISBN Number: 0-9614589-1-7

Printed in the United States of America

GRASS ROOTS PRODUCTIONS
444 West 54th Street
New York, NY 10019

CONTENTS

Still Crazy After all This Year...3
How To Use This Book..............4
USA Section
National Organizations............6
Regional Organizations............8
Arts Agencies.....................8
Ethnic & Foreign Language Orgs....9
Publications.....................12
Radio............................14
Film.............................15
Video............................16
Agents...........................17
Photographers....................18
Support Services.................18
  Mailing Lists; Record Production &
  Sound Reinforcement; Record Pres-
  sing & Cassette Duplication; Rec-
  ord Promotion; Travel Organizing
Songwriters......................19
Record Companies & Distributors..20
Books............................28
Instrument Build/Repair & Mail
  Order Stores...................30
Instruction......................33
Graduate Studies.................33
Archives.........................34
Dance............................35
Deaf Community...................36
Filk Music.......................36
Listings By State................37

Articles
"Taking Care of Business"
by Heather Wood..................159
"Records From Scratch"
by Leslie Berman.................161
"Enough About Me, What Do You
Think Of Me?" by Roger Dietz....164
Copyright Basics.................166
"The First Annual Festival of
Your Dreams" by Paula Ballan....167
"Collecting Folklore Before Its
All Gone" by Dr. Nancy Groce....170
The Deaf Community:
Some Definitions by Sherry Hicks
Glover, with an Introduction
by Leslie Berman.................173
"Local Dance On The Upswing"
by Andy Wallace..................175
Australia:
"An Insider's Report" and "Going
Legal: Australian Visas"
by Suzette Watkins...............176
Australia Section................178
Canada Section...................181
United Kingdom Section...........192
European Section.................210
Rest Of The World Section.......225
Survey Questionnaire.............231
Listing in Next Edition.........232

Still Crazy After All This Year

Welcome to the Second Edition of the Grass Roots International Folk Resource Directory. Thanks are due to all those who bought the last one, and to those who have waited patiently for this one. Thanks also to those who told us how useful they found the first edition, and to those who helped us improve the second.

Since the publication of the first edition, there have been major changes in the folk scene. Performers and organizations who followed the advice and used the resources of the first edition improved the quality of their pub-

licity efforts, and became more professional in their attitude. This helped improve the general public's image of the folk scene, and simultaneously attract more diverse audiences.

As well as working on this second edition, the editors attended conferences on the state of the folk scene, run by Hey Rube! in Minnesota, and by the Folk Arts Network in Boston. We met with officials of the English Folk Dance and Song Society in London, to discuss major upheavals in that august body. We attended festivals and performances in the U.S., the U.K., and Canada, and experienced firsthand the continuity from the oldtimers to the newcomers. We learned of many successes and a few failures. Overall, the folk scene appears healthy. But as our varied activities showed us, it is still fragmented.

The need for unity was most clearly brought home to us when we learned of the U.S. Immigration and Naturalization Service's proposed changes to the criteria for issuance of temporary work visas for foreign performers. Baldly stated, the new rules would deny visas to all but the most commercially successful performing artists. This would affect not only audiences, but also agents, promoters, record companies, and all the small adjunct businesses who base their livelihood on such tours, not only those on the folk scene, but in all performing arts movements.

We learned of all this when Leslie was researching an article for the Village Voice on the growing difficulties experienced by artists and their agents in obtaining temporary work visas for U.S. appearances. A chance remark by one interviewee alerted her to the INS's plans. Heather researched the proposed rules and determined that

they were particularly disastrous for the folk scene. Together we spread the alarm. The response was tremendous: letters and phone calls poured into the INS, and the campaign is continuing.

Our experiences in this campaign brought us to the realization that this was only one case out of many, where the folk scene suffered from the lack of one central clearinghouse organization that could coordinate efforts nationwide, to protect the rights and interests of its members. In particular, there is a need for a trade organization, like the American Dairy Council, or the Country Music Association, or indeed the National Ornament and Electric Lights Christmas Association, to enable the small businesses of the scene to enhance and applaud each other's efforts, and to raise the public profile of our industry. Grass Roots Productions is considering ways and means of setting up such an organization. To that end, we've included a pertinent questionnaire at the back of this book.

We wish you success in all your folk endeavors, and look forward to seeing you in the Third Edition.

How To Use This Book

We the editors have attempted to provide the most up-to-date and correct information in all our listings, however, we are well aware that errors are unavoidable. Organizations fold up their tents and steal away into the night, new ones spring up like mushrooms. People change. We neither endorse by inclusion, nor condemn by exclusion any persons or organizations in the field of folk. If we haven't catered to your particular interest, please write and tell us. We reserve the right to select listings for subsequent editions.

Courtesy
Most of the people in the folk music scene are dedicated volunteers. Many of the telephone numbers listed here are homes, not offices. Please be considerate about evening calls (especially across time zones). If you write to a club or organization, it may be helpful to enclose a stamped, self-addressed envelope. International Reply Coupons can be used between countries.

And Why
We hope that you will gain from this book, whether you are performers or audience, a feeling that there are a lot of us out there.

Those of us who love folk music in any or all of its various guises have almost a duty to share our love and our knowledge with others. Write to the press and to radio stations. Send out press releases. Encourage local folk organizations by attending, and also encourage non-folk organizations to participate. Let's make our presence felt. Sing, play, listen, organize - but most importantly: enjoy.

Order of Listings
We have tried to put the entries into a usable order. For example, national organizations are arranged alphabetically. Entries for a particular state are divided into broad categories: Venues (including clubs, concert promoters, and places to play), Print (including newspapers, newsletters, magazines and journals), Radio (including television) Festivals and Museums (self-explanatory), etc., then listed alphabetically by city, except Festivals, which are listed alphabetically by name within each state.

Codes
We have avoided codes, preferring rather to use abbreviations which we hope will be comprehensible: U or Univ for University, state two-letter codes, PG for a radio station's Program Guide, CP for a college's publication.

Publications and Radio Show Titles
These are all in capital letters. Two at one address are linked by lower-case "and." Where "and" appears in the actual title, it is signified by "&."

Symbols
Many areas of the folk scene have been very adequately covered by other publications and directories. We have not attempted to duplicate their efforts, but have listed them instead. The pointing finger symbol indicates such a directory. ☞

* New and updated entries are indicated by an asterisk.

INTERNATIONAL SECTION

We have tried to make international addresses conform with the customs of each country. European countries frequently have a country letter-code followed by a number preceding the city name. The English spelling of city and country names has been used. Telephone area codes/dialling codes have been enclosed in parentheses: this may not be the preferred form of the country concerned, for which we apologise.

Order of Listings
International listings are simply grouped by category under the individual country, and alphabetically by city within each category. Festivals are listed alphabetically by name within each country.

Political Statements
We have made only one political statement in this book, which is concerning South Africa, q.v. Decisions which may be construed politically: Northern Ireland listings have been included under United Kingdom; Southern Ireland has been included under Europe.

We tried again to think of a title for the Rest of the World section which wasn't too unwieldy, but you may notice that we haven't.

Where to find information
The Embassies and Consulates of the various nations are good sources, as are national tourist offices and national airlines. These may be found in your telephone directory.

N. Extremely B.
Please remember that many countries require you to have a visa even to visit, and some also expect innoculations and vaccinations. It is ILLEGAL to accept work, even unpaid work, in most countries where you are a foreigner. Check the regulations, and see our chapter on Australia Visas for some advice which is relevant for most countries.

NATIONAL ORGANIZATIONS

*ALLIANCE FOR CULTURAL
  DEMOCRACY
2262 W 119th Pl, Blue Island IL
60406 (312)388-3871. Allen
Schwartz. Community-based arts
programs and activist artists.

*AMERICAN ASSN FOR STATE
  & LOCAL HISTORY
172 2nd Ave N, #102, Nashville TN
37201 (615)255-2971. Directory of
Historical Societies.

*AMER COUNCIL FOR THE ARTS
570 7th Ave, New York NY 10018
(212)354-6655. Arts mangement and
advocacy.

*AMERICAN FOLKLIFE CENTER
Library of Congress, Washington DC
20540 (202)287-6590. Newsletter,
journal, other publications.

*AMER MUSIC FESTIVALS ASSN
3321 Granada Dr, Cameron Park, CA
95682 (916)677-3037.

*ASCAP - AMER SOC OF COMPOSERS,
  AUTHORS, & PUBLISHERS
1 Lincoln Plaza, New York NY 10023
(212)595-3050. Collects royalties
for publisher & songwriter members.
Workshops, awards, membership
directory.

*ARCHIVE OF CONTEMPORARY MUSIC
110 Chambers St, New York NY 10007
(212)964-2296. For all forms of
popular music. Wants samples
w/press kits. Info/research and
fact-checking service.

*ASSN OF COLLEGE, UNIVERSITY, &
  COMMUNITY ARTS ADMINISTRATORS
6225 University Ave, Madison WI
53705-1099 (608)233-7400. Holds
booking conferences, showcases,
etc. Info on facilities etc.
BLUEGRASS MUSIC ASSN
PO Box 16, Elm Spring AR 72728.
Newsletter.

*BMI - BROADCAST MUSIC INC
320 W 57th St, New York NY 10019
(212)586-2000. Collects royalties
for publisher & songwriter members.
Workshops, awards, membership
directory.

*JOHN C CAMPBELL FOLK SCHOOL
Brasstown NC 28902. Weekends
throughout the year. Music, dance,
instruments, stories.

*CTR FOR ARTS INFORMATION
625 Broadway, New York NY 10012
(212)677-7548. Library, info ctr,
help w/fundraising, organization.
Free list of publications.

*CONCERT MUSIC BROADCASTERS
c/o KKHI, Westin St. Francis Hotel,
San Francisco CA 94102 (415)986-
2151. Len Mattson.

*DISABLED ARTISTS NETWORK
PO Box 10781, New York NY 10025.
Sandra Aronson. Info exchange ctr.
List of resources for disabled
artists.

*FOLKLINE
(202)287-2000. Run by American
Folklife Ctr & Library of Congress.
Natl info on folklore & folklife,
inc job, grant, training openings.
24-hour taped service.

FOLKLORE INSTITUTE
504 N Fess St, Bloomington IN
47405. Various journals, research
lists, etc.

*FOUNDATION CENTERS
Provide funding info on corps and
foundations, info on non-profit org
management, fund-raising.
*312 Sutter St, San Francisco CA
94108 (415)397-0902.

*1001 Connecticut Ave NW, Washington
DC 20036 (202)331-1400.

*79 5th Ave, New York NY 10003
(212)620-4230.

*1442 Hanna Bldg, 1422 Euclid Ave,
Cleveland OH 33115-2001 (216)861-
1933.

*FREEDOM SONG NETWORK
885 Clayton, San Francisco CA
94110. Faith Petric.

*FUND RAISING SCHOOL
PO Box 3237, San Rafael CA 94912-
3237 (415)457-3520. Runs courses.

*HEY RUBE! ASSN FOR THE ADVANCEMENT OF TRADITIONAL PERFORMING ARTISTS
PO Box 14-6366, Chicago IL 60614. Member-based org of performers and others. Career assistance, inc gig list, radio list, group health insurance, instrument insurance. National info network. Nwsltr.

*HOSPITAL AUDIENCES, INC
1540 Broadway, New York NY 10036 (212)575-7681. Lynn Kable, In-facility Dir. For the cultural needs of the institutionalized and homebound.

*INDIAN ARTS & CRAFTS BOARD
US Dept of Interior, Rm 4004, Washington DC 20240.

INSTITUTE OF CELTIC STUDIES
4 Greenlay St, Nashua NH 03063. Annual Celtic Calendar.

*INTL BLUEGRASS MUSIC ASSN
PO Box 2277B, Nashville TN 37202. Peter V. Kuykendall, Chairman. To foster bluegrass. Info service, newsletter, directory, monthly press releases on bluegrass happenings.

*MUSIC CRITICS ASSN
6201 Tuckerman Ln, Rockville MD 20852 (301)530-9527.

*MUSICAL MAJORITY
c/o Gold Spaceship, 1416 N La Brea, Hollywood CA 90028 (213)469-2411. Danny Goldberg. Working to defend the rights of expression in music.

*NATL ACADEMY OF RECORDING ARTS & SCIENCES
303 N Glenoaks Blvd, #140, Burbank CA 91502 (818)843-8233. Join, and vote on the Grammys (there's a folk category!).

*NATL ACADEMY OF SONGWRITERS
6772 Hollywood Blvd, Hollywood CA 90028 (213)463-7178. Non-profit info clearinghouse.

*NATL ASSN FOR CAMPUS ACTIV
PO Box 6828, Columbia SC 29260 (803)782-7121. Holds showcases, conferences. Good for reaching college market.

*NATIONAL ASSN FOR THE PRESERVATION & PERPETUATION OF STORY-TELLING
PO Box 112, Slemons Hse, Fox St, Jonesborough TN 37659 (615)753-2171. Resource ctr, directory, archive, festivals. YARNSPINNER 12/yr, journal 4/yr. Mail order for books of stories.

*NATL ASSN OF INDEPENDENT REC DISTRIBUTORS & MANUFACTURERS
6935 Airport Hwy La, Pennsauken NJ 08109. (609)885-8085.

*NATL ENDOWMENT FOR THE ARTS
1100 Pennsylvania Ave NW, Washington DC 20506. Encourages & supports American arts and artists. Has Folk Arts funding program.

*NATL TRADITIONAL COUNTRY MUSIC ASSOCIATION
106 Navajo, Council Bluffs IA 51501 (712)366-1136. Bob Everhart. Holds annual Labor Day fest. TRADITION quarterly.

*NEW SONG LIBRARY
PO Box 295, Northampton MA 01061 (413)586-9485. Johanna Halbeisen. Members and others can access library of topical songs. Info & resource network for topical/political singers & songwriters. Radio show SING ABOUT IT.

*PEOPLE'S MUSIC NETWORK
for Songs of Freedom & Struggle
158 Cliff St, Norwich CT 06360. Charlie King. Political song org. SASSAFRASS. Conferences.

*MIDWEST PEOPLE'S MUSIC NETWORK
Box 8235, Lake St Sta, Minneapolis MN 55408.

*RIAA - RECORDING INDUSTRY ASSN OF AMERICA
888 7th Ave, New York NY 10106 (212)765-4330. Working against piracy.

*SOC FOR ETHNOMUSICOLOGY
PO Box 2984, Ann Arbor MI 48106 (313)665-9400. Journals, newsltr, conferences, monographs, etc.

SOC OF INTER-CELTIC ARTS
96 Marguerite Ave, Waltham MA 02154 (617)899-2204. K. Gilligan. Anual journal KELTICA.

ARTS AGENCIES

Listings include organizations and publications which cover more than one state. Some are duplications of state listings.

*ROBIN BLECHER MEMORIAL FUND
   CONFLICT CALENDAR (Northeast)
535 Concord Ave, Lexington MA 02173
(617)862-7837. Billie Hockett. To
promote Celtic and British trad
music. Calendar 4/yr.

*FAIRS & FESTIVALS IN THE
   NORTHEAST
Arts Extension Serv, Div of Cont
Ed, UMASS, Amherst MA 01003. lists
over 500 drafts, visual arts, and
musical events.

*FOLK ARTS NETWORK (New England)
PO Box 867, Cambridge MA 02238
(617)864-2970. Stephen H Baird.
Info/resource ctr. Directory.

*FOLKFARE (New England)
Box 586, Hadley MA 01035. Calendar
for folk events.

*FSGW NEWSLETTER (DC and area)
Box 19114, 20th St Stn, Washington
DC 20036-0114. Monthly listing of
music & dance events.

*THE FOLKNIK (CA and all over)
SFFMC, 885 Clayton St, San
Francisco CA 94117 (415)661-2217.
6/yr. Calendar, news, reviews, etc.

*THE HORNPIPE (Southeast)
PO Box 1618, Lexington SC 29072.
Daniel E Harmon. 6/yr. Calendar,
reviews, news, etc.

*KEEP PICKIN" (Tri-State area)
3005 N Anthony Blvd, Ft Wayne IN
46805. John P Brennan. Calendar.

*NY PINEWOODS FMC NEWSLETTER
   (NY, NJ, CT, etc)
26 Ravensdale Rd, Hastings-on-
Hudson NY 10706. Monthly. Annual
festivals list. Reviews, news, etc.

*NORTHEAST FOLKLORE SOC (New
   England & Eastern Canada)
S Stevens Hall, U of ME, Orono ME
04469. NE FOLKLORE 1/yr.

SW CELTIC MUSIC ASSN
PO Box 24222, Ft Worth TX 76124.
Ken Fleming.

*VOLUNTEER LAWYERS FOR THE ARTS
1560 Broadway, #711, New York NY
10036 (212)575-1150.

WELSH HARP SOCIETY
4204 Clark, Kansas City MO 64111.
Judith Brougham. Newsletter.

*WILD - WOMEN'S INDEP LABEL
   DISTRIBUTING NETWORK
PO Box 9012, Glendale CA 91205
(213)956-6624. Betsy York.

*WORLD FOLK MUSIC ASSN
PO Box 405553, Washington DC 20016.
To promote & preserve folk music.

REGIONAL ORGANIZATIONS

Some of the individual State Arts
Agencies are listed under their
respective states. Listed below are
associations of agencies. Many arts
agencies publish calendars of
events in their area, so be sure to
keep them informed of festivals,
concerts, etc. Arts agencies are
good sources of funding info, and
can help with publicity. Some
arrange block bookings for artists
in their area. They are a resource.
Use them.

ASSN OF STATE ARTS AGENCIES
   OF THE UPPER MIDWEST
528 Hennepin Ctr, #302, Minneapolis
MN 55403 (612)341-0775. IA, MN, ND,
SD, WI.

CPAC
PO Box 4204, Honolulu HI 96813
(808)524-6128. Pacific Arts and
Cultures: AK, AS, CA, CM, GU.

GREAT LAKES ARTS ALLIANCE
11424 Bellflower Rd, Cleveland OH
44106 (216)229-1098. IL, IN, MI,
OH.

MID-AMERICA ARTS ALLIANCE
20 W 9th St, #550, Kansas City MO
64105 (816)421-1388. AR, KS, MO,
NE, OK.

*MID-ATLANTIC STATES
  ARTS CONSORTIUM
11 E Chase St, #7-B, Baltimore MD
21202 (301)685-1400. Covers DE, DC,
MD, NJ, NY, PA, VA, WV.

*NATIONAL ASSN OF LOCAL
  ARTS AGENCIES
1785 Massachusetts Ave NW, #413,
Washington DC 20036 (202)483-8670.
Membership list available.

NATIONAL ASSN OF STATE
  ARTS AGENCIES
1010 Vermont Ave NW, Washington DC
20005 (202)347-6352. List
available.

NEW ENGLAND FOUNDATION
  FOR THE ARTS
25 Mt Auburn St, Cambridge MA 02138
(617)492-2914. CT, MA, ME, NH, RI,
VT.

SOUTHERN ARTS FEDERATION
1401 Peachtree St NE, #122, Atlanta
GA 30309 (404)874-7244. AL, FL, GA,
KY, LA, MS, NC, SC, TN, VA.

WESTERN ARTS FEDERATION
141 E Palace Ave, Santa Fe NM 87501
(505)988-1166. AZ, CO, ID, MT, NM,
NV, OR, UT, WA, WY.

ETHNIC & FOREIGN LANGUAGE

*AFRICAN-AMERICAN INSTITUTE
833 UN Plaza, New York NY 10016
(212)949-5666. For understanding
through education and cultural
programs.

*AMERICAN SCANDINAVIAN FNDN
127 E 73rd St, New York NY 10021
(212)879-9779. Quarterly magazine.

*ASSN OF HISPANIC ARTS
200 E 87th St, New York NY 10028
(212)369-7054. Jane Delgado. Info
on Hispanic arts, national resource
ctr. Newsletter.

*AUSTRIAN AMERICAN FEDN
31 E 69th St, New York NY 10021
(212)535-216.

*CARIBBEAN CULTURAL CTR
408 W 58th St, New York NY 10019
(212)307-7420. Marta Moreno.
Exhibitions, concerts, dances.
Journal 4/yr, festival.

*CHARAS
605 E 9th St, New York NY 10009
(212)982-0672. Carlos Gaarcia.
Concerts, dance presentations.
Workshops for kids and adults.

CHICANO STUDIES CENTER
405 Hilgard Ave, Los Angeles CA
90024. Journal 3/yr of Chicano
culture.

*CHINESE AMERICAN ARTS COUNCIL
27 Division St, New York NY (212)
431-9740.

*CHINESE MUSICAL &.THEATRICAL ASSN
181 Canal St, New York NY 10013
(212)226-8744.

*COMMONWEALTH SOC OF N AMERICA
2201 Wilson Blvd, #202, Arlington
VA 22201 (703)524-3121. Joan Young.

*COUNCIL ON INTL EDUCATIONAL
  EXCHANGE
205 E 42nd St, New York NY 10017
(212)661-1414 x 1209. Exchange
programs for students.

CZECH NATL COUNCIL/USA
2137 S Lombard Ave, Cicero IL
60650. For Czech Americans. Mag.

DUTCH IMMIGRANT SOCIETY
2216 Edgewood SE, Grand Rapids MI
49506. Magazine.

*EAST EUROPEAN FOLKLIFE CTR
3150 Portland St, Eugene OR 97405
(503)344-4519. Mark Levy, Dir.
Music & dance programs.

*EL CANEY DEL BARRIO
170 E 110th St, 2nd fl, New York NY
10029 (212)534-9555. William
Nieves. Concerts.

*EL MUSEO DEL BARRIO
1230 5th Ave, New York NY 10028
(212)831-7272.

*ENGLISH-SPEAKING UNION
16 E 69th St, New York NY 10021
(212)879-6800. Alice Boyne.

*ETHNIC ARTS CENTER
179 Varick St, New York NY 10013
(212)675-3741. Ethel Raim, Martin
Koenig. Fests, concerts, workshops,
etc. Calendar.

*FEDERATION OF TURKISH
  AMERICAN SOCIETIES
821 UN Plaza, New York NY 10016
(212)682-7688.

*FESTIVAL LATINO IN NY
Pulic Theater, 425 Lafayette St,
New York NY 10003 (212)598-7150.
Oscar Ciccone. 2-week intl fest of
music, film, theater. August.

*FRENCH CULTURAL SERVICES
Consulate, 3 Commonwealth Ave,
Boston MA 02116. LE CALENDRIER,
monthly listing of French cultural
events in Boston area.

*THE GERMAN SOCIETY
150 5th Ave, New York NY 10010
(212)989-2040.

*HEBREW ARTS SCHOOL
Abraham Goodman Hse, 129 W 67th St,
New York NY 10023 (212)362-8060.
Concerts, classes, other programs.

*HISPANIC SOC OF AMERICA
Broadway & 155th St, New York 10032
NY (212)690-0743.

*HOLLAND SOCIETY OF NEW YORK
  and HUGUENOT SOCIETY
122 E 58th St, New York NY 10022
(212)758-1675.

*INTER-CELTIC SOCIETY
96 Marguerite Ave, Waltham MA 02154
(617)899-2204. KELTICA, fests, arts
& crafts exhibitions.

*IRISH INSTITUTE
319 W 48th St, New York NY 10036
(212)581-1046.

*ITALIAN TRIBUNE NEWS
427 Bloomfield Ave, Newark NJ
07107. Weekly.

*JAPANESE-AMERICAN ASSN
7 W 44th St, New York NY 10036
(212)840-6942.

*JEWISH FOLK ARTS SOCIETY
10 Old Post Office Rd, Silver
Spring MD 20910 (301)589-6947.
David Shneyer, Dir. Festivals,
educational programs, publications.

KARIKAZO
Box 262, Bogota NJ 07630 (201)343-
5240. Judith Magyar. Hungarian folk
newsletter.

*KOSCIUSZKO FOUNDATION
15 E 65th St, New York NY 10021
(212)734-2120. Sponsors study
programs, grants, books, etc. on
Polish culture.

*LATIN AMERICAN MUSIC IN
  ALTERNATIVE SPACES (LAMAS)
PO Box 2207, Manhattanville Stn,
New York NY 10027 (212)281-5044.
Gustavo A. Paredes. Organizes
performances of LA music w/cultural
and community orgs. TV/radio progs.

MACEDONIAN TRIBUNE
542 S Meridian St, Indianapolis IN
46225. Weekly, social/cultural
news.

*MWATABU OKANTAH AFRO-AMER
  CULTURAL CENTER
UC 103, Cleveland State Univ,
Cleveland OH 44115 (216)687-3655.
Concerts, etc.

*NATL ASSN FOR ARMENIAN STUD
  AND RESEARCH
175 Mt Auburn St, Cambridge MA
02138 (617)876-7630. Journal 2/yr,
nwsltr 4/yr. Library. Distributes
Armenian books.

*NATL FNDN FOR JEWISH CULTURE
122 E 42nd St, New York NY 10168
(212)490-2280. Richard Siegel.
Seminars, festival. Grants. Events
calendar. Museum program. Major
national network/info ctr for
Jewish culture.

*NATL WELSH-AMERICAN FNDN
4900 Auburn Ave, #205, Bethesda MD
20814 (301)986-1859. P Howard
Patrick.

*NINNAU (Welsh)
11 Port Terr, Basking Ridge NJ
07920 (201)766-6736. Welsh
newspaper.

*NYABINGHI AFRIKAN SHOP
7 Flatbush Ave, Brooklyn NY
(718)855-5557. Records etc.

*POLISH AMERICAN VOICE
761 Filmore Ave, #201, Buffalo NY
14212 (716)891-8211. News, reviews
of music & fests, events coverage.

*POLISH ART
41 Katherine Rd, Watertown MA 02172
(617)926-8048. Basia Dziewanowska.
Folk costumes, gifts, etc.

*POLISH CONSULATE
Cultural Affairs Div, 233 Madison
Ave, New York NY 10016 (212)889-
8360. Info on study & travel.

*POLISH DANCE & FOLKLORE
3352 N Hackett Ave, Milwaukee WI
53211 (414)964-8444. Ada & Jas
Dziewanowski. Records, books,
instructions.

POLISH NATIONAL ALLIANCE
1201 N Milwaukee Ave, Chicago IL
60622. ZGODA semi-monthly.

*PUERTO RICAN FOLKLORE FIESTA
173 E 116th St, New York NY 10029
(212)427-8582.

*SOCIETY FOR ASIAN MUSIC
Hagop Kevorkian Ctr, 50 Washington
Sq S, New York NY 10012 (212)362-
0290. Kinza Schuyler. Concerts 9/yr
at Metropolitan Museum of Art.
Journal ASIAN MUSIC 2/yr.

*SOUTH AMERICAN MUSIC PROJECT
310 Lexington Ave, #10B, New York
NY 10016 (212)867-5521. Marco Rizo.
Concerts, schools programs,
workshops.

*UKRANIAN ACADEMY
206 W 100th St, New York NY 10025
(212)222-1866.

*UKRANIAN AMERICAN LEAGUE
85 E 4th St, New York NY 10012
(212)473-1762.

UKRANIAN WEEKLY
30 Montgomery St, Jersey City NJ
07302 (201)434-0237. Roma S
Hadzewycz.

WESTERN VIKING
2040 NW Market St, Seattle WA
98107. Weekly news of Norwegian
societies.

*WORLD ASSN OF ESTONIANS
243 E 34th St, New York NY 10016
(212)886-3356.

*WORLD MUSIC INSTITUTE
155 W 72nd St, #706, New York NY
10023 (212)362-3366 or 0290. Robert
Browning. Concerts, records, books,
radio shows.

*YIVO INSTITUTE
1048 5th Ave, New York NY 10028
(212)535-6700. Henry Sapoznik.
Yiddish culture. Archive. Concerts,
workshops, conferences. Nwsltr.

NATIONAL PUBLICATIONS

Publications listed here are available to the public. Journals etc. available only to members are listed under their organizations.

*ALTERNATIVE AMERICA
Resources, Box 134, Harvard Sq, Cambridge MA 02238. Directory of alternative resources.

AUTOHARPOHOLIC
PO Box 504, Brisbane CA 94005 (415)467-1700. 4/yr.

BANJO NEWSLETTER
Box 364, Greensboro MD 21639. Hub Nitchie.

*BILLBOARD
1515 Broadway, New York NY 10036 (212)764-7340. Major music-biz magazine. Reviews records and live shows.

*BILLBOARD INTL BUYERS' GUIDE
1515 Broadway, New York NY 10036. Lists record cos, etc. Write with your info to be included.

BLUEGRASS DIRECTORY
PO Box 412, Murphys CA 95247 (209)728-3379. Resource Guide.

*BLUEGRASS GAZETTE
PO Box 490, Toledo WA 98591.

*BLUEGRASS NEWSLETTER
5706 Reynolds Rd, Austin TX 78749.

*BLUEGRASS UNLIMITED
Box 1111, Broad Run VA 22014 (703)361-8992. Peter Kuykendall. Monthly. Festival guide in March.

*BLUES & RHYTHM
PO Box 2407, Hollywood CA 90078.

*BROADSIDE
PO Box 1464, New York NY 10023. Natl topical song magazine. 12/yr.

CASHBOX
1775 Broadway, New York NY 10019 (212)586-2640. Major music-biz mag. Reviews records.

CELTIC MUSIC RESOURCES
121 S 9th St, Reading PA 19602. Nina Mollico. Directory.

*CHILDREN'S FOLKLORE NEWSLTR
E Carolina U, Dept of English, Greenville NC 27834. C.W. Sullivan III.

*COME FOR TO SING
917 W Wolfram, Chicago IL 60657. Sadly deceased, but back issues available $2.50 each. SASE (37 cent stamp) for list.

*CONCERTINA & SQUEEZEBOX
Rte 1, Box 718, White Stone VA 23072. John Townley. 4/yr. Music, articles, interviews, reviews.

*COUNTRY HERITAGE
(formerly Resophonic Echoes)
RR1, Box 320, Madill OK 73446. Bev King. Monthly mag, for fans of Dobro and traditional country music. Interviews, info, lyrics, news, ads, etc. No reviews, but lists recordings and ordering info.

*DULCIMER PLAYER NEWS
PO Box 2164, Winchester VA 22601 (703)668-6152. Madeleine MacNeill. 4/yr for players and builders of hammer and fretted dulcimers.

*ETHNOMUSICOLOGY
Soc for Ethnomusicology, PO Box 2984, Ann Arbor MI 58106 (313)665-9400.

*FAST FOLK MAGAZINE + LP
178 W Houston St, #9, New York NY 10014. 12/yr.

*FLYPAPER
JAF Box 7095, New York NY 10116. Ed Haber. Newsltr/record mail-order for Richard Thompson/Fairport etc fans. Members-only rare cassette and record offers.

FOLK HARP JOURNAL
PO Box 161, Mt Laguna CA 92048. 4/yr.

*FOLK MUSIC SCENE
PO Box 878, N Arlington NJ 07032. Jake Conte. To our knowledge, there has only been one issue of this magazine so far, in early 1985.

*FOLKLIFE ANNUAL
Publishing Office, Library of Congress, Washington DC 20540. Pub by American Folklife Ctr.

*FOLKLIFE CENTER NEWS
American Folklife Ctr, Library of
Congress, Washington DC 20540 (202)
287-6590. 4/yr. Brett Topping.

*FOLKLIFE SOURCEBOOK
American Folklife Ctr, Library of
Congress, Washington DC 20540 (202)
287-6590. Superb resource guide,
esp to archives, degree courses.

*FOLKLISTINGS
Box 927, Estes Park CO 80517. 6/yr,
listings on folklife, music, dance.

*FRETS
Box 2120, Cupertino CA 95105
(408)446-1105. Jim Hatlo, Phil
Hood. Glossy monthly for acoustic
stringed instruments. Articles,
reviews, how-to info.

*GALACTIC CROSSROADS
PO Box 2352, Clarksburg WV 26301
(304)782-1061. Niles Hokkanen.
Mandolin-oriented news, reviews,
interviews, instruction. Compiling
directory of instrument builders -
send your info. Listings are free.

*GOLDMINE MAGAZINE
6 S 230 Cohasset Rd, Naperville IL
60540. Allen Shaw. For record
collectors.

*GRASS ROOTS INTERNATIONAL
    FOLK RESOURCE DIRECTORY
444 W 54th St, New York NY 10019
(212)957-8386. Leslie Berman,
Heather Wood. If you're not in, and
think you should be, send us the
information. Listings are free.

*THE GRASSOMETER
PO Box 56, Olustee FL 32072-0056.
Bluegrass news, info, record charts.

*GUITAR PLAYER
Box 2120, Cupertino CA 95105
(408)446-1105. Glossy monthly.

*HARP HERALD
PO Box 100, Pleasant View KY. 4/yr.

*HIGH FIDELITY
825 7th Ave, New York NY 10019
(212)265-8360. Ken Richardson.
Glossy monthly, reviews some folk
records.

*HOT WIRE
1321 Rosedale, Chicago IL 60660.
Toni Armstrong. Women's music and
culture.

INTERNATIONAL BANJO
PO Box 328, Kissimmee FL 32741.

*INTERNATIONAL BLUEGRASS
(newsletter of Intl Bluegrass Music
Assn) Rt 1, Box 710, Pittsboro NC
27312 (919)542-3997. Art Menius.
Worldwide bluegrass news, info ctr.

*LIVING BLUES
U of MS, Ctr for Study of Southern
Culture, University MS 38677
(601)232-5993. Frank W. Childrey,
Jr. 6/yr.

MEDIA RESOURCES DIRECTORY
1801 Eliott Ave, Bethlehem PA 18018
(215)865-2902. Annie Prince. For
political performers.

MUGWUMPS
15 Arnold Pl, New Bedford MA 02740
(617)993-0156. Michael Holmes.

*MUSIC ARTICLE GUIDE
PO Box 27066, Philadelphia PA
19118. (215)848-3540. Morris
Henken. 4/yr.

MUSIC CONNECTION
6640 Sunset Blvd, #201, Hollywood
CA 90028. J. Michael Dolan.

*MUSICAL AMERICA
825 7th Ave, New York NY 10019.
Shirley Fleming. Glossy bi-monthly.
Some good articles on folk music in
education.

*MUSICAL AMERICA DIRECTORY
825 7th Ave, New York NY 10019.
Mainly classical, but useful lists
of festivals, organizations, press,
etc. around the world.

NEW SOUNDS
Charlton Bldg, Derby CT 06418. John
Shelton Ivany, Editor.

*NO COMMERCIAL POTENTIAL
Box 3531, Omaha NE 68103. Good
lists of intl record distribs,
radio, publications. Reviews
records.

*ROLLING STONE
745 5th Ave, New York NY 10151
(212)758-3800. James Henke.

SEA HERITAGE NEWS
254-27 75th Ave, Glen Oaks NY 11004
(718)343-9575. Bernie Klay.

SING OUT!

*SING OUT
Box 1071, Easton PA 18042 (215)253-
8105. Mark Moss, Ed. 4/yr. Mag for
participating folksingers/players.
Songsheets, teach-ins, news,
reviews, and more. Now in its 36th
year of publication.

*SOUND CHOICE
PO Box 1251, Ojai CA 93023.
Contacts, reviews, etc.

STREET PERFORMERS' NEWS
PO Box 570, Cambridge MA 02238
(617)864-2970. Locations, legal
issues, resources.

*TALKIN' UNION
Box 5349, Takoma Park MD 20012.
Labor lore, music, history.

TWIN FIDDLE TREASURY
909 Humboldt St, Santa Rosa CA
95404. Music for Swedish and other
styles of fiddle-playing.

*TRADITION
NCTMA, 106 Navajo, Council Bluffs
IA 51501. Bob Everhart. 4/yr.

*VARIETY
154 W 46th St, New York NY 10036
(212)869-5700. Rich Gold. Reviews.
Has correspondents around the U.S.

*VOICES
478 W MacArthur Blvd, Oakland CA
94609. Newsltr of Redwood Records
Cultural & Educational Fund.

*WOMEN'S MUSIC PLUS
1321 Rosedale, Chicago IL 60660.
Toni Armstrong. Directory of
resources in women's music and
culture.

*WORLDWIDE BANJO DIRECTORY
Deering Banjo, 7936 Leicester Ave,
Lemon Grove, CA 92045. Everything
to do with banjos.

RADIO

Listed here are various radio shows
which are syndicated to several
stations around the US and abroad.
Also listed are organizations and
publications in this field.

*BLUEGRASS TODAY (show)
Rte 1, Box 719, Pittsboro NC 27312
(919)542-3997. Art Menius. Weekly
1hr show, music and interviews.

COLLEGE RADIO REPORT
Box 714, Bristol RI 02809. Shel
Kagan. Fortnightly paper.

*CONCERT MUSIC BROADCASTERS
c/o KKHI, Westin St Francis Hotel,
San Francisco CA 94102 (415)986-
2151. Len Mattson. Includes many
statins with folk programs.

*COUNTRY ROOTS (show)
Rte 1, Box 719, Pittsboro NC 27312
(919)542-3997. Art Mennius. Live
Sun night on WOW-AM, Omaha NE.

*THE FLEA MARKET (show)
WBEZ, 1819 W Pershing Rd, Chicago
IL 60609 (312)890-8241. Ken Gagne.
Live show, Sun 5-7 pm.

*THE FOLK SAMPLER (show)
Box 3012, Siloam Springs AR 72761
(501)524-5703. Mike Flynn, prod.
Distributed by American Public
Radio, also in Australia.

*IN TOUCH NETWORKS
322 W 48th St, New York NY 10036
(212)586-5588. Jasha M Levi. Broadcasting for the blind, stroke
victims, etc. Free national tapes.
Newspapers & periodicals.

*INTERCOLLEGIATE BROADCASTING
  SYSTEM
Box 592, Vails Gate NY 12584
(914)565-6710. Assn of school,
college, & university radio
stations.

*A MIXED BAG (show)
815 S Gary Pl, Tulsa OK 74104 (918) 585-5635. Bill Munger. Taped record show.

*MOUNTAIN STAGE (show)
WV Public Radio, Bldg 6, #424, Charleston WV 25305 (304)348-3239. Andy Ridenour, Larry Gross. Live acoustic music, 2nd & 4th Sun, 2-5 pm. Widely syndicated.

*MURRAY STREET ENTERPRISES
69 Murray St, New York KY 10007 (212)619-1475. Steve Rathe. Design & realization of radio programs.

*NATIONAL PUBLIC RADIO
2025 M St, Washington DC 20036 (202)822-2000. Various shows, inc "All Things Considered." Some festival coverage.

*PACIFICA PROGRAM SERVICE
  & RADIO ARCHIVE
5316 Venice Blvd, Los Angeles CA 90019 (213)931-1625.

*POLLUTION CONTROL
1725 E 115th St, Cleveland OH 44106 (216)791-7286. Pennie Stasik. Distribution of promotional recordings from indies to radio stations. Info network. Nwsltr.

*A PRAIRIE HOME COMPANION (show)
45 E 8th St, St Paul MN 55101 (612)221-1553. Garrison Keillor.

*SIMPLY FOLK (show)
WI Public Radio, 821 University, Madison WI 53706 (608)263-2243. Tom Martin-Erickson, Judy Woodward. Live shows, records, etc.

VOICE OF AMERICA
330 Independence Ave SW, Washington DC 20547. Russ Woodgate.

FILM

*ADAMS & ADAMS FILMS
706 Wayside Dr, Austin TX 78703 (512)477-8846.

*APPALSHOP FILMS
Appalshop, Box 743, Whitesburg KY 41858 (606)633-0108.

*BAYOU FILMS
Rte 3, Box 614, Cut Off LA 70345 (504)632-4100.

*LES BLANK, BRAZOS FILMS - see FLOWER FILMS

*CAROUSEL FILMS
1501 Broadway, New York NY 10036 (212)524-4126.

*CTR FOR DOCUMENTARY MEDIA
New Time Films Library, PO Box 315, Franklin Lakes NJ 07417.

CTR FOR SOUTHERN FOLKLORE
PO Box 40105, Memphis TN 38104.

*JOHN COHEN
Hazardous Films, RD 1, Box 304, Putnam Valley NY 10579. Films include HIGH LONESOME SOUND, WALTER PARDON.

*TOM DAVENPORT FILMS
Rte 1, Box 124, Delaplane VA 22025 (703)592-3701.

*EDUCATIONAL FILM SERVICES
28 Fisher Ave, Boston MA 02120 (617)440-7603.

*FILMS, INC
733 Greenbay Rd, Wilmette IL 60091 (800)323-4222.

*FLOWER FILMS
10341 San Pablo Ave, El Cerrito CA 04530 (415)525-0942. Les Blank.

*FOLKLORE FILMS
9 Vaughn Pl, New Rochelle NY 10801.

*MEDIA GENERATION
461 Eliot St, Milton MA 02187
(617)696-0231. John Bishop.

*OMNIFICENT SYSTEMS
1117 Virginia St E, Charleston WV
25301 (304)342-2624.

VIDEO

*CLEARWATER PUBLISHING
1995 Broadway, New York NY 10023
(212)873-2100. 38 hrs of Pete
Seeger videos.

*K-TWIN
1004 Marquette Ave S, Minneapolis
MN 55403 (612)338-1912. Tom
Pelissero. Distributor. Some folk.

*NATL FEDN OF LOCAL CABLE
  PROGRAMMERS
906 Pennsylvania Ave NE, Washington
DC 20003 (202)544-7272. Directory
of local cable producers, info/
resource ctr. Workshops, video,
print & music library, conferences,
special rates for equipment &
insurance, newsletter.

*VIDEO TAPE ARCHIVE PROJECT
2518 SE 17th Ave, Portland OR 97202
(503)231-6050. John Ullman. Many
traditional performers.

AGENTS

*BLADE AGENCY
PO Box 1556, Gainesville FL 32602
(904)372-8158.

*BLUE QUAIL PRODUCTIONS
PO Box 486, Chapel Hill NC 27514
(919)942-2023. Michael Gaffigan.

*ARNE BRAV ASSOCIATES
2862 Markbreit Ave, Cincinnati OH
45209 (513)631-3342. Arne Brav.

*NANCY CARLIN PRODUCTIONS
1930 Cameron Ct, Concord CA 94518
(415)686-1828. Nancy S Carlin.

*CRACKERBARREL ENTERTAINMENTS
168 Shore Rd, Clinton CT 06413
(203)669-6581. Ann Shapiro. Arts in
education programmers.

*JIM FLEMING & ASSOC
2055 Abbott, Ann Arbor MI 48104
(313)995-9066. Jim Fleming, David
Tamulevich, Tom Slothower.

*FOLKLORE PRODUCTIONS
1671 Appian Way, Santa Monica CA
90401 (213)451-0767. Manny & Mitch
Greenhill.

*HERSCHEL FREEMAN AGENCY
4212 Old Chapel Hill Rd, Durham NC
27707 (919)493-6208, 489-3898.

*GAYNES ENTERPRISES
1944 Rippleton Cross Rd, Cazenovia
NY 13035 (315)655-3308. Susie
Gaynes.

*GRASS ROOTS PRODUCTIONS
444 West 54th St, New York NY 10019
(212)957-8386. Heather Wood.

*IMMIGRANT MUSIC
25 Winsor Pl, Glen Ridge NJ 07028
(201)429-2273. Dan Behrman.
Specializes in non-English speaking
artists.

*INTERNATIONAL MUSIC NETWORK
PO Box 411, Mill Valley CA 94941
(415)383-3914. AnneMarie Martins.

ROBERT KENNY AGENCY
PO Box 1487, Milwaukee WI 53201
(414)224-9370. Ken Finkel.

*MUSIC BUSINESS AGENCY
611 Broadway, #822, New York NY
10022 (212)477-2320. Steve Martin.

*NOTEWORTHY TALENT
4 John St, #205, Tarrytown NY 10591
(914)631-8552. Thom Wolke.

*LEE OLSEN & ASSOC
PO Box 506, Lemont PA 16851 (814)
234-1647. Lee Olsen.

*PROPINQUITY MANAGEMENT
PO Box 9036, Denver CO 80209. Dan
Prendergast.

*REAL PEOPLE'S MUSIC
1825 W Larchmont, Chicago IL 60613
(312)281-4234. Josh Dunson.

*SCHNEIDER-DAVIS AGENCY
103 Bartlett Ave, Arlington MA
02174 (617)648-8204. Sharon Davis.

*TOUR CONSULTANTS
PO Box 1333, Montclair NJ 07042
(201)783-0778. Elizabeth Rush.

*TRADITIONAL ARTS SERVICES
2518 SE 17th Ave, Portland OR 97202
(503)231-6050. John Ullman. TOUR
BUILDER computerized resource
lists. Send SASE for info.

*VARIETY ARTISTS AGENCY
4120 Excelsior Blvd, Minneapolis MN
55416 (612)925-3440.

*DOUG YEAGER PRODUCTIONS
300 W 55th St, New York NY 10019
(212)245-0240.

PHOTOGRAPHERS

*JOHN COHEN
RD#1, Box 304, Putnam Valley NY
10579 (914)528-6453.

*ELLIOTT DABINSKY
886 Livingston Ave, N Brunswick NJ
08902 (201)846-2844.

*EMILY FRIEDMAN
917 W Wolfram, Chicago IL 60657.

*DAVE GAHR
New York NY. (212)675-7585.

*GERRY HINSON
3265 Bainbridge Ave, Bronx NY 10467
(212)652-2430.

*RIVERSIDE PHOTOGRAPHICS
1029 Garden St, #2, Hoboken NJ
07030 (201)792-5415, Dan Peck.

*THOM WOLKE
4 John St, #205, Tarrytown NY 10591
(914)631-8552.

*BOB YAHN
45 Patton Dr, E Brunswick NJ (201)
249-7877.

SUPPORT SERVICES

This category includes a lot of useful but otherwise unclassifiable oddments.

*ARTSMARKET
670 Front St, Marion MA 02738 (617)
748-1578. Consulting service for
arts organizations. Help with
budgets, marketing, PR, grant-
writing, events management.

*FRANKLIN PHOTOS
370 W 35th St, New York NY 10001
(212)279-1950. Copies photos, 8x10,
postcards, etc.

MAILING LISTS

*HEY RUBE!
PO Box 14-6366, Chicago IL 60614.

*MEDIA DISTRIBUTION CORP
2912 Daubeniss, #66, Soquel CA
95073 (408)462-6245 x 199. Rick
Sheridan. Lists of columnists and
publications, college radio stns,
bibliographies.

*RESOURCES
Box 134, Harvard Sq, Cambridge MA
02238 (617)876-2789. Will put your
mailing list on computer, also has
various lists for sale, other
business services.

*TOUR BUILDER
TAS, 2518 SE 17th Ave, Portland OR
97202. John Ullman. SASE for
details.

RECORD PRODUCTION & SOUND REINFORCEMENT

*BAY RECORDS
1516 Oak St, #320, Alameda CA 94501
(415)865-2040. Mike Cogan. Studio.

*CHARLES RIVER PRODUCTIONS
380 Broadway, Cambridge MA (617)
547-7781. Walter Lenk. Festival &
concert sound co, recording
specialists.

*COLLEGIUM SOUND
35-41 72nd St, Jackson Hts NY 11372
(718)426-8555. Don Wade. Sound co.

*HUMDINGER PRODUCTIONS
607 Piney Point Rd, Yorktown VA
23692 (804)898-8155. Record
production, inc sleeve design and
graphics. Publishing.

RECORD PRESSING & CASSETTE DUPLICATION

These companies specialize in small
orders. More complete lists can be
found either in the Billboard Studio Directory or Intl Buyers Guide.

*CP SOUND
200 Madison Ave, New York NY 10016
(212)532-5528. Peter Bengston.
Cassettes.

*DISCMAKERS
925 N 3rd St, Philadelphia PA 19123
(801)468-9353. Records & cassettes.

*EVA-TONE SOUNDSHEETS
4801 Ulmerton Rd, PO Box 7020,
Clearwater FL 33518 (800)EVA-TONE.
Producers of soundsheets (those
little floppy records) also other
promo stuff such as cassettes.

*EUROPADISK
75 Varick St, New York NY (212)226-
4401. Highest quality record
pressing.

*RAINBO RECORDS & CASSETTES
1738 Berkeley St, Santa Monica CA
90404 (213)829-0355/3476.

*RESOLUTION
Chace Mill, 1 Mill St, Burlington
VT 05401-1514 (800)862-8881. Real-
time cassette duplication (super
high quality).

*SOUTHERN AMERICAN RECORD
  PRESSING COMPANY
305 11th Ave S, Nashville TN 37203
(615)256-2521. John & Martha
Ivanits. Also cassettes, carts.

*WK STUDIO
611 Broadway, New York NY 10003
(212)473-1203. Casettes.

RECORD PROMOTION

*POLLUTION CONTROL
1725 E 115th St, Cleveland OH 44106
(216)791-7286. Mark Edwards, Pennie
Stasik. Sends packages of indie
records to radio stations. Much
other info.

TRAVEL

*ACFEA - Associate Consultants for
  Education Abroad
12 E 86th St, #200, New York NY
10028 (212)288-9000. Nancy Lee.
Exchange possibilities for US & UK
folk groups.

*CRIMSON TRAVEL SERVICE
39 John F Kennedy St, Cambridge MA
02138. Robbie O'Connell. Organizes
Ireland Folk Tour.

*FESTIVAL TOURS
1341 Ocean Ave, #276, Santa Monica
CA 90401 (213)395-2486. Nancy
Covey. Travel to folk events in the
British Isles, to the New Orleans
Jazz & Heritage Fest, and others.

SONGWRITING

If you write songs, you should read
the section on "Copyright Basics"
to make sure your works are
protected from piracy. To start
your own publishing company,
contact ASCAP or BMI.

We urge great caution when
dealing with companies who promise
to publish your songs, or to place
your songs with famous singers. We
also suggest that you avoid
companies which offer "30 actual
names and addresses for only $10."
This can only be termed a rip-off.
Billboard's Buyers Guide lists most
of the thousands of music
publishers in the world, and costs
maybe $40.

Many local schools offer courses
in songwriting, including the New
School in NYC.

*LOS ANGELES SONGWRITERS
  SHOWCASE
PO Box 93759, Hollywood CA 90093
(213)654-1666. Weekly showcase at
Gio's, 7574 Sunset Blvd, Hollywood.

Courses, seminars, monthly
MUSEPAPER, info service.

*NEW SONG LIBRARY
PO Box 295, Northampton MA 01061
(413)586-9485. Collection of
feminist and progressive songs.
Info service, song-finding
resource. Writers can send tapes
(all copyrights are respected).

*CHICAGO SONGWRITERS ASSN
PO Box 1541, Elk Grove IL 60009-
1541. Bill Batzkall, Exec Dir.

* N CALIF SONGGWRITERS ASSN
(415)327-8296.

*NASHVILLE SONGWRITERS ASSN
(714)997-4428. Doug Flaherty.

*SONGWRITER'S MARKET
Writer's Digest Books, 9933
Alliance Rd, Cincinnati OH 45242.
Annual, lists over 2000 song buyers
with royalty rates, submission
requirements, etc.

RECORD COs & DISTRIBs

The Archive of Folk Culture at the Library of Congress publishes a free list of folk-oriented record companies. A list of all the major record companies in the world may be found in the BILLBOARD BUYERS GUIDE (see entry under National Publications).

*A GENTLE WIND
Box 3103, Albany NY 12202. Jill Person. Music and tapes for kids.

*AARONSON & GREENE RECORDS
Box 7427, Dallas TX 75209.

*ACORN MUSIC
323 Marine St, #5, Santa Monica CA 90405.

ACOUSTIC REVIVAL RECORDS
1437 W Howard St, Chicago IL 60626.

*ADELPHI RECORDS
PO Box 7688, Silver Spring MD 20907 (301)434-6958.

ADIRONDACK RECORDS
Box 566, Massena NY 13662.

ADVENT PRODUCTIONS
PO Box 722, El Cerrito CA 94530 (415)525-1494. Frank Scott.

AFF RECORD SERIES
N AZ U, Box 5705, Flagstaff AZ 86011 (602)526-3547. Kathryn Cunningham.

*AIRWAYS RECORDS
6714 S Halstead St, Chicago IL 60621. Sunnyland Slim.

ALASKA FOLK MUSIC RECORDS
PO Box 4-1234, Anchorage AK 99509.

*ALCAZAR
Box 429, S Main St, Waterbury VT 05676 (802)244-8657. Joan Pelton. Catalog. Independent label, distributor, many imports.

*ALLIGATOR
PO Box 60234, Chicago IL 60660 (312)973-7736. Bruce Iglauer.

*ALPINE RECORDS
Red River NM 87558.

AMERICAN HERITAGE
1208 Everett St, Caldwell ID 83605.

*APPALACHIAN MUSEUM
CPO Box 2298, Berea College, Berea KY 40404.

*ARAF - see DISCS ARAF

*ARHOOLIE RECORDS
10341 San Pablo Ave, El Cerrito CA 94530 (415)525-7471. Chris Strachwitz.

*ARKA ARMENIAN RECORDS
4856 Santa Monica Blvd, Los Angeles CA 90029.

ARKANSAS TRADITIONS
Ozark Folk Ctr, Mountain View AR 72560.

ARLOCO RECORDS
250 W 57th St, New York NY 10107.

ATTEIRAM RECORDS
PO Box 606, Marietta GA 30061.

*AUGUSTA HERITAGE RECORDS
Davis & Elkins College, Elkins WV 26241 (304)636-1903. WV trad music.

*BALKAN ARTS RECORDS
EFA Ctr, 179 Varick St, New York NY 10013 (212)675-3741. Ethel Raim.

BANJAR RECORDS
Box 32164, Minneapolis MN 55432.

BARRELHOUSE RECORDS
PO Box 29014, Chicago IL 60629.

*BAY RECORDS
1516 Oak St, #320, Alameda CA 94501 (415)866-2040. Mike Cogan. Also a recording/production studio

*BEANCAKE RECORDS
Box 4211, Ann Arbor MI 48106.

*BERT & I RECORDS
35 Mill Rd, Ipswich MA 01928 (617) 356-0151. Robert Bryan, Pres.

*BIOGRAPH RECORDS
16 River St, Chatham NY 12037 (518) 392-3400. Arnold S. Caplin.

BIRCH RECORDS
PO Box 92, Wilmette IL 60091 (312)
251-7037. Dave Wylie, Pres.

BISHOP MUSEUM PRESS
PO Box 1900A, Honolulu HI 96819.

*BLACK TOP RECORDS
Box 56691, New Orleans LA 70156.

*BLIND PIG RECORDS
PO Box 2344, San Francisco CA 94126
(415)526-0373. Edward Chmelewski.

*BLIND PIG RECORDS
1304 W Schubert, Chicago IL 60614
(312)528-5455. Jerry del Guidice.
Regional office.

*BLUE DOG RECORDS
134 N 14th St, Lincoln NE 68502.

BLUE FLAME RECORDS
Box 49, Branford RI 02808.

*BLUES UNLIMITED
PO Box 1345, 415 N Parkerson Ave,
Crowley LA 70526 (318)783-1601. Jay
Miller.

*BLYTHEWOOD RECORDS
Box 344, Great Falls VA 22066.

*BONNIE BANKS RECORDS
PO Box 811, Camden ME 94743 (207)
236-2789. Glenn Jenks. Ragtime,
Maine artists.

*BUD'S RECORDS
PO Box 2784, Philadelphia PA 19120
(215)455-1385. Bud Manning.

*CAILLIER RECORDS
200 W Pine, Lafayette LA 70501.

*CANADIAN RIVER MUSIC
4106 Tyler St, Amarillo TX 79110.
Danna Garcia. Texas music. Catalog.

*CARTHAGE RECORDS
PO Box 667, Rocky Hill NJ 08553.
Geoff Muldaur.

*CASSANDRA RECORDS - see
SCHRODER MUSIC

*CENTIPEDE PRODUCTIONS
PO Box 371, Chapel Hill NC 27514.
Nyle Frank. Cassettes.

*CHESS RECORDS - see SUGAR
HILL RECORDS (NJ)

*CIMIRRON/RAINBIRD RECORDS
607 Piney Point Rd, Yorktown VA
23692 (804)898-8155. Lana Puckett,
Kim Peterson.

*CLOUDS RECORDS
6607 Marywood Rd, Bethesda MD
20817.

*COMMUNITY MUSIC
PO Box 5778, Takoma Park MD 20912
(301)270-3873. Sheila Kahn. Label
LIKEABLE.

*CORNBELT RECORDS
Box 3452, Madison WI 53704 (608)
256-7331. Lou & Peter Berryman.

*COVERED DISH RECORDS
PO Box 3005, Providence RI 02906.
Kate Katzburg, Steve Snyder.

*CRACKERBARREL ENTERTAINMENTS
168 Shore Rd, Clinton CT 06413.

*DELMARK RECORDS
4243 N Lincoln St, Chicago IL
60618.

*DEPOT RECORDS
PO Box 11, Kaneville IL 60144 (312)
557-2742. Lee Murdock.

*DISCS ARAF
3270 Kelton Ave, Los Angeles CA
90034. Music of Egypt and North
Africa.

*DOWN HOME MUSIC
10341 San Pablo Ave, EL Cerrito CA
94530 (415)525-1494. Distrib for
many labels. Catalog. Mail order.

*DRUMLESS RECORDS
Box 2228, Abington MA 02351.

*EARWIG MUSIC
Box 25235, Chicago IL 60625.

*EAST OF THE HEBRIDES
47 E Germantown Pike, Plymouth
Meeting PA 19462. William M. Reid.
Scottish imports, inc LISMOR.

*ELDERLY INSTRUMENTS
1100 N Washington, PO Box 14210,
Lansing MI 48901 (517)372-7890.
Chris Rietz. Distrib for many
labels. Catalog. Mail order. Takes
credit cards.

*LEONARD ELLIS PRODUCTIONS
PO Box 66002, Los Angeles CA 90066.

*END OF THE TRAIL MUSIC
Box 3157, Ridgewood NY 11385.

*EVEREST RECORDS
2020 Ave of the Stars, Century City
CA 90067.

*FANTASY RECORDS
10th & Parker, Berkeley CA 94710.

FESTIVAL RECORDS
161 Turk St, San Francisco CA
94102.

*FLAT TOWN MUSIC
PO Drawer 10, 434 E Main, Ville
Platte LA 70586 (318)363-2139. J
Floyd Soileau. Cajun/LA music. Also
SWALLOW RECORDS.

*FLYING FISH RECORDS
1304 W Schubert St, Chicago IL
60614 (312)528-5455. Bruce Kaplan.
Indepentent label. Free catalog.

FOLK ARTS PRODUCTIONS
PO Box 155, Huntington NY 11743
(516)231-0497.

*FOLK DANCER RECORDS
Folk Dance Ho, PO Box 2305, N
Babylon NY 11703.

FOLK TRADITION RECORDS
108 Stout St, Ambler PA 19002.

FOLK-LEGACY
*FOLK LEGACY RECORDS
Sharon Mountain Rd, Sharon CT 06069
(203)364-5661. Caroline Paton.

FOLKLORE & MYTHOLOGY CTR
UCLA, Los Angeles CA 90024.

FOLKRAFT RECORDS
10 Fenwick St, Newark NJ 07114
(201)824-8700.

*FOLKTELLERS
PO Box 1920, Asheville NC 28802.

*FOLKWAYS RECORDS
632 Broadway, New York NY 10003
(212)777-6606.

*FOUR DOTS RECORDS
Box 233, Denton TX 76201. carl
Finch.

FOX HOLLOW RECORDS
RD#1, Petersburg NY 12138.

*FOXFIRE RECORDS
PO Box B, Rabun Gap GA 30568

*FRECKLE RECORDS
PO Box 4005, Seattle WA 98104
(206)682-3200. Jack Burg.

*FRONT HALL RECORDS
PO Box 307, Voorheesville NY 12186
(518)765-4193. Andy & Bill Spence.
Free catalog.

FRONT PORCH RECORDS
Abraham Baldwin Agricultural Coll,
Tifton GA 31794.

*FUSE MUSIC
1230-1/2 Garden St, Santa Barbara
CA 93101 (805)963-1034. Rob
Rosenthal.

*GNP CRESCENDO
8400 Sunset Blvd, Los Angeles CA
90069.

*GALAX OLD FIDDLERS CONV
PO Box 655, Galax VA 24333.

*GATEWAY RECORDS
234 Forbes Ave, Pittsburgh PA
15222.

*GLOBAL VILLAGE MUSIC
Box 2051, Cathedral Stn, New York
NY 10025 (212)749-2284. Michael
Schlesinger. Casette & record
production/distribution.

*GOLDBAND RECORDS
313 Church St, Lake Charles LA
70601.

GOLDDUST RECORDS
115 E Idaho Ave, Las Cruces NM
88001 (505)524-1889. Emmit H
Brooks.

*GOOD COMPANY PRODUCTIONS
Box 429, Newton Centre MA 02159
(617)926-2591. Artist-directed
music production network.

GRAMAVISION
260 W Broadway, New York NY 10013
(212)226-7075. Jonathan Rose.

*GREAT DIVIDE RECORDS
178 W Houston St, #9, New York NY
10013 (212)989-7088. Jack Hardy.

*GREAT SOUTHERN RECORDS
PO Box 13977, New Orleans LA 70185.

*GREAT SOUTHERN RECORDS
PO Box 13977, New Orleans LA 70185.

*GREEN LINNET RECORDS
70 Turner Hill Rd, New Canaan CT
06840 (203)966-0864. Wendy Newton.
Independent label. Irish and
Scottish trad and ritual. Catalog.

GREEN TREE RECORDS
2340 Sierra Ct, Palo Alto CA 94303
(415)856-6529. Miriam Patchem.

GREENHAYS RECORDINGS
7A Locust Ave, Port Washington NY
11050. Jean Ritchie.

GUSTO RECORDS
1900 Elm Hill Pike, Nashville TN
37210 (615)889-8000. Moe Lytle.

*GYPSY GULCH
561B N H
LADY OF CARLISLE RECORDS
152 Wolf Rock Rd, Carlisle MA
01741. Paul Beck.

*HEARTWOOD RECORDS
PO Box 8266, Salem MA 01971.

HEIRLOOM RECORDS
RFD32, Wiscasset ME 04578.

*HEPATICA MUSIC
119 Clover Rd, State College PA
16801. Carrie Crompton. Dulcimer.

HERITAGE RECORDS
Rte 3, Box 278, Galax VA 24333
(703)454-2350. Bobby F Patterson.

*HIGH WATER RECORDS
Coll of Communications & Fine Arts,
Memphis State Univ, Memphis TN
38152 (901)454-2350. Dr David
Evans.

*HIGH WINDY PRODUCTIONS
Rte 6, Box 572, Fairview NC 28730.

HISTORIC NEW ORLEANS COLL
533 Royal St, New Orleans LA 70130.

*HOGEYE MUSIC
1920 Central St, Evanston IL 60201
(312)475-0260. Jon C Burda, VP.
Distributor.

HUNGARIA RECORDS
PO Box 2073, Teaneck NJ 07666 (201)
343-5240. Kalman Magyar.

*IN THE TRADITION
PO Box 223, Deer Isle ME 04627
(207)348-6884. Debbie Suran.
Amazing catalog of international
folk stuff.

INDIAN HOUSE RECORDS
Box 472, Taos NM 87571 (505)776-
2953. American Indian Music.

*INDIAN RECORDS
PO Box 47, Fay OK 73646 (405)887-
3516. Songs from many American
Indian nations.

JACK RABBIT RECORDS
4323 Woodglen Dr, Moorpark CA
93021.

*JAZZOLOGY RECORDS
3008 Wadsworth Mills Pl, Decatur GA
30032 (404)288-1480. Also
SOUTHLAND RECORDS.

JEWEL RECORDING CO
1544 Kinney Ave, Cincinnati OH
45231.

*JEWEL RECORDS
Box 1125, Shreveport LA 71102 (318)
222-0673/0795. Stanley Lewis.

JOLIET RECORDS
PO Box 67201, Los Angeles CA 90062.

*JUNE APPAL RECORDINGS
PO Box 743, Whitesburg KY 41858
(606)633-0108. Pat Martin. Music
from the Southern Mountains.

KALEIDOPHONE RECORDS
3740 Kanawha St NW, Washington DC
20015.

*KALEIDOSCOPE RECORDS
PO Box 0, El Cerrito CA 94530 (415)
234-4100. Tom Diamant.

*KERRVILLE MUSIC FEST
Box 1466, Kerrville TX 78029 (512)
257-3600. Rod Kennedy.

*KICKING MULE RECORDS
PO Box 158, Alderpoint CA 95411
(707)926-5312. Catalog.

*KINGSTON KORNER
6 S 230 Cohasset Rd, Naperville IL
60540.

*LA LOUISIANE RECORS
711 Stevenson St, Lafayette LA
70501.

LADY OF CARLISLE RECORDS
152 Wolf Rock Rd, Carlisle MA
01741. Paul Beck.

*LADYSLIPPER
PO Box 3130, Durham NC 27705 (919)
683-1570. Women's music label and
distrib, wholesale and retail. Over
2000 titles.

*LANOR RECORDS
PO Box 233, Church Point LA 70525.
Lee Lavergne.

*LARK IN THE MORNING
Box 1176, Mendocino CA 95460 (707)
964-5569. Catalog.

LEGEND ENTERPRISES
909 W Armitage St, Chicago IL 60614.

*LERIC MUSIC
Box 12229, Chicago IL 60612.

*LIBRARY OF CONGRESS
Recorded Sound Div, Washington DC
20540 (202)287-5705.

*LIKEABLE RECORDS - see
   COMMUNITY MUSIC.

LINCOLN RECORDS
23 Valentine St, Cambridge MA 02139
(617)491-7780. John V Wright.

LIVING FOLK RECORDS
59 Magazine St, Cambridge MA 02139.
Peter Johnson.

*LISMOR RECORDS - see EAST OF
   THE HEBRIDES.

LOG CABIN RECORDS
PO Box 255, Historical Corp, Battle
Ground IN 47920.

*LOUISIANA FOLKLIFE RECORDS
PO Box 44247, Baton Rouge LA 70176.

*LYRICHORD DISCS
141 Perry St, New York NY 10014
(212)929-8234. Peter Fritsch, Pres.
Varied international music.

MAGIC CROW RECORDS
3 Salem St, Cambridge MA 02139.
Geoff Bartley.

MAMLISH RECORDING CO
PO Box 417, Cathedral Stn, New York
NY 10025 (212)783-7711. Don Kent.

*MANHATTAN MUSE
80 Fifth Ave, #706, New York NY
10003 (212)929-1585. Virginia
Giordano. Distribs independents,
women's music, etc.

*MARIMAC RECORDINGS
PO Box 5, Little Ferry NJ 07643.

MARJON INTERNATIONAL
159 Easton Rd, Hermitage PA 16146
(412)347-4726. John T Krizancic.

MENORAH RECORDS
36 Eldridge St, New York NY 10002
(212)925-7573.

MERIWEATHER RECORD CO
Arts Commission, 502 E Main St,
Bowling Green KY 42101.

MINERAL RIVER RECORDS
Box 292, Dover NH 03820 (603)749-
4694. Bill Staines.

MISSOURI FRIENDS OF THE
   FOLK ARTS
Box 307, New Haven MO 63068.

MONITOR RECORDS
156 5th Ave, New York NY 10010
(212)989-2323. Michael Stillman.

*MONTANA FOLKLIFE PROJECT
c/o Montana Arts Council, 35 S Last
Chance Gulch, Helena MT 59620 (406)
444-6430. Michael Korn.

MORE (MINORITY-OWNED RECORDS)
1205 Lester Dr NE, Albuquerque NM
87105.

MORGAN PRODUCTIONS
168 Shore Rd, Clinton CT 06413
(203)669-6648. The Morgans.

NATL OLDTIME FIDDLERS
Chamber of Commerce, 25 W Idaho St,
Weiser ID 83672.

*NATL COUNCIL FOR THE
   TRADITIONAL ARTS
1346 Connecticut Ave NW, #1118,
Washington DC 20036.

*NIGHTHAWK RECORDS
Box 15856, St Louis MO 63114.

NORTHEAST FIDDLERS ASSN
RFD#1, Stowe VT 05672.

*OASIS RECORDS
Box 287, Mt Sunapee NH 03772 (603)
763-9788. Tom Pirozzoli.

*OCOOCH MOUNTAIN RECORDS
Rte 2, Box 163A, Viola WI 54664.
Traditional Wisconsin music.

*OLD HOMESTEAD RECORDS
Jaymore Pub Co, PO Box 100,
Brighton MI 48116 (313)227-1997.
John Morris.

*OLIVIA RECORDS
4400 Market St, Oakland CA 94608
(415)655-0364. Judy Dlugacz.
Largest and most varied label in
women's music.

OMAC RECORDS
23207 52nd Ave W, Mountlake Terrace
WA 98043 (206)776-2806. Mark
O'Connor.

*ONE SKY MUSIC
129 Columbia Hts, Brooklyn NY
11201. Judy Gorman-Jacobs.

ORIGIN JAZZ LIBRARY
PO Box 85, Santa Monica CA 90406
(213)395-5735. Bill Givens.

*ORIGINAL MUSIC
RD1, Box 190, Lasher Rd, Tivoli NY
12583. John Storm Roberts. Huge
catalog of varied world musics.

OUTLET RECORDS
Box 107A, Rte 1, Ferrum VA 24088
(703)483-1538. W Rod Shively.

*PACIFIC CASCADE RECORDS
47534 McKenzie Hwy, Vida OR 97488.

PEACOCK RECORDS
c/o MCA, Universal City Plaza,
Universal City CA 90048 (213)508-
4000.

*PHILO RECORDS
c/o Rounder, 1 Camp St, Cambridge
MA 02140 (617)354-0700. Ken Irwin,
Marion Leighton.

PINE BREEZE RECORDS
Pine Breeze Ctr, Hamilton Ave,
Chattanooga TN 37405.

PIONEER RECORDS
161 Pelham Rd, Amherst MA 01002.

*PLAYBOY RECORDS
8560 Sunset Blvd, Los Angeles CA
90069.

POCA RIVER RECORDS
PO Box 563, Fairmont WV 26555
(304)363-3107. Kenneth Davidson.

*POLYGRAM RECORDS
810 7th Ave, New York NY 10019
(212)399-7067.

PRAIRIE SCHOONER RECORDS
PO Box 3022, St Louis MO 63130.

*PRAIRIE SMOKE RECORDS
250 W 99th St, #8c, New York NY
10025.

PROGRAM IN ETHNOMUSICOLOGY
UCLA, Dept of Music, Los Angeles CA
90024.

PURITAN RECORS
Box 44, 512 Jewitt St, Battle
Ground IN 47920.

*RAINBOW MORNING MUSIC
2121 Fairland Rd, Silver Spring MD
20904.

*RAINLIGHT RECORDS
900 E 5th, #111, Austin TX 78702.

*RAMPUR RECORDS
2018 Delaware St, Berkeley CA 94709
(415)848-0283. Dev Singh.

*RAMPUR RECORDS
6546 N Glenwood Ave, #2S, Chicago
IL 60626. Branch office.

*RED BEANS RECORDS
2240 N Magnolia, Chicago IL 60614
(312)472-4787. Pete Crawford, Erwin
Helfer.

*RED HOUSE RECORDS
PO Box 4044, St Paul MN 55104 (612)
646-9382. Bob Feldman.

*RED PAJAMAS RECORDS
Box 233, Seal Beach CA 90740. The
music of Steve Goodman.

*REDWOOD RECORDS
476 W MacArthur Blvd, Oakland CA
94609 (415)428-9191. JoLynne
Worley. Independent label. Catalog.

*REVELS RECORDS
Box 290, Cambridge MA 02238.

REVONAH RECORDS
Box 217, Ferndale NY 12734 (914)
292-5965. Paul Gerry.

RICHEY RECORDS
PO Box 12937, Ft Worth TX 76116
(817)731-7375. Slim Richey.

*ROADWORK
1475 Harvard St NW, Washington DC
20009 (202)234-9308.

ROOSTER BLUES
2615 N Wilton Ave, Chicago IL 60614
(312)281-3385. Jim O'Neal.

ROOSTER RECORDS
RFD#2, Bethel VT 05032 (802)234-
5094. William Wright. Free catalog.

*ROSETTA RECORDS
115 W 16th St, New York NY 10011

*ROUNDER RECORDS
1 Camp St, Cambridge MA 02140 (617)
354-0700. Ken Irwin, Marion
Leighton. Large catalog.

*ROUNDER DISTRIBUTION
1 Camp St, Cambridge MA 02140 (617)
354-0700. George Thomas.
Distributes to stores. ARTIST
INDEX discography.

*ROUNDUP RECORDS
PO Box 154, N Cambridge MA 02140.
Catalog of over 150 labels.

*RUBY SLIPPERS RECORDS
6 Franklin Ct, Northampton MA
01060. Judy Polan.

RURAL RHYTHM RECORDS
PO Box A, 10634 E Live Oak St,
Arcadia MA 01060. Uncle Jim O'Neal.

SAMPLER RECORDS
197 Melrose St, Rochester NY 14619.

*SCHRODER MUSIC CO
1450 6th St, Berkeley CA 94710
(415)524-5804. Nancy Schimmel.
Publishes Malvina Reynolds books
and records, and others.

SE MUSIC
375 Airport Dr, Worcester MA 01602
(617)757-6369. Gil Markle, Pres.

SELO RECORDS - see FESTIVAL
  RECORDS

*SHANACHIE RECORDS
1 Hollywood Ave, Ho-Ho-Kus NJ 07423
(201)445-5561. Dan Collins, Richard
Nevins. Independent label. Catalog
with some excellent material, inc
imports and licensed albums.

SHILOH RECORDS
14902 Sabre Lane, Huntigton Beach
CA 92647.

*SIERRA RECORDS
PO Box 5853, Pasadena CA 91107
(818)355-0181. John M Delgatto.

*SILO
Box 429, S Main St, Waterbury VT
05676 (802)244-5178. Carol Senning.
Domestic & imported records.

*SILVER STREAM MUSIC
20 Wills Ave, Stanhope NJ 07874
(201)398-7444. Elaine Silver.

*SKANDISK
3424 S 19th Ave, Minneapolis MN
55407 (612)724-6561. Scandinavian
records and other goodies.

*SKYLARK PRODUCTIONS
1108A Post Rd, RR5, Wakefield RI
02879 (401)783-1178. Patrick Sky.

SLAVYANKA CASSETTES
1521 Campus Dr, Berkeley CA 94708.
E European music.

*SLEEPY MORNING RECORDS
Box 393, Scarsdale NY 10583.

*SMILER MUSICS
1739 Ward St, Berkeley CA 94703
(415)548-7597. Barry Smiler.

*SMITHSONIAN COLLECTION
900 Jefferson Dr NE, Washington DC
20560 (202)357-1300. Felix Lowe.

SMITHSONIAN RECORDINGS
PO Box 10230, Des Moines IA 50336.

*SNOWY EGRET MUSIC
234 Eliot St, S Natick MA 01760
(617)653-8290. Rick, Lorraine Lee.

SOLID SMOKE RECORDS
Box 22732, San Francisco CA 94122
(415)731-0500. Rico Tee.

SONYATONE RECORDS
PO Box 576, Santa Barbara CA 93102
(805)967-7837. Peter P Feldman.

SOUND IMAGE RECORDS
Box 550, Kenmore Stn, Boston MA
02215.

SOUNDCHIEF'S ENTERPRISE
PO Box 1944, Lawton OK 73501.

*SOUTH STREET SEAPORT MUSICS
16 Fulton St, New York NY 10038
(212)608-0642.

*SOUTHERN FOLK CULTURAL
REVIVAL PROJECT
339 Valeria St, Nashville TN 37210.

SOUTHERN FOLKLORE RECORDS
PO Box 40105, 1216 Peabody Ave,
Memphis TN 38104.

*SOUTHLAND RECORDS - see
JAZZOLOGY RECORDS

*SPECIALTY RECORDS
8300 Santa Monica Blvd, Los Angeles
CA 90069.

*SPIVEY RECORDS
65 Grand Ave, Brooklyn NY 11205.
Some great blues albums.

*STASH RECORDS
611 Broadway, #725, New York NY
10012 (212)477-6277. Bernard
Brightman.

*STAT RECORDS
1304 Fletcher Rd, Tifton GA 31794
(912)382-6257. Gus P Statiras.

STINSON RECORDS
PO Box 3415, Granada Hills CA 91344
(213)368-1612. Jack McKall.

*SUGAR HILL RECORDS
PO Box 4040, Duke Stn, Durham NC
27706 (919)489-4349. Penny Parsons.
Bluegrass.

*SUGAR HILL RECORDS
96 West St, Englewood NJ 07631
(201)569-5170. Sylvia Robinson.
Blues. Owns Chess catalog.

SUNNY MOUNTAIN RECORDS
PO Box 14592, Gainesville FL 32604.
Barbara & William Koehler.

*SUOMI SOUNDS
221 S Lamar, Austin TX 78704 (512)
479-0367 or 280-3291. Phillip Page.
Finnish imports.

*SWALLOW RECORDS - see FLAT
TOWN MUSIC.

SWALLOWTAIL RECORDS
Box 843, Ithaca NY 14580 (607)844-
4539. Phil Shapiro.

TAMBUR RECORDS
c/o Tara Pubs, 29 Derby Ave,
Cedarhurst NY 11516 (516)299-2290.
Velvel Pasternak.

TANNEHILL RECORDS
7846 Kendalia St, Houston TX 77036.

TENNESSEE FOLKLORE SOCIETY
Box 201, Mid-TN State University,
Murfreesboro TN 37132 (615)898-
2576. Charles Wolfe.

TENNVALE RECORDINGS
PO Box 1264, Huntsville AL 35807.

*THREE FEATHERS MUSIC
311 6th Ave, Brooklyn NY 11215
(718)965-3886 or 0741. Lydia Adams
Davis.

*THRUSHWOOD RECORDS
PO Box 111, Pomfret CT 06258 (203)
928-2619. Sally Rogers.

*TOMORROW RIVER MUSIC
PO Box 165, Madison WI 53701.
Robbie Clement.

*TRADITIONAL RECORDS
PO Box 8, Hwy 32, Cosby TN 37722
(615)487-5543. Jean & Lee
Schilling.

*TRAIN ON THE ISLAND RECORDS
PO Box 9701, Minneapolis MN 55440.
Catalog.

*TRIX RECORDS
Drawer AB, Rosendale NY 12472 (914)
687-9573. Peter B Lowry.

TURNEROUND RECORDS
6470 8th Ave, Grandville MI 49418
(616)457-2172. Donald A Round.

*TURQUOISE RECORDS
HC-84, Box 1358, Whitesburg KY
41858 (606)633-0485.

*TURTLE MOUNTAIN MUSIC
PO Box 340, Belcourt ND 58316.
Music from Turtle Mtn Reservation.

UNIV OF NORTH CAROLINA PRESS
PO Box 2288, Chapel Hill NC 27514.

UNIV OF UTAH PRESS
USB 101, Salt Lake City UT 84112.

UNIV OF WASHINGTON PRESS
U of Washington, Seattle WA 98105.

*VSP
Preservation Hall, 726 St Peter St,
New Orleans LA 70116.

*VANGUARD RECORDING SOCIETY
71 W 23rd St, New York NY 10010
(212)255-7732. Maynard Solomon.

VETCO RECORDS
5825 Vine St, Cincinnati OH 45216
(513)2422-8000. Lou Ukelson.

*VOYAGER RECORDS
424 5th Ave, Seattle WA 98122 (206)
323-1112. Vivian Williams. Catalog.
Fiddle, old time music.

*WEST VIRGINIA UNIV PRESS
Wise Library, PO Box 6069,
Morgantown WV 26506-6069.

WHEATLAND RECORD CO
1414 Congress St, Lansing MI 48906.

*WILDWOOD RECORDS
Box 48, Hillside Colony, Stillwater
NY 12170.

*WINDHAM HILL
PO Box 9388, Stanford CA 94305.

*WOODPECKER RECORDS
PO Box 1134, Portsmouth NH 03801.
Harvey Reid.

*WORKSHOP RECORDS
PO Box 49507, Austin TX 78765 (512)
452-8348. Dan Huckabee.

*WORLD MUSIC ENTERPRISES
717 Avondale St, Kent OH 44240
(216)673-3763. Terry E Miller.
World musics, esp SE Asia.

XALMAN LABEL
601 E Montecito St, Santa Barbara
CA 93103. La Casa de la Raza
Cultural Arts.

*YAZOO RECORDS
245 Waverly Pl, New York NY 10014.

*YELLOW ORCHID MUSIC
Box 212, Pomfret Ctr MA 06259 (203)
974-2829. Peggy Morgan, Bette
Phelan.

*ZOMBA RECORDS
1348 Lexington Ave, New York NY
10128 (212)410-4774. Barry Weiss.

BOOK PUBLISHERS

Information about currently-avail-
able books on folklore, folk music,
and related topics can be four in
BOOKS IN PRINT, which may be
consulted at your local public
library.

*AMERICAN FOLKLIFE CTR
Library of Congress, Washington DC
20540.

*ARNO PRESS
3 Park Ave, New York NY 10016
(212)725-2050. International
Folklore Series.

*CAPTAIN FIDDLE PUBLICATIONS
4 Elm Ct, Newmarket NH 03857. Ryan
J. Thomson. "Fiddler's Almanac."

*CTR FOR SOUTHERN FOLKLORE
1216 Peabody Ave, PO Box 4081,
Memphis TN 38104.

*CHURCH HYMNAL CORP
800 2nd Ave, New York NY 10017
(212)661-6700.

COLUMBIA PUBLICATIONS
16333 NW 54th Ave, Hialeah FL
33014. Dulcimer instruction, etc.

*COUNTRY BOOKSHOP
Plainfield VT 05667. Benjamin &
Alexandra Koenig. Wonderful, wide
selection of folklore books.
Catalog.

*COYOTE PRESS
PO Box 641, Eugene OR 97440. Percy
Milo.

*THE CROSSING PRESS
PO Box 640, Main St, Trumansburg NY
14886 (607)387-6217. Books,
postcards, calendars.

*CRYING CREEK PRESS
Cosby TN 37722.

*DOVER PUBLICATOINS
180 Varick St, New York NY 10014
(212)255-3755. Very wide range.
Free catalogs. Cut-price showroom.
Will consider re-publishing out-of-
print books if you have a copy.
Highly recommended.

*ELDERLY INSTRUMENTS
1100 N Washington, PO Box 14218,
Lansing MI 48901 (517)372-7890.
Distributes all kinds of folk
books: instruction, reference,
songbooks, folklore, children's,
international, biography, etc.

FARM & WILDERNESS TUNES
Plymouth VT 05056.

FIDDLECASE BOOKS
Box 540, Peterborough NH 03458.
Traditional tune-books.

*FOLK PUBLICATIONS
PO Box 52755, Atlanta GA 30355.
Walt Hulgren.

*FOLKLORE PUBLICATIONS GROUP
Folklore Institute, 504 N Fess St,
Bloomington IN 47401.

GOURD MUSIC
PO Box 585, Felton CA 95018.
Dulcimer chord-books.

*HUMANITIES PRESS INTL
171 1st Ave, Atlantic Highlands NJ
07748.

IWW - WOBBLIES
3435 N Sheffield, #202, Chicago IL
60657. Little Red Songbook.

*LEGACY BOOKS
PO Box 494, 12 Meetinghouse La,
Hatboro PA 19040. Books on
folklore, songs, etc. COME-ALL-YE
newsletter.

*MUSIC IN ACTION
PO Box 204, E Stroudsburg PA 18301.
Books for music educators.

*NATL STORYTELLING RESOURCE
PO Box 112, Slemons Hse, Fox St,
Jonesborough TN 37659. Books of
stories for telling, etc.

*NEW ENGLAND FREE PRESS
60 Union Sq, Somerville MA 02143.
"Working Women's Music."

OAK PUBLICATIONS
5 Bellvale Rd, Box 572, Chester NY
10919. Major US publisher of
instruction and songbooks.

*PELICAN PUBLISHING CO
Box 189, Gretna LA 70053.

*PRINCETON BOOK CO
PO Box 109, Princeton NJ 08542
(609)737-8177. Dance books, inc
Playford.

*PURPLE MOUNTAIN PRESS
PO Box E-3, Fleischmanns NY 12430
(914)254-4062. Wray & Loni
Rominger. Publisher & bookseller of
NY regional books.

QUINLIN CAMPBELL BOOKS
Box 651, Boston MA 02134. Free
list. Traditional Irish tunes.

*RESCAN ASSOCS
401 Boyden Ave, Maplewood NJ 07040.
"Folk Music Chronicles" by Roger
Deitz.

*ROBINSON-LYNN PUBLISHERS
100 Walnut Pl, Brookline MA 02146.
"Partially Sage."

SACRED HARP BOOK CO
108 E Main St, Samson AL 36477.

SETS IN ORDER
462 N Robertson Blvd, Los Angeles
CA 90048. Dance books.

*SHOESTRING PRESS
2659 Club Park Rd, Winston-Salem
NC 27104. Bill Stevens. O'Carolan
tunes arranged for guitar.

*SMITHSONIAN INSTITUTION
Folklife Program, Washington DC
20560.

*SYRACUSE UNIV PRESS
1600 Jamesville Ave, Syracuse NY
13210. "Traditional American Folk
Songs from the Anne & Frank Warner
Collection," others.

*TEN-SPEED PRESS
Box 7123, Berkeley CA 94707.

*UNIV OF CALIFORNIA PRESS
2223 Fulton St, Berkeley CA 94720.

*UNIV OF CHICAGO PRESS
5750 Ellis Ave, Chicago IL 60637.

*UNIV OF ILLINOIS PRESS
Urbana IL 61801.

*UNIVERSITY PRESS OF KENTUCKY
102 Laffert Hall, Lexington KY
40506.

*UNIV OF MISSOURI PRESS
PO Box 1653, Hagerstown MD 21741.
"Ozark Folksongs" by Vance
Randolph.

*UNIV OF PENNSYLVANIA PRESS
3933 Walnut St, Philadelphia PA
19104.

*UNIV OF TENNESSEE PRESS
293 Communications Bldg, Knoxville
TN 37912. Folk life & lore catalog.

*UNIV OF TEXAS PRESS
PO Box 7819, Austin TX 78712.
American Folklore Soc publications.

*WEST VIRGINIA UNIV PRESS
Wise Library, PO Box 6069.
Morgantown WV 26506-6069.

*WORLD AROUND SONGS
Rte 5, Box 398, Burnsville NC
28714.

*YELLOW MOON PRESS
PO Box 1316, Cambridge MA 02238.

INSTRUMENT REPAIR/BUILD
& MAIL ORDER OUTLETS

*ACORN MUSIC
323 Marine St, #5, Santa Monica CA
90405 (213)392-6473. Tony Elman.
Hammered dulcimers, tune books.

*ALFIERI GUITARS
9 Oak Dr, New Hyde Park NY 11040
(516)437-4377. Don Alfieri. Buy and
sell. Repairs, restorations. Keep a
"wanted" list.

AMAZING GRACE MUSIC
111 Redhill Ave, San Anselmo CA
94960 (415)456-0414. Guitars,
repairs, restorations, lessons.

RALPH ASHMEAD, LUTHIER
1141 Evelyn, Albany CA 94706
(415)526-6254. Instruments,
repairs.

AUTOHARPS
1415 Waukegan Rd, Northbrook IL
60062 (800)323-4173. Oscar Schmidt.

BONES BY PERCY DANFORTH
1411 Granger Ave, Ann Arbor MI
48104 (313)662-3360. Sales,
workshops, instruction tapes and
books.

*BREEZY RIDGE INSTRUMENTS
PO Box 295, Center Valley PA 18034
(215)282-3319. John Pearse.
Strings, picks, accessories.

*CASTIGLIONE ACCORDION CO
12644 E 7-Mile Rd, Detroit MI 48205
(313)527-1595. New and used
accordions, concertinas, melodeons,
Martin and Ovation guitars.

*CASWELL HARPS
14690 Carrier La, Guerneville CA
95446 (707)869-0997. Theresa
Caswell. Celtic harp kits, books,
records, supplies. Free list.

THOMAS OLIVER CROEN
6214 Florida St, #1, Oakland CA
94618 (415)655-1510. Violins,
violas, cellos. Make/repair.

D'ADDARIO STRINGS
East Farmingdale NY 11735

*DOTY DULCIMERA
3773 Wychemere, Memphis TN 38128.

DOUGLAS/STRINGFELLOW
85 N Whitney St, Amherst MA 01002
(413)253-7532. Concert harps, all
types of guitars. Make and repair.

*ELDERLY INSTRUMENTS
1100 N Washington, PO Box 14210,
Lansing MI 48901 (517)372-7890. 24-
hr machine 372-4161. Instruments,
books, records, etc. Free lists.
Monthly used instrument list. Huge
selection. inc accessories.

30

FIDDLER'S CHOICE
41 E Main St, Joffrey NH 03452
(603)532-8440. Instruments,
repairs, workshops.

*FOLKCRAFT INSTRUMENTS
Cnr High & Wheeler Sts, Winsted CT
06098 (203)379-9857.

*FOLKCRAFT INSTRUMENTS
Webatuck Craft Vill, Rte 55,
Wingdale NY 12594 (914)832-6057.

Both centers have instruments,
kits, wood, fittings, records,
books, etc. Dulcimers, harps,
psalteries, kanteles, kankles,
banjos, mandolins. Catalog.

FRETTED INSTRUMENT WORKSHOP
47 S Pleasant St, Amherst MA 01002
(413)256-6217. Buy, sell, repair.

GENE'S GUITAR SHOP
451 Judah St, San Francisco CA
94100 (415)753-8776. Gene Mitchell.
Instruments, repairs, lessons.

GHS STRINGS
2813 Wilbur Ave, Battle Creek MI
49015.

GRAINNE YEATS
PO Box 1033, Houlton ME 04730
(207)532-9051. Irish harps.
Workshops on making and playing.

*GUILD OF AMERICAN LUTHIERS
8222 South Park, Tacoma WA 98408.
Non-profit educational org for art
of stringed instrument construction
and repair. Membership open. Natl
convention/exhibition held even
years, different locations.

*HALCYON HARPS
Box 1393, Montpelier VT 05602
(802)229-0446. Daniel Hecht. Handmade small harps, same string
spacing as concert harps. Optional
sharping levers, cases available.

*HANDLEY CROSS CONCERTINAS
PO Box 705, Bellingham WA 98227
(206)671-6381. Joel M Cowan. Used
English-made concertinas. Repairs.

HOFFMAN GUITARS
2219 E Franklin Ave, Minneapolis MN
55404 (612)338-1079. Make & repair
guitars. Rep for Martin and Gibson.
Store, good range of accessories.

HOHNER HARMONICAS
PO Box 15035, Richmond VA 23227.

TOM HOSMER
726 Euclid Ave, Syracuse NY 13210.
Fiddle maker, instrument repairer.

*HOUSE OF MUSICAL TRADITIONS
7040 Carroll Ave, Takoma Park MD
20912 (301)270-0222/9800. David
Eisner. Instruments, books,
records, workshops, etc.

*INTERMOUNTAIN GUITAR & BANJO
712 E 100 S, Salt Lake City UT
84102 (801)322-4682. New & used
instruments.

*JAWHARPS
Leonard Fox, 278-A Meeting St,
Charleston SC 29401. Handmade
imports from Austria. 3 sizes.
Wholesale & retail.

*LANHAM'S STRINGED INSTRUMENT
  REPAIR & CUSTOM BANJO SHOP
PO Box 4781, Nashville TN 37216
(615)262-4891. Marty Lanham

LARK IN THE MORNING
Box 1175, Mendocino CA 95460
(707)964-5569. Instruments, books,
records.

*LIBERTY BANJO COMPANY
245 Nancy Dr, Bridgeport CT 06606
(203)374-7072. Instruments, parts,
repairs. Free catalog.

MAIN STREET CASE CO
Main St, Tetonia ID 83452 (208)456-
2233. Free catalog.

*MANDOLIN BROS.
629 Forest Ave, Staten Island NY
10310-2576 (718)981-3226. Stanley
M. Jay. Vintage & new mandolins;
guitars inc Dobro, National, pedal
steel; banjos. 10-5, Mon-Sat.

MAPLE LEAF MUSIC
49 Elliott St, Brattleboro VT
05301 (802)254-5559. New & used
guitars.

*MARTIN GUITARS
510 Sycamore St, Nazareth PA 18064
(215)759-2837.

MCSPADDEN DULCIMERS
Drawer ESO, Mountain View AR 72560
(501)269-4313. Free brochure.

MUSIC EMPORIUM
2018 Massachusetts Ave, Cambridge
MA 02140 (617)661-2099.
Instruments, books, records. SASE
for lists.

*THE MUSICIAN'S FRIEND
PO Box 869, Eagle Point OR 97524
(503)826-9545. Instruments,
accessories, books, etc. Mail
order. Free catalog.

NEW ENGLAND ACCORDION CTR
PO Box 4656D, 36 Massabesic St,
Manchester NH 03108 (603)669-0424.
Accordions, concertinas, etc.

KEVIN O'DWYER
5502-1/2 W Devon Ave, Chicago IL
60646 (312)774-4372. Irish
instruments.

*OME BANJO COMPANY
4575 N Broadway, Boulder CO 80302
(303)449-0041.

*JOHN PEARSE STRINGS
(see BREEZY RIDGE INSTRUMENTS)

*SANDY'S MUSIC
896A Massachusetts Ave, Cambridge
MA 02138 (617)491-2812. Records,
instruments, instruction books.

SAUVE GUITARS
121 Union St, N Adams MA 02147
(413)663-3060. Make/repair.

*DAVID SHEPPARD INSTRUMENTS
AND REPAIRS
1820 Spring Garden St, Greensboro
NC 27403 (919)274-2395. Warranty
repairs to Martin, Sigma, Gibson,
Epiphone, Alvarez-Yairi. Builds,
restores, repairs stringed insts.

*SHUBB CAPOS
1701 Woodhaven Way, Oakland CA
94611.

*SOUTHERN HIGHLAND ACCORDIONS
1010 S 14th St, Slaton TX 79364.
Stinson Behlen. Accordions and
concertinas, new & used, repairs.

SWEETHEART FLUTE CO
32 S Maple St, Enfield CT 06082
(203)749-4494. New & antique
flageolettes, flutes, fifes. Free
brochure.

THIN MAN STRINGS
5232-1/2 Santa Clara Ave, Alameda
CA 94501 (415)521-2613. Larry
White. String sets for most
instruments. catalog.

THIRD HAND CAPO CO
716-1/2 W Lincoln, Dekalb IL 60115
(815)758-8818. Clamp any string at
any fret.

*MATT UMANOV GUITARS
273 Bleecker St, New York NY 10012
(212)675-2157. New & used, sale and
repair.

*VERMONT MUSICAL INSTRUMENT
BUILDERS CO-OPERATIVE
RD1, Box 2250, Plainfield VT 05667
(802)479-0862, 476-6097. Susan
Norris, Fred Carlson, Daniel Hecht.
Make/repair instruments. Workshops
for all ages on homemade
instruments.

VINTAGE FRET SHOP
20 Riverside Dr, Ashland NH 03217
(603)968-3326. Instruments,
repairs, records, etc.

DENNIS G WARING
60 Home Ave, Middletown CT 06457
(203)346-8597. Ethnic & early
instruments.

*HARRY & JEANIE WEST
PO Box 17067, W Durham Stn, Durham
NC 27705 (919)383-5750. New &
vintage instruments & accessories.
SASE for lists. Free advice!

RANDY WOODS
31 Cornus Dr, Savannah GA 31406
(912)352-2655. Guitar maker.

*SYLVIA WOODS HARP CTR
PO Box 29521, Los Angeles CA 90029
(818)247-4177. Celtic harps, books,
records, tapes of harp music.

WOODWORKERS DREAM
14 S Broad St, Nazareth PA 18064.
Dick Book. Exotic woods, woodwork
shop, instrument kits.

TEACHING AIDS

BELLA ROMA MUSIC
4442A Walnut St, #197, Berkeley CA
94709. Janet Smith. Finger-style
guitar.

*CAPTAIN FIDDLE PUBLICATIONS
4 Elm Ct, Newmarket NH 03857.
Fiddle tapes and books.

*COLUMBIA PUBLICATIONS
158000 NW 48th Ave, Hialeah FL
33014. Dulcimer instruction etc.

*STEFAN GROSSMAN'S GUITAR
WORKSHOP
PO Box 804, Cooper Stn, New York NY
10276. Many guitar styles. Free
catalog.

*HOMESPUN TAPES
Box 694, Woodstock NY 12498
(914)679-7832. Happy Traum. Tapes
and videos, many instruments and
styles.

JUNE APPAL INSTRUCTIONAL
Appalshop, Box 743, Whitesburg KY
41858 (606)633-0108. Dulcimer
tapes.

KICKING MULE RECORDS
PO Box 158, Alderpoint CA 95411
(707)926-5312. Instruction tapes.

*LARK IN THE MORNING
PO Box 1176, Mendocino CA 95460
(707)964-5569. Video music lesson
series, inc folk harp, fiddle,
flute, dulcimer, clogging.

*MANDOLIN INSTRUCTION
6330 Flamingo Rd, Melbourne FL
32904. Niles Hokkanen. Free
catalog. Book/tape instruction.

*OFF-CENTAUR PUBLICATIONS
PO Box 424, El Cerrito CA 94530
(415)528-3172. Instruction for
various kinds of harp. catalog.

*VALLEY OF THE MOON
SCOTTISH FIDDLING SCHOOL
1938 Rose Villa St, Pasadena CA
91107 (415)668-0612, (818)793-3716.
Instruction for all levels. Other
instruments too.

*WORKSHOP RECORDS
PO Box 49507, Austin TX 78765
(512)452-8348. Dan Huckabee.
Courses for many instruments.
Tapes, books, and videos.

YELLOW MOON PRESS
1725 Commonwealth Ave, Brighton MA
02135. Lorraine Lee. Tape/book
instruction for mountain dulcimer.

FOLKLORE DEGREE PROGRAMS

For a complete list, see J Am Folklore, p 391, Jan-Mar 1986, and the
Folklife Sourcebook. Courses are
available for degrees noted.

*COOPERSTOWN GRADUATE PROG
Cooperstown NY 13326 (607)547-2586.
Program in History Museum Studies.

*DUQUESNE UNIVERSITY
Tamburitzans Inst of Fok Arts,
Pittsburgh PA 15219 (412)434-5185.
Walter W Kolar. MA.

*GEORGE WASHINGTON UNIV
Folklife Program, Dept of
Anthropology, Washington DC 20052
(202)676-7244. John M. Vlach. MA.

*INDIANA UNIVERSITY
Folklore Inst, 504 N Fess St,
Bloomington IN 47405 (812)335-1027.
W Edson Richmond. MA, PhD.

*STATE U OF NY AT BUFFALO
Dept of English, Buffalo NY 14260
(716) 636-2560. Bruce Jackson. MA,
PhD.

*UNIV OF CALIFORNIA
Dept of Anthropology, Berkeley CA
94720 (415)642-2092. Alan Dundes.
MA.

*UNIV OF CALIFORNIA
405 Hillgard Ave, Folklore Group,
Los Angeles CA 90024 (213)825-3962.
Robert A Georges. MA, PhD.

*UNIV OF NORTH CAROLINA
Curriculum in Folklore, Greenlaw
Hall 066A, Chapel Hill NC 27514
(919)962-4065. Daniel W Patterson.
MA, PhD.

*UNIV OF PENNSYLVANIA
Folklore Dept, Box 13, Logan Hall,
Philadelphia PA 19104 (215)898-
7352. Dr Kenneth Goldstein, Chmn.
MA, PhD.

*UNIV OF TEXAS AT AUSTIN
Folklore & Ethnomusicology Ctr,
SSB3, 106, Austin TX 78712 (512)
471-1288. Richard Bauman. MA, PhD.

*WESTERN KENTUCKY UNIV
Ctr for Intercultural/Folk Studies,
Bowling Green KY 42101 (502)745-
2401. Burt Feintuch. MA.

ARCHIVES

Most archives are open to the public by appointment (if at all).
A complete list is in "Folklife
Sourcebook," a directory of folklife resources in the U.S. and
Canada, published by the American
Folklife Ctr, and available from
the AFC, Library of Congress, Washington DC 20540, for $10 mail, $8
in their store.

ACADIAN & CREOLE FOLKLORE
U of SW LA, Lafayette LA 70504.

*ARCHIVE OF AMERICAN
    MINORITY CULTURES
PO Box S, University AL 35486 (205)
348-5512. Brenda McCallum, Dir.
Research/resource ctr. Cassettes,
tapes, slides, photos, video.
Various folk styles.

*ARCHIVE OF FOLK CULTURE
Library of Congress, Washington DC
20540 (202)287-5510. Joe Hickerson.
Research facility, publications,
35,000 recordings, etc, info &
referral service, intern program.

*E C BECK COLLECTION
Clarke Historical Library, Mt
Pleasant MI 48858 (517)774-3352.
William H Mulligan, Jr, Dir.

BEN BOTKIN PAPERS
U of NE, Lincoln Library, Lincoln
NE 68508.

JOHN EDWARDS MEMORIAL FNDN
UNC, Folklore Dept Library, Chapel
Hill NC 27514.

J S HALL GREAT SMOKY MOUNTAINS
    COLLECTION
1455 Lemoyne St, Los Angeles CA
90065.

*JOE HEANEY COLLECTION
See Univ of Washington.

*JEHILE KIRKHUFF OLD TIME
    MUSIC FUND
RD4, Box 39, Montrose PA 18801. Ed
& Geraldine Berbaum. Field
recordings in PA and upstate NY.

W E KOCH FOLKLORE COLL
Kansas State U, Denison Hall,
Manhattan KS 66502.

BASCOM LAMAR LUNSFORD COLL
Mars Hill Coll, Mars Hill NC 28754.

*NORTHEAST ARCHIVES OF
    FOLKLORE & ORAL HISTORY
Rm B, S Stevens Hall, U of ME,
Orono ME 04469. Edward D Ives.
Tapes, photos, mss, esp on lumber
trade in the Northeast. Does field
recordings and research.

PEABODY MUSEUM
Harvard U, Cambridge MA 02138.

*SMITHSONIAN FOLKLIFE PROGRAM
Smithsonian Institution, Washington
DC 20560.

SOUTHERN FOLKLORE COLLECTION
UNC, Wilson Library, Chapel Hill NC
27514.

TRADITIONAL CRAFT ARCHIVE
435 Main St, Oneida NY 13421.

*UNIVERSITY OF WASHINGTON
Ethnomusicology Archives, Seattle
WA 98103. Includes Joe Heaney Coll
of over 160 tapes, plus Asian,
Indonesian, and intl material.

URBAN FOLKLIFE ARCHIVE
Rutgers Univ, Conklin Hall, Newark
NJ 07102.

WEATHERFORD-HAMMOND COLL
Berea Coll Library, Berea KY 40403.

WORLD MUSIC ARCHIVES
Wesleyan U, Dept of Music,
Middletown CT 06457.

YIVO INSTITUTE
1048 5th Ave, New York NY 10028
(212)535-6700. Jewish and Yiddish
language archives.

DANCE

AMERICAN MORRIS NEWSLETTER
438 NE 4th St, Minneapolis MN
55413. 4/yr.

*AMERICAN SQUARE DANCE SOC
462 N Robertson Blvd, Los Angeles
CA 90048-1799. Dance books.

*COUNTRY DANCE & SONG SOC
505 8th Ave, New York NY 10018
(212)594-8833. Newsletter.

*DANCE MAGAZINE/COLLEGE GUIDE
33 W 60th St, New York NY 10023
(212)245-9050. Mainly classical
dance, but guide lists colls where
various ethnic dance styles are
taught at all levels.

*DURANGO INTL FOLK DANCERS
Sawmill Rd, CR-142, Durango O 81301
(303)259-0987 or 385-4278. Meet Sat
at Park School Gym, 623 5th St.

*EARLY DANCE & MUSIC INST
PO Box 531, Amherst MA 01004
(413)586-4218. Classes, fests.

*FOLK DANCE FEDN OF CALIF, SOUTH
13250 Ida Ave, Los Angeles CA 90066
(213)306-7898.

*FOLK DANCE SYMPOSIUM
PO Box 2692, Hollywood CA 90028
(213)467-6341. Annual meeting at
UCA Santa Barbara.

*FRIENDS OF FIDDLE & DANCE
RD1, Box 489, W Hurley NY 12491
(914)338-2996. Jay Ungar. Nwsltr,
dance camps, info/resource guide.

*HARLEY'S TRADING POST
105 E 5th St, Loveland CO 80537
(303)663-1156. Polka records.

*KENTUCKY DANCE INSTITUTE
Held at Morehead Univ. 460 Long
Needle Rd, Brandenburg KY 40108.
Stew Shacklette. Aug.

*OLD SONGS DANCE FESTS
PO Box 197, Guilderland NY 12084
(518)765-2815. Dances, workshops,
demonstrations.

*PEOPLES FOLK DANCE DIRECTORY
PO Box 8575, Austin TX 78713. Sue
Hovorka, John Steele, editors.
Directory of intl folk dance groups
listing bands, business, record
suppliers, etc.

*POLISH DANCE & FOLKLORE
3352 N Hackett Ave, Milwaukee WI
53211 (414)964-8444. Ada & Jas
Dziewanowski. Records, books,
instructions.

*POLISH DANCE COSTUMES
41 Katherine Rd, Watertown MA 02172
(617)926-8048. Basia Dziewanowska.

*PRINCETON BOOK CO
PO Box 109, Princeton NJ 08542
(609)737-8177. Specializes in dance
books, inc. Playford.

*QUARTER TURN
644 Sembler St, Sebastian FL 32958
(305)589-5219. Judy Tremblay.
Monthly. Natl round dance mag.

*STOCKTON FOLK DANCE CAMP
Univ of the Pacific, Stockton CA
95211. Jack McKay, Dir.

*VT FOLK ARTS NETWORK
Hartland Hill, Woodstock VT 05091
(802)457-1759. Ruby Herzig. Monthly
New England & NY dance calendar.

*VILTIS
1337 Marion St, Denver CO 80218
(303)839-1589. V F Beliajus. 6/yr.
America's oldest folkdance mag.

THE DEAF COMMUNITY

NOTE: TDDs are nifty devices which allow printed copy to be sent via phone lines. Some phone nos below are tagged V for voice, TDD when such a device is connected.

*DEAF ARTISTS OF AMERICA
Box 2332, Westfield NJ 07091 (201)232-6677 (V/TTD). Tom Willard. Clearinghouse for info related to deaf people and the arts. Helps hearing-impaired artists. Newsltr 4/yr. Directory of artists.

*NATL CAPTIONING INSTITUTE
5203 Leesburg Pike, Falls Church VA 22041 (703)998-2400 (V/TDD). John Ball, Pres. Provides closed-caption service for TV, video. Works with producers.

*NATL INFO CTR ON DEAFNESS
Gallaudet Coll, Kendall Green, Washington DC 20002 (202)651-5109 (V); 651-5976 (TDD). Schools, college, and info clearinghouse. Keeps list of performance groups of and for deaf people.

*NATL TECH INST FOR THE DEAF
Public Info Office, 1 Lomb Memorial Dr, PO Box 9887, Rochester NY 14623-0887 (716)475-6824 (V/TDD). Deaf students, also research ctr. Trains those who work with hearing-impaired. Info to the public. Visitors welcome: 475-6405 (V); 475-2181 (TDD).

*REGISTRY OF INTERPRETERS FOR THE DEAF
814 Thayer Ave, Silver Spring MD 20910 (301)588-2406 (V/TDD). Dennis Cokely, Pres. Certifies, evaluates interpreters. Info center. Newsltr, journal.

TRAINING

Many sign-language classes are available around the country. The Natl Info Ctr on Deafness suggests checking w/local education depts, schools, community info & referral ctrs, vocational rehab services, deafness-related groups, etc.

*AMERICAN ANNALS OF THE DEAF
814 Thayer Ave, Silver Spring MD 20910. April reference issue has list of services, school, and classes for the deaf. Good place to locate signing classes. Check your library.

FILK MUSIC

Filk songs tend to get sung at science fiction conventions, post-revel meetings of the Society for Creative Anachronisms, and other gatherings of like-minded persons. Some traditional, some parodies, some brand new. Our thanks for this info to Ernest Clark, editor of the 2nd Wurm Wald Post-Revel Songbook, published by Off-Centaur (below). "Filk" was originally a misprint for folk in an SF convention program. It stuck.

*THE FILK FOUNDATION
34 Barbara Drive, Little Rock AR 72204. Margaret Middleton. Newsltr HARPINGS 6/yr; songbook KANTELE.

*OFF-CENTAUR PUBLICATIONS
PO Box 424, El Cerrito CA 94530. Records, tapes, books, theirs and others. Catalog. "The folk music of the future - Today."

*PEGASUS PUBLISHING
PO Box 9394, Ft Worth TX 76107. Tapes, books, distributor.

*THE PHILK FEE-NOM-EE-NON
PO Box 4128, Panorama City CA 91412 (818)989-5912. Monthly magazine.

*SOCIETY FOR CREATIVE ANACHRONISMS
PO Box 360743, Milpitas CA 95035 (408)262-5250. Cliveden Chew Haas.

*WAIL SONGS
PO Box 29888, Oakland CA 94604. Cassettes.

LISTINGS BY STATE

ALABAMA

*BIRMINGHAM PUBLIC LIBRARY
2020 Park Pl, Birmingham AL 35203
(205)254-2541. Funding info.

VENUES

AUBURN UNIVERSITY
316 Foy Union, Auburn AL 36849
(205)826-5292. Some concerts. CP:
AUBURN PLAINSMAN weekly 19K.

UNIV OF NORTHERN ALABAMA
PO Box 5347, Univ Stn, Florence AL
35630 (205)766-4100. Some concerts.
CP: FLOR-ALA weekly 4500.

*SOUTHERN APPALAACHIAN
  DULCIMER ASSN
Rte 1, Box 473, Helena AL 35080.
Charles Ellis.

*HUNTSVILLE MOUNTAIN
  DULCIMER ASSN
416 Green Acres Dr NW, Huntsville
AL 35805. J R Maulsby.

*TENN VALLEY OLDTIME FIDDLERS
305 Stella Dr, Madison AL 35758.
THE DEVIL'S BOX.

UNIVERSITY OF SOUTHERN ALABAMA
Student Union, Univ Stn, Mobile AL
36688 (205)460-7144. Some concerts.
CP: VANGUARD weekly 7000.

TROY STATE UNIVERSITY
Adams Ctr, Troy AL 36081 (205)566-
3000. Some concerts. CP: TROPOLITAN
weekly 4000.

*ALABAMA FOLKLIFE ASSN
U of AL, c/o McCallum, Box S,
University AL 35486.

FESTIVALS

ALABAMA STATE FAIR
PO Box 3800-B, Birmingham AL 35208
(205)787-2641.

*MAY ON THE MOUNTAINS FEST
Held at Louvin Bros Music Park.
Rte 2, Box 156-A, Henagar AL 35978.
Bluegrass. May.

*TALLADEGA COLLEGE ARTS FEST
Talladega AL 35160 (205)362-0206.
Varied arts. April.

*VANDIVER BLUEGRASS FEST
Rte 1, Box 106, Vandiver AL 35176
(205)672-9500. Late June.

MUSEUMS

*ANNISTON MUSEUM
4301 McClellan Blvd, PO Box 1587,
Anniston AL 36202 (205)237-6766.
Annual ethnic festival.

*W.C. HANDY MUSEUM
620 W College St, Florence AL 35630
(205)766-7410. Birthplace.

*AL DEPT OF ARCHIVES & HISTORY
624 Washington Ave, Montgomery AL
36130 (205)832-6510.

*THE OLD TAVERN
Capitol Park, PO Box 1665,
Tuscaloosa AL 35401 (205)758-8163.

PRINT

ATHENIAN
Athens State Coll, Athens AL 35611
Monthly 1500.

*BIRMINGHAM NEWS
PO Box 2553, Birmingham AL 35202
(205)325-2222. Oliver Roosevelt.

*BIRMINGHAM POST-HERALD
PO Box 2553, Birmingham AL 35202
(205)325-2222. Mitch Mendelssohn.

HILLTOP NEWS
Birmingham-Southern, 800 8 Ave N,
Birmingham AL 35254. Weekly 1000.

EXECUTIVE
Geo Wallace State Comm College,
Dothan AL 36303. Monthly 2000.

*GADSDEN TIMES
401 Locust St, Gadsden AL 35999
(205)547-7521. Deirdre Coakley.

EXPONENT
U of AL, 4701 Univ Dr, Huntsville
AL 35899. Weekly 4500.

HUNTSVILLE TIMES
PO Box 1487, West Stn, Huntsville
AL 35807.

CHANTICLEER
Jacksonville State U, Jacksonville
AL 37265. Weekly 6000.

*MOBILE PRESS/REGISTER
304 Government St, Mobile AL 36630
(205)433-1551. Gordon Tatum, Jr.

SPRINGHILLIAN
Springhill Coll, 4307 Old Shell Rd,
Mobile AL 36608. 2x monthly 1000.

ALABAMIAN
U of Montevallo, Montevallo AL
35115 (205)665-2521. 2x mthly 2500.

GARGOYLE
Huntingdon Coll, 1500 Fairview Ave,
Montgomery AL 36106. 2x mthly 750.

*MONTGOMERY ADVERTISER
PO Box 1000, Montgomery AL 36192
(205)262-1611.

MAROON & WHITE
Alabama A&M U, Normal AL 35762.
Weekly 2500.

ALABAMA MONTHLY
PO Drawer 16, Tuscaloosa AL 35402
(205)752-28144.

CAMPUS DIGEST
Tuskegee Institute, Tuskegee AL
36083. 2x monthly 4500.

RADIO

*WEGL (91)
Auburn Univ, 1239 Haley Ctr, Auburn
AL 36830 (205)826-5184. Jeff
Bradley.

WBHM
U of AL, 1028 7th Ave S, Birmingham
AL 35294. CP: KALEIDOSCOPE 2x
weekly 8000.

*WEXP (91.5)
Gadsen State JC, 100 Wallace Dr,
Gadsen AL 35903 (205)546-0484 x
259. Ken Stokes. CP: COURIER
monthly 1000.

*WLRH (NPR-89.3)
222 Holmes Ave E, Huntsville AL
35801 (205)539-9405. Tom Godel. 9
hrs folk. PG.

WELR
Box 709, Roanoke AL 36274.

WUAL
U of AL, PO Box 100, University AL
35486. CP: CRIMSON WHITE daily 15K.

ALASKA

*ANCHORAGE LIBRARY
U of AK, 3211 Providence Dr,
Anchorage AK 99504 (907)263-1848.
Funding info.

VENUES

*ABOTMA - ALASKA BLUEGRASS &
  OLD-TIME MUSIC ASSOCIATION
601 E Northern Lights Blvd, #199,
Anchorage AK 99503. Festival,
concerts, newsletter. Monthly jams
at 2605 Eide St. Ken Terry
(907)333-1217.

*AMERICAN PIE SHOPPE
555 W Northern Lights Blvd,
Anchorage AK (907)272-7569. Some
folk evenings.

*DANCING BEARS
Box 3-366, ECB, Anchorage AK 99501.

*FLY BY NIGHT CLUB
Spenard Rd, Anchorage AK.

*GRAND CENTRAL STATION
549 W Intl Airport Rd, Anchorage.

*MOUNTAIN VIEW COMMUNITY CTR
315 Price St, Anchorage AK. Dances,
jams.

BULL'S EYE
Box 81324, College AK 99708
(907)488-3992. Laine St. John.

INST OF ALASKAN NATIVE ARTS
PO Box 80583, Fairbanks AK 99708.
Newsletter.

ALICE'S CHAMPAGNE PALACE
PO Box 1244, Homer AK 99603 (907)
235-7650. Lu Lovelace.

FESTIVALS

*ALASKA FESTIVAL OF MUSIC
PO Box 10325, Anchorage AK 99510
(907)238-1898. At Anchorage
Community Coll. Classical, some
folk. Early Sept.

*ALASKA FOLK FESTIVAL
PO Box 1748, Juneau AK 99802. Apr.

*ALASKA STATE FAIR
Box 1128, Palmer AK 99645 (907)745-4827. Late Aug.

*KSKA ALASKA BLUEGRASS &
  FOLK MUSIC FESTIVAL
Run by KSKA, Alaska Pacific U, 4101
Univ Ave, Anchorage AK 99508 (907)
561-1161. Wendy Kamrass. July.

*KSKO BLUEGRASS FESTIVAL
Run by KSKO, Box 4, McGrath AK
99627 (907)524-3001. Organizer:
Will Peterson. July.

*SITKA FOLK FESTIVAL
Box 3023, Sitka AK. Nancy
Mitashval. Early Oct.

*SUMMER SOLSTICE BLUEGRASS FEST
State Campground, nr Anchorage. Run
by ABOTMA (above). June.

The ABOTMA Newsletter lists other
festivals, including the following:

*NENANA RIVER DAYS - early June.
Free. On banks of Tatana River.

*SUTTON MUSIC FESTIVAL
Sutton. (907)745-2328. Charlie
Overby. Mid-June.

*TALKEETNA BLUEGRASS FEST
Goose Creek, Parks Hwy. (907)495-6518. Dirty Ernie. Early August.

MUSEUMS

*ANCHORAGE HISTORICAL &
  FINE ARTS MUSEUM
121 W 7th St, Anchorage AK 99501
(907)264-4326.

*UNIV OF ALASKA MUSEUM
907 Yukon Dr, Fairbanks AK 99701
(907)474-7505.

*ALASKA INDIAN ARTS
23 Ft Seward Dr, PO Box 271, Haines
AK 99827 (907)766-2160. Dance
recitals.

*ALASKA STATE MUSEUM
Subport, Pouch FM, Juneau AK 99811
(907)465-2901.

*BARAANOF MUSEUM
Erskine Ho, 101 Marine Way, Box 61,
Kodiak AK 99615

PRINT

ANCHORAGE NEWS
200 Patten Dr, Pouch 6616, Anchorge
AK 99502.

*ANCHORAGE TIMES
Box 40, Anchorage AK 99510 (907)
263-9000. Carmen Dybdahl.

*FAIRBANKS NEWS-MINER
Box 710, Fairbanks AK 99707 (907)
456-6661.

RADIO

*KABN (830AM)
334 E 2 Ave, Anchorage AK 99501
(907)276-3881. Scott Waterman,
Tricia King. Interviews.

*KSKA (NPR-103.1)
Alaska Pacific U, 4101 Univ Ave,
Anchorage AK 99508 (907)276-3000.
Sharon Harris, Wendy Kamrass. PG.

KBRW
Box 109, Barstow AK 99723.

KDLG (NPR-670AM)
Box 670, Dillingham AK 99723.

KUAC (NPR-104.7)
U of AK, Fairbanks AK 99704 (907)
474-7491. Michael Berndt. 10 hrs
folk. PG. CP: SUN-STAR wkly 3000.

*KHNS (NPR-102.3)
PO Box 245, Haines AK 99827.

*KBBI (NPR-1250AM)
PO Box 1085, 215 E Main Ct, Homer
AK 99603 (907)235-7721. Charles
Andrews. PG. Celtic, live folk
fests.

*KTOO (NPR-104.3)
224 4th St, Juneau AK 99801.

*KXMT (NPR-100.1)
PO Box 484, Kodiak AL 99615 (907)
486-3181. Jamie Rodriguez. 12%
folk. PG. 13000 audience.

KOTZ (NPR-720AM)
Box 78, Kotzebue AK 99752.

*KSKO (NPR-870AM)
Box 4, McGrath AK 99627 (907)524-3001. Folk programs. Runs Bluegrass Festival in July.

*KFSK (NPR-100.9)
PO Box 149, Petersburg AK 99833. A MIXED BAG 9pm Sunday.

*KCAW (NPR-104.7)
Box 520, Sitka AK 99835 (907)747-5877. Jake Schumacher. Folk, blues, bluegrass, diverse musics.

ARIZONA

*PHOENIX PUBLIC LIBRARY
Social Sciences, 12 E McDowell Rd, Phoenix AZ 85004 (602)262-4782. Funding info.

*TUCSON PUBLIC LIBRARY
200 S 6th Ave, Tucson AZ 85701 (602)791-4393. Funding info.

VENUES

COCHISE COLLEGE
Student Union, Douglas AZ 85607 (602)364-79443. Some concerts. CP: APACHE monthly 3000.

*ARIZONA FRIENDS OF FOLKLORE
N AZ U, Box 5705, Flagstaff AZ 86011 (602)526-3547. Kathryn Cunningham. SOUTHWEST FOLKLORE quarterly.

CHARLY'S
23 N Laroux, Flagstaff AZ 86011 (602)779-1919. Charly Spining.

*COCONINO CENTER FOR THE ARTS
PO Box 296, Flagstaff AZ 86002. (607)779-5944. David Schaub.

NORTHERN ARIZONA UNIVERSITY
Student Union, Flagstaff AZ 86011 (602)523-2391. Some concerts. CP: LUMBERJACK weekly 11000.

ROCKY MTN FOLKLORE CAUCUS
N AZ U, Flagstaff AZ 86011. Newsletter.

*AZ BLUEGRASS ASSN
4044 N 44th Pl, Phoenix AZ 85018.

EMERY-RIDDLE AERO UNIVERSITY
Student Union, Prescott AZ 86302 (602)778-4130. Some concerts. CP: PIONEER monthly 900.

WAREHOUSE
130 E University Dr, Tempe AZ 85281 (602)966-7788.

*SOUTHERN AZ OLDTIME FIDDLERS
PO Box 5334, Tucson AZ 85703. FIDDLESTICKS.

*SOUTHWEST FOLKLORE CTR
U of AZ, 1524 E 6th St, Tucson AZ 85721 (602)621-3392. Jim Griffith.

*TUCSON FRIENDS OF TRAD MUSIC
PO Box 40654, Tucson AZ 85717 (602) 626-3487. Newsletter.

ARIZONA WESTERN COLLEGE
Student Union, Yuma AZ 85364 (602) 726-1000. Some concerts. CP: WESTERN PRESS weekly 1000.

FESTIVALS

*ARIZONA FOLK FAIR
Tempe Historical Museum, 3500 S Rural Rd, PO Box 272394, Tempe AZ 85282 (602)966-7253. April.

*SW TRADITIONAL MUSIC FEST
HCR Box 412, Benson AZ 85602 (602)624-6646. Anna Duff. Trad, contemp, old-time. Workshops. Mid-June.

*STATE CHAMPIONSHIP OLD-TIME FIDDLERS CONTEST
1480 E Bethany Home Rd, #180, Phoenix AZ 85014 (602)474-4515. Late September.

MUSEUMS

*THE AMERIND FOUNDATION
PO Box 248, Dragoon Rd, Dragoon AZ 85609 (602)586-3003. Ethnohistory of the Southwest & Mexico.

*TEMPE HISTORICAL MUSEUM
3500 S Rural Rd, PO Box 272394, Tempe AZ 85282 (602)966-7253.

PRINT

CACTUS
Central Arizona College, Coolidge
AZ 85228. Weekly 3000.

VOICE
Glendale CC, 6000 W Olive Ave,
Glendale AZ 85302. Weekly 4000.

*MESA TRIBUNE and others
PO Box 1547, Mesa AZ 85201 (602)
898-6520. Pat Conner.

LEGEND
Mesa Community College, Mesa AZ
85201. Weekly 10000.

*ARIZONA LIVING
5046-C N 7 St, Phoeniz AZ 85014
(602)264-4295. Joe Kullman.

*ARIZONA REPUBLIC
120 E Van Buren St, Phoenix AZ
85004 (602)271-8979.

NEW TIMES
111 W Monroe, #819, Phoenix AZ
85004.

*PHOENIX
4707 N 12, Phoenix AZ 85014 (602)
248-8900. Jeff Burger. Monthly mag.

PHOENIX GAZETTE
PO Box 1950, Phoenix AZ 85001.

CAMPUS NEWS
Scottsdale Community College,
Scottsdale AZ 85251. Wkly 3000.

GILA MONSTER
E AZ State Coll, Thatcher AZ 95552.
Weekly 1400.

ARIZONA DAILY STAR
PO Box 26807, Tucson AZ 85726. Pam
Parrish.

AZTEC PRESS
Pima CC, 2202 W Anklam Rd, Tucson
AZ 05709. Weekly 8500.

*TUCSON CITIZEN
PO Box 26767, Tucson AZ 85726 (602)
573-4626. Chuck Graham.

TUCSON STAR
PO Box 26807, Tucson AZ 85726.

RADIO

KASR
AZ State U, 123 E University, Tempe
AZ 85281 (602)965-4163. Lisa Macek.
CP: STATE PRESS daily 18000.

KNCC
Navajo Comm Coll, Tsaile AZ 06556.

*KUAT
Univ of AZ, MLB Rm 222, Tucson AZ
85721 (602)621-7548. Interviews.
CP: AZ DAILY WILDCAT, 22500.

KXCI
145 E Congress St, Tucson AZ 85701.

*KNNB
PO Box 310, Whiteriver AZ 85944.

KAWC (NPR-1320AM)
PO Box 929, Yuma AZ 85364.

ARKANSAS

Happy 150th Birthday in 1986!

*ARKANSAS SESQUICENTENNIAL
PO Box 1986, Little Rock AR 72203
(501)371-1500. Statewide events.

*AR DEPT OF PARKS & TOURISM
1 Capitol Mall, Little Rock AR
72201. Calendar of Events.

*ARKANSAS CULTURAL HERITAGE
225 E Markham, #200, Little Rock AR
72201 (501)371-1639. Concerts,
contests, festivals, etc.

*LITTLE ROCK PULIC LIBRARY
Reference Dept, 700 Louisiana St,
Little Rock AR 72201 (501)370-5950.
Funding info.

VENUES

HENDERSON STATE UNIVERSITY
Student Union, Arkadelphia AR 71923
(501)246-5511. Some concerts. CP:
ORACLE weekly 3000.

*ARKANSAS COLLEGE
Student Activities, Batesville AR
72501 (501)793-9813 x 242. Mark
Wood, PR Director. Some concerts,
Scottish Festival.

OZARK STATES FOLKLORE SOCIETY
Arkansas Coll, Batesville AR 72501.

*AR TRAVELLER FOLK & DINNER
  THEATRE
Box 536, Hardy AR 72542 (501)856-
2256. Late May-late Aug.

ARKANSAS COUNTRY DANCE SOC
31 Hampshire Circle, Little Rock AR
72212. Neil Kelley. ARKANSAS
COUNTRY DANCER.

*OZARK FOLK CENTER
Mountain View AR 72560 (501)269-
3851. Concerts, workshops, craft
demos, conferences. Folk culture
museum, record & tape library.

FOLKLIFE SOCIETY
324 Walnut, Newport AR 72112 (501)
523-6250.

RACKENSACK FOLKLORE SOC
Mountain View AR 72560.

ARKANSAS TECHNICAL UNIVERSITY
Student Activities Board,
Russellville AR 72801 (501)968-
0368. Some concerts. CP: ARKA TECH
weekly 2500.

*SALEM COUNTRY MUSIC ASSOC
PO Box 848, Salem AR 72576 (501)
895-2491. Concerts, contests, etc.

*TEXARKANA REGIONAL ARTS &
  HUMANITIES COUNCIL
PO Box 1171, Texarkana, AR-TX
75504-1171 (214)792-8681. Concerts.

*OZARK NATIVE ARTS & CRAFTS
RR2, Box 139, Winslow AR 72959
(501)634-3791. Exhibits, fairs.

FESTIVALS

*ARKANSAS FOLK FESTIVAL
Held at Ozark Folk Ctr. PO Box 500,
Mountain View AR 72560 (501)269-
3851. Elliott Hancock. Trad crafts
and music. April.

ARKANSAS FIDDLERS CONVENTION
Chamber of Commerce, PO Box 939,
Harrison AR 72601 (501)741-2659.
Mid-March.

*ARKANSAS HERITAGE WEEK
Events statewide. 225 E Markham,
#200, Little Rock AR 72201
(501)371-1639. Music, tours,
crafts, exhibits, history. May.

*FIDDLE CONTEST/SPRING FEST
Chamber of Commerce, Box 551,
Eureka Springs AR 72632 (501)253-
8737. Mid-April.

*LESTER FLATT MEMORIAL PARK
Otto AR. info: O.G. Kuykendall,
1 Beth Dr, Gravel Ridge AR 72076
(501) 835-2451. Various fests, inc
GOSPEL MUSIC May, Aug; MOUNTAIN
MUSIC July, Aug.

GOSPEL SINGING CONVENTION
Held at Spring Park. 1200 W Main,
Heber Springs AR 72543 (501)362-
2641. D.F. Magness. Mid-July.

*MOUNTAIN & HAMMERED
  DULCIMER WEEKEND
Held at Ozark Folk Ctr. PO Box 500,
Mountain View AR 72560 (501)269-
3851. Late April.

OLD TIMERS' DAY
Events along historic Main Street.
Chamber of Commerce, PO Box 652,
Van Buren AR 72956 (501)474-2761.
Music, crafts, etc. Early May.

OZARK FOLK FESTIVAL
Held in City Auditorium. PO Box 88,
Eureka Springs AR 72632 (501)253-
8737. Max Hunter. Trad music,
crafts. Late Oct.

*TURKEY TRACK BLUEGRASS FEST
PO Box 419, Waldron AR 72958 (501)
637-3862. Bill Churchill. Oct.

MUSEUMS

*MILES MUSICAL MUSEUM
Hwy 62 W, PO Box 488, Eureka
Springs AR 7262232 (501)253-8961.
Over 100 stringed instruments.

*BUFFALO NATIONAL RIVER
PO Box 1173, Harrison AR 72601
(501)741-5443. 700-vol library on
Ozark folklife.

RADIO

*SOUTHWEST TIMES RECORD
920 Rogers Ave, Ft Smith AR 72901
(501)785-7746. Jane Ramos.

PIONEER EXPRESS
N AR Community College, Harrison AR
72601. Monthly 1000.

LAKER
Garland City Community College, Hot
Springs AR 71901. 2x monthly 2000.

*ARKANSAS DEMOCRAT
Box 2221, Little Rock AR 72203
(501)378-34472. Eric Harrison.

*ARKANSAS GAZETTE
PO Box 1821, Little Rock AR 72203
(501)371-3373724. Kelley Bass.

*ARKANSAS TIMES
PO Box 34010, Little Rock AR 72203
(501)375-2985.

FORUM
U of AR, 33rd & University, Little
Rock AR 72204. Weekly 4500.

ARKANSAWYER
U of AR, Cedar St N, Pine Bluff AR
71601. Monthly 4000.

MID-SOUTH FOLKLORE
AR State, English Div, Box 779,
State University AR 72467. William
M. Clements.

RADIO

KJWH
Box 606, Camden AR 71701.

KHDX
Hendrix College, Conway AR 72032.

KUCA (91.3)
U of Central AR, Box A, Conway AR
72032 (501)450-3161. Cary
Shillcutt.

*KESP
PO Box 547, Eureka Springs AR
72632.

KVAF
U of AR, 103 N Duncan, Fayetteville
AR 72701. Folk interest. CP:
ARKANSAS TRAVELER 2x wkly 8000.

*KABF
1501 Arch, Little Rock AR 72202.
Mark Oswald.

*FOLK SAMPLER
Box 3012, Siloam Springs AR 72761
(501)-524-5703. Mike Flynn. Show
syndicated to 40 US, 30 Australian
stations.

KASU
AR State U, PO Box 2160, State
University AR 72467 (501)972-3070.
Sherry Williford. CP: HERALD 2x
weekly 7250.

CALIFORNIA

*CA COMMUNITY FOUNDATION
1151 W South St, Los Angeles CA
90017 (213)413-4719. Funding info.

*CA PRESENTERS BOOKING NET
U of CA, University Events Office
B-009, La Jolla CA 92093-0001 (619)
452-4090. Lynne Peterson. Booking
consortium.

*U OF CA INTERCAMPUS ARTS
ICE Program Q-055, U of CA, La
Jolla CA 92093 (619)452-4929.
Michael Addison. Booking
consortium.

VENUES

*HUMBOLDT FOLKLIFE SOC
Box 1061, Arcata CA 95521 (707)822-
7150. Calendar 6/yr.

*HUMBOLDT STATE UNIV
CenterArts, Arcata CA 95521 (707)
826-4411. Peter Pennekamp.
Concerts.

*JAMBALAYA CLUB
915 H St, Arcata CA 95521 (707)822-
4766. Jake McCarthy. Some folk.

*ASHKENAZ MUSIC & DANCE CAFE
1317 San Pablo Ave, Berkeley CA
94702 (415)525-5054. David Nadel.
Dances, folk and other.

ASIAN FOLKLORE STUDIES GROUP
U of CA, 206 Stephens Hall,
Berkeley CA 94720. Newsletter.

*ASUC SUPERB PRODUCTIONS
201 Student Union, U of CA,
Berkeley CA 94720 (415)642-7477.
Concerts. CP: BERKELEY REVIEW
weekly 1300, DAILY CALIFORNIAN
20000.

*BERKELEY MORRIS
58527-1/2 Patton, Oakland CA 94618
(415)658-5341. Terry O'Neal.

*BERKELEY SOC FOR PRESERVATION
OF TRADITIONAL MUSIC
1827 San Pablo Ave, Berkeley CA
94702.

*CAMPS, INC
1744 University Ave, Berkeley CA
94703 (415)549-2396. Music & dance
camps in Summer.

FOLKLORE ALLIANCE
U of CA, Kroeber Hall, Berkeley CA
94720. Newsletters.

*FREIGHT & SALVAGE
1827 San Pablo Ave, Berkeley CA
94720 (415)548-1761. Varied
acoustic music. Weds-Sun. Seats 80.

*JULIA MORGAN THEATER
2640 College Ave, Berkeley CA 94704
(415)548-2687. Sean McCallough, Amy
Gorman. Mostly theater, some music.

*JULIE'S PLACE
Unitarian Fellowship Hall, 1606
Bonita Ave @ Cedar St, Berkeley CA
94709. Mostly Sat. Acoustic music,
natl/internatl performers. Booking:
Barry Smiler, (415)526-8470 1023
Key Rte Blvd, Albany CA 94706.

*LA PENA
3105 Shattuck Ave, Berkeley CA
94705 (415)849-2568. Cultural,
info, fund-raising resource ctr.
Concerts. Newsletter. La Tienda
consignment gift shop retails items
for solidarity orgs. Cafe Violeta.

*STARRY PLOUGH
3101 Shattuck, Berkeley CA 94705
(415)841-2082. Irish pub sessions
on Mon.

*UNIV OF CA
Committee for Arts & Lectures, 101
Zellerbach Hall, Berkeley CA 94720
(415)642-0212. Ella Baff. Intl folk
dance groups, occasional concerts.

*SOUTHERN CA OLDTIME FIDDLERS
Star Rte, Box 89, Caliente CA
93518. Howard & Joy Moore.
Newsletter.

*FOLK MUSIC SOC OF MONTEREY
26380 Val Verde Dr, Carmel CA
93923. Joe Broadman.

*CENTRAL CA OLDTIME FIDDLERS
2805 Charlotte Ave, Ceres CA 95307.
Alva Davis.

CALIFORNIA STATE UNIV
Bell memorial Union, Chico CA 95929
(916)895-5701. Some concerts. CP:
NEWS & REVIEWS weekly 29000; ORION
weekly 7200.

*CHICO FOLK CLUB
PO Box 3406, Chico CA 95927 (916)
891-5192. Pete La Velle.

*FOLK MUSIC CENTER
220 Yale Ave, Claremont CA 91711
(714)624-2928. Charles & Dorothy
Chase. Music store, some concerts/
workshops. Annual Spring festival.

*CITY OF CONCORD
PO Box 6166, Concord CA 94524-1166
(415)671-3270. John Toffoli, Jr.
Concerts.

*ORANGE COAST COLLEGE
Community Services, 2701 Fairview
Rd, Costa Mesa CA 92628 (714)432-
5880. George Blanc.

*COTATI CABARET
85 La Plaza, Cotati CA 94928
(707)795-7783. Mark Bronstein,
Leslie Swanson. Seats 250. NOTEBOOK.

*SONOMA COUNTY FOLK SOCIETY
PO Box 555, Cotati CA 94938 (707)
542-4586. Nancy DiBello. Monthly
meetings, some concerts, newsltr.

*PALMS PLAYHOUSE
726 Road 103, Davis CA 95616 (916)
756-8502. Linda McDonough.

*BASEMENT COFFEEHOUSE
1226 N Alvarado St, Echo Park CA
(213)413)9111. Open Mike Sat.

*FOLK SONG SOC OF SAN DIEGO
1715 Somerland St, El Cajon CA
92021. Joy Bloom.

AMUSEMENT CONSPIRACY
PO Box 517, Encino CA 91316 (213)
981-9433. Art Newberger. Concerts.

*ASSN OF HUMBOLDT ARTISTS
422 First St, Eureka CA 95501
(707)442-0278. Arts org.

*OLD TOWN BAR & GRILL
327 2nd St, Eureka CA 95501
(707)445-2971 or 3168. Deborah
Lasio. Seats 300.

HILDERAND'S WINE BAR
85 Bolinas Rd #9, Fairfax CA 94930
(415)457-1394. Local acts. Sat.

*CAL FOLK ARTS SOCIETY
609 Sutter St, Folsom CA 95630
(916)985-3411. Jeff & Penny Cloud.
Concerts in various venues.

*FINN MACCOOL'S
2220 Tulare St, Fresno CA (209)485-
3466. Mary Hanson. Bar, with Celtic
concerts Tues-Sat.

FRESNO FOLKLORE SOC
PO Box 4617, Fresno CA 93728. Glen
Delpit. FLYER.

*POLESTAR PRODUCTIONS
4838 N Blackstone Ave, #A, Fresno
CA (800)344-7383.

CALIFORNIA STATE UNIV
Students Union 202, Fullerton CA
90007 (213)741-7561. Some concerts.
CP: DAILY TROJAN 11000; ROW RUN
2x monthly 5000.

*FRIENDS OF FOLK MUSIC
7111 Talbert Ave, Huntington Beach
CA 92648.

*COLLEGE OF MARIN
Public Events, Kentfield CA 94904
(415)485-9319. Steven Barclay.
Concerts.

*ON STAGE MUSIC
PO Box 683, Kentfield CA 94914
(415)459-2862. Jan Tangen, Pres.
Performance classes, camps.

*OLD TIME CAFE
1464 N Hwy 101, Leucadia CA 92024
(619)436-4030. Pearl Wolf. Varied
acoustic music. Seats 50. Sometimes
2 shows nightly.

*LONG BEACH TRADITIONAL
   FOLK MUSIC CLUB
4714 Clark Ave, Long Beach CA
90844. (213)429-2774. Vickie
Thompson. 3rd Fri.

*BLUES UNLIMITED
3701 W 54th St, Los Angeles CA
(213)294-5127.

CALIFORNIA FOLKLORE SOC
U of CA, Folklore & Mythology
Program, Los Angeles CA 90024 (213)
825-7041. FOLKAL POINT, FOLKLORE
& MYTH, WESTERN FOLKLORE.

CALIFORNIA STATE UNIVERSITY
5154 State University Dr, Los
Angeles CA 90032 (213)224-2123.
Some concerts. CP: UNIVERSITY TIMES
daily 8000.

*FOLK DANCE FEDN OF CA, SOUTH
13250 Ida Ave, Los Angeles CA
90066.

*GORKY'S
536 E 8th St, Los Angeles CA (213)
627-4060. Varied music most nights.

*JAPANESE AMERICAN
   CULTURAL CENTER
244 S San Pedro Rd, Los Angeles CA
90012 (215)628-2725. Concerts.

*LEDAY'S LOUNGE
1321 N La Brea Blvd, Los Angeles CA
(213)419-7726. Live blues Thur-Sat.

UNIV OF CALIFORNIA
Campus Programs, Los Angeles CA
90024 (213)825-7471. Some concerts.
CP: UCLA DAILY BRUIN 20000.

*OCEAN PRODUCTIONS
2035 Estridillo St, Martinez CA
94553 (415)229-2710. James Ocean.
Concert production, coffeehouse.

*PENINSULA MOUNTAIN
   DULCIMER CLUB
PO Box 104, Menlo Park CA 94026.
Newsletter.

*BREAD & ROSES
78 Throckmorton Ave, Mill Valley CA
94941 (415)381-0320. Pam Cleland.
Artists volunteer to play in
hospitals etc.

*SWEETWATER
153 Throckmorton Ave Mill Valley CA
94941 (415)388-2820. Jay & Jeannie
Patterson. R & B. Seats 65.

*HOUSE CONCERTS
390 Alcatraz Ave, Oakland CA 94609
(415)655-8604. Doug Faunt.

*RIDGDEWAY CAFE
208 Ridgeway Ave, Oakland CA
(415)653-8866. Heidi Barton. House
concerts chez Heidi.

*OJAI FOLK CONCERTS
301 Bald St, Ojai CA 93023 (805)
646-5163. Tom & Becky Lowe. Various
venues, inc house concerts.

*CAL STATE OLDTIME FIDDLERS
PO Box 1703, Oroville CA 95965.
SOUND POST.

*HAMMER DULCIMER SOC
PO Box 60766, Palo Alto CA 94306
(415)494-3117. Events, workshops,
newsletter.

*IN TOTO
2381 Middlefield Rd, Palo Alto CA
94301 (415)322-9441. One concert a
week. Folk, Latino, political.
Seats over 100.

*PALO ALTO MORRIS & SWORD
PO Box 51555, Palo Alto CA 94303
(415)327-0269. Susan L. Pross.

*SPANGENBERG THEATER COMPLEX
780 Arastradero Rd, Palo Alto CA
94306 (415)855-8242. Galen Wolf.
Concerts.

*AMBASSADOR INTERNATIONAL
   CULTURAL FOUNDATION
300 W Green St, Pasadena CA 91129
(818)304-6166. Wayne Shriket.
Concerts.

*VALLEY OF THE MOON
   SCOTTISH FIDDLING SCHOOL
1938 Rose Villa St, Pasadena CA
91107. Jan Tappan (818)793-3716,
Bonnie Thompson (415)668-0612,
Sally Ashcraft (415)331-3241.
Tuition, ceidlidhs, camps.

MARIPOSA FEEDBACK THEATER
Box 155, Raymond CA 93653 (209)966-
2748. Bob & Doi DeWitt. Concerts.

*PRISM MUSIC
4795 Friendship La, Redding CA
96001. Dan Howard, (916)244-9421;
Jane Ryder (916)241-9374.

*BARN COFFEEHOUSE
UC Riverside, 1531 Ransom Rd,
Riverside CA 92506 (714)682-3621.
Dot Harris.

*RIVERSIDE FOLK SONG SOCIETY
880 Navajo Dr, Riverside CA 92507.

*EAST BAY CENTER FOR THE
   PERFORMING ARTS
339 11th St, Richmond CA 94804
(415)234-5624. Sylvia Tucker.
Concerts.

CALIFORNIA STATE COLLEGE
1801 E Cotati Ave, Rohnert Park CA
94928 (707)664-2391. Some concerts.
CP: HOMEGROWN.

*FIFTH STRING
5522 H St, Sacramento CA (916)447-
8282. Skip Green. Tues-Weds.

MARIN COUNTY FOLKSONG SOC
7 Morningside Dr, San Anselmo CA
94960 (415)456-0427. John Barger.
Singarounds every other Friday.

*PENINSULA FOLK MUSIC CLUB
PO Box 53, San Carlos CA 94070
(415)591-9579. Meets at Burton
Park. FOLK NOTES.

*BAY AREA COUNTRY DANCE SOC
PO Box 22165, San Francisco CA
94110. Contact Joyce & David Uggla,
2235 Ralmar, E Palo Alto CA 94303
(415)321-2773.

*US/SCOTTISH FIDDLING REVIVAL
1938 Rose Villa St, Pasadena CA
91107.

*CALIFORNIA BLUEGRASS ASSN
PO Box 11287, San Francisco CA
94110. BLUEGRASS BREAKDOWN.

*CASTLE FOLK CLUB
Edingburgh Castle, 950 Geary, San
Francisco CA (415)885-4074. Res:
Allan Macleod, Dick Holdstock,
Redmond O'Connell. 1st & 3rd Thurs.
Bookings: Allan Macleod, 4438 Park
Blvd, Oakland CA 94602 (415)531-
0339.

*GREAT AMERICAN MUSICHALL
859 O'Farrell, San Francisco CA
94109 (415)885-0750. Lee Brenkman.
Varied music, many nights.

*LAST DAY SALOON
Clement St, San Francisco CA
(415)387-6343. David Dahner.
Bluegrass most eves. Seats 200.

*MUSIC & ARTS INSTITUTE
2622 Jackson St, San Francisco CA
94115 (415)567-1445. Ross McKee.
Concerts, lectures, courses.

*PLOUGH & STARS
116 Clement, San Francisco CA 94118
(415)751-1122. Irish music most
nights.

*PLOWSHARES
Bldg C, Rm 300, Ft Mason Ctr,
Marina at Laguna St, San Francisco
CA 94123 (415)441-8910. 1 or 2
concerts a month, Sep-Jun. Seats
200. Varied acoustic music.

*SAN FRANCISCO FOLK MUSIC CLUB
885 Clayton St, San Francisco CA
94117 (415)661-2217. Faith Petric.
Singarounds alt Fridays, pot-luck
suppers, dances, camps, festivals,
newsletter 6/yr, and more fun stuff
than you can possibly imagine.

*SAN FRANCISCO MAIN LIBRARY
Civic Ctr, San Francisco CA 94102.
Free concerts. Bookings: Fay
Cuthbertson (415)731-2527. Low pay.

SANTA CLARA VALLEY FIDDLERS
1260 Branham Ave, San Jose CA
95158. Meets 1st Sunday.

*LINNAEA'S PLACE
1530 Broad, San Luis Obispo, CA
93401 (805)541-2463 or 5888. Small
folk concerts.

SANTA CRUZ BLUEGRASS SOC
De Laveago Park, Santa Cruz CA
95065. Meets 4th Sunday.

*AT MY PLACE
1026 Wilshire Blvd, Santa Monica CA
90401 (213)451-8985. Matt Kramer.
Several nights. Mostly rock, but
will book folk openers.

*MCCABE'S
3101 Pico Blvd, Santa Monica CA
90405 (213)828-8037, concert info
828-4403. John Chelow. Club and
guitar store. Seats 120.

*SANTA MONICA TRADITIONAL
    FOLK MUSIC CLUB
143 S Kenter Ave, Los Angeles CA
90049 (213)472-7662. April Wayland.
Meetings 1st Fri (call for venue).
Newsletter.

WOODHAVEN WEST
Methodist Church, 19848 Prospect,
Saratoga CA 95070 (408)252-8268 or
379-4090. Concerts 1/mo Sep-May.

*CENTRL SIERRA ARTS COUNCIL
19411 Village Dr, Sonora CA 95370
(209)532-2787.

MNTN VIEW FOLK MUSIC CLUB
257 Arriba Dr, #12, Sunnyvale CA
94086.

*CA TRADITIONAL MUSIC SOC
4401 Trancas Pl, Tarzana CA 91356
(818)342-7664. Elaine & Clark
Weissman. House concerts 10/yr, New
Year camp, festival. Journal 2/yr,
reviews, listings, etc. 10K circ.

FESTIVALS

CALIFORNIA STATE FAIR
PO Box 15649, Sacramento CA 95813
(916)641-2311. August.

*FREE FOLK FESTIVAL
Held at Ft Mason Bldgs A & C.
SFFMC, 885 Clayton St, San
Francisco CA 94117 (415)661-2217.
Mid-June.

*INTERNATIONAL FOLK DANCE
Held at Dorothy Chandler Pavilion,
LA Music Ctr. 1124 Summit Dr,
Beverly Hills CA 90210 (213)272-
5539. Irwin Parnes. January.

*LARK IN THE MORNING
    MUSIC FESTIVAL
Held at Mendocino Woodlands Camp.
PO Box 1176, Mendocino CA 95460
(707)964-5569. Mickie Zekeley.
Varied acoustic music and dance.
August, for 10 days.

*PAUL MASSON SUMMER SERIES
Held at Paul Masson Winery. 13150
Saratoga Ave, Saratoga CA 95070
(408)725-4236. Bruce Labadie. Folk,
blues, jazz, classical. Jun-Aug.
Free.

*MIDSUMMER BLUEGRASS FEST
Held at Nevada Cnty Fairgrounds,
Grass Valley. 741 East St, #198,
Woodland CA 95695-4144 (916)662-
5691 or 2906. Early Aug.

PARADISE ARTS FESTIVAL
Various public locations. 6686
Brook Way, Paradise CA 95969
(916)877-8360. Thomas E. Wilson.
Classical, Dixieland, pop.

REDLANDS BOWL SUMMER MUSIC FEST
PO Box 466, Redlands CA 92373 (714)
793-7316. Mrs. Raymond Beeler.
Classical, dance, some folk. Free.

*REDWOOD MUSIC FEST
Redwood Records, 478 W MacArthur
Blvd, Oakland CA 94609 (415)428-
9191. Sept. Redwood artists.

SAN DIEGO FOLK FESTIVAL
UCSD, La Jolla CA (619)282-7833.
Late Apr.

*SANTA ROSA OLDTIME
 FIDDLE CONTEST
1784 Allan Way, Santa Rosa CA 95404
(707)545-2218. May.

*STERN GROVE MIDSUMMER
 MUSIC FESTIVAL
1090 Sansome St, San Francisco CA
94111 (415)398-6551 or 673-1090.
Patricia Kristof Moy. Free. Sundays
mid-June to mid-Aug. Varied music
and dance.

*SUMMER SOLSTICE FEST
CTMS, 4401 Trancas Pl, Tarzana CA
91356 (818)342-7664. Elaine
Weisman. Varied music and dance.

*TOPANGA BANJO FIDDLE CONTEST
5922 Corbin, Tarzana CA 91356
(818)345-3795.

*VARIOUS FESTS including the
Pitchin' Cookin' & Spittin'
Hullabaloo. Calico Ghost Town,
PO Box 638, Yermo CA (619)254-2122.

MUSEUMS

*MALKI MUSEUM
Morongo Indian Reservation, 11-795
Fields Rd, Banning CA 92220
(714)849-7289. Indian artifacts inc
music.

*MINGEI INTERNATIONAL MUSEUM
 OF WORLD FOLK ART
4495 La Jolla Village Dr, PO Box
553, La Jolla CA 92038 (619)453-
5300. Exhibits, library.

*CRAFT AND FOLK ART MUSEUM
5814 Wilshire Blvd, Los Angeles CA
90036 (213)937-5544. Mask festival.

*SOUTHWEST MUSEUM
234 Museum Dr, Los Angeles CA
90065. Folklore collection.

*PACIFIC ASIA MUSEUM
46 N Los Robles Ave, Pasadena CA
91101 (213)449-2742. Asian folk art
collections. Concerts.

*MENDOCINO COUNTY MUSEUM
400 E Commercial St, Willits CA
95490 (707)459-2736. Local history.
Living History Days.

PRINT

*ANAHEIM BULLETIN
PO Box 351, Anaheim CA 92804 (714)
634-1567.

VOICE
Cabrillo Coll, Aptos CA 95003. 2x
monthly 5000.

*BAKERSFIELD CALIFORNIAN
PO Box 440, Bakersfield CA 93302
(805)395-7500.

RENEGADE RIP
Bakersfield Coll, 1801 Panorama,
Bakersfield CA 93305. weekly 10K.

EXPRESS
Box 3198, Berkeley CA 94703. Bart
Bull.

GOLDEN WEST BLUEGRASS
PO Box 341, Bonsall CA 92003.

BURBANK DAILY REVIEW
220 E Magnolia Blvd, Burbank CA
91502 (213)843-6700. Ellen Reagan.

BULL'S EYE
Cal State U, Dominguez Hills,
Carson CA 90747. Weekly 6000.

ORION
Cal State U, Chico CA 95929. Weekly
7200.

COLLAGE
Claremont Coll, Claremont CA 91711.
Weekly 5000.

COAST REPORT
Orange Coast Coll, Costa Mesa CA
92626. Weekly 10000.

*ORANGE COAST DAILY PILOT
PO Box 1560, Costa Mesa CA 92626
(714)642-4321.

HOOFBEAT
Cypress Coll, Cypress CA 90630.
Weekly 5000.

*DAVIS ENTERPRISE
PO Box 1078, 315 G St, Davis CA
95617 (916)756-0800. Del McColm.

*FRESNO BEE
1626 E St, Fresno CA 93786 (209)
441-6111.

RAMPAGE
Fresno City Coll, 1101 E Univ,
Fresno CA 93741. Weekly 5000.

*FULLERTON NEWS-TRIBUNE
701 W Commonwealth Ave, Fullerton
CA 92632 (714)871-2345. Art
Aguilar, Entertainment Editor.

EL VAQUERO
Glendale Coll, 1500 N Verdugo,
Glendale CA 91208. Weekly 5000.

*LEADER NEWSPAPER GROUP
(Burbank Leader, Glendale News-
Press, Foothill Leader)
111 N Isabel St, Glendale CA 91206
(818)241-4141. Patti Roberts.

PIONEER
Cal State U, Hayward CA 94542. 2x
weekly 5000.

BRANDING IRON
Goldenwest Coll, 15744 Goldenwest,
Huntington Beach CA 92647. Weekly
6000.

IRVINE WORLD NEWS
PO Box 19512, Irvine CA 92713.

UNION JACK
PO Box 1823, La Mesa CA 90241. Andy
Bairden (freelance).

*LONG BEACH PRESS-TELEGRAM
604 Pine Ave, Long Beach CA 90844
(213)435-1161.

VIKING
Long Beach City Coll, 4901 E
Carson, Long Beach CA 90808. Weekly
8000.

DAILY TROJAN and ROW RUN
U of Southern CA, Los Angeles CA.
DT: 11000. RR: 2x monthly 5000.

EXPLORER
LA SW Coll, 1600 W Imperial Hwy,
Los Angeles CA 90047. 2x mo 5K.

*LOS ANGELES DAILY NEWS
14539 Sylvan St, Van Nuys CA 91411
(818)997-4081.

*LOS ANGELES HERALD EXAMINER
1111 S Broadway, Los Angeles CA
90015 (213)774-8000.

*LOS ANGELES TIMES
Times Mirror Sq, Los Angeles CA
90053 (213)972-7745.

*L A WEEKLY
5325 Sunset Blvd, Los Angeles CA
90027. Bill Bentley, Craig Lee.

NOMMO (Black)
PACIFIC TIES (Asian-American)
TEN PERCENT (Gay/Lesbian)
TOGETHER (Women's)
U of CA, Los Angeles CA 90024. All
monthly 10000.

UCLA DAILY BRUIN
U of CA, Los Angeles CA 90024. 20K.

LARIAT
Saddleback Coll, 28000 Marguerite,
Mission Viejo CA 92692. Weekly 7K.

*MODESTO BEE
PO Box 3928, Modesto CA 95352 (209)
578-2310. Leo Stutzin.

*MONTEREY PENINSULA HERALD
PO Box 271, Monterey CA 93942
(408)646-4338.

CAMPUS NEWS
E Los Angeles City Coll, Monterey
Park CA 91754. Weekly 5000.

TALON MARKS
Cerritos Coll, Norwalk CA 90650.
Weekly 9000.

*BAM
5951 Canning St, Oakland CA 94609
(415)652-3810.

*OAKLAND TRIBUNE
PO Box 24424, Oakland CA 94623
(415)645-2647.

*PENINSULA TIMES TRIBUNE
Box 300, Palo Alto CA 94302 (415)
853-5211. Karen Smith, Music Ed.

*STAR-NEWS
525 E Colorado Blvd, Pasadena CA
91109 (818)578-6469. Luaine Lee.

PROGRESS-BULLETIN
PO Box 2708, Pomona CA 91766
(714)622-1201. Joseph H. Firman.

*RIVERSIDE PRESS-ENTERPRISE
PO Box 792, Riverside CA 92502
(714)684-1200. Doug List.

AMERICNA RIVER CURRENT
American River Coll, 4700 College
Oaks, Sacramento CA 95841. Weekly
7000.

PONY EXPRESS
Sacramento CC, 3835 Freeport Blvd,
Sacramento CA 95841. Weekly 5000.

*SACRAMENTO BEE
PO Box 15779, Sacramento CA 95852
(916)446-9211. Scott Leber.

*SACRAMENTO UNION
301 CAPITOL MALL, SACRAMENTO CA
95814 (916)442-7811.

*SAN BERNADINO SUN
399 N D St, San Bernadino CA 92401
(714)889-9666. Tom Jacobs.

*SAN DIEGO TRIBUNE and UNION
350 Camino de la Reina, San Diego
CA 92108 (619)299-3131.

BAY GUARDIAN
2700 19th St, San Francisco CA
94110 (415)824-7660. Bruce
Brugmann. Listings, reviews. Free
weekly.

FORUM
U of SF Law School, San Francisco
CA. Monthly 6000.

*SAN FRANCISCO CHRONICLE
901 Mission St, San Francisco CA
94119 (415)777-7116.

*SAN FRANCSICO EXAMINER
PO Box 7260, San Francisco CA 94120
(415)777-7937.

*SAN JOSE MERCURY NEWS
750 Ridder Park Dr, San Jose CA
95190 (408)920-5656 or 5914.

MUSTANG DAILY
CA Poly State U, San Luis Obispo CA
93407. 7000.

*TIMES
1080 S Amphlett Blvd, San Mateo CA
94402 (415)348-4338. Barbara
Bladen.

*INDEPENDENT-JOURNAL
PO Box 330, San Rafael CA 94915
(415)883-8600.

EL DON
Santa Ana Coll, 1530 W 17th, Santa
Ana CA 92706. Weekly 6000.

*REGISTER
625 Grand Ave, Santa Ana CA 92711
(714)835-1234. Jim Washburn.

*SANTA BARBARA NEWS-PRESS
Drawer MN, Santa Barbara CA 93102
(805)966-3911.

SANTA CLARA
U of Southern CA, Santa Clara CA
95060. Weekly 5000.

*EVENING OUTLOOK
1920 Colorado Ave, Santa Monica CA
90404 (213)829-6811.

*PRESS DEMOCRAT
PO Box 569, Santa Rosa CA 95401
(707)546-2020.

BARD CHORD
Songmakers, PO Box 5488, Sherman
Oaks CA 91413.

*STOCKTON RECORD
PO Box 900, Stockton CA 95201
(209)943-6397.

*DAILY BREEZE
5215 Torrance Blvd, Torrance CA
90509 (213)540-5511. Don Lechman,
Music Ed.

WARWHOOP
El Camino Coll, 16007 Crenshaw,
Torrance CA 90506. Weekly 8000.

VALLEY STAR
LA Valley Coll, 5800 Fulton, Van
Nuys CA 91401. Weekly 7500.

VAN NUYS DAILY NEWS
14539 Sylvan St, Van Nuys CA 91411.
Kevin Henry.

MOUNTAINEER WEEKLY
Mt. San Antonio Coll, 1100 N Grand,
Walnut CA 91789 (714)595-9925. 6000.

*SAN GABRIEL VALLEY TRIBUNE
1210 N Azusa Canyon Rd, W Covina CA
91790 (818)962-8811. Barbara
Tarshe.

EL PAISANO
Rio Hondo Coll, Whittier CA 90600.
2x monthly 8000.

ROUNDUP
LA Pierce Coll, 6201 Winnetka,
Woodland Hills CA 91371. Weekly 5K.

RADIO

*KHSU (NPR-90.5)
Humboldt State U, Arcata CA 95521
(707)826-3758 or 4807. Paul Keegan,
Jim Kurland. Folk. CP: LUMBERJACK
weekly 6000.

*KIWI
5252 Standard St, Bakersfield CA
93308 (805)325-5494. Robert Duffy.

KALX
U of CA, Eshelmann Hall, Berkeley
CA 94704 (415)642-1111. Max
Hechter.

*KPFA (94.1)
2207 Shattuck Ave, Berkeley CA

94704 (415)261-7386 or 647-3475.
Nancy Guinn, others. Much folk.

*FOLKSCENE MUSIC
23457 Schoolcraft St, Canoga Park
CA 91307 (213)346-4112 or 883-7557.
Roz & Howard Larmen. Producers &
hosts for KPFK, KCRW. Tapes shows,
interviews, etc.

KCHO (NPR-91.1)
Chico State U, 1st & Normal Sts,
Chico CA 95929.

*KSPC (88.7)
Pomona Coll, Thatcher Music Bldg,
Claremont CA 91711 (714)621-8157.
Kevin Gardner, Liz Milner, David
Murray. Folk Sat & Sun. Wants to
interview visiting performers. CP:
STUDENT LIFE weekly 2200.

*KKUP (91.5)
PO Box 547, Cupertino CA 95014.
Bill Hazzard. Varied folk.

*KDVS (90.3)
U of CA, 14 Lower Freeborn, Davis
CA 95616 (916)752-0728. CP:
PEOPLE'S MONITOR 2x mnthly;
CALIF AGGIE daily 13000.

KDAC
Box 1248, Ft Bragg CA 95437.

KOHL
Fremont Newark CC, PO Box 3909,
Fremont CA 94538 (415)657-KOHL.

KFCF
PO Box 4364, Fresno CA 93744.

*KFSR (90.7)
Cal State U, Shaw at Maple, Fresno
CA 93740 (209)294-2598. Kirk
Biglione. CP: DAILY COLLEGIAN 5000;
LA VOZ 2x monthly 6K; INSIGHT
weekly 6000.

*KSJV (91.5)
PO Box 12682, Fresno CA 93778.

KVPR (NPR-89.3)
754 P St, Fresno CA 93721 (209)486-
7710. Wayne Angerame, PD.

*KFCR (91.3)
Fullerton Coll, 321 E Chapman Ave,
Fullerton CA 92634 (714)871-2426.
Chuck Range.

KIEV
PO Box 1051, Hawthorne CA 90250
(213)672-4333. Tom Girvin. SOUNDS
O' THE ISLES.

*KIDE (91.13)
PO Box 1220, Hoopa CA 95546.

*KUCI
U of CA, Box 4362, Irvine CA 92717
(714)856-6868. John Talley. CP: NEW
UNIVERSITY weekly 11000.

*KSDT (95.7 cable)
U of CA, B-015, La Jolla CA 92093
(619)452-4225. CP: GUARDIAN 2x
weekly 11000.

*KULV (89.5)
U of LaVerne, 1950 3rd St, LaVerne
CA 91750 (714)596-1693. Lucy
Beloian. CP: CAMPUS TIMES weekly
2000.

KLPN (NPR-88.1)
Cal State U, 1250 Bellflower, Long
Beach CA 90840. CP: 49'ER daily
10000; UNION weekly 10000.

KFJC
Foothill Coll, 12345 El Monte Rd,
Los Altos Hills CA 94022 (415)948-
8590 x 268. CP: FOOTHILL SENTINEL
weekly 4000.

*KFAC (Mutual-92.3)
6735 Yucca St, Los Angeles CA 90028
(213)466-9566. Ed Argow.

*KSCR
U of Southern CA, SU 404, Los
Angeles CA 90089 (213)743-5727.
Terry Nelson.

*KXLU (88.9)
Loyola Marymount U, 7101 W 80th St,
Los Angeles CA 90045 (213)642-2866.
Rick Winward. CP: L A LOYOLAN
weekly 3000.

*KLA
UCLA, 308 Westwood Plaza, Los
Angeles CA 90024.

*PACIFICA RADIO FOUNDATION
5316 Venice Blvd, Los Angeles CA
90019. Radio programming service.
KBOQ (92.7)
223 Reindollar Ave, Marina CA 93933
(408)384-5755. Laura Hopper, MD.

KMFB
14200 Prairie Way, Mendocino CA
95460.

KSBR (NPR-88.5)
Mission Viejo CA 92692.

KRJB (97.7)
Broadcasting Hse, Box 230, Monte
Rio CA 95462 (415)375-1242. PG.
N Kafeley, MD.

KSMC
St Mary's Coll, Box 233, Moraga CA
94575 (415)376-1242. CP: COLLEGIAN
2x monthly 2000.

KSFH
St Francis Coll, 1855 Miramonte
Ave, Mountain View CA 94040 (415)
968-5374.

*KHYV
PO Box 3131, Modesto CA 95353
(209)523-7756. Tom & Freda Ehrman.

*KVMR (89.5)
Box 328, Nevada City CA 95959.

KPFK (90.7)
3729 Cahuenga Blvd W, N Hollywood
CA 91604 (213)877-2711. Clare
Spark, MD, Andree Enthall. Varied
format. PG.

*KCSN (88.5)
18111 Nordhoff St, Northridge CA
91330 (818)885-3089. Michael
Turner. CP: DAILY SUNDIAL 10K.

KOVA (105.5)
1205-1 Maricopa Rd, Ojai CA 93023
(805))646-1434. Richard Bailey, MD.

*RADIO CHAPMAN (90.1 cable)
Chapman Coll, 333 Glassell St,
Orange CA 92666. Chuck Martin. CP:
PANTHER weekly 1500.

*KAZU (90.3)
PO Box 206, Pacific Grove CA 93950.

*KZSU (90.1)
Palo Alto. Gwen Orell. Folk.

KPCC (89.3)
Pasadena CC, 1580 E Colorado Blvd,
Pasadena CA 91106 (213)578-7231.
Gary Nissley, MD. Ethnic. CP: PC
COURIER 2x monthly 5500.

*KCPK
Cal State Polytechnic Inst, 3801 W
Temple Ave, Pomona CA 91768
(714)598-4565.

*KUOR (89.1)
U of Redlands, 1200 E Colton Ave,
Redlands CA 92373 (714)792-0951.
John Cloud.

KUCR
U of CA, 691 Riverside, Riverside
CA 92521. CP: HIGHLANDER wkly 5K.

KSUN
Cal State Sonora, 1701 E Cotati,
Rohnert Park CA 94928.

*MICHAEL CURRY
4417 76th St, Sacramento CA 95820
(916)456-4181. Produces shows for
KALW San Fran, KYDS. House
concerts. Would like to interview
visiting performers.

*KVMR (89.5)
Sacramento. Much varied folk.

KXPR (NPR-88.9)
Cal State U, 6000 J St, Sacramento
CA 95819 (916)454-6222. Charles
Starzynski. Varied format. CP:
STATE HORNET weekly 10000.

*KVCR (NPR-91.9)
701 S Mt Vernon Ave, San Bernadino
CA 92410-2798 (714)888-6511 x 305.
Steve Ward, MD/PD. PG. 8hrs/week
bluegrass, host Bill Eason.

KBOS (NPR-89.5)
San Diego CA.

*KCR (89.1)
San Diego State U, 5300 Campanile
Dr, San Diego CA 92182 (619)265-
6280. Joel Quirt. CP: DAILY AZTEC
13000.

KFSD (CMN-94.1)
1650 6th Ave, San Diego CA 92101
(714)239-9091. Brian Stuart, MD.

*KALW (NPR-91.7)
2905 21st St, San Francisco CA
94110 (415)648-1177. Folk.

*KDFC
2822 Van Ness Ave, San Francisco CA
94109 (415)441-5332. Ed Davis.

KFAX
1470 Pine St, San Francsico CA
94109. Ethnic programming.

*KKHI (95.7)
335 Powell St, Hotel St Francis,
San Francisco CA 94102 (415)986-
2151. Gordon Engler.

*KQED (NPR-88.5)
500 8th St, San Francisco CA 94103
(415)553-2129. Laura Brodian. Folk.

*KSFS
SF State U, 1600 Holloway Ave, San
Francsico CA 94132.

*KUSF
U of San Francisco, 2130 Fulton St,
San Francisco CA 94117 (415)666-
6206. Steve Lionetti.

KSJS
San Jose State U, Washington Sq,
San Jose CA 95192 (408)277-2766.
Rob Garnier, MD. CP: INDEPENDENT
WEEKLY, SPARTAN DAILY 10000.

KCBX (NPR-90.1)
Box 95, San Luis Obispo CA 93406
(805)541-1295. Matt Elmore, MD,
Duane Tenglish. PG.

*KCPR
Cal Poly, San Luis Obispo CA 93407
(805)544-4640.

*KSM
Palomar Coll, Rm Q3, San Marcos CA
92069 (619)727-7558.

KCSM (NPR-91.1)
1700 W Hillsdale Blvd, San Mateo CA
94402 (415)574-6425. Mike Davidson,
MD. Various folk. PG.

*KTIM (100.9)
1623 5th Ave, San Rafael CA 94901
(415)456-1510.

*KCSB (91.9)
U of CA, PO Box 13401, Santa
Barbara CA 93107 (805)961-2424.
Patrice J. Cardenas (805)966-6698
hosts BLACK NAG Sat 10-12am. CP:
DAILY NEWS 11000.

KDB (93.7)
23 W Micheltorena Rd, Santa Barbara
CA 93101 (805)966-4131. Bob Scott.

*KSCU (103.3)
Santa Clara U, PO Box 1207, Santa
Clara CA 95053 (408)984-4414. Steve
Rudicel.

*KUSP (88.9)
PO Box 423, Santa Cruz CA 95061.

KZSC
U of CA, Santa Cruz CA 95064
(408)429-2811. Sarah Cardin, Andre
Jones, Maryanne Biskups. CP: CITY
ON A HILL PRESS weekly 11000.

*KCRW (NPR-89.9)
Santa Monica Coll, 1900 Pico Blvd,
Santa Monica CA 90405 (213)450-
5183. Ton Schnabel, Rene Engel,
Isobel Holt. Folk. Interviews. CP:
CORSAIR WEEKLY 5000.

*KBBR (89.1)
PO Box 7189, Santa Rosa CA 95401.

*JOHN DAVIS
PO Box 128, Sierra Madre CA 91204.
Programs for KPFK.

*KZSU (90.1)
Stanford U, PO Box 5788, Stanford
CA 94305 (415)328-2000. Frank Bird.
CP: STANFORD DAILY 16000.

*KUOP (91.3)
U of the Pacific, 3601 Pacific Ave,
Stockton CA 95211 (209)946-2582.
Jack Guilder hosts MUSICAL CHAIRS.
CP: PACIFICAN weekly 4500.

*KRCL
California Lutheran Coll, 60 W
Olson Rd, Thousand Oaks CA 91360
(805)492-0194. CP: KINGSMAN ECHO
weekly 1500.

KUKI
1400 Kuki La, Ukiah CA 95482.

KWIN
2397 N State St, Ukiah CA 95482.

*KPFK (90.7)
Box 8639, Universal City CA 91608.

STORES

*AMAZING GRACE MUSIC
111 Redhill Ave, San Anselmo CA
94960 (415)456-0414. Acoustic
guitars. Lessons, repairs.

*GENE'S GUITAR SHOP
451 Judah St, San Francisco CA
(415)753-8776. Gene Mitchell.
Repairs, sales, lessons.

*MCCABE'S GUITAR SHOP
3101 Pico Blvd, Santa Monica CA
90405 (213)828-4497. Instruments,
books, records, etc.

COLORADO

*COLORADO FOLK ARTS COUNCIL
PO Box 1226, Denver CO 80201. Vyte
Beliajus.

*DENVER PUBLIC LIBRARY
Sociology Div, 1357 Broadway,
Denver CO 80203 (303)571-2190.
Funding info.

*ROCKY MOUNTAIN CONSORTIUM
CO State U, Lory Student Ctr, Ft
Collins CO 80523 (303)491-6626.
Mims Harris. Booking consortium.

VENUES

*ARVADA CTR FOR THE ARTS
6901 Wadsworth Blvd, Arvada CO
80003 (303)431-3080. Kathy
Hotchner.

KALEIDOSCOPE
Pachamama's, 18th & Pearl, Boulder
CO 80302 (303)447-0580. Open stage
Mondays.

ASPEN CITY LIMITS
4501 E Virginia, Denver CO 80222
(303)377-2701. Blues.

CONLEY'S NOSTALGIA
554 S Broadway, Denver CO 80209
(303)777-3921. Open stage Tues.

*MUSIC ASSOC OF SWALLOW HILL
1905 S Pearl St, Denver CO 80210.
John Wolf. School, concerts,
workshops.

*UNIVERSITY OF DENVER
Cultural Programs, 2050 E Evans
Ave, Denver CO 890210 (303)753-
3527. Ellen . Markey, Dir. Some
concerts. CP: CLARION 2x wkly 10K;
FURTHERMORE monthly 8000.

*COLORADO FOLKLORE SOCIETY
Ft Lewis Coll, Durango CO 81301.
Kenneth Perlman.

*COLORADO STATE UNIVERSITY
Cultural programs, Lory Student
Ctr, Ft Collins CO 80523 (303) 491-
6626. Miriam B. Harris. Some
concerts. CP: COLLEGIAN daily 14K.

UNIV OF NORTHERN COLORADO
University Ctr, Greeley CO 80639
(303)351-2871. Some concerts. CP:
MIRROR 3x weekly 7500.

COLORADO FRIENDS OF OLDTIME
PO Box 192, Idledale CO 80453 (303)
697-0510. Music, dance. Newsletter.

*CO BLUEGRASS MUSIC SOC
13546 Omega Dr, Littleton CO
80124.Concerts, festival, jams.
Nwsltr.

*TOWN HALL ARTS CTR
2450 W Main St, Littleton CO 80120
(303)794-2787. Glenda G. Watson.

NORTHERN STAR CONCERTS
PO Box 74, Masonville CO 80541
(303)667-2416. Folk concerts.
Newsletter.

FESTIVALS

COLORADO FOLKLIFE FEST
At Four Mile Historic Park. 715 S
Forest St, Denver CO 80222 (303)
399-1859. Music, contests, crafts,
dance, food, folklife. Mid-Aug.

CO STATE DULCIMER FEST
PO Box 3050 AF, Estes Park CO 80517
(303)586-4431. Concerts, workshops,
craft demos. Early Jun.

COLORADO STATE FAIR
Fairgrounds, Pueblo CO 81004 (303)
561-8484. August.

LONGS PEAK SCOTTISH FEST
Box 3050 AP, Estes Park CO 80517
(303)586-4431. Music, dance,
crafts. Historic Buckskinners camp.
Early Sept.

*TELLURIDE BLUEGRASS FEST
Box 7212, 860 Union, Boulder CO
80302. June.

MUSEUMS

*FOUR MILE HISTORIC PARK
715 S Forest St, Denver CO 80222
(303)399-1859. Reconstructed
houses. Rural life. Festival.

*FLORENCE PIONEER MUSEUM
Pikes Peak Ave & Front St, Florence
CO 81226 (303)784-3157. Folklore
collection, library.

*FORT FRANCISCO MUSEUM
La Veta, Co 81055 (303)738-1107.
Musical instruments, taped library
of oral histories.

*OVERLAND TRAIL MUSEUM
I-76 & Hwy 6E, Sterling CO 80751
(303)522-3895. Local history,
musical instrument collection.

PRINT

*DAILY CAMERA
PO Box 591, Boulder CO 80306 (303)
442-1202.

*GAZETTE TELEGRAPH
PO Box 1779, 30 S Prospect St,
Colorado Springs CO 80903 (303)
632-5511. Linda DuVal.

DENVER MAGAZINE
899 Logan St, Denver CO 80203 (303)
832-5400. Dick Griffin, Ed, Geri
meyers, diary, Glossy monthly.

*DENVER POST
650 15th St, Denver CO 80202 (303)
820-1624. Glen Giffin, Music Ed.

METROPOLITAN
Meetro State Coll, 250 14th Ave W,
Denver CO 80204. Weekly 10000.

*ROCKY MOUNTAIN NEWS
400 W Colfax Ave, Denver CO 80204
(303)892-5447. Joe Rassenfoss.

VILTIS FOLKLORE MAGAZINE
PO Box 1226, Denver CO 80201.

WESTWORD
PO Box 5970, Denver CO 80217 (303)
534-4613. Weekly listings etc.

OREDIGGER
CO School of Mines, Golden CO
80401. Weekly 4000.

*CHIEFTAIN and STAR JOURNAL
PO Box 36, Pueblo CO 81002 (303)
544-3520. Bob Thomas, Music Ed.

RADIO

*KASF (90.9)
Adams State Coll, Alamosa CO 81101
(303)589-7154. M. Bowannie; D.
Davis. CP: SOUTH COLORADAN weekly
2200.

*KAIR (660 AM & cable 104FM)
U of CO, Campus Box 207, Boulder CO
80309 (303)492-5031. Penny Birtner.
Some blues. CP: COLORADO DAILY,
CAMPUS PRESS weekly 12000.

*KGNU (NPR-88.5)
PO Box 885, 2049 Broadway, Boulder
CO 80306 (303)449-4885. Paul
Metters, MD. Folk, blues, gospel,
international.

*KDNK (90.5)
PO Box 1388, Carbondale CO 81623.
Wick Moses.

*KRCC (91.5)
Colorado College, 117 E Cache la
Poudre, Colorado Springs CO 80903
(303)473-4801. Denise Soss, MD.

KCFR (NPR-90.1)
2056 S York, Denver CO 80208 (303)
753-3437. Jack Winter, MD. Jazz,
classical, bluegrass.

*KVOD
1601 W Jewell Ave, Denver CO (303)
936-3428. John Sampson: DOWN
TO EARTH.

*KDUR
Ft Louis Coll, PO Box 7339, Durango
CO 81301 (303)247-7262.

*KCSU
Lory Student Ctr, CO State U, Fort
Collins CO 80523 (303)491-7611.
Dawn Greening. Folk.
KMSA (91.3)
Mesa Coll, Box 2647, Grand Junction
CO 81502 (303)248-1240. Darrell
Burke, MD; David Pipe.

KUNC (NPR-91.5)
U of Northern CO, Greeley CO 80639
(303)351-2916. Bruce Clement. Folk,
jazz, classical. PG. CP: MIRROR 3x
weekly 7500.

*KDBR (89.5)
7932 S La Mar Ct, Littleton CO
80123.

*KVNF (90.9)
PO Box 538, Paonia CO 81428.

*KOTO (91.7)
PO Box 1069, Telluride CO 81435.

STORES

ARS ANTIQUA
827 E 5th St, Denver CO 80218.
Denise Schroeder.

CRIPPLE CREEK DRY GOODS
1423 Larimer Sq, Denver CO 80202
(303)572-3132. Instruments etc.

ZITHER SHOP
525 E Ohio, Denver CO 80209 (303)
733-3015. Instruments, books,
records, accessories.

CONNECTICUT

*D.A.T.A.
81 Saltonstall Ave, New Haven CT
06513 (203)776-0797. Funding info.

*NEW ENGLAND PRESENTERS
Bushnell Mem Hall, Sta A, Box 6420,
Hartford CT 06106 (203)527-3123.
Judith Allen. Booking consortium.

VENUES

*BRANFORD FOLK MUSIC SOCIETY
Box 441, Branford CT 06405 (203)
488-7715. Debbie Winograd. Trinity
(Episcopal Church) Coffeehouse. 2nd
Sat Oct-May; every Sat Jun-Sep.
Seats 175.

*NEW HARMONY COFFEEHOUSE
Held at Roaring Brook Nature Ctr,
Gracey Rd, Canton. Booking: PO Box
310, W Simsbury CT 06092 (203)658-
2493. Gary Bargatze. Sat. Seats
130.

FAIRFIELD UNIVERSITY
Students Union, Fairfield CT 06430
(203)255-5411. Some concerts. CP:
MIRROR weekly 5000.

*COMMON TREASURY
Falls Village CT. Booking: Denise J
Sinley, RD1, Box 112, Poplar Ave,
Pine Plains NY 12567.

GOSHEN SUMMER CONCERT SERIES
Recreation Dept, Town Hall, Goshen
CT 06756 (203)491-2249. Lui
Collins.

MANCHESTER COMMUNITY COLLEGE
Student Program Board, Manchester
CT 06040 (203)646-4900. Some
concerts. CP: COUGAR 2x mthly 5K.

NEW HAVEN COUNTRY DANCE
379 Edgewood Ave, New Haven CT
06511. Barbara Loeb.

*SOUTHERN CT STATE UNIV
Students Union, 501 Crescent St,
New Haven CT 06515 (203)397-4434.
Joseph Maciorowski. Some concerts.
CP: SOUTHERN NEWS weekly 6000.

*YALE CENTER FOR BRITISH ARTS
Yale University, 1080 Chapel St,
New Haven CT 06511 (203)436-3013.
Barbara Mulligan. Sun 3-4pm. Folk
occasionally.

YALE UNIVERSITY ART GALLERY
1111 Chapel Hill, New Haven CT
06520 (203)436-2490. Janet Dickson.
Concerts Sun.

*CELLAR DOOR
66 Forest Dr, Newington CT 06111
John Merino. At Elmwood Club, 26
Newington Rd, W Hartford. 2 & 4
Sats.

*HOKUS POKUS ARTS
RD#1 Peterson Rd, Box 132, Pomfret
Ctr CT 06259 (203)974-1705. Jan
Kirchner. 1x Thurs/mo.

*STAMFORD MUSEUM
39 Schofieldtown Rd, Stamford CT
06903 (203)322-1646. Jerry
Rasmussen. Concert 1 Sat/mo. Early
New England farm.

*UNIVERSITY OF CONNECTICUT
Jorgenson Auditorium, #U-104,
Storrs CT 06268 (203)486-4228. Jack
G Cohan, Dir. Some concerts.

*RABBIT HILL *174 Anso St,*
518 Valley Rd, Stratford CT 06497
(203)378-4764. Mary-Ellen Kachuba.
United Methodist Church, Rte 57,
Westport. 1st Fri. Seats 150.

*SOUNDING BOARD *349-1518*
290 Middletown Rd, Wethersfield CT
06109 (203)563-3263. Len Domler.
Congregational Church, W Hartford.
Sat. Seats 200. Newsletter.

FESTIVALS

*AUTUMN HILLS DULCIMER FEST
Held at Camp Sequassen. Box 807,
Winsted CT 06098 (203)379-9857.
Concerts, workshops, dance. Food,
canoes, free camping. Late Sept.

*CT FAMILY FOLK FESTIVAL
Held at Elizabeth Park, Hartford.
290 Middletown Ave, Wethersfield CT
07109 (203)563-3263. Len Domler.
Varied music, free. Mid-Aug.

*CT SACRED HARP CONVENTION
Wesleyan U, RD2, Box 8, S Main St,
Terryville CT 06786. Late July.

CONNECTICUT STATE FAIR
Durham CT 06422 9203)349-9495. Jul.

*INDIAN NECK
Box 5, Torrington CT 06970. May.

*SEA MUSIC FESTIVAL
Mystic Seaport Museum, Rte 27,
Mystic CT 06355 9203)572-0711.
Concerts, workshops, dance, pub
sings. Early June.

MUSEUMS

*BATES-SCHOFIELD HOMESTEAD
45 Old Kings Hwy, Darien CT 06820
(203)655-9233. Archives, folklore.

*MONROE HISTORICAL SOCIETY
Wheeler Rd, PO Box 212, Monroe CT
06468 (203)268-5403. Folklore.

*MYSTIC SEAPORT MUSEUM
Greenmanville Ave, Mystic CT 06355
(203)57277-0711. Sea stuff.

*YALE UNIV COLLECTION OF
  MUSICAL INSTRUMENTS
15 Hillhouse Ave, PO Box 2117, New
Haven CT 06520 (203)436-4935.

PRINT

*BRIDGEPORT POST and TELEGRAM
333 Beechwood Ave, Bridgeport CT
06604 (203)366-9444. Richard W.
Day, Arts Ed.

*NEWS-TIMES
333 Main St, Danbury CT 06810
(203)744-5100. Jean Buoy, Music
Editor.

*CONNECTICUT MAGAZINE
636 Kings Hwy, Fairfield CT 06430
(203)576-6978.

*HARTFORD COURANT
285 Braod St, Hartford CT 06115
(203)241-3718. Steve Metcalf.

*HERALD
1 Herald Sq, New Britain CT 06050
(203)255-4601.

*NEW HAVEN REGISTER and
    JOURNAL-COURIER
40 Sargent Dr, New Haven CT 06511
(203)562-1121.

NORTHEAST SEM NEWSLETTER
U of New Haven, World Music Dept,
New Haven CT 06516. Audrey Mazur.

YALE REVIEW
PO Box 1902A, Yale Stn, New Haven
CT 06520. Kai T. Erikson.

*NORWICH BULLETIN
66 Franklin St, Norwich CT 06360
(203)887-9211. James Hunyardi.

*ED MCKEON
312 Stonegate Rd, Southington CT
06489. Freelance reviewer. Hosts
show on WWUH.

*ADVOCATE
75 Tresser Blvd, Stamford CT 06901
(203)964-2200. Steve Klein,
Stephanie Schorow.

*AMERICAN and REPUBLICAN
PO Box 2090, 309 Meadow St,
Waterbury CT 06720 (203)574-3636.
Theresa Rousseau.

INFORMER
U of Hartford, West Hartford CT
06091. Weekly 5000.

CONNECTICUT TODAY
PO Box 5186, Westport CT 06880
(203)227-5679. Robert Fort.

RADIO

*WPKN (89.5)
244 University Ave, Bridgeport CT
06602 (203)576-4895. Anne Camp.

*WXCI (91.7)
Western CT State Coll, 181 White
St, Danbury CT 06810 (203)792-8666.
Morgan Williams. CP: WESTCONN ECH
weekly 4500.

*WLNV (90.1)
246 Main St, Derby CT 06148.

*WSHU
Sacred Heart Univ, PO Box 6460,
Fairfield CT 06606 (203)371-7989.
Stephen J. Winters: PROFILES
IN FOLK.

WNPR (NPR-89.1)
24 Summit St, Hartford CT 06106
(203)527-0905. Midge Ramsey.

*WRTC (89.3)
Trinity Coll, Summit St, Hartford
CT 06106 (203)527-0447. Michelle
Roubal. CP: TRINITY TRIPOD weekly
3000.

*WESU
Wesleyan U, Box 2300, Middletown CT
06457 (203)347-0050. E. Seidel.

*WFCS (97.9)
Central CT State Coll, 1615 Stanley
St, New Britain CT 06050 (203)223-
6767. Brad Farley.

*WYBC (94.3)
Yale U, Box WYBC, Yale Stn, New
Haven CT 06520 (203)43-MUSIC. Helen
Yee. CP: YALE DAILY NEWS 3000.

*WCNI
Connecticut Coll, Box 1333 New
London CT 06320 (203)447-7636. Wiff
Stenger.

*WHUS (91.7)
U of CT, Box U-8, Storrs CT 06268
(203)486-4007. Anne Castellano. CP:
DAILY CAMPUS 10000.

*WHNU (88.7)
U of New Haven, 300 Orange Ave,
West Haven CT 06516 (203)934-8888.
Pete Ghadosik. CP: NEWS weekly 3K.

*WWUH (91.3)
U of Hartford, 200 Blomfield Ave,
W Hartford CT 06117 (203)243-4703.
Andy Taylor, MD. Folk 6-9 am every
weekday. Bill Domler (trad,
eclectic); Ed Savagae (Celtic); Ed
McKeon (rogue, Brit, US, ethnic);
Tom Bowman (bluegrass); John Marino
(eclectic acoustic). Interviews,
live performances.

STORES

*MUSIC VALE
188 S Whitney St, Hartford CT 06105
(203)232-6924. Eclectic record
store.

*FOLKCRAFT INSTRUMENTS
Box 807, High & Wheeler Sts,
Winsted CT 06098 (203)379-9857.
Instruments, books, kits, records.

DELAWARE

*DELAWARE FOLKLIFE PROJECT
2 Crestwood Pl, Wilmington DE
19809.

*HUGH MORRIS LIBRARY
U of DE, Newark 19711 (302)738-
2965. Funding info.

VENUES

DELAWARE STATE COLLEGE
King Ctr, Dover DE 19901 (302)678-
5133. Some concerts. CP: HORNET
monthly 2500.

*BRANDYWINE FRIENDS OF OLDTIME
Box 3504, Greenville DE 19807 (302)
654-3930. Carl Goldstein. MORNING
STAR.

UNIVERSITY OF DELAWARE
Student Activities Ctr, Newark DE
19711 (302)738-1296. Some concerts.
CP: REVIEW 2x weekly 13500.

*EASTERN SHORE BLUEGRASS ASSN
86 Jamore Dr, Seaford DE 19973

*FOLK SURVIVORS
2228 Grubb Rd, Wilmington DE 19810
(302)475-2599. John Gallagher. Odd
nights, various venues.

*GREEN WILLOW
226 Filbert Ave, Wilmington DE
19805 (302)994-0495. Mike & Carla
Dinsmore. 2 concerts/month.

FESTIVALS

*BRANDYWINE MOUNTAIN MUSIC
Held at Fair Hill, MD. Box 3504,
Greenville DE 19807 (302)654-3930.
Carl Goldstein. Trad music & dance.
Mid-July.

MUSEUM

*BUREAU OF MUSEUMS
PO Box 1401, Dover DE 19901 (302)
736-5316. Various sites &
collections. History of Delaware.

PRINT

*DELAWARE STATE NEWS
PO Box 737, Dover DE 19803 (302)
674-3600. Chris Ritchie.

FINE TIMES
Box 226, Montchanin DE 19710.

DELAWARE ALTERNATIVE PRESS
PO Box 4592, Newark DE 19711. Vic
Sadot.

*MORNING NEWS and others
831 Orange St, Box 1111, Wilmington
DE 19899 (302)573-2000. Penny Cope.

RADIO

*WXDR
U of DE, 307 Student Ctr, Newark DE
19711 (302)451-2701. Susie Wallen-
berg, Mike Dinsmore. Folk programs.
CP: REVIEW 2x weekly 13500.

DIST. OF COLUMBIA

See also nearby areas of Virginia and Maryland.

VENUES

*BLUES ALLEY
1073 Wisconsin Ave, Georgetown, Washington DC (202)337-4141. Live music, mainly jazz, some blues & folk.

*CONRADH NA GAELIGE
3549 Quesada St, Washington DC 20015 (202)864-2385 or 244-6367. Myron Bretholz. Concerts. AN NUAIDHEACHT.

DUBLINER
4 F St NW, Washington DC 20001 (202)737-3773. Irish pub.

*FOLKLORE SOCIETY OF GREATER WASHINGTON
Box 19114, 20th St Stn, Washington DC 20036 (703)281-2228. Concerts, workshops (including dance, gospel, Sacred Harp sings), festivals, newsletter.

*GAELIC LEAGUE OF DC AREA
4916 49th Ave, Hyattsville MD 20781 (301)864-2385. Judy Walsh.

*GEORGE WASHINGTON UNIV
800 21st St NW, Washington DC 20052 (202)676-6500. Folklife Assn; East Asian Culture Series. CP: HATCHET 2x week 12K; SEQUENT monthly 8000.

HOWARD UNIV STUDENT ASSN
Howard U, Blackburn Ctr, #104, Washington DC 20059 (202)636-7007. Lanny Braud. Some concerts. CP: HILLTOP weekly 12000.

IRELAND'S FOUR PROVINCES
3412 Connecticut Ave NW, Washington DC 20008 (202)244-0860. Irish pub.

IRISH CONNECTION
1737 De Sales St NW, Washington DC 20036 (202)737-7322. Irish pub.

ITALIAN FOLKLORE GROUP
2500 Wisconsin Ave NW, Washington DC 20007. Lucy Baldessarini.

*9:30 CLUB
930 F St NW, Washington DC (202)393-0930. Occasional folk.

*ROADWORK
1875 Harvard St NW, Washington DC 20009 (202)234-9308. Amy Horowitz. Women's cultural org.

*ROXY
1214 18th St NW, Washington DC (202)296-9292.

FESTIVALS

*SMITHSONIAN FOLKLIFE FEST
Smithsonian Institution, Washington DC 20560 (202)357-1300. Late Jun.

*WASHINGTON FOLK FEST
Held at Glen Echo Park, MD. FSGW, Box 19114, 20th St Stn, Washington DC 20036 (703)281-2228. Early June.

MUSEUMS

*B'NAI BRITH KLUTZNICK MUSEUM
1640 Rhode Island Ave, Washington DC 20036 (202)857-6583. Jewish folk and ceremonial art.

*LIBRARY OF CONGRESS
Washington DC 20540. Archive of Folk Culture and other interesting collections.

PRINT

ALL METRO COLLEGIAN
Univ of DC, 4200 Conn Ave NW, Washington DC 20008. Monthly 20K.

CITY PAPER
919 6th St NW, Washington DC 20001 (202)289-0520. Mark Perry, Joe Sasfy. Reviews, listings.

*KEN ROSEMAN (freelance)
PO Box 744, Arlington VA 22216 (703)522-3290.

*THIS WEEK
5428 MacArthur Blvd NW, Washington DC 2016 (202)362-6848. Terri Cooke. Free weekly. Listings.

TOWER
Catholic Univ, 620 Michigan Ave NE, Washington DC 20064. Weekly 6000.

*WASHINGTON POST
1150 15th ST NW, Washington DC
20071 (202)334-7549. Richard
Harrington, Geoffrey Hines.
Reviews, previews.

*WASHINGTON TIMES
3600 New York Ave NE, Washington DC
20002 (202)636-3000. Michael Dolan.

RADIO

*MUSIC AMERICANA
5428 MacArthur Blvd, #205,
Washington DC 20016. Doris Justis,
Dick Cerri.

*NATIONAL PUBLIC RADIO
2025 M St NW, Washington DC 20036
(202)822-2000. Bob Wisdom, Peg
Shea, Thurston Briscoe.

*PACIFICA NEWS BUREAU
425 13th St NW, #334, Washington DC
20004.

*WAMU (88.5)
American Univ, Washington DC 20016
(202)885-1030. Lee M. Dempsey, MD.
Bluegrass. CP: EAGLE weekly 10000.

*WETA (NPR - 90.9)
Box 2626, Washington DC 20013
(703)998-2970. Mary Cliff. Folk
progs. Interviews, record reviews.

*WPFW (Pacifica-89.3)
700 H St NW, Washington DC 20001.

*WRGW
George Washington Univ, 730 21st St
NW, Washington DC 20052 (202)676-
6385.

FLORIDA

*COMMUNITY FUNDING RESOURCE CTR
Leon Cnty Public Library, 1940 N
Monroe St, Tallahassee FL 32303
(904)487-2665. Funding info.

*FL DIVISION OF TOURISM
126 Van Buren St, Tallahassee FL
32301.

*FLORIDA FOLKLORE SOC
Florida Folklife Programs, Box 265,
White Springs FL 32096.

*FL PROFESSIONAL PRESENTERS
Broward Community Coll, 225 E Las
Olas Blvd, Ft Lauderdale FL 33301-
2208. Ellen Chandler-Manning.
Booking consortium.

VENUES

*RICHARD R BAUMGARTNER CTR
   FOR THE PERFORMING ARTS
Managed by Pact, 1111 McMullen
Booth Rd, Clearwater FL 33519 (813)
725-5573. Andrew Fishman. Some folk
concerts.

*BROWARD COMM COLL
Special Events Series, 225 E Las
Olas Blvd, Ft Lauderdale FL 33301
(305)761-7490. Some concerts. CP:
PHOENIX weekly 6000.

*SW FL BLUEGRASS ASSN
Box 734, Ft Myers FL 33902.

HARMONICA JOE'S
Gainesville FL 32601.

HIPPODROME
25 SE 2nd Pl, Gainesville FL 32601
(904)373-5968. Seats 300.

*SMOKEY'S JUNCTION
1850 N State Rd 7, Hollywood FL.
Bluegrass Fri/Sat.

APPLEJACKS
1402 San Marco Blvd, Jacksonville
FL 32207 (904)398-2111. Alex
Gregory. Thur-Sat. Seats 150.

FLORIDA INTL UNIVERSITY
151 St & Biscayne, Student
Activities, Miami FL 33181 (305)
940-5804. Some concerts. CP: NEW
INTERNATIONAL weekly 7500.

*SOUTH FL BLUEGRASS ASSN
20050 Bel Aire Dr, Miami FL 33157.
Virginia Schweitzer. Meets 1st Sun.
Ives Optimist Club, NE 15th Ave,
Miami FL.

*SOUTHEAST BLUEGRASS ASSN
9760 SW 165th Terr, Miami FL 33157.

*TOBACCO ROAD
615 S Miami Ave, Miami FL (305)
428-0917. Blues Sat-Sun.

*EMERALD PUB
100 W Flagler St, Miami Beach FL
33110 (305)371-7292. Irish music.

*PHOENIX PARK PUB
17300 Collins Ave, Miami Beach FL
33110 (305)945-3551. Irish music
Fri/Sat.

*SOUTH FLORIDA FOLK CLUB
PO Box 19-1878, Miami Beach FL
33119 (305)531-3655. Michael Stock.
Fri/Sat, at Underground Cafe, under
Shelborne Hotel, 1801 Collins Ave.
Fri & Sat. Concerts, festival,
newsletter. Hotlines: (303)531-
FOLK; 666-6656 (blues).

*FLORIDA STATE FIDDLERS ASSN
Box 713, Micanopy FL 32667.

*ARTS COUNCIL OF NW FLORIDA
PO Box 731, Pensacola FL 32594
(904)432-9906. Dian Magie, Dir.
Some concerts.

*FRIENDS OF FLORIDA FOLK
1625 Vereda Verde, Sarasota FL
33582 (813)377-9256. Jean Hewitt.
Annual meeting at FL Folk Fest.
Monthly newsletter/calendar.

NATURE'S WAY
Tallahassee FL 32301 (904)224-4525.
Robert Sorrent. Fri, dinner & show.
Seats 50.

FLORIDA FRIENDS OF BLUEGRASS
7318 Sequoia Dr, Tampa FL 33617.
Newsletter.

*PEANUT GALLERY
11329 N Nebraska, Tampa FL 33603
(813)977-7782. Varied folk, blues.

FESTIVALS

DUNEDIN HIGHLAND GAMES
1425 US 19-S, Bldg 9-107,
Clearwater FL 33546 (813)531-2348.
Chuck Peterson. late Mar.

*FLORIDA FOLK FEST
Held at Stephen Foster Ctr. PO Box
265, White Springs FL 32096
(904)397-2192. Ormond Loomis. FL
performers, trad FL folklife. Late
May.

FLORIDA STATE FAIR
PO Box 11766, Tampa FL 33680
(813)621-7821. Mar.

*PIONEER FLORIDA DAY
Pioneer Museum, N Hwy 301, Dade
City FL 34297 (904)576-0262. Labor
Day.

*SEVEN LIVELY ARTS FEST
PO Box 737, Hollywood FL 33022
(305)920-7809. Late Feb.

*STEPHEN FOSTER WEEK
S Foster State Folk Culture Ctr, PO
Drawer G, White Springs FL 32096
(904)397-2733. Mid-Jan.

MUSEUMS

*PIONEER FLORIDA MUSEUM
N Hwy 301, PO Box 335, Dade City FL
34297 (904)567-0262. Pioneer life.
Oldtime music contests.

*MORIKAMI MUSEUM OF
  JAPANESE CULTURE
4000 Morikami Park Rd, Delray Beach
FL 33446 (305)499-0631. Japanese
folk art.

*PINE CASTLE CTR OF THE ARTS
5903 Randolph St, Orlando FL 32809
(305)855-7461. Pioneer Days Folk
Fest. Oral history tapes.

*STEPHEN FOSTER STATE
  FOLK CULTURE CTR
PO Drawer G, White Springs FL 32096
(904)397-2733. Musical instruments,
minstrel show material, Foster mss.

PRINT

*SOUTHERN TRADITIONS
PO Box 2278, Dade City FL 34297.
6/yr. Calendar of S FL folk events,
songs, interviews, etc.

*HIGH RISER
4009 NE 5th Terr, Ft Lauderdale FL
33334 (305)563-3311. Bob Freund.

*FT LAUDERDALE NEWS and
  SUN SENTINEL
101 N New River Dr NE, Ft
Lauderdale FL 33302 (305)761-4000.
Tim Smith.

SOUTHERN FOLKLORE QUARTERLY
U of FL, 13th & W Univ Ave,
Gainesville FL 32611.

*SUN-TATTLER
2500 N 29th Ave, Hollywood FL 33020
(305)929-8100. Lori Mirrer.

*MIAMI/SOUTH FLORIDA
PO Box 140008, Miami FL 33114
(305)374-5011. Nina L. Diamond,
Nightlife. Glossy monthly.

*MIAMI HERALD
1 Herald Plaza, Miami FL 33101
(305)376-3656. James Roos, Mus Ed.

*SUN REPORTER (for various cities)
1771 West Ave, Miami Beach FL 33139
(305)532-4531. Anslie M. Stark,
Entertainments Ed.

*TALLAHASSEE DEMOCRAT
PO Box 990, Tallahassee FL 32302
(904)599-2149. Mark Hinson.

*TAMPA TRIBUNE
PO Box 191, Tampa FL 33601
(813)272-7570.

RADIO

WHRS (NPR-90.7)
505 S Congress Ave, Boynton Beach
FL 33425 (305)732-7850. Steve
Carlson, MD.

WRCC
Box 189, Cape Coral FL 33910 (813)
283-1034. Rob Abplanalp.

*WVUM (90.5)
U of Miami, SU Bldg 1306, Stanford
Dr, Coral Gables FL 33124 (305)284-
3131. Monty Q. CP: HURRICANE 2x
weekly 10000.

*WDQQ (102)
PO Box 102, 750 Root St, Daytona
Beach FL 321028 (904)255-1456. Ken
Myer.

WQCS (NPR-88.3)
3209 Virginia Ave, Ft Pierce FL
33450 (305)464-2000. William Dake.

*WRUF
U of FL, Box 14444, Gainesville FL
32604 (904)392-0771.

*WUFT
U of FL, Coll of Journalism,
Gainesville FL 32611. B. Brenesal.
CP: INDEP FL ALLIGATOR daily 28K.

*WFAM (91.1)
Jones Coll, Arlington Expwy,
Jacksonville FL 32211 (904)743-
1122.

WJCT (NPR-89.9)
1444 E Adam St, Jacksonville FL
32202 (904)358-6349. Madge Bruener.

*WFIT
FL Inst of Tech, 150 State
University Blvd, Melbourne FL 32901
(305)768-8777. John Hammerlund. CP:
CRIMSON 2x monthly 2500.

VOICE OF AMERICA
51 SW 1st Ave, #1518, Miami FL
33130. Greg Flakus.

*WDNA (88.9)
PO Box 558636, Ludlum Branch, Miami
FL 33155.

*WLRN (91.3)
172 NE 15th St, Miami FL 33132
(305)350-3228. Michael Stock. Folk,
interviews, live performances.

WTMI (CMN-93.1)
2951 S Bayshore Dr, Miami FL 33133
(305)433-2521. Dave Connor.

*WUCF (89.9)
U of Central FL, 4000 Central
Florida Blvd, Orlando FL 32816
(305)2755-2133. Brenda Layman. CP:
FUTURE NEWS weekly 12000.

WKGC (NPR-90.7)
5230 W Hwy 98, Panama City FL 32401
(904)769-52421. Wallace Crawford.

WUWF (NPR-88.1)
U of W FL, Pensacola FL 32514. Jan
Holly. PG. CP: VOYAGER weekly 2400.

*WECR
Eckerd Coll, St Petersburg FL 33733
(813)867-1166 x 419.

WAMF
A & M Univ, 314 Tucker Hall,
Tallahassee FL 32307. CP: FAMUAN 2x
monthly 6000.

*WFSU
FL Inst of Tech, 150 W University
Blvd, Tallahassee FL 32306 (305)
7242-0915. Dan McDonald. Jazz or
classically-oriented folk. CP:
FLORIDA FLAMBEAU daily 21000.

WEDU
1300 North Blvd, Tampa FL 33607.

*WMNF (88.5)
3838 Nebraska Ave, Tampa FL 33603
(813)226-3003. Robert Lorej, PD.
Folk, blues, international, bluegrass. Live shows and interviews.

*WUSF (89.7)
U of Southern FL, 4202 Fowles Ave,
Tampa FL 33620 (813)974-2215. PG.
CP: ORACLE daily 16000.

*WRPK
Rollins Coll, Box 1155, Winter Park
FL 32789 (305)646-2000.

STORES

*MUSICIAN'S EXCHANGE
729 W Sunrise Blvd, Ft Lauderdale
FL (305)944-2627.

*BANJO SHOP
5653 Johnson St, Hollywood FL 33021
(305)981-8040. Dave & Paul Stype.
Instruments etc. Repairs, tuition,
new & used. Jams on Sat.

GEORGIA

*ATLANTA PUBLIC LIBRARY
1 Margaret Mitchell Sq, Carnegie
Way, Atlanta GA 30303 (404)688-
4636. Funding info.

VENUES

*ATHENS FOLK MUSIC & DANCE SOC
Box 346, Athens GA 39693.

UNIV OF GEORGIA
229 Memorial Hall, Athens GA 30602
(404)542-7774. Some concerts. CP:
RED & BLACK daily 16000.

GEORGIA INST OF TECH
Student Ctr, 225 North NW, Atlanta
GA 30332 (404)658-2234. Some
concerts. CP: TECHNIQUE weekly 10K.
*MUSIKWORKS
696-A Cleburne Terr, Atlanta GA
30306 (404)876-7971. John Miller.
Concerts, workshops, school of
traditional music.

*ATLANTA FRIENDS OF FOLK MUSIC
1535 Danbury Dr, Norcross GA 30093.
Don Smith.

NIGHT FLIGHT CAFE
113 River, Savannah GA 31401 (912)
236-7309. Tim Coy, Scott Alexander.

GEORGIA SOUTHERN COLL
Box 8063, Student Union, Statesboro
GA 30460 (912)681-5409. Some
concerts. CP: GEORGE-ANNE wkly
5500.

FESTIVALS

*DAHLONEGA BLUEGRASS FEST
PO Box 98, Hwy 60S, Dahlonega GA
30533 (404)864-7203. Late June.

GEORGIA STATE FAIR
PO Box 5260, Macon GA 31208 (912)
746-7184. Oct.

*HAMBY MNTN BLUEGRASS FESTS
Baldwin GA (404)376-5929. June,
Sept.

*NORTH GEORGIA FOLK FEST
PO Box 352, Athens GA 30603 (404)
354-2670. Oct.

MUSEUMS

*COLUMBUS MUSEUM
1251 Wynton Rd, Columbus GA 31906
(404)323-3617. Southern folk
culture.

*OKEFENOKEE HERITAGE CTR
N Augusta Ave, Waycross GA 31501
(912)285-4260. Oral history.

PRINT

*ALBANY HERALD
138 Pine Ave, Albany GA 31703
(912)888-9300.

*BANNER HERALD and DAILY NEWS
1 Press Pl, Athens GA 30613 (404)
549-0213. Masie Underwood.

*ATLANTA JOURNAL-CONSTITUTION
72 Marietta St NW, Atlanta GA 30303
(404)526-5454.

DIGEST
Atlanta Univ Ctr, 112 Chestnut St
SW, Atlanta GA 30314. Weekly 10000.

*CHRONICLE and HERALD
PO Box 1928, Augusta GA 30913 (404)
724-0851. Dahlia Wren, Sunday Ed.

*LEDGER & ENQUIRER
PO Box 771, Columbus GA 31994 (404)
571-8580. Sandra Okamato, Ents Ed.

*RANT & REEL
234 Melrose Ave, Decatur GA 30030.
Lindsay Morris. Chattahoochee
Dancers.

*MACON TELEGRAPH & NEWS
PO Box 4167, Macon GA 31213 (912)
744-4347. Jeffrey Day.

*FOXFIRE
Rabun Gap. GA 30568. George
Reynolds.

*EVENING PRESS and MORNING NEWS
PO Box 1088, Savannah GA 31402
(912)236-9511. Lila Moore, Mus Ed.

RADIO

WJAZ
PO Box 505, Albany GA 31702. John
Benford.

*WUOG (90.5)
Box 2065, Memorial Stn, Athens GA
30602 (404)542-1700. Randy Tattle.

WABE (NPR/APR-90.1)
740 Bismark Rd NE, Atlanta GA 30324
(404)873-4477. Jonathan Phelps.

WRAS (88.5)
Georgia State U, University Plaza,
Atlanta GA 30303 (404)658-2240.
Jane Davis. CP: SIGNAL wkly 12000.

*WREK
Box 32743, 225 North Ave, Atlanta
GA 30332 (404) 894-2468. Bob Goff,
Bill Petterson.

*WRFG Radio Free Georgia (89.3)
PO Box 5332, Atlanta GA 30307.

WTBS
1065 Williams St, Atlanta GA 30309.
Bill Tullis.

*WWGC (90.7)
W GA COll, PO Box 10014, Carrollton
GA 30118 (404)834-1355. Danny
Brewton. CP: W GEORGIAN wkly 4500.

*WXCG (88)
Georgia Coll, PO Box 3124,
Milledgeville GA 31061 (912)453-
4101. Charlotte Cook.

WHCJ
Savannah State Coll, Box 20484,
Savannah GA 31404.

WQTT
127 Upper Factors Walk, Savannah GA
31406. Judy Lammers.

WSVH (NPR-91.1)
409 E Liberty St, Savannah GA 31401.

*WVGS
Georgia Southern Coll, Landrum Box
11619, Statesboro GA 30460 (912)
681-5525. Travis Late.

WVVS (90.9)
Valdosta State Coll, Box 142,
Valdosta GA 31698 (912)333-5660.
Robin Atkins. CP: SPECTATOR
weekly 4000.

STORE

*MUSIKWORKS
696-A Cleburne Terr, Atlanta GA
30306 (404)876-7971. John Miller.
Store open 10-10 Mon-Sat.
Instruments, accessories, books,
records. Repairs, workshops,
tuition. Expert luthiers.

HAWAII

*THOS HALE HAMILTON LIBRARY
U of HI, 2550 The Mall, Honolulu HI
96822 (808)948-7214. Funding info.

VENUES

*UNIV OF HAWAII
2465 Campus Rd, Community Services
Div, Honolulu HI 96822 (808)948-
8242. Barbara Furstenberg, Dir.
Some concerts. CP: KA LEO O HAWAII
3x weekly 15K.

*KAUAI COMMUNITY COLLEGE
Special programs, 3-1901 Kaumuali
Hwy, Lihue HI 96766 (808)245-8271.
R.K. Carter, Dir. Some concerts.

*LEEWARD COMMUNITY COLLEGE
Special programs, 96-045 Ala Ike,
Pearl City HI 96782 (808)455-0230.
Pikake Wahilani, Dir. Some
concerts.

FESTIVALS

50TH STATE FAIR
Aloha Stadium, Honolulu HI 96707
(808)682-5767. May.

*INTERARTS HAWAII
1221 Griffiths St, Honolulu HI 96826
(808)941-5388. Marian Kerr.
Classical, ethnic. Jun-July.

*KAPALUA MUSIC FEST
1 Bay Dr, Kapalua, Maui HI 996761
(808)669-4844. Yizhak Schotten.
Classical, ethnic. May.

MUSEUMS

*LAHAINA RESTORATION FNDN
Dickenson & Front Sts, Box 338,
Lahaina, Maui HI 96761 (808)661-
3262. Local history, whaling.

*PACIFIC WHALING MUSEUM
Sea Life Park, Waimanalo HI 96795
(808)259-5177.

PRINT

*HONOLULU ADVERTISER and others
605 Kapiolani Blvd, Honolulu HI
96813 (808)525-8000.

NOVUS
PO Box 162, Honolulu HI 96810.
Local music paper. Listings.

RADIO

KHPR (NPR-88.1)
1335 Lower Campus Rd, Honolulu HI
96822 (808)955-8821. Alan Campbell.

KNDI
1734 S King St, Honolulu HI 96826.

*KTUH
U of HI, 2445 Campus Rd, #202,
Honolulu HI 96822 (808)948-7431.
Randy Sylva. CP: KA LEO O HAWAII
3x weekly 15000.

IDAHO

*CALDWELL PUBLIC LIBRARY
1010 Dearborn St, Caldwell ID 83605
(208)459-3242. Funding info.

VENUES

*BOISE FOLKLORE SOCIETY
1210 N 16, Boise ID 83702 (208)345-
8409. Ginny DeFoggi. Sun. Dance 1st
weekend.

*BOISE STATE UNIV
Morrison Ctr, 1910 University Dr,
Boise ID 83725. Some concerts.

*COEUR D'ALENE FOLKLORE SOC
307 S 19th, Coeur d'Alene ID 83814
(208)667-4178. Thomas Orjala.
Monthly concert, dance 1st Sat.

*CREEKSIDE
PO Box 2235, Ketchum ID 83340 (208)
726-8200. Mark Wheaton. Summer: 2-3
concerts/mo; Winter: 6/week. Ski
Center.

*UNIVERSITY OF IDAHO
Campus Program Coordinator, ASUI
Student Union, Moscow ID 83843
(2080855-6484.

IDAHO STATE UNIV
Student Union, Box 8118, Pocatello
ID 83208 (208)236-4561. Some
concerts. CP: BENGAL weekly 5500.

*SUN VALLEY CTR FOR THE ARTS
PO Box 656, Sun Valley ID 83353
(208)622-9371. Jacqueline Schuett.
Concerts, Northern Rockies Fest in
August. Institute of the American
West (cowboy lore).

IDAHO OLDTIME FIDDLERS ASSN
c/o Signal-American, Box 709,
Weiser ID 83672. Contests.

FESTIVALS

*EASTERN IDAHO STATE FAIR
PO Box 250, Blackfoot ID 83221
(208)785-2480. Sept.

*NATL OLDTIME FIDDLERS CONTEST
Chamber of Commerce, 8 E Idaho St,
Weiser ID 83672 (208)549-0450.
Judee Parsons. 300 entrants, age 5-
91, 31 states. Mid-June.

*NORTHERN ROCKIES FOLK FEST
Sun Valley Ctr, Box 656, Sun Valley
ID 83353 (208)622-9371. Kit Neraas.
Early August.

MUSEUMS

*ST GERTRUDE'S MUSEUM
Box 107, Cottonwood ID 83522 (208)
962-3224. Local history, music.

*TWIN FALLS COUNTY MUSEUM
Rte 2, Files ID 83328 (208)734-
7358. Local history, musical
instruments.

*INTERMOUNTAIN CULTURAL CTR
Paddock La, PO Box 307, Weiser ID
83672 (208)549-0205. Music,
folklore.

PRINT

*IDAHO STATESMAN
PO Box 40, 1200 N Curtis, Boise ID
83707 (208)37-6444. Tim Burroughs,
Features Editor.

*IDAHO STATE JOURNAL
305 S Arthur, Pocatello ID 83201
(208)232-4161. Joy S. Morrison,
Music Editor.

RADIO

*KBSU
Boise State, 1910 University Dr,
Boise ID 83725 9208)385-3637. David
Browne. CP: UNIVERSITY NEWS weekly
15000.

KYME (740 AM)
1002 W Franklin St, Boise ID 83702
(208)343-9393. Kim Day.

KJLG
Lewis-Clark U, 6th St @ 8th Ave,
Lewiston ID 83501 (208)746-2341.

*KUOI (89.3)
U of ID, Student Union Bldg, Moscow
ID 83843 (208)885-6433. David
Hanson. CP: IDAHO ARGONAUT
2x weekly 6000.

STORES

*GUITAR'S FRIEND
309 S Main, Moscow ID 83842 (208)
882-1823. Instruments etc.
Concerts, workshops.

*ANDERSEN STRINGED INSTRUMENTS
PO Box 371, Sandpoint ID 83864
(208)264-5725. Steven Andersen.
Makes guitars, mandolins, mandolas.

ILLINOIS

VENUES

CHICAGO BLUEGRASS MUSIC SOC
717 Webster, Algonquin IL 60102
(312)274-7333. Marguerite Vaness.

*FOX VALLEY FOLKLORE SOC
755 N Evanslawn, Aurora IL 60506
(312)897-3655. Juell Ulven. Open
mike, singarounds, concerts, workshops, etc. Fest Labor Day weekend.

*OLD QUARTER COFFEEHOUSE
8520 Brookfield Ave, Brookfield IL
60513 (312)485-3712. Dave Reynolds.
Fri-Sat.

UNIV OF ILLINOIS
Student Activities, Champaign IL
61820. Some concerts. CP: DAILY
ILLINI 13000.

EASTERN IL UNIV
University Board, Charleston IL
61920 (217)581-5117. Some concerts.
CP: DAILY EASTERN NEWS 8500.

*AURAL TRADITION
PO Box 14407, Chicago IL 60614
(312)897-3655. Juell Ulven.
Concerts, newsletter.

*BIDDY MULLIGAN'S
7644 N Sheridan, Chicago IL 60626
(312)761-6532. Blues, R&B, rock.

B.L.U.E.S.
2519 N Halsted, Chicago IL 60614
(312)528-1012. Live blues.

BYFIELD'S
1301 N State Parkway, Chicago IL
60610 (312)787-6433. Some folk.

*CHICAGO AREA BLUEGRASS
    & PICKING SOCIETY
1437 W Howard, Chicago IL 60626
(312)274-7333.

*CHICAGO IRISH FOLKLIFE SOC
Box 42845, Chicago IL 60642.

CROSSCURRENTS
3206 N Wilton, Chicago IL 60657
(312)472-7778. Tom Goodman.

DE PAUL UNIVERSITY
2324 N Seminary, Chicago IL 60614
(312)321-7980. Some concerts. CP:
DE PAULIAN weekly 10000.

*ETHNIC CULTURAL
    PRESERVATION SOCIETY
4012 Archer Ave, Chicago IL 60632.

*FLEA MARKET
WBEZ, 1819 W Pershing Rd, Chicago
IL 60609 (312)840-8241. Ken Gagne,
prod; Jim Post, host. 2-hr live
show, recorded Sunday 5-7p.m. On
various stations nationwide. 4 acts
per show.

HOBSON'S CHOICE
5101 N Clark, Chicago IL 60640
(312)271-0400. Wed-Sun.

*HOLSTEIN'S
2464 N Lincoln, Chicago IL 60613
(312)327-3331. Ed Holstein. Most
nights, varied music. Seats 150.

*HOUSE CONCERT
6970 N Glenwood, Chicago IL 60626
(312)743-3344. Music 7 nights.

KINGSTON MINES
2548 N Halsted, Chicago IL 60614
(312)477-4646. Live blues.

*OLD TOWN SCHOOL OF FOLK
909 W Armitage, Chicago IL 60614
(312)525-7793. Concerts, workshops,
info/coordination ctr.
*U OF CHICAGO FOLKLORE SOC
Box 7, Faculty Exchange, Chicago
60637. Laura Gloger. Fest late Jan.
UNIVERSITY OF ILLINOIS
Student Activities, Chicago IL
60680 (312)996-2645. Amy Levant.
Some concerts. CP: CHICAGO ILLINI
wkly 21K.

WISE FOOLS PUB
2270 N Lincoln, Chicago IL 60614
(312)929-1510. Blues, gospel.

*NEW PRAIRIE CAFE
N IL U, DeKalb IL (815)753-1421.
Weds. Seats 300.

*TWO-WAY STREET COFFEEHSE
1047 Curtiss, Downers Grove IL
60515 (312)969-9720 or 968-5526.
David L. Humphreys. Varied folk
music, Fri.

LEVY CENTER
1700 Maple, Evanston IL 60201
(312)525-7793. Some concerts.

*DAVID ADLER CULTURAL CTR
School of Folk & Old-time Music,
1700 N Milwaukee Ave, Libertyville
IL 60048 (312)367-0707. Doug
Miller. Concerts, dances, classes,
workshops, research & documentation
of Illinois folk music.

*NEW FRIENDS OF OLDTIME MUSIC
Braden Auditorium, Rm 146, ISU,
Normal IL 61761 (309)438-3212. Jane
Campagne, advisor.

*SONGSMITH SOC
PO Box 2601, Northbrook IL 60065
(312)272-9199. James Durst. Some
concerts. Artist co-op, distribs
records & cassettes.

BRADLEY UNIVERSITY
901 N Elmwood, Peoria IL 61606
(309)672-3887. Some concerts. CP:
BRADLEY SCOUT weekly 6000.

*CHARLOTTE'S WEB
(815)965-9017. Bookings: Brian
Livingston (815)877-4966, 3600 N
Main, Rockford IL 61103.

*ROCK RIVER FRIENDS
    OF FOLK MUSIC
PO Box 1583, Rockford IL 61110
(815)987-3200. Sam Schaeffer. Fest
in July.

*IL OLDTIME FIDDLERS ASSN
211 W South 4th St, Shelbyville IL
62565.

*CLAYVILLE FOLK ARTS GUILD
PO Box 1674, Springfield IL 62705
(217)626-1132. Don Tebbe, Dan
Keding. 4th Thurs.

*PRAIRIE GRAPEVINE
Springfield IL (217)528-9218. Dave
Landreth.

FOLKWORKS
908 Fairlawn, Urbana IL 61801
(217)328-6836. Bruce Williams.

*DULCIMER SOC OF N ILLINOIS
777 Locust St, Winnetka IL 60093.
Rosamund Campbell.

FESTIVALS

*BLUEGRASS COUNTRY MUSIC
  KICKOFF
1328 Lumber St, Crete IL 60417
(312)672-5259. Mid-May.

*CHICAGO FOLK FESTIVAL
U of Chicago, Box 7, Faculty
Exchange, Chicago 60637. Laura
Gloger. Late Jan.

*CLAYVILLE MUSIC FESTIVAL
Clayville Rural Life Ctr, Pleasant
Plains IL 62677 (217)626-1132. Don
Tebbe, Dan Keding. Varied folk,
kids' events, workshops, story-
telling. 1850s food & setting.
Early Aug.

DUQUOIN STATE FAIR
PO Box 182, Duquoin IL 62832
(618)542-4705.

*FOX VALLEY FESTIVAL
755 N Evanslawn, Aurora IL 60506
(312)897-3655. Juell Ulven. Sun of
Labor Day weekend.

*HARMONY PINES
RR2, Box 151, Gilson IL 61436
(309)876-2381. Bluegrass. May,
Sept.

MUSEUMS

*UNIVERSITY MUSEUM
S IL U, Faner 2469, Carbondale IL
629021 (618)453-5388. Folklore,
oral history, ethnomusicology.

*BALZEKAS MUSEUM OF
  LITHUANIAN CULTURE
4012 S Archer Ave, Chicago IL 60632
(312)847-2441. Lithuanian folklore.
Folk art classes.

*CHICAGO PUBLIC LIBRARY
  CULTURAL CENTER
78 E Washington St, Chicago IL
60602 (312)269-2820. Coll of
musical instruments. Cultural
traditions.

*POLISH MUSEUM OF AMERICA
984 N Milwaukee Ave, Chicago IL
60622 (312)384-3352. Polish
culture.

*OFFICE OF CULTURAL ARTS
S IL U, Box 150, Edwardsville IL
62026 (618)69629-2996. Folklore
archive, musical instrument coll.

*MITCHELL INDIAN MUSEUM
2408 Orrington Ave, Evanston IL
(312)866-1395. American Indian
material.

*CLAYVILLE RURAL LIFE CTR
RR 125, Pleasant Plains IL 62677
(217)626-1132. IL history and
folklife.

PRINT

*BEACON-NEWS
101 S River St, Aurora IL 60506
(312)844-5891. James V. Gill.

*THE PANTAGRAPH
301 W Washington, Bloomington IL
61701 (39)829-9411.

*CHAMP-URBANA NEWS-GAZETTE
PO Box 677, Champaign IL 61820
(217)351-5368.

*CHICAGO MAGAZINE
303 E Wacker Dr, Chicago IL 60601
(312)565-5080. Listings.

*CHICAGO SUN-TIMES
401 N Wabash Ave, Chicago IL 60611.
Don McLeese.

*CHICAGO TRIBUNE
435 N Michigan, Chicago IL 60611.
Lynne van Matre.

*HOT WIRE
1321 W Rosedale, Chicago IL 60660.
Toni Armstrong. Women's music and
culture. 3/yr.

*READER
11 E Illinois, Box 11101, Chicago
IL 60611 (312)828-0350. Robert A.
Roth, Neil Tesser. Free weekly.
News, reviews, interviews,
listings.

*DECATUR HERALD & REVIEW
601 E William St, Decatur IL
62523(217)429-5151.

FOLKTIVITIES
1331 Washington St, Evanston IL
60202. Monthly dance news.

*HERALD-NEWS
399 Caterpillar Dr, Joliet IL 60436
(815)729-6161. Pat Gleason, City
Editor.

*MOLINE DISPATCH
1720 5th Ave, Moline IL 61255 (309)
764-4344.

ILLINOIS ENTERTAINER
PO Box 356, Mt Prospect IL 60056
(312)298-9333. Listings.

GOLDMINE MAGAZINE
6 S 230 Cohasset Rd, PO Box 543,
Naperville IL 60540. Allen Shaw.

*PEORIA JOURNAL-STAR
1 News Plaza, Peoria IL 61643 (309)
686-3000.

*QUINCY HERALD-WHIG
5th & Jersey, Quincy IL 62301 (217)
223-5100.

*ARGUS
1724 4th Ave, Rock Island IL 61201
(309)786-6441. Charles H. Sanders.

*ROCKFORD REGISTER STAR
99 E State St, Rockford IL 61105
(815)987-1343.

*STATE JOURNAL-REGISTER
PO Box 219, 1 Copley Plaza,
Springfield IL 62705 (217)788-1540.

*NEWS-SUN
100 W Madison St, Waukegan IL 60085
(312)578-7205. Chris Cashman.

RADIO

*WESN
Illinois Wesleyan U, Box 2900,
Bloomington IL 61701.

WIDB (600AM)
Southern IL Univ, Carbondale IL
62901 (618)536-2361. Vic Lantini.
CP: DAILY EGYPTIAN 25500.

WSIU (NPR-91.9)
S IL U, Box 73, Carbondale IL 62901
(618)453-4343. Jane Fisher. CP:
DAILY EGYPTIAN 25500.

*WEFT
113 N Market, Champaign IL 61820
(217)359-9338. Mary-Ellen Page.
Folk progs, also concert series.

*WBEZ
1819 W Pershing Rd, Chicago IL
60609 (312)840-8241. Folk programs
inc FLEA MARKET (above).

*WCRX (88.1)
Columbia Coll, 600 S Michigan Ave,
Chicago IL 60605 (312)663-1693.
Jeff Kapuga. CP: COLUMBIA
CHRONICLE 2x monthly 5000.

WCYC
12801 S Ridgdeway Ave, Chicago IL
60623.

*WFMT (98.7)
500 N Michigan Ave, Chicago IL
60611 (312)565-5000. Ray
Nordstrand, Studs Terkel. Folk. PG:
CHICAGO magazine.

*WHPK (88.3)
U of Chi, 5706 S University Ave,
Chicago IL 60637 (312)962-8289.
David Toub, Tom Uhl. CP: CHICAGO
MAROON 2x weekly 12000.

WKCK
6800 S Wentworth Ave, Chicago IL
60621.

WLUW (88.7)
Loyola U, 820 N Michigan Ave,
Chicago IL 60611 (312)670-3205.
Mary Devous. CP: LOYOLA PHOENIX
weekly 9000.

WNIB (97.1)
12 E Delaware, Chicago IL 60611
(312)337-5252. Ron Ray.

WOUI
IL Inst of Tech, 3300 S Federal St,
Chicago IL 60616 (312)567-3075.

WTTW-TV Channel 11 Public TV
5400 N St Louis Ave, Chicago IL
60625 (312)583-5000.

WUIC (88.1)
U of IL, Circle Campus, Box 4348,
Chicago IL 60680 (312)996-2645. CP:
CHICAGO ILLINI weekly 21000.
WXRT
4949 W Belmont, Chicago IL 60641.
John Mrvos.

WZRD (88.3)
Northeast IL U, 5500 St Louis Ave,
Chicago IL 60625 (312)583-4789. Bob
St Clair. CP: NIU PRINT wkly 7K.

WKDI (93.5)
N IL U, 544 College Ave, De Kalb IL
60115 (815)753-1278. Steve Anderson
*WNIU (89.5)
N IL U, DeKalb IL 60115 (815)753-
0212. Mark Kellner. CP: NORTHERN
STAR daily 17500.

*WJMU
Milliken U, 1184 W Main, Decatur IL
62522 (217)424-6377. Scott
Schuller.

WSIE (NPR-88.7)
Southern IL U, Box 73, Edwardsville
IL 62026 (618)692-2228. Fred
Criminger. CP: ALESTLE 2x wkly 7K.

WNUR (89.3)
Northwestern U, 1905 Sheridan Ave,
Evanston IL 60201 (312)492-7101.
Bruce Isaacson. Folk progs. CP: NW
REVIEW 2x monthly 7000; DAILY
NORTHWESTERN 8500.

*WDCB
Coll of DuPage, Glen Ellyn IL 60137
(312)858-2800. Folk progs. Would
like to interview visiting artists.

*WMXM (88.9)
Lake Forest Coll, Lake Forest IL
60045 (312)234-5480. Cara Jepsen.

WIUM (NPR-91.3)
Western IL U, Macomb IL 61455
(309)298-1248. Malcolm Hinrichs,
CP: WESTERN COURIER 3x wkly 7K.

*WGLT (NPR-89.1)
IL State U, Normal IL 61761 (309)
438-2255. Eric Landon, John Burk.
CP: DAILY VIDETTE 16000.

WCBU (NPR-89.9)
1501 W Bradley Ave, Peoria IL 61625
(309)673-7100. Peter Carroll.

WRRG (88.9)
Triton Coll, 2000 5th Ave, River
Grove IL 60171 (3212)456-0300. CP:
TRIDENT 2x monthly 5000.

WVIK (NPR-90.1)
Augustana Coll, Rock Island IL
61201 (309)794-7777. Lowell Darman,
CP: OBSERVER weekly 2800.

*WLRA
Lewis U, Rte 53, Romeoville IL
60441 (815)838-0700.

WSSR (NPR-91.1)
Sangamon State U, Shepherd Rd,
Springfield IL 62708 (217)786-6516.
John Fisher. CP: PRAIRIE STAR
2x monthly 2500.

WILL (NPR-90.9)
810 S Wright St, Urbana IL 61801
(217)333-0850. Grace Babakhanian.

STORES

TOBIAS MUSIC
5013 Fairview Ave, Downers Grove IL
60515 (312)960-2455. Guitars, etc.

*THE MUSIC WORKS
5210 S Harper, Harper Ct, Hyde Park
IL (312)955-2635. Instruments,
accessories, books, tuition,
repairs.

INDIANA

INDIANA TOURISM
1 N Capitol, #700, Indianapolis IN
46204 (317)232-8860. In IN: (800)
622-4464; in IL KY MI OH TN MO:
(800)858-8073. Festival map with
listings.

*INDIANAPOLIS-MARION COUNTY
   PUBLIC LIBRARY
40 E St Clair St, Indianapolis IN
46204 (317)283-4259. Funding info.

VENUES

*BLOOMINGTON COALITION FOR
   BETTER CONCERTS
105 E 14th, Bloomington IN 47401
(812)339-3076. Lee Williams. House
concerts, festival.

BLUEBIRD
216 N Walnut, Bloomington IN 47401
(812)336-2473. Some folk.

*HOOSIER FOLKLORE SOC
504 N Fess, Bloomington IN 47401
(812)335-8048. Harry Gammerdinger.
Indiana & nearby folklore, ethnic
traditions, etc. Newsletter.

LARK PRODUCTIONS
PO Box 277, Bloomington IN 47402.
Concerts.

*EVANSVILLE BLUEGRASS ASSN
2001 S Parker Dr, Evansville IN
47714.

INDIANA-PURDUE UNIV
Student Union Board, Ft Wayne IN
46805 (219)482-5616. Some concerts.
CP: COMMUNICATOR weekly 5500;
SAGAMORE weekly 12000.

*TRI-STATE FOLK MUSIC SOC
532 W Packard Ave, Ft Wayne IN
46807 (219)456-8046. Dave Dawkins,
Pres. KEEP PICKIN' monthly. Ed:
John Brennan, 3005 N Anthony Blvd,
Ft Wayne IN 46805 (219)483-4768.
Concerts, workshops, dances, etc.
at various venues.

PURDUE UNIVERSITY
Calumet Campus, Hammond IN 46323
(219)844-0520. Some concerts. CP:
PURDUE CHRONICLE 2/mo 5000.

*BORDEN BLUEGRASS ASSN
Henryville Fire Dept, Henryville IN
47162.

HUMMINGBIRD CAFE
2131 E 71st St, Indianapolis IN
46205 (317)253-4428. Caroline
Webster.

*INDIANA FRIENDS OF
  BLUEGRASS
Rte 2, Box GM-8, New Palestine IN
46163. Carmen Westington.

*MICHIGAN SONGMAKERS
1214 Academy Pl, Columbia Hall,
Notre Dame IN 46616.

NOTRE DAME UNIV
La Fortune Student Ctr, Notre Dame
IN 46556 (219)283-7308. Some
concerts. CP: OBSERVER daily 12K;
SCHOLASTIC monthly 7500.

*SOUTHERN IN FIDDLERS ASSN
Rte 3, Salem IN 47167. Carl
Nicholson.

FESTIVALS

*FESTIVAL PROMOTIONS
6695 Egbert Rd, Martinsville IN
46151 (317)831-3180.

BATTLE GROUND FIDDLERS'
  GATHERING
Box 225, Battle Ground IN
47920 (317)567-2147. Jun or Jul.

*DUNELAND HARVEST FESTIVAL
Indiana Dunes National Lakaeshore,
1100 N Mineral Springs, Porter IN
46304 (219)926-7561. W Snyder.
Music, dance. Late Sept.

FIESTA INDIANAPOLIS
Held at Veterans Memorial Plaza.
617 E North St, Indianapolis IN
46204 (317)636-6551. Elba Gonzalez.
Hispanic Heritage celebration.

FOUNDERS' DAY & INDIANA
  FOLK FESTIVAL
1119 W Main St, Madison IN 47250
(812)265-5080. Dixie McDonough.
German bands, food, costumes,
crafts. Early June.

INDIANA OFFICIAL FIDDLING
  CONTEST
Held at American Legion Post. RR#1,
Winslow IN 47598 (812)789-2162.
Tony Rothrock. Banjo & fiddle
contests, etc. Early June.

INDIANA STATE FAIR
Held on State Fairgrounds. 1202 E
38th St, Indianapolis IN 46205
(317)927-7500. Sid Hutchcraft. Aug.

*NATIONAL WOMEN'S MUSIC FEST
Held at Indiana Univ. PO Box 53217,
Bloomington IN 47402 (812)876-6785.
Mary Byrne.

NATIVE AMERICAN FESTIVAL
Held at Angel Mounds Memorial. 8215
Pollack, Evansville IN 47715 (812)
853-3956. Jancie B Luth. Face
painting, dance, stories, food.
Early August.

*SWISS ALPINE FESTIVAL
PO Box 151, Vevay IN 47043
(812)427-3511. Judy Moore. Polka
music, dance, food, clogging,
crafts. Early August.

*WABASH VALLEY BLUEGRASS
  JAMBOREE
RR 24, Terre Haute IN 47802 (812)
894-2975. Eugene Smith. Music,
food, dance, workshops, pig roast.
Late May.

MUSEUMS

*FORT WAYNE HISTORICAL SOC
302 E Berry St, Ft Wayne IN 46802
(219)426-2882. Sheet music
collection. Local history.

*MUSEUM OF INDIAN HERITAGE
6040 DeLong Rd, Eagle Creek Park,
Indianapolis IN 46254 (3170293-
4488. American Indian history &
culture.

PRINT

*EVANSVILLE COURIER
201 NW 2nd St, Evansville IN 47702
(812)464-7459. Patricia Smith.

*JOURNAL-GAZETTE
PO Box 88, Ft Wayne IN 46801 (219)
461-8427.

*POST-TRIBUNE
1065 Broadway, Gary IN 46402 (219)
881-3143.

*TIMES
417 Fayette St, Hammond IN 46320
(219)932-3100.

*INDIANAPOLIS NEWS
307 N Pennsylvania St, Indianapolis
IN 46204 (317)633-9226. Charles B
Staff, Jr.

*LAFAYETTE JOURNAL & COURIER
217 N 6th St, Lafayette IN 47901
(317)423-5511. Kathy Mather.

*NEWS-DISPATCH
121 W Michigan Blvd, Michigan City
IN 46360 (219)874-7211. John Mabin.

*MUNCIE EVENING PRESS
125 S High St, Muncie IN 47302
(317)747-5700. Keith Roysdon.

*MUNCIE STAR
125 S High St, Muncie IN 47302
(317)747-5700. Bruce Douglas.

*SOUTH BEND TRIBUNE
225 W Colfax Ave, South Bend IN
46626 (219)233-6161. John D Miller.

*TRIBUNE-STAR
PO Box 149, Terre Haute IN 47808
(812)231-4281. Martin W Jasicki.

PURDUE ENGINEER
Purdue U Engineering School, W
Lafayette IN 47907. Monthly 6000.

RADIO

*WFIU (NPR-103.7)
Indiana U, Bloomington IN 47405
(812)335-1357. 4 hrs folk. CP: IN
DAILY STUDENT 10500.

WCNB
PO Box 619, Connersville IN 47331.
Randy Klemme.

*WVPE (88.1)
2424 California Rd, Elkhart IN
46514. Tim Eby, Bill Prochon. Folk.

*WUEV (91.5)
U of Evansville, PO Box 329,
Evansville IN 47702 (812)479-2022.
Jon B Klotz. CP: CRESCENT weekly
5000.

WBNI (89.1)
2000 N Wells St, Ft Wayne IN 46808
(219)423-1629. Bernie Lochmullen.

WGCS (91.1)
Goshen Coll, Goshen IN 46256
(219)533-3161. CP: RECORD weekly
2000.

WAJC (Mutual-104.5)
4600 Sunset Blvd, Indianapolis IN
46208 (317)283-9500. James
Phillippe.

WIAN (NPR-90.1)
931 Fletcher Ave, Indianapolis IN
46203 (317)266-4141. Jim Walsh.
Folk programs.

WICR
1400 E Hanna Ave, Indianapolis IN
46227.

WBST (NPR-92.1)
Ball State U, Muncie IN 47306 (307)
285-4174. Kent Leslie. CP: DAILY
NEWS 14000.

WPUM
St Joseph's Coll, Box 651,
Rensselaer IN 47978.

*WECI
Earlham Coll, Box E-1239, Richmond
IN 47374 (317)962-3451. CP: EARLHAM
POST 2x monthly 1200.

WBAA (920 AM)
Purdue Univ, W Lafayette IN 47906
(317)494-5920. Caryl Matthews. CP:
PURDUE EXPONENT daily 18000.

*WCCR
Purdue Univ, Box M, Cary Quad, W
Lafayette IN 47906 (317)494-9773.
CP: see above.

IOWA

*DES MOINES PUBLIC LIBRARY
*DES MOINES PUBLIC LIBRARY
100 Locust St, Des Moines IA 50308
(515)283-4259. Funding info.

VENUES

*STONE CITY GENERAL STORE
RR1, Anamosa IA 52205 (319)462-
4733. Mike Richards, Mitch
Mitchell. Fri-Sun. Seats 125. Folk,
blues, bluegrass, ethnic, light
jazz.

*DRAKE UNIVERSITY
Student Activities Board, Des
Moines IA 50311 (516)271-3711. Some
concerts. CP: TIMES-DELPHIC 2x
weekly 4000.

IOWA FRIENDS OF OLDTIME MUSIC
329 N Lucas, Iowa City IA 52240.
Tom Gillespie.

MILL RESTAURANT
120 E Burlington, Iowa City IA
52240 (319)351-9529. Keith
Dempster. Thur-Sun.

*SANCTUARY
405 S Gilbert St, Iowa City IA
52240 (319)351-5692. Darrell
Woodson. Fri-Sat.

*U OF IA FRIENDS OF OLDTIME
U of IA, Dept of English, Iowa City
IA 52240 (319)351-555 or 353-7663.
Harry Oster. Some concerts.

*DECKER HOUSE
128 N Main, Maquoketa IA. (319)652-
2170. Rule Bell. 1 weekend night
per week. Seats 100.

FESTIVALS

*BUTLER COUNTY BLUEGRASS
RR#6, Cedar Falls IA 50613
(319)266-4329. End May, also end
June.

*IOWA STATE FAIR
State Hse, Des Moines IA 50319
(515)262-3111. Mid-Aug.

*NEW ACOUSTIC MUSIC FEST
Inn at Stone City, Rte 1, Anamosa
IA 52205 (319)462-4733. Early Sept.

*OLD-TIME COUNTRY MUSIC FEST
Held at Pottawattamie Fairgrounds.
106 Council Bluffs IA 51501
(720)366-1136. Bob Everhart.
Contests, crafts, dancing, music.
Late August.

MUSEUMS

*LITTLE YELLOW SCHOOLHOUSE
303 6th St, Allison IA 50602 9319-
267-2526. Local history, music.

*STATE HISTORICAL SOC
402 Iowa Ave, Iowa City IA 52240
(319)338-5471. Iowa history &
culture. Broadsides.

*MIDWEST OLD SETTLERS &
  THRESHERS ASSN
RR1, Mt Pleasant IA 52641 (319)385-
8937. Local history, folk theater.

*MITCHELL COUNTY
  HISTORICAL MUSEUM
North 6th, Osage IA 50461 (515)732-
4118. Musical instruments.

PRINT

*AMES DAILY TRIBUNE
PO Box 380, Ames IA 50010 (515)232-
2160. Dan W Geiser.

*CEDAR RAPIDS GAZETTE
500 3rd Ave NE, Cedar Rapids IA
52401 (319)398-8329. Cindy Cullen
Chapman, Arts & Entertainment Ed.

*THE NONPAREIL
117 Pearl St, Council Bluffs IA
51501 (712)328-1811.

*TRADITION
106 Navajo, Council Bluffs IA
51501. Bob Everhart.

*QUAD-CITY TIMES
PO Box 3828, Davenport IA 52808
(319)383-2325. Sarah Bowden.

*DES MOINES REGISTER
715 Locust St, Des Moines IA 50304
(515)284-8000.

*TELEGRAPH-HERALD
8th & Bluff Sts, Dubuque IA 52001
(319)588-5671. Ken Amundson.

*GLOBE-GAZETTE
300 N Washington, Mason City IA
50401 (515)423-4270.

*SIOUX CITY JOURNAL
6th & Pavonia Sts, Sioux City IA
51102 (712)279-5075. Bruce Miller.

*WATERLOO COURIER
PO Box 540, Waterloo IA 50704 (319)
291-1461. Phyllis Singer.

RADIO

*KPGY
Iowa State U, 1199 Friley Hall,
Ames IA 50012 (515)294-9292. CP:
IOWA STATE DAILY 16000.

*KUNI (91.1)
U of N IA, Cedar Falls IA 50614
(319)23-6400. Phil Nusbaum. CP:
NORTHERN IOWAN 2x weekly. 9000.
Folk shows, interviews.

*KCCK
Kirkwood Community Coll, PO Box
2068, Cedar Rapids IA 52406 (319)
398-5446. Dave Becker. Folk progs.

KIWR (89.7)
1700 College Rd, Council Bluffs IA
51501 (712)325-3254. Roger Dobrick.
Folk programs.

KDEC
Box 1240, Highland Dr, Decorah IA
52101.
KWLC
Luther Coll, Decorah IA 52101 (319)
387-1023.

*KDIC
Grinnell Coll, Box 805, Grinnell IA
50112 (515)236-1838. Jean
Silverberg. CP: SCARLET & BLACK
weekly 2000.

*KRUI (89.7)
U of IA, 570 S Quad, Iowa City IA
52242 (319)353-5500. Mimi
Schneider. CP: DAILY IOWAN 20000.

KSIU (NPR-91.7)
U of IA, 3300 EB, Iowa City IA
52242 (319)353-5665. John Monick.
CP: DAILY IOWAN 20000.

*KRNL
Cornell Coll, Mt Vernon IA 52314
(319)895-8821.

KIGC
W Penn Coll, N Market & Trueblood,
Oskaloosa IA 52577 (515)673-8311.

KDCR (88.5)
Dordt College Campus, Sioux Center,
IA 51250 (712)722-0885. Cindy
Holtrop.

KMSG
1501 Morningside Ave, Sioux City IA
51106.

KWIT (NPR-90.3)
Box 265, Sioux City IA 51102
(712)274-2600. Bill Reynolds.

KWAR
Wartburg Coll, Waverley IA 50617
(319)352-1200. CP: WARTBURG TRUMPET
weekly 2000.

STORES

*WOOCK'S HANDCRAFT MUSIC
113 Elk Run St, Elk Run Hts,
Waterloo IA 50707.

KANSAS

*WICHITA PUBLIC LIBRARY
223 S Main, Wichita KS 67202 (316)
262-0611. Funding info.

VENUES

*COFFEYVILLE COMMUNITY COLL
11th & Willow, Coffeyville KS 67337
(316)251-7700. Kenneth Burchinal.
Some concerts.

*EMPORIA STATE UNIVERSITY
Special Events, Mem Union, Emporia
KS 66801 (316-343-1200 x 481. Mary
Downing, Dir. Some concerts.

*UNIVERSITY OF KANSAS
Student Union Activities, KS Union,
Lawrence KS 66045 (913)864-3477.
Some concerts. CP: DAILY KANSAN
16000.

*MISSOURI VALL FOLKLIFE SOC
10408 Caenen St, Overland Park KS
66215. Arlen Schubert.

*PRAIRIE DULCIMER SOCIETY
9540 Walnut St, Overland Park KS
66212. Harvey L Prinz.

*PITTSBURG STATE UNIVERSITY
1700 S Broadway, Student Union,
Pittsburg KS 66762 (316)231-7000.
Some concerts. CP: COLLEGIO weekly
5000.

*SALINA ARTS COMMISSION
PO Box 1281, Salina KS 67401
(913)827-4640. Martha Rhea, Dir.
Some concerts.

*KANSAS BLUEGRASS ASSN
2781 Hiram, Wichita KS 67217.

*KANSAS FOLKLORE SOCIETY
Wichita State U, Dept of English,
Wichita KS 67208. P.J. Wyatt, James
Hay. Newsletter. CP: SUNFLOWER 3x
weekly 12000.

*WALNUT VALLEY ASSOCIATION
PO Box 245, Winfield KS 76156 (316)
221-3250. Bob Redford. WALNUT
VALLEY OCCASIONAL.

FESTIVALS

KANSAS STATE FAIR
State Fairgrounds, Hutchinson KS
67501 (316)662-6611.

SUMMERFIELD IRISH FEST
Summerfield KS 66541. Sharon
Cameron.

*WALNUT VALLEY NATIONAL
  FLATPICKING CHAMPIONSHIPS
Held at Winfield Fairgrounds. Box
245, 918 Main, Winfield KS
(316)221-3250. Bob Redford. Varied
music, contests. Camping. Sep.

MUSEUMS

*PIONEER MUSEUM
430 W 4th, Ashland KS 67831 (316)
635-2227. Pioneer life, musical
instruments.

*BOOT HILL MUSEUM
Front St, Dodge City KS 67801 (316)
227-8188. Frontier history.

*PIONEER ADOBE HOUSE & MUSEUM
Ash & D Sts, Hillsboro KS 67951
(316)947-3775. Folklore collection.

*KS STATE HISTORICAL SOCIETY
120 W 10th ST, Topeka KS 66612
(913)296-3251.

*FELLOWS-REEVE MUSEUM
2100 University, Wichita KS 67213
(316)261-5800. Collection includes
musical instruments.

PRINT

*HUTCHINSON NEWS
300 W 2nd St, PO Box 90, Hutchinson
KS 67504-0190 (316)662-3311.

*KANSAN
901 N 8th St, Kansas City KS 66104
(913)371-4300. Andrea Stewart.

DAILY JOURNAL WORLD
Lawrence KS 66044. Chuck Twardy.

*SALINA JOURNAL
333 S 4th St, PO Box 740, Salina KS
67402-0740 (913)823-6363.

*TOPEKA CAPITAL-JOURNAL
6th & Jefferson, Topeka KS 66607
(913)295-1195. Nancy Nowick.

*WICHITA EAGLE BEACON
925 Douglas Ave, PO Box 820,
Wichita KS 67201-0820 (316)268-
6000.

RADIO

KVCO
2221 Campus Dr, Concordia KS 66901.

*KHCC (NPR-90.1)
815 N Walnut, #300, Hutchinson KS
67501 (316)665-3555. Ken Krehbiel,
MD. Performers should contact News
Dir Patsy Terrell for interviews.

*KANU (NPR-91.5)
U of KS, Broadcasting Hall,
Lawrence KS 66044 (913)864-4530.
Michael Allen, Rick Desko. FLINT
HILLS SPECIAL Sun 7-midnight. CP:
DAILY KANSAN 16000.

KJHK (90.7)
U of KS, 217 Flint Hall, Lawrence
KS 66045 (913)864-4745. John
Cheney.

*KSDB (88.1)
Kansas State U, McCain Auditorium,
3rd fl, Manhattan KS 66506
(913)532-6960. Lori Coffey. CP: KS
COLLEGIAN daily 15000.

*KANZ (91.1)
1 Broadcast Plaza, Pierceville KS
67868 (316)335-5120. Steve Olson,
MD. Some folk, blues.

KMUW (NPR-89.1)
3317 E 17th St, Wichita KS 67208
(316)682-5737. Patrick Daly. PG.

KENTUCKY

*ASSN OF FOLKLORISTS
  IN THE SOUTH
Western KY U, Folk Studies, Bowling
Green KY 42101. Camilla Collins,
Bert Feintuch. Newsletter.

*KENTUCKY FOLKLORE SOCIETY
Western KY U, Box 169, Bowling
Green KY 42101. KENTUCKY FOLKLORE
RECORD.

*LOUISVILLE COMMUNITY FNDN
623 W Main St, Louisville KY 40202
(502)585-4649. Funding info.

VENUES

*PARAMOUNT ARTS CENTER
PO Box 1546, Ashland KY 41101
(606)324-3175. Some concerts.

*BEREA COLLEGE
CPO 2339, Berea KY 40404 (606)986-
9341 x 496. John J. Crowden. Some
concerts. CP: PINNACLE 2x monthly
1700.

*EASTERN KY BLUEGRASS ASSN
Hazard High School, Hazard KY
41701.

NORTHERN KENTUCKY UNIVERSITY
University Ctr, #366, Highland Hts
KY 41075 (606)292-5146. Some
concerts. CP: NORTHERNER wkly 7500.

LEXINGTON/FAYETTE DEPT OF
  PARKS & RECREATION
545 N Upper St, Lexington KY 4058.
Lara Way, Cultural Arts Specialist.
Concerts & other programs.

*UNIVERSITY OF KENTUCKY
Student Activities, 203 Student
Ctr, Lexington KY 40506 (606)257-
8867. John H. Herbst. Some
concerts.

*KENTUCKY CTR FOR THE ARTS
5 Riverfront Plaza, Louisville KY
40202 (502)562-0100. Dick Van
Kleeck. Concert series, Folk Arts
Program in libraries, etc. Nwsltr.

*MOREHEAD STATE UNIVERSITY
University Ctr, Student Activities,
Morehead KY 40351 (606)783-3213.
S. Redwine, Assoc Dir. Concerts.
CP: TRAIL BLAZER weekly 6500.

MURRAY STATE UNIVERSITY
Student activities Board, Murray KY
42071 (502)762-6922. Some concerts.
CP: TRAIL BLAZER wkkly 9000.

*LOUISVILLE DULCIMER SOC
208 Ash Ave, Pewes Valley KY 40056.
Betty Stuedle.

*EASTERN KENTUCKY UNIVERSITY
Student Activities, 128 Powell
Bldg, Richmond KY 40475 (8606)623-
3855. Dr. Hayward Daugherty, Jr.
Some concerts. CP: EASTERN PROG
weekly 10000.

FESTIVALS

*FRALEY FAMILY MOUNTAIN
  MUSIC FESTIVAL
Carter Caves State Resort Park,
Olive Hill KY (606)286-4411. J P
and Annadeene Fraley. Concerts,
workshops, jams. Guaranteed no
bluegrass. Camping, cave tours.
Early Sept.

*KENTUCKY FRIED CHICKEN
  BLUEGRASS FESTIVAL
PO Box 32070, Louisville KY 40232
(502)456-8607. Early Sept.

*OLD JOE CLARK BLUEGRASS FEST
Rte 5, Box 142, Berea KY 40403.
Mid-July.

MUSEUMS

*THE KENTUCKY MUSEUM
W KY U, Bowling Green KY 42101
(502)745-2592. Traditional tools,
musical instruments, etc.

*MOUNTAIN LIFE MUSEUM
State Park, London KY 40741
(606)878-8000. Folklore collection.

*BLUE LICKS BATTLEFIELD MUSEUM
Blue Licks park, Mt Olivet KY 41064
(606)289-5507. Folklore collection.

PRINT

ASHLAND INDEPENDENT
PO Box 311, Ashland KY 41101.

*LEXINGTON HERALD-LEADER
100 Midland Ave, Lexington KY 40507
(606)231-3252. Tom Carter.

LEXINGTON TRAD DANCE NEWS
Boxz 1538, Bluebird La, Lexington
KY 40503. Peter Rogers.

*LOUISVILLE TIMES and
    COURIER-JOURNAL
525 W Broadway, Louisville KY 40202
(502)582-4011. William Mootz.

*MESSENGER-INQUIRER
PO Box 1480, 1401 Frederica St,
Owensboro KY 42302 (502)926-0123.
Ann W. Whittinghill, People Ed.

*PADUCAH SUN
PO Box 2300, Paducah KY 42001
(502)443-1771. Don Pepper.

RADIO

*WDNA
Berea Coll, CPO 381, Berea KY 40404
(606)986-9341 X 617. Jeff Lipscomb.

WKYU (NPR-88.9)
Western KY U, Bowling Green KY
42101 (502)745-5489. Mark
Vogelzang. PG. CP: COLLEGE HEIGHTS
HERALD 2x weekly, 10000.

WRVG
Georgetown Coll, Georgetown KY
40324.

*WNKU (89.7)
Northern KY U, 301 Landrum Academic
Ctr, Highland Hgts KY 41076
(606)572-6500. Richard F. Pender,
GM. Kentucky folk radio. CP:
NORTHERNER weekly 7500.

WBKY (NPR-91.3)
U of KY, 340 McVey Hall, Lexington
KY 40506 (606)257-3221. Don
Wheeler. CP: KENTUCKY KERNEL daily
18000.

WFPL (NPR-91.9)
Public Library, 4th & York Sts,
Louisville KY 40203 (502)584-4151.
Brady Miller.

*WLCV (870AM)
U of Louisville, S 3rd St,
Louisville KY 40208 (502)588-6966.
CP: ACTION 2x monthly; LOUISVILLE
CARDINAL weekly 15000.

WOUL (NPR-90.5)
U of Louisville, Louisville KY
40292 (502)588-6467. David
Brownstein. PG. CP: see WLCV.

*WMKY
Morehead State U, Morehead KY
40351.

*WKMS (NPR-91.3)
Box 2018, University Stn, Murray KY
42071 (502)762-4359. Pat O'Neill,
MD. Folk programs. PG.

WEKU (NPR-88.9)
Eastern KY U, Richmond KY 40475
(606)622-2474. Loy W. Lee. PG.

LOUISIANA

*LOUISIANA FOLKLIFE PROGRAM
666 N Foster Dr, PO Box 44247,
Baton Rouge LA 70804 (504)925-3930.
Maida Bergeron, Nicholas Spitzer.
Producers of a wonderful and
comprehensive book, "Louisiana
Folklife." Lists of fests etc.

*LOUISIANA OFFICE
  OF TOURISM
PO Box 94291, Baton Rouge LA 70804-
9291 (504)925-3877. Dennis Bryant.
Advertising and publicity.

*SHREVE MEMORIAL LIBRARY
424 Texas St, Shreveport LA 71101
(318)226-5894. Funding info.

VENUES

LOUISIANA FOLKLORE SOC
LSU, Dept of English, Baton Rouge
LA 70803. Frank de Cara. Nwsltr.

*CALVIN FOLKLORE SOC
Calvin High School, Calvin LA
71410. THE SASSAFRAS.

*GRAMBLING STATE UNIV
Concert & Lecture Series, Favrot
Student Union, Grambling LA 71235
(318)247-6941 x 205. Eddie
Henderson, Chmn. Concerts.

SOUTHEAST LOUISIANA UNIV
Student Activities Board, Hammond
LA 70402 (504)549-2041. Some
concerts. CP: LIONS ROAR wkly 3500.

*ACAADIANA ARTS COUNCIL
PO Box 53762, Lafayette LA 70505
(318)233-7080. Julie Carter.
Concerts.

UNIV OF SW LOUISIANA
100 E University, Lafayette LA
70504 (318)264-6381. Some concerts.
CP: VERMILLION weekly 12000.

*FOLKLIFE SOCIETY OF LOUISIANA
NW State U, Dept of Languages,
Nachitoches LA 71457 (318)375-6511.
Don Hatley. Newsletter.

*ECUADOR CLUB
856 Carondelet, New Orleans LA
70130.

LOUISIANA FOLKLORE SOC
U of New Orleans, Anthropology
Dept, New Orleans LA 70148 (504)
283-0338. LA FOLKLORE MISCELLANY.

*SOUTH CENTRAL GOSPEL MUSIC
   CONFERENCE
Box 1956, Shreveport LA 71166.
Concerts, meetings.

*NICHOLLS STATE UNIVERSITY
Student Entertainment Board,
Student Union, Thibodaux LA 70301
(504)446-8111. William Borskey.
Some concerts. CP: NICHOLLS WORTH
weekly 6000.

FESTIVALS

*BATON ROUGE BLUES FESTIVAL
427 Laurel St, Baton Rouge LA 70801
(504)344-8558. Held on the levee,
Lower Mississippi Vall performers,
April.

CAJUN FEST
1502 Industrial St, Vinton LA 70668
(318)589-7358. Clarence LeBlanc.
Mid-Sept.

*FEST DE LA MUSIQUE ACADIENNE
Held in Girard Park. Ctr for LA
Studies, USL, Lafayette LA 70504
(318)231-6350. Cajun & Creole
music. Sept.

*FRENCH ACADIAN MUSIC FEST
Held at Knights of Columbus Hse.
209 N Bailey Ave, Abbeville LA
70510 (318)893-1257. Robert P
Prejean, Chairman. Mid-April.

LOUISIANA STATE FAIR
PO Box 9100, Shreveport LA 71139
(318)635-1361. C Ed Nelson. Late
Oct.

*LA STATE FIDDLE CHAMPIONSHIPS
Box 127, Marthaville LA 71450
(318)472-6255. Last wkend May.

*MAMOU CAJUN MUSIC FEST
Held in Jaycee Park. PO Box 200,
Mamou LA 70554 (318)468-5555. Paul
Tate, Jr. 1st Fri-Sat in June.

*NACHITOCHES FOLK FESTIVAL
Held in Prather Coliseum. Folklife
Ctr, NSU, Box 363, Nachitoches LA
71457-0014 (318)357-4332. Trad
music, foods, crafts. Each year
focuses on an industry that has
shaped Louisiana. 2nd wkend July.

*NEW ORLEANS JAZZ & HERITAGE FEST
PO Box 2350, New Orleans LA 70176
(504)522-4786. Trad New Orleans
jazz, Mardi Gras Indians, R&B,
Cajun, zydeco. 10 days, 10 stages
simultaneously. Apr/May.

MUSEUMS

*LSU RURAL LIFE MUSEUM
6200 Burden La, Baton Rouge LA
70808 (504)766-8241.

*STATE CAPITOL FOLKLIFE EXHIBIT
State Capitol Bldg, Baton Rouge LA
70804 (504)925-3930.

*ZIGLER MUSEUM
411 Clara St, Jennings LA 70546
(318)824-0114. Oral history etc.

*ACADIAN VILLAGE
Rte 3, Box 1976, Lafayette LA 70506
(318)981-2364. Folk buildings round
man-made bayou.

*LOUISIANA STATE MUSEUM
757 Chartres St, PO Box 2458, New
Orleans LA 70116 (504)568-6968.
Folk artifacts, folk art.

PRINT

*ALEXANDRIA TOWN TALK
3rd & Washington, Alexandria LA
71306 (318)487-6397. Alice B
Thomas, Focus Ed.

FOLK DANCE SCENE/BATON ROUGE
4431 Blecker Dr, Baton Rouge LA
70809.

*MORNING ADVOCATE and STATE TIMES
PO Box 588, Baton Rouge LA 70821
(504)383-1111.

PIONEER AMERICA
PO Box 22230, Baton Rouge LA 70893.

*DAILY ADVERTISER
PO Box 3268, Lafayette LA 70502
(318)235-8511.

*LOUISIANE (French)
PO Box 3936, Lafayette LA 70502.
Promotes use of French language.

*LAKE CHARLES AMERICAN PRESS
PO Box 2893, Lake Charles LA 70602
(318)439-2781.

*NEWS-STAR-WORLD
411 N 4th St, Monroe LA 71203
(318)322-8161.

*NEW ORLEANS TIMES-PICAYUNE/
   STATES-ITEM
3800 Howard Ave, New Orleans LA
70140 (504)586-3687.

WAVELENGTH
PO Box 15667, New Orleans LA 70175.
Record reviews.

*SHREVEPORT JOURNAL and TIMES
PO Box 31110, Shreveport LA 71130
(318)459-3218.

RADIO

*WPRG (107.3)
LA State U, 107 E Stadium, Baton
Rouge LA 70803 (504)388-2826. CP:
DAILY REVEILLE 16000.

KGRM
Grambling State U, Grambling LA
71245 (318)247-6941. CP:
GRAMBLINITE weekly 5500.

WRKF (NPR-89.3)
15862 Frenchtown Rd, Greenwell
Springs LA 70739 (504)261-0679.
Constence Nourahl.

*KRVS
Burke Hall, USL, Lafayette LA
70504. Cajun & Creole programs.

*KNLU (88.7)
NE LA U, Monroe LA 71212 (318)342-
4072. Chris Lea. CP: POW-WOW weekly
8000.

*KNWO
NW State U, Nachitoches LA 71497
(318)357-4422.

*WWOZ (90.7)
PO Box 51840, New Orleans LA 70151
(504)568-1234. Steve Pierce, PD.
Folk, cajun, zydeco, world music.
PG: ALL RIGHT.

*WYES-TV
916 Navarre Ave, New Orleans LA
70124 (504)486-5111. Some folk
documentaries.

*KLPI (89.1)
LA Tech U, Box 5358, Tech Sta,
Ruston LA 71272 (318)257-4851. Doug
Lathan.

*KSCL (91.3)
Centenary Coll of LA, 2911
Centenary Rd, Shreveport LA 71104
(318)869-5296. Tom Hibbs.

KVFG
Box 2664, Univ Sta, Thibodaux LA
70301 (504)446-8111.

*WTUL (91.5)
Tulane Univ Ctr, 6823 St Charles
Ave, Tulane LA 70118 (504)865-5887.
Gina Forsyth. Folk programs.

MAINE

*MAINE ARTS SPONSORS ASSN.
PO Box 2352, Augusta ME 04330 (207)
62207131 x 271. Andrea Stander.
Booking consortium.

*U OF S ME, CTR FOR RESEARCH
246 Deering Ave, Portland ME 04102
(207)780-4411. Funding info.

VENUES

*UNIVERSITY OF MAINE
Augusta ME 04330 (207)622-7131 x 271. Bronwen Tudor, Exec Dir. Concerts.

*CTR FOR THE ARTS
804 Washington St, Bath ME 04530-2617 (207)442-8455. Suzanne L Weiss. Conerts.

DOWNEAST FRIENDS OF FOLK ARTS
461 College St, Lewiston ME 04240.

FO'C'SLE
U of ME, Memorial Union Cafe, Orono ME 04469. (207)581-1734. Bobbie Ives. Mainly student performers, some guests.

*NORTHEAST FOLKLORE SOC
U of ME, S Stevens Hall, Orono ME 04469 (207)581-1891. Edward Ives. Annual meeting. Publishes monograph series. Also covers Maritime Provinces of Canada.

*PORTLAND FOLK CLUB
80 Quebec St, Portland ME 04101 (207)773-9459. Charlie Ipcar.

*UNIV OF SOUTHERN MAINE
Chair, Speakers & Cultural Events Committee, Student Activities, Bedford St, Portland ME 04103 (207)780-4096. John Bell. Works with Portland FC.

FESTIVALS

BANGOR STATE FAIR
100 Dutton St, Bangor ME 04401 (207)947-3542. 942-9000

BAR HARBOR FESTIVAL
93 Cottage St, Bar Harbor ME 04609 (207)288-5744. Classical, folk. Jul-Aug.

*DOWNEAST DULCIMER FESTIVAL
Chamber of Commerce, Box 158, Bar Harbor ME 04609 (207)288-5653. Mid-July.

*THOMAS PT BEACH BLUEGRASS FEST
Rte 24, Cooki Corner, Brunswick ME 04011 (207)725-6009. Late Aug.

MUSEUMS

*CAMDEN-ROCKPORT HISTORICAL SOC
Camden Rd, PO Box 897, Camden ME 04843. Historic houses, folklore.

*ALLIE RYAN MARITIME COLLECTION
Quick Hall, Maine Maritime Academy, Castine ME 04333 (207)326-4311. Maritime history, broadsides.

*WILLOWBROOK AT NEWFIELD
Main St, Newfield ME 04056 (207) 793-2784. C19 history, musical instrument collection.

*SHAKER MUSEUM
Sabbathday Lake, Poland Spring ME 04274 (207)926-4597. Folk art.

*VINALHAVEN HISTORICAL SOC
Mayflower Hill, Waterville ME 04901 (207)873-1133. Folklore.

PRINT

*BANGOR DAILY NEWS
491 Main St, Bangor ME 04401 (207) 942-4881. Robert H Newall, Arts Ed.

*BAR HARBOR TIMES
66 Main St, Bar Harbor ME 04609 (207)288-3311. Rebecca Byers, Arts Ed. Listings.

*LEWISTON DAILY SUN and
  LEWISTON EVENING JOURNAL
104 Park St, Lewiston ME 04240 (207)784-5411. Mark Leslie.

*PORTLAND EVENING EXPRESS,
  PRESS HERALD, MAINE
  SUNDAY TELEGRAM
PO Box 1460, Portland ME 04104 (207)775-5811.

SWEET POTATO
PO Box 385 DTS, Portland ME 04112 (207)799-2643. Bennie Green. Robin Downs, listings.

RADIO

*WHSN (89.3)
Husson Coll, Bangor ME 04401 (207) 947-3987.

*WBOR (99.3)
Bowdoin Coll, Moulton Union, Brunswick ME 04011 (207)725-5008. Dan Covell.

*WUMF (92.3)
U of ME, 86 Main St, Farmington ME
04938 *207)778-4522/4533. Michael
Keating.

*WMPG
U of ME, 37 College Ave, Gorham ME
04038 (207)780-5416. J C Ball.

WRNE
16 Cary St, Houlton ME 04730.

*WRBC
Bates Coll, Lewiston ME 04240 (207)
581-2333. Jose Diaz.

*WMEB (91.9)
U of ME, East Annex, Orono ME 04469
(207)581-2333. Dana Snyder. CP:
MAINE CAMPUS daily 5000.

WMGX
477 Congress St, Portland ME 04101.

WPBN
PO Box 1628, Portland ME 04101.
Susan Wark.

WPOR
562 Congress St, Portland ME 04101.

WUPI
U of ME, Box 64, Normal Hall,
Presque Isle ME 04769.

WDCS (106.3)
10 Oak Hill Terr, Scarborough ME
04074 (207)883-9596. Alan Ellstrom.

WTOS
Box 159, Skowhegan ME 04976.

*WMHB
Colby Coll, Roberts Union,
Waterville ME 04901.

STORES

MUSIC WORKS
95 Lisbon St, Lewiston ME 04240
(207)783-6699.

*AMADEUS MUSIC
332 Fore St, Portland ME 04101
(207)772-8416. Record store.

MARYLAND

Many Maryland events can be found
in the Folklore Soc of Greater
Washington's Newsletter. See them
in DC.

*ENOCH PRATT FREE LIBRARY
Social Science & History Dept, 400
Cathedral St, Baltimore MD 21201
(301)396-5320. Funding info.

*OFFICE OF TOURIST DEVELOPMENT
45 Calvert St, Annapolis MD 21401
(301)269-3517. Events calendar.

VENUES

*BALTIMORE DANCE COUNCIL
817 Corktree Rd, Baltimore MD
21220. Monthly square dances.

*BALTIMORE FOLK MUSIC SOCIETY
PO Box 7134, Waverly Sta, Baltimore
MD 21218 (301)462-6993. Linda Baer.
Sat. Seats 300.

*BERTHA'S MUSSELS
734 S Broadway, Baltimore MD 21231.
(301)327-5795. Tony & Laura Norris.
Thurs-Fri. Seats 75.

*DUNBAR PERFORMING ARTS CTR
1515 E North Ave, Baltimore MD
21213 (301)396-3181. Norman E Rose.

JOHNS HOPKINS UNIVERSITY
Student Actvities, Hopkins Union,
Baltimore MD 21218 (301)338-8208.
Some concerts. CP: NEWSLETTER
weekly 6000.

*MT VERNON PLACE COFFEEHSE
Methodist Church, 10 E Mt Vernon
Pl, Baltimore MD 21202 (301)462-
6993. Linda Baer, 1609 Park Ave,
Baltimore MD 21217. Fri. Seats 100.

*UNIVERSITY OF MARYLAND
Student Entertainment Enterprises,
1211G Stamp Union Bldg, College
Park MD 20742 (301)454-4546. Judy
Davidson, Prog Advisor. CP:
RETRIEVER weekly 6000.

*MOUNT ST MARY'S COLLEGE
Artists, Lecturers, & Performers
Series. Emmitsburg MD 21727
(301)447-6122 x 369. Patricia M
Fergus, Chmn.

GAELIC LEAGUE OF DC AREA
4916 49th Ave, Hyattsville MD 20718
(301)864-2385. Judy Walsh.

MARYLAND THEATRICALS
PO Box 539, Owings Mills MD 21117
(301)363-0460. Concerts.

*ROCKVILLE DEPT OF REC
City Hall, Maryland Ave & Vinson
St, Rockville MD 20850 (301)424-
8000. Some concerts.

WESTERN MD FOLKLORE SOC
Rte 1, Box 52A, Smithburg MD 21783
(301)739-5265. Dances 1st Sat at
Mens Club, Shepherdstown WV.

*KOINONIA ESTATE
1400 Greenspring Rd, Stevenson MD
(301)484-2604. Will Werley. Some
concerts.

*HOUSE OF MUSICAL TRADITIONS
7040 Carroll Ave, Takoma Park MD
20912 (301)270-9090 or 0222. David
Eisner. Concerts Mon, Takoma Cafe.
Workshops.

*TAKOMA CAFE
1 Columbia Ave, Takoma Park MD
20912 (301)270-2440. Music Thurs-
Mon. Seats 60.

*WESTERN MD COLLEGE
Westminster MD 21157 (301)848-7000.
Kathleen Dawkins. Some concerts.

FESTIVAL

*TAKOMA PARK FOLK FEST
Held at Takoma Pk Jr High School.
7611 Piney Branch Rd, Takoma Pk MD
20912 (301)829-8802. Sara Green.
Early Sept.

MUSEUMS

*NATIONAL COLONIAL FARM
3400 Bryan Pt Rd, Accokeek MD 20607
(301)283-2113. Folklore.

*CHESAPEAKE BAY MARITIME MUSEUM
Navy Point, PO Box 636, St Michaels
MD 21663 (301)745-2916.

PRINT

*BALTIMORE NEWS AMERICAN
301 E Lombard St, Baltimore MD
21202 (301)528-8000.

*BALTIMORE SUN
PO Box 1377, 501 N Calvert St,
Baltimore MD 21278 (301)332-6176.

*GEOFFREY HIMES
3720 Greenmount Ave, Baltimore MD
21218. Journalist, reviews records,
concerts, & books.

*COLUMBIA FLIER and others
10750 Little Patuxent Pkwy,
Columbia MD 21044 (301)730-3620.
Geoffrey Himes, Music Ed.

*HAGERSTOWN HERALD and DAILY MAIL
100 Summit Ave, Hagerstown MD 21740
(301)733-5131. David C Elliott.

RADIO

WLOM
PO Box 829, Annapolis MD 21404.

WBJC (NPR-91.5)
2901 Liberty Hts Ave, Baltimore MD
21215 (301)396-0404. Bill Quinn.

WFMM
611 Hardwood Ave, Baltimore MD
21212. Lawrence Smith.

*WJHU (88.1)
Johns Hopkins U, 34th & Charles St,
Baltimore MD 21218 (301)338-8400.
Bill Barnett.

WHFS
4853 Cordell Ave, Bethesda MD 20014
(301)656-0600.

WMUC (88.1)
U of MD, Box 99, College Park MD
20742 (301)454-3688. Tony Lombardi.
CP: DIAMONDBACK daily 21K; MIZPEH
weekly; BLACK EXPLOSION 2x monthly
4000.

*WMTB
Mt St Mary's Coll, Emmitsburg MD
21727 (301)447-6122 x 488.

*WECC
Essec Community Coll, Essex MD
21237 (301)682-6000. Chris Peach.

*WVCT (89.7)
Towson State U, Media Ctr, Towson
MD 21204 (301)321-2898. Chris
Roberts. CP: TOWERLIGHT wkly 11000.

STORES

*MAGGIE'S MUSIC STUDIO
940 Bay Ridge Ave, Annapolis MD
(301)268-3592. Maggie Sansone.
Instrument classes: recorder,
banjo, mandolin, guitar, hammered
dulcimer (rentals available).

*HOUSE OF MUSICAL TRADITIONS
7040 Carroll Ave, Takoma Park MD
20912 (301)270-9090 or 0222. David
Eisner. Instruments, records,
books, classes, accessories.

MASSACHUSETTS

*ASSOCIATED GRANTMAKERS OF MA
294 Washington St, #501, Boston MA
02108 (617)426-2608. Funding info.

VENUES

*BOSTON FOOD CO-OP COFFEEHSE
449 Cambridge St, Allston MA 02134
(617)787-1416. Concerts Fri-Sat. N.6.

*KINVARA PUB
34 Harvard Ave, Allston MA 02134
(617)254-9737. Jerry Quinn. Thur-
Sun. Irish & American music.

*TRANSFIGURED NIGHT COFFEEHSE
Allston Congregational Church, 41
Quint Ave, Allston MA (617)524-
7692. Michael Kane.

HAMPSHIRE FOLK MUSIC SOCIETY
Hampshire Coll, Amherst MA 01002.

*HISTORICAL DANCE & MUSIC INST
Room 111, University Library,
Amherst MA 01003 (413)486-4218.
Medieval & Baroque. Classes, fests.

*CABLE COFFEEHOUSE
81 Mystic St, Arlington MA 02174
(617)646-2462. 1st Wed. Taped for
local cable release.

*FOLKTREE CONCERTMAKERS
Box 313, Arlington MA 02174 (617)
641-1010. Harry Lipson. Major folk
& acoustic concerts in greater
Boston area. Season tickets
available. books BERKLEE PERFORMANCE
+ DeCORDOVA MUSEUM Sun 9-1
M-F 10-6

*UNCLE SAM'S BACKYARD
At Wood & Strings, 493 Mass Ave,
Arlington MA 02174 (617)641-2131.
Bookings: Matt Weiss (617)646-2462,
26 Park St, Arlington MA. 3rd Fri.

*BERKLEE PERFORMANCE CENTER
136 Massachusetts Ave, Boston MA
(617)492-7679. Concerts.

*FOLK SONG SOCIETY
  OF GREATER BOSTON
PO Box 492, Somerville MA 02143.
Info tape: (617)623-1806. For
bookings, write Chairman, Booking
Committee. Monthly concerts,
various venues.

NORTHEASTERN UNIVERSITY
Student Activities, Boston MA 02115
(617)437-2642. Some concerts. CP:
NE NEWS weekly 12000.

*WHEELOCK COLL
New Campus Ctr, Riverway, Boston
MA. Some concerts.

*OFF THE COMMON COFFEEHOUSE
52 School St, Bridgewater MA 02324
(617)697-8575 or 947-9162. Al
Silva, Tricia Tumino, 65 Summer St,
Middleboro MA 02346. 2nd & 4th Sat.

*CAMBRIDGE ADULT EDUC CTR
42 Brattle St, Cambridge MA 02138
(617)547-6789. Rosalie & Paul de
Crescendo. Concerts Thurs.

*COUNTRY DANCE SOCIETY
*FOLK ARTS CTR OF NEW ENGLAND
*NEW ENGLAND FOLK FEST ASSN
595 Massachusetts Ave, Cambridge MA
02139 (617)491-6084. Anne Goodwin.
Dance info, folk dance records,
classes.

*DANCES
7 Temple St, Cambridge MA (617)354-
1340. Varied dancing, all levels,
several nights.

*FOLK ARTS NETWORK
PO Box 867, Cambridge MA 02238
(617)864-2970. Stephen Baird.
Concerts, workshops, etc.
Community events. FAN RESOURCE
GUIDE - annual and invaluable.

*JONATHAN SWIFT'S
30 JFK St, Cambridge MA 02138
(617)661-9887. Music 7 nights. Some
folk, blues.

*NAMELESS COFFEEHOUSE
3 Church St, Cambridge MA 02138
(617)864-1630. Anne Goodwin. Fri &
Sat. 5 sets/night, local artists.
Trad, bluegrass, oldtime. Free.

*PASSIM'S —SAME MACHINE AS BERKLEE
47 Harvard Sq, Cambridge MA 02138
(617)492-7679. Bob & Rae Ann
Donlin. Tues-Sun. Live show on WERS
Sun. Varied acoustic music.

*CHICOPEE FOLK MUSIC SOC,
  STAINED GLASS COFFEEHOUSE
621 Broadway, Chicopee MA 01020
(413)598-8976. Jim & Charlene
Murphy. 1 Sat/mo.

*OLD IRISH ALE HOUSE
2-4 Bridge St, Dedham MA 02026
(617)329-6034. Michael Hagerty.

*FIRST ENCOUNTER COFFEEHOUSE
At Unitarian Church, Samoset Rd,
Eastham MA 02651 (617)255-5438.
Karie Miller, Box 490, N Eastham MA
02651. 1st & 3rd Sat.

*NORTHERN LIGHTS
First Parish Church, Upper Common,
Fitchburg MA 01420 (617)537-1299.
Dick Wales. Fri, Sept-May.

*J P JUNCTION COFFEEHSE
At Central Congregational Church,
85 Seaverns Ave, Jamaica Plains MA
02130 (617)524-3343. Dennis Bailey.
4th Fri, Sep-May. Square dance 3rd
Fri.

*RED BOOK STORE
92 Green St, Jamaica Plain
(617)522-3303. Folk on Sun.

*SOUTH SHORE FOLK MUSIC CLUB
31 Smith's Lane, Kingston MA 02364
Steve & Gail Mattern. Music Fri,
dance 1st Sat, at Beal House, Rte
106, Kingston. Seats 250. Newsltr.

*DE CORDOVA & DANA MUSEUM
Sandy Pond Rd, Lincoln MA 01773 1982
(617)259-8355. Concerts Sun. Gail Rich

*ME AND THEE COFFEEHSE
At Unitarian Church, 28 Mugford St.
PO Box 1084, Marblehead MA 01945
(617)631-7930. Ralph Silva. Fri.

*SAT NIGHT IN MARBLEHEAD
At St. Andrew's Church, Lafayette
St, Marblehead MA 01945. Kevin &
Barbara Cross (617)631-4951; Bob
Franke (617)535-3331, 106 Winona
St, W Peabody MA 01960. Seats 150.

GATES OF DAWN COFFEEHOUSE
St Andrew's, 26 Pleasant St,
Medfield MA 02052 (617)359-4602.
Janet DiNapoli.

*THE FOLK GUILD
Needham Congregational Church, 1154
Great Plain Ave, Needham MA 02192
(617)384-8784. Jon Roper, PO Box
323, Westwood MA 02090. 1st Fri.

*HOMEGROWN COFFEEHOUSE
First Parish Unitarian Church,
Dedham & Great Plain Ave, Needham
MA 02192 (617)444-7478. Jim
Sargent. Sat, 2/mo.

*TRYWORKS COFFEEHOUSE
Parish Hse, First Unitarian Church,
8th & Union Sts, New Bedford MA
02719 (617)996-5295. Maggi Peirce,
544 Washington St, Fairhaven MA
02719. Sats.

*SMU COFFEEHOUSE
Southeastern MA U, N Dartmouth MA
02747 (617)999-8134. Phil Young.
Tues. Free.

*FOLK GUILD
Needham Congregational Church, 1154
Great Plain Ave, Needham MA 02192
(617)384-8784. John Roper, PO Box
323, Westwood MA 02090. 1st Fri.
Seats 300.

*IRON HORSE
20 Center St, Northampton MA 01060
(413)584-0610. Jordi Herold. Varied
music, most nights. Seats 85.

*PIONEER VALLEY FOLKLORE SOC
PO Box 803, Northampton MA 01061
(413)586-5285. Concerts, school
programs, newsletter.

SALEM STATE COLLEGE
Campus Ctr, Salem MA 01970
(617)745-4732. Some concerts. CP:
LOG weekly 5000.

*SOMERVILLE THEATRE
Davis Sq, Somerville MA 02143
(617)862-7837. Some concerts.

*EVENSONG COFFEEHOUSE
Old S Union Church, Columbia Sq, S
Weymouth MA 02190 (617)471-1675.
Terri Hoitt. Bookings: Randy
Perkins (617)878-4835. Sat.

*U 'N' I COFFEEHOUSE
At First Unitarian Universalist
Church, 245 Porter Lake Dr,
Springfield MA 01106 9413)562-3990.
Ed & Beth Brown, 10 Grandview Dr,
Westfield MA 01085. Monthy Sep-May.

CHOLMONDELEY'S
Brandeis U, 415 South St, Waltham
MA 02254 (617)647-2167. CP: JUSTICE
weekly 5000.

*SOCIETY OF INTER-CELTIC
  ARTS AND CULTURE
96 Marguerite Ave, Waltham MA 02154
(617)899-2204. Kevin Gilligan.
Concerts. KELTICA, 1/yr.

SCOTTISH ARTS
45 Norder St, W Newton MA 02165.
Concerts, workshops, newsletter.

*WOODS HOLE FOLK MUSIC SOC
174 Lakeshore Dr, E Falmouth MA
02536 (617)540-0320. Clyde Tyndale.
Held at Woods Hole Community Hall.
1st & 3rd Sun, Oct-May. Seats 150.
Newsletter.

*JOHN HENRY'S HAMMER
  COFFEEHOUSE
At First Unitarian Church, 90 Main
St, Worcester MA 01605. Info: (617)
752-2012. Bookings: Gene Petit
(617)752-7517 (WICN - see below).

WORCESTER AREA FOLK SOC
68 Bouyce St, Auburn MA 01501 (617)
752-2019.

FESTIVALS

*BOSTON AREA DULCIMER FEST
77 Bigelow Ave, Watertown MA 02172
(617)926-0307. Gail Rundlett.
Concerts, workshops. Early May.

*EISTEDFODD   bus hrs
Southeastern MA U, N Dartmouth MA
02747 (617)999-8166. Jean Salzman.
Late Sept.

*FESTIVAL OF LIGHT & SONG
√ PO Box 27, Cambridge MA 02140
(617)861-0649. Celebrations of
Winter & Summer solstices, Boston
and NYC.

*LAS POSADAS
Held at Strand Theater, Boston. 249
Lowell St, Wilmington MA 01887
(617)938-0854. Eileen Tannian.
Multi-cultural fest, with workshops
in earlier months. Dec.

√ MASSACHUSETTS STATE FAIR
Wilson St, Spencer MA 01562
(617)885-2635. Sept. bus hrs

*NEFFA FOLK FESTIVAL
√ Held at Natick High School, Natick
MA. 309 Washington St, Wellesley MA
01760 (617)234-6181. Late April.

MUSEUMS

*OLDE COLONIAL COURTHOUSE
Main St, Barnstable MA 02630 (617)
775-4811. Folk tales recordings.

*BERLIN ART & HISTORICAL COLL
51 South St, PO Box 87, Berlin MA
01503 (617)838-2502. Folklore.

*HISTORIC DEERFIELD
The Street, PO Box 321, Deerfield
MA 01342 (413)774-5581. Folklore.

*MUSEUM OF OUR NATIONAL HER
33 Marrett St, PO Box 519,
Lexington MA 02183 (617)861-6559.

*NEW BEDFORD WHALING MUSEUM
18 Johnny Cake Hill, New Bedford MA
02740 (617)997-0046.

*HANCOCK SHAKER VILLAGE
Rte 20, PO Box 898, Pittsfield MA
01202 (413)443-0188. 20 bldgs,
craft demonstrations.

*KENDALL WHALING MUSEUM
27 Everett St, PO Box 297, Sharon
MA 02057 (617)784-5642. Bob Webb.
Exhibits, library, 2 concerts a
year, workshops, newsletter

*OLD STURBRIDGE VILLAGE
Sturbridge MA 01566 (617)347-3362.
Living history.

PRINT

*BOSTON GLOBE
135 Morrisey Blvd, Boston MA 02107
(617)929-2000. Listings Thurs,
reviews, interviews.

*BOSTON HERALD
1 Herald Sq, Boston MA 02106 (617)
426-3000. Listings Thurs, reviews.

*BOSTON PHOENIX
100 Massachusetts Ave, Boston MA
02115 (617)536-5390. Milo Miles.
News, reviews, interviews,
listings.

*BOSTON ROCK
1318 Beacon St, #7, Brookline MA
02146 (617)734-7043. Michael
Dreese. News, reviews, interviews.

*SWEET POTATO
PO Box B, Astor Sta, Boston MA
02123 (617)254-6321. Richard
Cromonic. Some concert & record
reviews.

*THE ENTERPRISE
60 Main St, Brockton MA 02403
(617)586-6200. Joseph Sherman.

*CAMBRIDGE CHRONICLE
678 Mass Ave, Cambridge MA 02139
(617)868-7400. Listings, reviews.

*HERALD-NEWS
207 Pocasset St, Fall River MA
02722 (617)676-8211.

*MIDDLESEX NEWS
33 New York Ave, Framingham MA
01701 (617)872-4321.

*GREENFIELD RECORDER
14 Hope St, Greenfield MA 01301
(413)772-0261.

VALLEY ADVOCATE
87 School St, Hatfield MA 01038
(413)247-9301. David Sokol.

*TRANSCRIPT-TELEGRAM
120 Whiting Farms Rd, Holyoke MA
01040 (413)536-2300.

*LOWELL SUN & SUNDAY SUN
PO Box 1477, Lowell MA 01853 (617)
458-7100. Carol McQuaid.

*DAILY EVENING NEWS
PO Box 951, Lynn MA 01903 (617)593-
7700. Bill Brotherton, Mus Ed.

*NEW BEDFORD STANDARD-TIMES
555 Pleasant St, New Bedford MA
02742 (617)997-7411. Earl J Dias.

*THE TAB
217 California St, Newton MA 02158
(617)969-0340, 964-2400. Dean
Johnson, Rhea Becker. Listings.

*BERKSHIRE EAGLE
33 Eagle St, Pittsfield MA 01202
(413)447-7311. Andrew L Pincus.

*PATRIOT LEDGER
13-19 Temple St, Quincy MA 02169
(617)786-7066. Jon Lehman.

*SPRINGFIELD DAILY NEWS and
    SPRINGFIELD UNION & REPUBLICAN
1860 Main St, Springfield MA 01102
(413)788-1306.

VALLEY ADVOCATE
1113 Main St, Springfield MA 01103
(413)481-1900. F S Frail.

*WORCESTER EVENING GAZETTE and
    WORCESTER TELEGRAM
20 Franklin St, Worcester MA 01613
(617)793-9100.

RADIO

WAMH
Amherst Coll, Box 318, Sta 2,
Amherst MA 01002. CP: AMHERST
STUDENT 2x weekly 3000.

*WFCR (NPR-88.5)
U of MA, Hampshire Hse, Amherst MA
01003 (413)545-0100. Mary
DesRosiers. Folk programs. CP:
DAILY COLLEGIAN 19000.

WMUA
U of MA, 42 Marston Hall, Amherst
MA 01003 (413)545-2425. Al
Flanagan. Folk programs. CP:
DAILY COLLEGIAN 19000.

WBUR (NPR-90.9)
630 Commonwealth Ave, Boston MA
02215 (617)353-2790. Marcia Heets,
→Peter Stockerson. Folk. Live M-F 9-5
concerts.

*WERS (88.9)
Emerson Coll, 130 Beacon St, Boston
MA 02116 (617)267-7821. Brad Paul.
Folk. CP: BERKELEY BEACON 2x
monthly 2000.   578-8892 bus office

WNEV
7 Bullfinch Pl, Boston MA 02114.
Angela Rippen.

*WGBH (NPR-89.7)
125 Western Ave, Boston MA 02134
(617)492-2777. Ellen Kraft, Asst
Mgr, Dick Pleasants. Folk progs.
PG. A great station.

*WUMB (91.9)
U of MA, Harbor Campus, Boston MA
02125 (617)929-7919. Tom Callahan.
Over 10 hrs of folk per day.
Welcomes interviews. CP: MASS MEDIA
weekly 8000.

WHRB (95.3)
Harvard U, 45 Quincy St, Cambridge
MA 02138 (617)495-4818. Sinc &
Lynn. Folk. CP: HARVARD CRIMSOM
daily 3500, and others.

WMBR (88.1)
3 Ames St, Cambridge MA 02142
(617)494-8810. Dave Palmeter. Folk.

WZBC (90.3)
Boston Coll, Box K151, Chestnut
Hill MA 02167 (617)552-4686. Jim
McKay. Folk. CP: HEIGHTS weekly
12000.

WAQU
45 Fisher Ave, E Longmeadow MA
02108.

WVCA (104.9)
2 Duncan St, Gloucester MA 01930
(617)283-3700. Simon Geller.

WPOE
154 Federal St, Greenfield MA
01301.

WRSI (95.3)
Box 910, Greenfield MA 01302 (413)
774-2321. Ed Skudnick. Folk.

*WCCH (103.5)
Holyoke Community Coll, 303
Homestead Ave, Holyoke MA 01040.
Ed & Beth Brown, 10 Grandview Ave,
Westfield MA 01085 (413)562-3990,
THE ACOUSTIC ALTERNATIVE.

WREB
560 Dwight St, Holyoke MA 01040.

*WCOD
105 Stevens St, Hyannis MA 02601.
Joan Orr: CAPE ACOUSTICS.

WJUL
1 University Ave, Lowell MA 01854.

WATD (95.9)
PO Box 487, Marshfield MA 02050
(617)837-1168. Dick Pleasants.
Folk. Live broadcasts.

*WMFO (91.5)
Tufts Univ, Medford MA 02153 (617)
381-3800. Noah Osnos. Folk. CP:
TUFTS DAILY; TUFTS OBSERVER wkly
6500.

WNTN (1550AM)
143 Rumford Ave, Newton MA (617)
969-1500. John Curran. Irish folk.

*ANDREW NAGY
589 California St, Newtonville MA
02160 (617)244-8624. Programs for
WBRS, WGBH; writes for Boston
Globe.

WJMQ (1170AM)
PO Box 1170, Norfolk MA 02036 (617)
329-1170. Martin Haley.

WHMP
78 Main St, Northampton MA 01060.

WKZE
Bog Hollow Rd, Orleans MA 02653.
Joan Orr.

WQVR
41 Wheelock Rd, Oxford MA 01540.

WTBR
PO Box 1885, Pittsfield MA 01202.
James Thompson.

*WOMR (91.9)
PO Box 975, Provincetown MA 02657.
(617)487-2106. Steve Russo, Jacqui
McDonald. Folk each morning 9-12.

WHMC
Mt Holyoke Coll, S Hadley MA 01075.
CP: MT HOLYOKE NEWS weekly 2600.

*WTCC
Springfield Tech Community Coll,
Box 9000, Springfield MA 01101-9000
(413)736-2781. Jim & Charlene
Murphy: JUST FRIENDS & FOLK.
Interviews, records.

*WBRS
415 South St, Waltham MA 02154
(617)893-7080. George Brown, Andrew
Nagy. Folk.

WCRB (102.5)
750 South St, Waltham MA 02154
(617)893-70680. George Brown.

WKKL
Cape Cod CC, Rte 132, W Barnstable
MA 02668 (617)362-2131.

WAAF
19 Norwood St, Worcester MA 01608.

*WCUW (91.3)
910 Main St, Worcester MA 01601
(617)753-1012. Folk.

*WICN (NPR-90.5)
75 Grove St, Worcester MA 01605
(617)752-7517. Gene Petit. Folk
programs.

STORES

*WOOD & STRINGS
493 Massachusetts Ave, Arlington MA
02174 (617)641-2131. Rick Cyge.
Instruments, books, records,
repairs, lessons, etc.

*SANDY'S MUSIC
896A Massachusetts Ave, Cambridge
MA 02139 (617)491-2812.
Instruments, books, records, etc.

MICHIGAN

*PURDY LIBRARY
Wayne State U, Detroit MI 48202
(313)577-4040. Funding info.

VENUES

*AACTMAD
11029 Westaire Way, Ann Arbor MI
48103 (313)996-8359. Don Theyken.

ANN ARBOR FRIENDS OF TRAD
720 Linda Vista, Ann Arbor MI
48103. Suzanne Davidson.

*THE ARK
637-1/2 S Main, Ann Arbor MI 49104
(313)761-1451. David Siglen. Varied
music, most nights.

COUNCIL FOR TRAD MUSIC
875 S 1st St, #3, Ann Arbor MI
48103.

MICHIGAN FOLKLORE SOC
1471 Kensington, Ann Arbor MI
48103. Yvonne Lockwood.

*DETROIT COUNTRY DANCE SOC
32705 Bellvine Trail, Birmingham MI
48010. Burt & Marie Schartz Nils-
Bels.

*SPIRIT OF THE WOODS MUSIC ASSN
11171 Kerry Rd, Brethrem MI 49619.
Tim & Wanda Josephs. Bookings: Joe
Ferrer 840 Cemetery Rd, Manistee MI
49660 (616)723-6447. Concerts,
square dances 1/mo, school and
community progs. Seats 300.
Festival in June.

*GOPHERWOOD MUSIC CO-OP
243 Marble St, Cadillac MI 49601
(616)825-2113. Fred Hentenen,
Shelley Youngman.

*GREENSTONE MUSIC CO-OP
Rte 1, Box 33A, Calumet MI 49923
(906)337-4843. Jill VanderMeer.

WAYNE STATE UNIV
Student Ctr, Detroit MI 48202 (313)
574-9442. Some concerts. CP: SOUTH
END daily 1800.

*LANSING AREA FOLKSONG SOC
MI State U, PO Box 447, E Lansing
MI 48823 (517)372-2898. Eliot
Singer. Concerts, workshops,
dances.

*LOOKING-GLASS MUSIC
  & ARTS ASSN
PO Box 1403, E Lansing MI 48823
(517)372-9048.

*TEN-POUND FIDDLE
Box 6167, E Lansing MI 48823 (517)
694-7505. Catherine Madsen. Fri,
Sep-May.

*SOUTHFIELD FOLKTOWN COFFEEHSE
29648 Lockmoor, Farmington Hills
MI 48018 (313)855-9848. Ken
Knoppow.

*DELTA COUNTY FRIENDS OF FOLK
6065 Country Club La, Gladstone MI
49837 (906)428-3157. Dustin & Susan
Pease.

*GRAND RAPIDS FOLKLORE SOC
924 Carrier Creek NE, Grand Rapids
MI 49506 (616)457-8642. Margaret
Clouse.

*WESTERN MI UNITED BLUEGRASS
  PICKERS ASSN
200 College NE, #2, Grand Rapids MI
49503.

*GRASSROOTS MUSIC CO-OP
Rte 3, Hart MI 49420 (616)873-2330.
Bruce Bartin.

*CALUMET THEATRE
PO Box 86, Hubbell MI 49934 (906)
296-9624. Jim O'Brien.

*INTERLOCHEN CTR FOR THE ARTS
Interlochen MI 49643 (616)276-9221.
Donna Shugart, Special Events.

*FRIENDS OF FOLK MUSIC
122 Hughitt, Iron Mountain MI 49801
(906)779-1561. Mike Felten.

*NORTH COUNTRY FOLK ARTS
PO Box 189, Ironwood MI 49938 (906)
932-2727. Phil Kucera.

*MARQUETTE FOLK DANCERS
Rte 1, Box 2, Ishpeming MI 49849
(906)486-9941. Bob Railey.

*KALAMAZOO FOLKLIFE ORG
PO Box 1421, Kalamazoo MI 49001
(616)375-6853. Chuck Dineen. Runs
Celery City Music Hall. Sat, Sep-
Apr, except hols.

*AURA FIDDLERS' JAMBOREE
Rte 1, Box 217, L'Anse MI 49946
(906)524-7178. Fred Waisanen,
Helmer Toyras.

*ORIGINAL MI FIDDLERS ASSN
2221 Libbie Dr, Lansing MI 48917.
Robert Murphy. Regular fiddle-and-
dance jamborees. Newsletter.

*HIAWATHA MUSIC CO-OP
PO Box 414, Marquette MI 49855 (906)
228-6969. Jack Bowers, Sec.

*WILD RICE MUSIC CO-OP
402 43rd Ave, Menominee MI 49858
(906)863-8568. Mike Kettu.

*FOLK MUSIC SOC OF MIDLAND
1878 Hicks Rd, Midland MI 48640.
Dave Bowen.

SAGINAW VALLEY FOLKLORE SOC
1501 Bayberry, Midland MI 48640.
Dave Bowen.

*FRIENDS OF FOLK
304 Oak, Munising MI 49862 (906)
387-4055. Wendy Olson.

*MUSIC CONSERVANCY/BLISS FEST
421 Howard, Petoskey MI 49770
(616)347-2381. Jim Gillespie.

*ALLEGAN WOODS FOLK ARTS
Pleasant Hills Farms, Pennville MI
49408.

*WHEATLAND MUSIC ORGANIZATION
PO Box 22, Remus MI 49340 (517)561-
2873. Bruce & Jan Bauman. Community
events, school programs, festival.

*SAULT STE MARIE FRIENDS OF FOLK
726 Eureka, Sault Ste Marie MI
49783 (906)632-7488. Simon Couvier.

DETROIT FOLKLORE SOC
232428 Plumbrook, Southfield MI
48075.

FOLK ARTS
18605 Hilton, Southfield MI 48075.

*PAINT CREEK FOLKLORE SOC
4874 Brittney, Sterling Heights MI
48079. Rick Ott.

*BAYSIDE TRAVELERS
1004 Lincoln, Traverse City MI
49684 (616)947-3624. Ed Hargis.

FESTIVALS

*FLINT BLUEGRASS & FOLK ARTS FEST
913 E 2nd St, Flint MI 48503. Aug.

*GRAND MARAIS MUSIC &
  ARTS FESTIVAL
PO Box 118, Grand Marais MI 49839
(906)494-2766. Tom & Kathy Baker.

*HIAWATHA TRAD MUSIC FEST
PO Box 414, Marquette MI 49855 (906)
228-6969. Jack Bowers, Sec. Varied
music. Family-oriented. Workshops,
camping. July.

*LOOKING-GLASS MUSIC & ARTS FEST
Held in Riverfront Park. PO Box
1403, E Lansing MI 48823 (517)372-
9048. Ethnic, trad, blues, oldtime.
Late July.

MICHIGAN STATE FAIR
State Fairgrounds, Detroit MI 48203
(313)368-1000. August.

*SALT RIVER BLUEGRASS FESTIVAL
775 N Homer Rd, Midland MI 48640
(517)631-7659. George Carr.

*SOUTHERN MI DULCIMER FEST
1660 W Kimmel Rd, Jackson MI 49201
(517)784-6210. Late June.

*SPIRIT OF THE WOODS MUSIC
  ASSN FOLK FESTIVAL
Held at Manistee County
Fairgrounds, Onekama. 11171 Kerry
Rd, Brethrem MI 49619. Tim & Wanda
Josephs. Bookings: Joe Ferrer 840
Cemetery Rd, Manistee MI 49660
(616)723-6447. June.

MUSEUMS

*STEARNS COLL OF MUSICAL
  INSTRUMENTS
U of MI, School of Music, Ann Arbor
MI 48109 (313)763-4389. Western &
non-Western instruments.

*IRON COUNTY MUSEUM
Museum La, Hwy 42, Box 272, Caspian
MI 49915 (906)265-3942. Local
folklore & history.

*YOUR HERITAGE HOUSE
110 E Ferry, Detroit MI 48202 (313)
871-1667. Children's music.

*MI STATE UNIV MUSEUM
W Circle Dr, E Lansing MI 48824-
1045 (517)355-2370. Marsha
MacDowell, Curator of Folk Arts.
FOLKLINE publication.

*MICHIGAN HISTORICAL MUSEUM
208 N Capitol Ave, Lansing MI 48918
(517)373-0515. Folklore coll.

PRINT

*ANN ARBOR NEWS
PO Box 14-147, Ann Arbor MI 48106
(313)994-6825.

*BATTLE CREEK ENQUIRER
155 W Van Buren St, Battle Creek MI
49016 (616)964-7161. James A Dean.

*BAY CITY TIMES
311 5th Ave, Bay City MI 48706
(517)895-8551.

*DETROIT FREE PRESS
321 W Lafayette Blvd, Detroit MI
48231 (313)222-6459.

*DETROIT MONITOR
33490 Groesbeck, Fraser MI 48026
(313)296-6007. Horst Mann, Ed.

*DETROIT NEWS
615 W Lafayette Blvd, Detroit MI
48231 (313)222-2283.

FOLKLORE WOMEN'S COMMUNICATION
Wayne State U, Dept of English,
Detroit MI 48201. Janet Langlais.

METRO TIMES
2111 Woodward, Detroit MI 48201
(313)961-4060. Ron Williams, Ed;
Angeline Kaimala, listings.

*ESCANABA DAILY PRESS
600 Ludington St, Escanaba MI 49829
(906)786-2021.

*FLINT JOURNAL
200 E 1st St, Flint MI 48502 (313)
767-0660.

*GRAND RAPIDS PRESS
Press Plaza, 155 Michigan St,
Grand Rapids MI 49503 (616)459-
1400.

*CITIZEN PATRIOT
214 S Jackson St, Jackson MI 49204
(517)787-2300.

*KALAMAZOO GAZETTE
401 S Burdick St, Kalamazoo MI
49003 (616)345-3511.

STATE-JOURNAL
120 E Lenawee St, Lansing MI 48919
(517)487-4611.

*MUSKEGON CHRONICLE
981 3rd St, Muskegon MI 4943 (616)
722-3161.

*OAKLAND PRESS
PO Box 9, 48 W Huron St, Pontiac MI
48056 (313)332-8181. Kenn Jones.

DAILY TRIBUNE
210 E 3rd St, Royal Oak MI 48067
(313)541-3000. Michael A Beeson.

*SAGINAW NEWS
203 S Washington Ave, Saginaw MI
48605 (517)776-9707. Janet I
Martineau.

RADIO

*WGVC (88.5)
Grand Vall State Coll, Allendale MI
49401 (616)895-3128. Henry Hardy.

*WCBN (88.3)
U of MI, 530 SAB Bldg, Ann Arbor MI
48109 (313)7764-3501. Gretchen
Lindensmith. Folk progs. CP:
MICHIGAN DAILY 5000.

WAUS (NPR-90.7)
University Ctr, Box 113, Berrien
Springs MI 49104 (616)471-3400.
Vaida Smith.

*WRKX
Ferris State Coll, Big Rapids MI
49307 (616)7796-0461. Ken McCloud.

*WUMD
U of MI, 4901 Evergreen Rd,
Dearborn MI 48128.

*WAYN
Wayne State U, 672 Putnam, Detroit
MI 48202 (313)577-4200.

WCAR
8079 Evergreen Rd, Detroit MI
48228. Mike McCanhon.

*WDET
5057 Woodward, Detroit MI 48202
(313)577-4147. Judy Donlin. Folk
progs. Interviews, listings. PG.

*WKAR (90.5)
MI State U, 283 Communication Arts
Bldg, E Lansing MI 48824. THE FOLK
TRADITION, prod/host Bob Blackman.
CP: STATE NEWS daily 38000.

*WORB (90.3)
Oakland Community Coll, 27055
Orchard Lake Rd, Farmington Hills
MI 48024 (313)476-9400 x 505. Jean
St Germaine.

WFBE (95.1)
605 Crapo St, Flint MI 48503 (313)
762-1148. David Tamulevich. Folk.

*WTHS
Hope Coll, Dewitt Ctr, Holland MI
49423 (616)394-6452.

*WGGL (MPR/APR/NPR-91.1)
Michigan Tech U, PO Box 45,
Houghton MI 49931 (906)482-8912.
Jim Neumann. Occasional folk. May
do interviews. CP: TECH LODE weekly
5500.

WIAA
Ctr for the Arts, Interlochen MI
49684 (616)276-9221.

*WMTU
Michigan Tech, W Wadsworth Hall,
Houghton MI 49931 (906)487-2333.
Fortune Tuchowski.

*WJMD
Kalamazoo Coll, Kalamazoo MI 49007
(616)383-1686. Tom Miars.

*WMUK (NPR-102.1)
W MI U, Friedman Hall, Kalamazoo MI
49008 (616)383-1921. Folk progs
Sat-Sun. CP: WESTERN HERALD 3x
weekly 13000.

WLCC
430 N Capital Ave, Lansing MI
48901.

*WNMU
N MI U, Marquette MI 49855
(906)227-2600. Bill Hart. Folk
progs. CP: NORTHWIND wkly 6K.

*WMHW
Central MI U, 180 Moore Hall, Mount
Pleasant MI 48859 (517)772-3511 or
774-7287. John Scheffler. CP:
CENTRAL MI LIFE 3X weekly 15500.

*WNMC (90.9)
N MI Coll, 1701 Front St, Traverse
City MI 49684 (616)922-1091. Jim
Frixen. Folk progs.

WEMU
E MI U, Ypsilanti MI 48197
(313)487-2229. CP: EASTERN ECHO 3x
weekly 10000.

STORES

*GOLD RUSH MUSIC
757 W Michigan, Kalamazoo MI 49007
(616)342-2154. Jan Bloom.

*GITFIDDLER
302 E Main, Northville MI 48167.

*WHITE BROS
4245 Okemos Rd, Okemos MI 48864.
Instruments, accessories.

MINNESOTA

*MINNEAPOLIS PUBLIC LIBRARY
Sociology Dept, 300 Nicollet Mall,
Minneapolis MN 55401 (612)372-6555.
Funding info.

MN COUNCIL FOR TRAD ARTS
PO Box 9524, Minneapolis MN 55440.

*MN STATE ARTS BOARD
Folk Arts Program, 432 Summit Ave,
St Paul MN 55102 (612)297-1121.
Phil Nussbaum. Encourages
presenters, does public
programming, advice on funding.

VENUES

*HARDANGER FIDDLE ASSN
325 Howtz St, Duluth MN 55811.

*ORPHEUM CAFE
201 E Emperor St, Duluth MN 55802.
run by Friends of Music, Jim
Ofsthun, 2105 Kenwood Ave, Duluth
MN 55811 (218)724-2247. 2/mo. Seats
100.

MANKATO STATE UNIV
Student Union, Mankato MN 56001
(507)389-6075. Some concerts. CP:
REPORTER 2x weekly 8000.

*MINNESOTA FOLKLIFE SOCIETY
103 Park Ave, Marshall MN 56258.

*COFFEEHOUSE EXTEMPORE
416 Cedar Ave, Minneapolis MN 55454
(612)370-0004. Jack Hayes. Varied
music, many nights. Women's music
Thurs – contact Jill Jacoby (612)
781-0138.

*DULANO'S PIZZA
607 W Lake, Minneapolis (612)827-
1726. Bluegrass Fri-Sat.

*HOMESTEAD PICKIN' PARLOR
6625 Penn Ave S, Minneapolis MN
(612)861-3308. Marv Menzel.
Concerts, workshops, classes.

*MN BLUEGRASS & OLDTIME MUSIC
PO Box 9782, Minneapolis MN 55440.
Larry Jones, Pres (612)374-3391.
Concerts, festival. INSIDE
BLUEGRASS 12/yr.

UNIV OF MINNESOTA
Coffman Union Program Council,
Minneapolis MN 55455 (617)373-0373.
Some concerts. CP: MN DAILY 40K.

*ST CLOUD STATE UNIV
Atwood Ctr, St Cloud MN 56301
(612)255-2205. Brent Greene.
Concerts. CP: CHRONICLE 2x wkly 7K.

*IRISH MUSIC & DANCE ASSN
Box 65187, St Paul MN 55165.

*NORTH SHORE MUSIC ASSN
Box 2127, Tofte MN 55615 (800)642-
6036.

BERT WHITCOMBE
Rte 2, Underwood MN 56586 (218)495-
3235. Concerts in Fergus Falls.

FESTIVALS

*FESTIVAL OF NATIONS
1694 Compo Ave, St Paul MN 55108
(612)647-0191. April.

*MINNESOTA BLUEGRASS FESTIVAL
MBOTMA, PO Box 9782, Minneapolis MN
55440 (612)874-3391. Early Aug.

MINNESOTA STATE FAIR
St Paul MN, 55108 (612)645-2781.
Aug.

*NORTH SHORE MUSIC FESTIVAL
Box 2127, Tofte MN 55615 (800)642-
6036. Early July.

*SWAYED PINES FOLK FEST
St John's Univ, Collegeville MN
56374. April.

MUSEUMS

*POLK COUNTY HISTORICAL SOC
Hwy 2, PO Box 214, Crookston MN
56716 (218)281-1038. Folklore.

*COOK COUNTY MUSEUM
Grand Marais MN 55604 (218)387-
1678. Folklore collection.

*AMERICAN SWEDISH INSTITUTE
2600 Park Ave, Minneapolis MN 55407
(612)871-4907. Swedish folklore.

*GOODHUE COUNTY HISTORICAL SOC
1166 Oak St, Red Wing MN 55066
(612)388-6024. Folklore.

*VASA LUTHERAN CHURCH MUSEUM
Rte 1, PO Box 63, Welch MN 55089
(612)258-4274. Musical instruments
& songbooks.

PRINT

*DULUTH NEWS-TRIBUNE & HERALD
424 W 1st, Duluth MN 55801 (218)
723-5281.

*FREE PRESS
418 S 2nd St, Mankato MN 56001
(507)625-4451. Tim DeMarce.

CITY PAGES
Box 8467, Minneapolis MN 55408.

*MINNEAPOLIS STAR & TRIBUNE
425 Portland Ave, Minneapolis MN
55488 (612)372-4445. Jon Bream.

*TWIN CITIES READER
Butler Sq, Minneapolis MN. Martin
Keller.

*ST CLOUD DAILY TIMES
3000 N 7th St, St Cloud MN 56301
(612)255-8750. Deborah Hudson.

*ST PAUL PIONEER PRESS & DISPATCH
345 Cedar St, St Paul MN 55101
(612)228-5580. Robert L Protzman,
Jim Tarbox.

RADIO

KBSB (89.7)
Bemidji State U, Deputy Hall,
Bemidji MN 56601 (612)222-5011.
Dave Kaiser. CP: NORTHERN
STUDENT weekly 5000.

KSJR (NPR-90.1)
Collegeville MN 56321 (517)774-
3105. Mark Conway.

*KDTH
U of MN, 2400 Oakland Ave, Duluth
MN 55812 (218)726-7126. CP:
STATESMAN weekly 7000.

KUMD
U of MN, 130 Humanities Bldg,
Duluth MN 55812. 8 hrs folk.

WSCD (NPR-92.9)
1200 Kenwood Ave, Duluth MN 55811
(218)728-3657. M Barone. 10 hrs
folk and bluegrass.

*KAXE (91.7)
1841 Hwy 169 E, Grand Rapids MN
55744-3398. Dan Salin, Susan Huju.
Folk, ethnic.

KICC (Longhorn-91.5)
Rainy River Community Coll,
International Falls MN 56649
(218)283-4498. Mary Ann Tarro.

*PETRA HALL
3111 12th Ave S, Minneapolis MN
55407. Does show on KFAI, high-
lighting women's music. Others too.
Interviews.

*KBEM
Minneapolis MN. Folk progs: FLEA
MARKET, A MIXED BAG, others.

*KFAI (90.3)
3104 16th Ave S, Minneapolis MN
55407 (612)721-5011. Everett Forte.
Folk progs. PG.

KMOJ
810 5th Ave N, Minneapolis MN
55405.

KCCM (NPR-90.1)
Concordia Coll, Box 72, Moorhead MN
56560 (218)299-3666. CP: CONCORDIAN
weekly 1500.

KUMM
U of MN, Morris MN 56267 (612)589-
2220. Bryan J Minder, MD. CP:
MORRIS WEEKLY 1400.

*KRLX (88.1)
Carleton Coll, Northfield MN 55057
(507)663-4000 x 4102. MD Kim
Sollenberger. Folk progs. CP:
CARLETONIAN weekly 2000.

*WCAL (NPR-89.3)
St Olaf Coll, Northfield MN 55057
(507)663-3071. Gordy Abel. Folk.
CP: MANITOU MESSENGER weekly 4K.
KRSW (NPT-91.7)
Worthington Comm Coll, Piperstone
MN 56187 (507)372-2904. James Boyd.

KLSE (NPR-91.1)
735 Marquette Bank Bldg, Rochester
MN 55901 (507)282-0810. John Gadda.

KVSC
St Cloud State U, 140 Stewart Hall,
St Cloud MN 56301 (612)255-2205.
CP: CHRONICLE 2x weekly 7000.

KCTA TV
1640 Como Ave, St Paul MN 55108
*612)646-4611. Kathi Riley. Have
filmed at Winnipeg Festival.

*KSJN (NPR-91.1)
45 E 8th St, St Paul MN 55101 (612)
221-11500. Dale Connolly. Folk
progs, interviews. PRAIRIE HOME
COMPANION.

WMCN
Macalester Coll, 1600 Grand Ave, St
Paul MN 55015 (612)647-6297. CP:
MAC WEEKLY 2500.

KQAL
Winona State U, Winona MN 55987
(507)457-5226. Paul Marszalek. CP:
WINONAN weekly 4000.

KSMR (90.9)
St Mary's Coll, Box 29, Winona MN
55987 (507)452-4430 x 1428.

STORES

*BENEDICT'S MUSIC
3400 Lyndale Ave S, Minneapolis MN
(612)822-7335. Handmade & vintage
guitars, banjos, repairs, mods,
accessories. Instruction.

*HOMESTEAD PICKIN' PARLOR
6625 Penn Ave S, Minneapolis MN
(612)861-3308. Marv Menzel.
Instruments, accessories,
instruction, repairs.

*SCHMITT MUSIC AUDITORIUM
88 S 10th St, Minneapolis MN
(612)339-4811. Instruments,
accessories, clinics.

*HERE, INC
RR4, Red Wing MN 55066.

MISSISSIPPI

*JACKSON METROPOLITAN LIBRARY
301 N State St, Jackson MS 39201
(601)944-110. Funding info.

VENUES

*MISSISSIPPI FOLKLORE SOC
E Central JC, English Div, Box 697,
Decatur MS 39327. Ovid S Vickers.
Newsletter.

*U OF SOUTHERN MISSISSIPPI
University Activities Council,
Hattiesburg MS 39406 (601)266-4985.
Some concerts. CP: STUDENT
PRINTZ 2x weekly 7000.

*MS VALLEY STATE U
Box 1488, Itta Beria MS 38941 (601)
254-9041 x 6462. George White. Some
concerts.

MISSISSIPPI STATE U
Union Program Board, PO Box 5368,
Mississippi State MS 39762 (601)
325-2513. Some concerts. CP:
REFLECTOR 2x weekly 7000.

*CENTER FOR THE STUDY OF
    SOUTHERN CULTURE
U of MS, University MS 38677 (601)
232-5993. LIVING BLUES.

UNIV OF MISSISSIPPI
Student Activities, University MS
38677 (601)232-7222. Some concerts.
CP: DAILY MISSISSIPPIAN 10K.

*YAZOO ARTS COUNCIL
PO Box 965, Yazoo MS 38184 (601)
746-6062. Lois Russell, Exec Dir.
Some concerts.

FESTIVALS

DELTA BLUES FESTIVAL
Freedom Village, Greenville MS
(601)335-3523. Sep-Nov.

*FALL ARTS FESTIVAL
Chamber of Commerce, PO Box 187,
Ocean Springs MS 39564 (601)875-
4424. Music, crafts, food. Early
Nov.

INDIAN FESTIVAL
Grand Indian Village, Natchez MS
(601)446-6502. Dances, crafts. Sep.

*JIMMIE RODGERS MEMORIAL FEST
PO Box 790, Meridian MS 39301
(601)693-1306. Late May.

MISSISSIPPI STATE FAIR
PO Box 892, Jackson MS 39212 (601)
353-1187. Oct.

MUSEUMS

*DELTA BLUES MUSEUM
1109 State St, PO Box 280,
Clarksdale MS 38614 (601)624-4461.
Books, records, videos of blues
artists. Produces films, radio, &
TV programs.

*MS STATE HISTORICAL MUSEUM
N State & Capitol Sts, PO Box 571,
Jackson MS 39205 (601)354-6222.
Social history, folk crafts.

*JIMMIE RODGERS MUSEUM
PO Box 1928, Meridian MS 39301
(601)485-1808.

*MS CRAFTS CENTER
Natchez Trace Pkwy, PO Box 69,
Ridgeland MS 39157 (601)856-7546.
Exhibits and craft demnos.

*CASEY JONES MUSEUM
Main St, Vaughan MS 39179 (601)673-
9864.

PRINT

*SUN/DAILY HERALD
PO Box 4567, Biloxi MS 39531 (601)
896-2331. Jerry Kinser.

MS FOLKLORE REGISTER
Box 418, Southern Sta, Hattiesburg
MS 39401.

BLUE & WHITE FLASH
Jackson State U, Jackson MS. 2x
monthly 7000.

*CLARION-LEDGER
311 E Pearl St, Jackson MS 39205
(601)961-7280.

*MERIDIAN STAR
810-12 22nd Ave, Meridian MS 39301
(601)693-1551. Dean Lamb.

RADIO

PUBLIC RADIO IN MISSISSIPPI
PO Drawer 1101, Jackson MS 39204.

WHJT (93.5)
MS Coll, Box 4207, Clinton MS 39058
(601)924-4505. Donn Kenyon, Sr,
Robert Nations.

WMUW
Box W-940, Columbus MS 39701.

*WMSB
MS State U, PO Drawer PF,
Mississippi State MS 39762 (601)
325-3910. Janet Harris.

MISSOURI

*METROPOLITAN ASSN FOR PHIL
5600 Oakland, G324, St Louis MO
63110 (314)647-2290. Funding info.

MISSOURI DIV OF TOURISM
PO Box 1055, Jefferson City MO
65102 (314)751-4133. Calendar.

VENUES

*MISSOURI FOLKLORE SOCIETY
PO Box 1757, Columbia MO 65205.
Newsletter, journal.

*MO STATE OLD TIME FIDDLERS
Box 7423, Columbia MO 65205.

MO FIDDLERS & COUNTRY MUSIC
8245 Whitecliff Park La, Crestwood
MO 63126. Newsletter.

*TRI-STATE BLUEGRASS ASSN
RR1, Kahoka MO 63445.

*BLAYNEY'S
415 Westport Rd, lower level,
Kansas City MO (816)561-3747. Music
Mon-Sat. Jazz, blues, R&B.

*FOOLKILLER
2 W 39th, Kansas City MO 64111
(816)756-3754. Carol Smith. Varied
music, various nights.

*GRAND EMPORIUM
3832 Main, Kansas City MO (816)531-
1504. Blues, zydeco. Varied music
Mon-Sat.

*HURRICANE
4048 Broadway, Kansas City MO 64111
(816)753-0884. Music most nights,
some folk.

*JIMMY'S JIGGER
39th & State Line, Kansas City MO
(816)753-2444. Music most nights,
some folk.

*THE LONE STAR
4117 Mill St, Kansas City MO 64111
9816)561-1881. Music Mon-Sat,
blues, zydeco, R&B, reggae.

*MISSOURI VALLEY FOLKLIFE SOC
PO Box 5916, Kansas City MO 64116
(816)523-4351. Concerts, workshops,
dances. Info center.

*NORTHEAST MO STATE U
Student Activities, Kirksville MO
63501 (816)785-4222. Some concerts.
CP: INDEX weekly 5600.

ST LOUIS FOLK MUSIC CLUB
415 Emerson Ave, Kirkwood MO 63112
(314)TRI-4970. Janet Boyer.

*SOC FOR THE PRESERVATION OF
  BLUEGRASS MUSIC OF AMERICA
Box 95, Lake Ozark MO 65049.

*BLACK SNAKE HILLS
  DULCIMER PLAYERS
Box 274, St Joseph MO 64506.

*CHILDGROVE COUNTRY DANCERS
416 S Meramec Ave, St Louis MO
63105.

*FOCAL POINT
7427 Chamberlain, St Louis MO 63130
(314)726-4707. Judy Stein. Varied
folk. Mostly Fridays. Other events
include parties, open mike nights.
Nwsltr inc other area events.

*MO FRIENDS OF THE FOLK ARTS
410 S Meramec Ave, St. Louis MO
63105.

*NOT-SO-DULCIMER SOCIETY
St Louis MO (314)429-7385. Pam.
Monthly meeting, nwsltr.

*PLAIN LABEL CONCERT HALL
3724 Blair, St Louis MO (314)231-
6982. Paul & Leigh Stamler. House
concerts.

ST LOUIS UNIVERSITY
221 N Grand Blvd, St Louis MO
63103 (314)658-2811. Some concerts.
CP: UNIVERSITY NEWS weekly 7000.

UNIV OF MISSOURI
262 University Ctr, St Louis MO
63121 (314)553-5536. Some concerts.
CP: CURRENT weekly 7500.

*OZARK FOLKLORE SOCIETY
1240 W Westview, Springfield MO
65804. Max F Hunter.

FESTIVALS

FAMILY BLUEGRASS WEEKEND
Held at Pomme de Terre State Park.
Parks Div, PO Box 176, Jefferson
City MO 65102 (314)751-2479.

FRONTIER FOLKLIFE FEST
11 N 4th St, St Louis MO 63102
(314)425-6004. Aug.

JUBILEE DAYS
Benton County Ents, Warsaw MO 65355
(816)438-6312. Mahlon K White. Old
fiddlers contest, music, crafts.
Early June.

MAIFEST
Held around the town. Box 88,
Hermann MO 65041. Music, dancing,
food, costumes. Mid-May.

MISSOURI STATE FAIR
Held in Sedalia. 1616 Missouri
Blvd, Jefferson City MO 65101
(314)751-4645. Aug.

*ST LOUIS SUMMER FOLK FEST
7417 Chamberlain, St Louis MO 63130
(314)726-4707. Judy Stein. Aug.

*SHADY HILL'S BLUEGRASS FESTIVAL
Rte 2, Box 163A, Neosho MO 64850
(417)451-2260. Gene & Betty Hale.
Mid-July.

STORYTELLING FEST
Held at Gateway Arch. Visitors
Bureau, 10 S Broadway, St Louis MO
63102 (314)421-1023. Varied
stories. Early May.

MUSEUMS

*MISSOURI TOWN 1855
Lake Jacomo, Blue Springs MO 64015
(816)881-4431. Folklore.

*RALPH FOSTER MUSEUM
School of the Ozarks, Point Lookout
MO 65726 (417)334-6411. Music room
dedicated to country, western, &
other Ozark music.

*MISSOURI HISTORICAL SOC
Lindell & De Baliviere, St Louis MO
63112 (314)361-1424.

PRINT

*JOPLIN GLOBE
117 E 4th St, Joplin MO 64801 (417)
623-3480.

*KANSAS CITY STAR and TIMES
1729 Grand Ave, Kansas CIty MO
64108 (816)234-4380. Blake Samson.

*KC PITCH
4128 Broadway, Kansas City MO 64111
(816)561-2744. Donna Trussell. Free
entertainment monthly. Listings,
some reviews. Folk & Country
column.

UNIVERSITY NEWS
U of MO, 5100 Rockhill Rd, Kansas
City MO 64110. Weekly 10000.

*ST JOSEPH NEWS-PRESS
9th & Edmond Sts, St Joseph MO
64502 (816)279-5671. Don Thornton.

*ST LOUIS GLOBE-DEMOCRAT
710 N Tucker Blvd, St Louis MO
63101 (314)342-1354.

*ST LOUIS POST-DISPATCH
900 N 12th St, St Louis MO 63101
(314)622-7077.

STUDENT LIFE
Washington U, St Louis MO 63100. 2x
weekly 9000.

BEAR TIMES and SW STANDARD
SW MO State U, Springfield MO
65800. Both weekly, 10000.

*SPRINGFIELD LEADER & PRESS,
    DAILY NEWS, NEWS READER
651 Boonville, Springfield MO 65801
(417)836-1100. Bill Tatum.

MULESKINNER
Central MO State U, Warrensburg MO.
Weekly 6500.

RADIO

KRCU
SE Mo State U, 900 Normal, Cape
Girardeau MO 63701. CP: CAPAHA
ARROW weekly 7000.

KBIA (NPR-91.3)
PO Box 758, Columbia MO 65205 (314)
882-3431. Jim Armstrong.

*KOPN (89.5)
915 E Broadway, Columbia MO 65201
(314)874-5676. Josh Adelstein.

KLUM
1004 E Dunklin St, Jefferson City
MO 65101.

KCUR (NPR-89.3)
5100 Rockhill Rd, Kansas City MO
64110 (816)276-1551. Dave Brown,
BALLADS, BARDS & BAGPIPES.

*MIDEAST RADIO PROJECT
PO Box 6126, Kansas City MO 64110.

KWPB
William Jewwell Coll, Liberty MO
64068 (816)781-3806. CP: STUDENT
weekly 1200.

KNOS
MO Valley Coll, Marshall MO 65340
(816)886-6924.

KXCV (NPR-90.5)
NW MO State U, Maryville MO 64468
(816)582-2076. Sharon Shipley. CP:
NW MISSOURIAN weekly 5000.

KSOZ (NPR-91.7)
School of the Ozarks, Point Lookout
MO 65726 (417)334-6411. David
Paisley.

*KMNR
U of Mo, 203A Mining Bldg, Rolla
MO 65401 (314)341-4266. Rich
Arkenberg. CP: MISSOURI MINER
weekly 6000.

*KUMR (NPR-88.5)
U of Mo, G-6 Library, Rolla MO
65401 (314)341-4386. Jess Stoll.
CP: MISSOURI MINER weekly 6000.

KCLC
Lindenwoowd COll, Kings Hwy, St
Charles MO 63301. Ernie Nowlin.

*KWMU (NPR-90.7)
8001 Natural Bridge Rd, St Louis MO
63121 (314)553-5968. Mary Edwards.
Folk progs.

*KTAD (88.1)
2601 N 11th St, St Louis MO 63106.

KSMU (NPR-91.1)
901 S National, Springfield MO
65804 (417)836-5831. Randy Stewart.

STORES

*PENNY LANE
Chain of record stores. 844
Massachusetts, Lawrence MO
(913)749-4211; 4128 Broadway,
Westport MO (816)561-1580; 103rd &
State Line, S Kansas City MO (816)
941-3970.

MONTANA

*MON-DAK HERITAGE CENTER
PO Box 50, Sidney MT 59270.
Exhibitions etc.

*MONTANA STATE LIBRARY
930 E Lyndale Rd, Helena MT 59601
(406)449-3004. Funding info.

VENUES

*MONTANA STATE FIDDLERS ASSN
3901 Becroft La, Billings MT 59101.
Bonnie Stark.

*MONTANA STATE UNIV
ASMSU Concerts, Rm 282-B, Strand
Union Bldg, Bozeman MT 59717
(406)994-3389. Clay Baker. Some
concerts.

*HELENA PERFORMING ARTS SERIES
Civic Ctr 1700, 9 Placer St, Helena
MT 59601 (406)443-0287. Arnie
Malina, Exec Dir. Concerts.

*FLATHEAD VALLEY COMM COLL
1 1st St SE, Kalispell MT 59901.
Dr D Gatzke, Counselling Office.

*MISSOULA FOLKLORE SOCIETY
538 N 3rd W, Missoula MT 59802
(406)549-3665. Rick Ryan. Concerts.

*UNIV OF MONTANA
ASUM Programming, Performing Arts
Series, Univ Ctr 104, Missoula MT
59812 (406)243-6661. David Buckley.
Some concernts. CP: MONTANA KAIMIN
daily 6300.

FESTIVALS

FESTIVAL OF NATIONS
Red Lodge MT. Bob Moran. Celebrates
eight nationalities: music, crafts,
food. Early August.

MONTANA STATE FAIR
PO Box 1524, Great Falls MT 59403
(406)452-6401. August.

MONTANA STATE FIDDLERS
  CHAMPIONSHIIPS
39801 Becraft La, Billings MT 59101

*NORTH AMERICAN INDIAN DAYS
Museum of the Plains Indian, Hwy
89, PO Box 400, Browning MT 59417
(406)338-2230. July.

MUSEUM

*RICHEY HISTORICAL MUSEUM
Box 218, Richey MT 59259 (406)733-
5656. Musical instrument
collection, rural life.

PRINT

*BILLINGS GAZETTE
PO Box 2507, Billings MT 59103
(406)657-1243.

*MONTANA STANDARD
25 W Granite St, Butte MT 59701
(406)782-8301.

*GREAT FALLS TRIBUNE
PO Box 5468, Great Falls MT 59403
(406)761-6666. Paula Wilmot.

*MISSOULIAN
PO Box 8029, Missoula MT 59807
(406)721-5200. Judy Gibbs, Ed.

RADIO

*KEMC (NPR-91.7)
1500 N 30th St, Billings MT 59101
(406)657-2941. Steve Hollander.
Folk shows Sat, Sun. PG.

KGLT (91.1)
Montana State, Strand Union Bldg,
Bozeman MT 59717 (406)994-3001. Jim
Kehoe. CP: EXPONENT 2x weekly 8000.

*BLACKFEET MEDIA DEPT
PO Box 850, Browning MT 59417.

KMSM
Montana Tech, Student Union, Butte
MT 59701. CP: TECHNOCRAT wkly 2000.

*KGRZ
105 California St, Missoula MT
59801.

*KUFM
U of Montana, Missoula MT 59812
(406)542-2468. John Tisdell. Folk
show.

NEBRASKA

*ARTS ALLIANCE-NEBRASKA
PO Box 3393, Omaha NE 68103.
R. Jerry Hargitt. Advocacy for arts
funding.

*NEBRASKA ARTS COUNCIL
1313 Farnam-on-the Mall, Omaha NE
68102 (402)554-2122. Artists in
Schools: Barbara Berger.

*NEBRASKANS FOR THE ARTS
PO Box 3702, Omaha NE 68103. Help
in promoting the arts.

*W DALE CLARK LIBRARY
215 S 15th St, Omaha NE 68102 (402)
444-4822. Funding info.

VENUES

*KEARNEY STATE COLLEGE
Artists & Lecture Series, Fine Arts
Bldg, Kearney NE 68849 (308)234-
8611. Nancy Whitman, Chmn. Some
concerts. CP: ANTELOPE weekly 5000.

*BENNET MARTIN PUBLIC LIBRARY
14th & N St, Lincoln NE. Concerts,
lectures, exhibitions.

*LINCOLN ASSN FOR TRAD ARTS
1943 Euclid Ave, Lincoln NE 68502
(402)474-2275. Liz Warner. Nwsltr.

UNIVERSITY OF NEBRASKA
Student Union, Lincoln NE 68588
(402)472-2452. Some concerts. CP:
DAILY NEBRASKAN 17500.

*CORNHUSKER COUNTRY MUSIC
PO Box 42, Louisville NE 68037.
Newsletter.

*CREIGHTON UNIVERSITY
2500 California St, Omaha NE 68178
(402)280-509. Some concerts. CP:
CREIGHTONIAN wkly 5000.

*NEVILLE CENTER FOR THE
    PERFORMING ARTS
Rte 1, Box 428, North Platte NE
69101 (308)532-9119. Concerts.

*NORFOLK ARTS CENTER
804 Norfolk Ave, Norfolk NE 68701
(402)371-7199. Juliana Hammond,
Exec Dir.

UNIVERSITY OF NEBRASKA
Student Ctr, 60th & Dodge Sts,
Omaha NE 68182. Some concerts. CP:
GATEWAY 2x weekly 9000.

*WEST NEBRASKA ARTS CTR
PO Box 62, Scottsbluff, NE 69361
(308)632-2226. Phyllis A.
Harrison, folklorist-in-residence.

FESTIVAL

NEBRASKA STATE FAIR
PO Box 81223, Lincoln NE 68501
(402)474-5371. August.

MUSEUMS

*PLAINSMAN MUSEUM
210 16th St, Aurora NE 68818 (402)
694-6531. Ethnic groups in Nebraska.

*STATE HISTORICAL MUSEUM
131 N Centennial Mall,Lincoln NE
68508 (402)471-3270.

*THOMAS P KENNARD HOUSE
    NE STATEHOOD MEMORIAL
1627 H St, Lincoln NE 68508 (402)
471-3270. Folk life programs.

*PIONEER VILLAGE
Minden NE 68959 (308)832-1181.

*GREAT PLAINS BLACK MUSEUM
2213 Lake St, Omaha NE 68110
(402)344-0350. Black history.
Collection of old jazz 45s.

PRINT

*LINCOLN STAR
926 P St, Lincoln NE 68508 (402)
473-7312.

*FLATWATER ARTS COMPANION
NE Arts Council, 1313 Farnam-on-the
Mall, Omaha NE 68102 (402)554-2122.
John McNamara, Ed.

*OMAHA WORLD-HERALD
World-Herald Sq, Omaha NE 68102
(402)444-1000. Rick Ansorge.

RADIO

KDCV
Dana Coll, Blair NE 68008. CP:
HERMES 2x monthly 600.

KUCV (90.9)
3800 S 48th St, Lincoln NE 68506
(402)48-0996. Bev Johnson. PG.

*KREG
423 N 47th, Omaha NE 68132
(402)551-2124. Paul Krigler.

*KZUM (89.5)
1038 S 23rd St, Lincoln NE 68510
(402)474-5086. Joe Janacek.

KVNO
6625 Dodge St, Omaha NE 68132.

NEVADA

*CLARK COUNTY LIBRARY
1401 E Flamingo Rd, Las Vegas NV
89109 (702)733-7810. Funding
information.

VENUES

JIMMY & NANCY BORSDORF
PO Box 2456, Carson City NV 89707
(702)883-3499. Concerts.

*CHARLESTON HEIGHTS ARTS CTR
800 S Brush, Las Vegas NV 69107
(702)386-6384.

NEVADA OLDTIME FIDDLERS ASSN
7969 Rodeo Rd, Las Vegas NV 89119.
Don Germain.

*UNIVERSITY OF NEVADA
4505 Maryland Pkwy, Las Vegas NV
89154 (702)739-3535. Some concerts.
CP: YELL weekly 5000.

S NEVADA BLUEGRASS SOCIETY
PO Box 3704, N Las Vegas NV 89030.
BLUEGRASS NEWS. Radio Show
BLUEGRASS EXPRESS.

*UNIVERSITY OF NEVADA
Lawlor Events Ctr, Reno NV 89557-
0096 (702)784-4659. Some concerts.

FESTIVALS

*NATIONAL BASQUE FESTIVAL
Chamber of Commerce, PO Box 470,
Elko NV 89801 (702)738-7135. Games,
Arinak Dancers, Irrintzi (Basque
Yell) contest, food, music, pelota,
other traditional activities. July.

NEVADA STATE FAIR
PO Box 2723, Reno NV 89504
(702)785-4280. Sep.

MUSEUM

*NORTHEASTERN NEVADA MUSEUM
1515 Idaho St, PO Box 2550, Elko NV
89801 (702)738-3418. Local history,
inc Pony Express.

PRINT

*LAS VEGAS SUN
121 S Highland Ave, Las Vegas NV
89106 (702)385-3111.

*REVIEW-JOURNAL
PO Box 70, Las Vegas NV 89125 (702)
383-0271.

*RENO EVENING GAZETTE
PO Box 22000, Reno NV 89520 (702)
788-6397.

RADIO

KNPR (NPR-89.5)
5151 Boulder Hwy, Las Vegas NV
89122 (702)456-6695. Lamar
Marchese. Bluegrass. PG.

*KUNV (91.5)
U of NV, 4505 Maryland Pkwy, Las
Vegas NV 89254 (702)739-3877. Ken
Jordan.

KUNR (NPR-88.7)
U of NV, Education Bldg #106, Reno
NV 89557 (702)784-6591. Tim Jones.
CP: SAGEBRUSH 2x wkly 5000.

MIKE REED
804 Gear, Reno NV 89503. Radio show
Sat.

NEW HAMPSHIRE

*NH CHARITABLE FUND
1 South St, PO Box 1335, Concord NH
03301 (603)225-6641. Funding info.

*NH STATE VACATION TRAVEL
PO Box 856, Concord NH 03301
(603)271-2665. Lists of fests and
events.

VENUES

*CANTERBURY FOLK CLUB
Canterbury NH 03224. Dudley
Laufman.

WAPACK FOLK ARTS COUNCIL
PO Box 160, Greenville NH 03048
(603)878-2255. Randy Crosby.

*MUSKEG MUSIC
Box 212, Lebanon NH 03766. Karen
Porter. Concerts, dances, pub
sings.

*MONADNOCK FOLKLORE SOCIETY
Nelson Village, Minsonville NH
03457.

MERRIMACK VALL FOLK MUSIC
Nashua NH 03060 (603)883-2348.
David Larlee, James Murray, Robert
Daniels. Concerts.

*STONE CHURCH
Zion's Hill, PO Box 202, Newmarket
NH 03857 (603)659-6321. Richard
Hurd. Music Wed-Sun, mostly R&B.

*APPLETREE COFFEEHOUSE
Unitarian Church, Old Wilton Ctr,
NH 03086 (603)878-3247. Randy
Crosby. 4th Sat.

*THE FOLKWAY
85 Grove St, Peterborough NH 03458
(603)924-7484. Widdie Hall. Varied
music, several nights. Good food
too.

*THE PRESS ROOM
77 Daniel St, Portsmouth NH 03801
(603)431-5186. Jay Smith. Bar with
varied music 7 nights. Seats 100.

FESTIVALS

*ARTS JUBILEE
Box 647, Conway NH 03860. Folk,
dance, puppets, other. Jul-Oct.

CHESHIRE CNTY BLUEGRASS FEST
Held at Rte 12 Fairgrounds. Keene
NH (603)357-4740. Late May.

INTL ZUCCHINI FESTIVAL
Harrisville NH (603)827-3033.
Vegetable songs. Late Aug.

*NH HIGHLAND GAMES
Held in Lincoln NH. PO Box 130,
Cambridge MA 02238 (617)864-8945.
Stephen Avery, Evelyn Murray.
Games, fiddle & harp championships,
ceilidh, SCD Ball, crafts, food,
Scottish imports. 2nd weekend after
Labor Day.

MUSEUMS

*EFFINGHAM HISTORICAL SOCIETY
Rte 153, center Effingham NH 03882
(603)569-2469. Local history.

*LANCASTER HISTORICAL SOCIETY
226 Main St, Lancaster NH 03584.
Local history.

*NEW HAMPSHIRE FARM MUSEUM
Rte 16, Plummer's Ridge, PO Box
644, Milton NH 03851. Oral
histories.

*STRAWBERRY BANKE
Hancock & Marcy Sts, PO Box 300,
Portsmouth NH 03801 (603)436-8010.
Social and cultural history.

PRINT

*NEW HAMPSHIRE PROFILES
109 N Main St, PO Box 1175, Concord
NH 03301.

NEW HAMPSHIRE TIMES
PO Box 35, Concord NH 03301
(603)224-9100. weekly.

*UNION LEADER
PO Box 780, Manchester NH 03104
(603)668-4321. James Adams.

*TELEGRAPH
PO Box 1008, Nashua NH 03061 (603)
882-2741.

RE:PORTS
Box 1472, Portsmouth NH 03801
(603)4823. William Paarlberg, Ed;
Cate Goodson, listings.

RADIO

*WEVO (NPR-89.1)
26 Pleasant St, Concord NH 03301
(603)228-8910. Philip Bragdon PD;
Judy Ellior. Listings, interviews.

WBNC/WMWV
Box 2008, E Main St, Concord NH
03818.

WUNH (91.3)
U of NH, Mem Union Bldg, Durham NH
03824 (603)862-2541. Sarah
Reynolds, Ryan Thomson. CP: NEW
HAMPSHIRE 2x weekly 10000.

WFRD (NBC-99.1)
Dartmouth Coll, Box 957, Hanover NH
03755 (603)646-3313. Chuck Steidel. ·
CP: DARTMOUTH daily 4K; REVIEW wkly
8K; HARBINGER monthly 5K.

*MARY DESROSIERS
PO Box 196, Harrisville NH 03450.
Programs for WMDK among others.

WNEWC (91.7)
New England Coll, Danforth Library,
Henniker NH 03242 (603)428-2278.
Diane THibault. CP: NEW ENGLANDER
weekly 3000.

WKKNH
Keene State U, Elliot Hall, Keene
NH 03431. Kate McNally. CP: EQUINOX
weekly 3000.

WSLE
Peterborough NH 03458.

STORES

*VINTAGE FRET SHOP
20 Riverside Dr, Ashland NH 03217-
0562 (603)968-3346. Bobbie Herron.
Fine folk instruments bought, sold,
traded.

DADDY'S MUSIC STORE
77 Congress St, Portsmouth NH 03801
(603)436-1142.

NEW JERSEY

*THE SUPPORT CENTER
744 Broad St, #1106, Newark NJ
07102 (201)643-5774. Funding info.

VENUES

PERIMETER II COFFEEHOUSE
240 W Atlantic Ave, Audubon NJ
08106 (609)546-5016. Anne Deeney.
At W Collingwood Railroad Stn. Fri.
Seats 80.

*MINSTREL SHOW COFFEHOUSE
At SCEEC, 190 Lord Sterling Rd,
Basking Ridge NJ (201)766-2489.
Bookings: Mike Agranoff (201)335-
9489. Fri. Seats 250.

*FOLK MUSIC SOC OF NORTHERN NJ
36 Osborne St, Bloomfield NJ 07003
(201)731-0103. Roger Deitz. Runs
Closing Circle (qv) & other events.

*MIDDLE ATLANTIC FOLKLIFE ASSN
Box 11, E Millstone NJ 08873. Sue
Samuelson.

*CLINTON HISTORICAL MUSEUM
Rte 78, Exit 15, Clinton NJ (201)
735-4101. Concerts Aug.

*RIDGEWOOD COUNTRY DANCERS
532 Prospect St, Glen Rock NJ
07452. Carl Petri.

*MAXWELL'S
1039 Washington St, Hoboken NJ
07030 (201)656-9632. Steve Fallon.
Some folk.

*BLUEGRASS & OLDTIME MUSIC
   ASSN OF NEW JERSEY
185K Farrington Dr, Matawan NJ
07747. Mr Farmer.

*FOLK PROJECT
PO Box 41, Mendham NJ 07945 (201)
335-9489. Mike Agranoff. Runs
Minstrel Show (qv), spring and fall
camps.

*WHOLE THEATRE
544 Bloomfield Ave, Montclair NJ
(201)744-2996. Summer concert
series.

*NJ DULCIMER SOCIETY
141 Hawthorne Dr, Mt Holly NJ
08060. Silvia Mellon.

*MINE STREET COFFEEHOUSE
First Reformed Church, Neilson &
Bayard Sts, New Brunswick NJ 08901
(201)581-2326. Sat.

*NEW JERSEY FOLKLORE SOCIETY
Box 747, New Brunswick NJ 08903.
*COMMON GROUND COFFEEHOUSE
Grange Hall, W Nelson St, Newton NJ
07860 (201)948-3586. 3rd Sat.

*HURDY GURDY FOLK MUSIC CLUB
Held at Central Unitarian Church,
156 Forest Ave, Paramus NJ 07652.
81-A Primrose Lane, Paramus NJ
07652 (201)845-8260. Gerry Rogers.
1st Sat. Seats 400.

*STOCKTON FOLKLORE SOCIETY
Campus Activities, Stockton State
Coll, Pomona NJ 08240.

*PRINCETON COUNTRY DANCERS
Box 427, Princeton NJ 08540. Marge
Scott.

*PRINCETON FOLK MUSIC SOCIETY
PO Box 427, Princeton NJ 08540
(609)924-9143. Isabel Abelson.
Concerts usually 3rd Sat, various
house concerts.

*HUNTERDON COUNTY FOLK EXCH
PO Box 321, Quakertown NJ 08868
(201)782-8656. Jim King, Pres.
House concert 1st Sat.

*CLOSING CIRCLE COFFEEHOUSE
Held at 621 Eagle Rock Ave,
Roseland NJ 07068. Run by FMS of N
NJ. Bookings: Roger Dietz (201)731-
0103. 3rd Sat. Seats 120.

*WATERLOO VILLAGE
Stanhope NJ (201)347-0900. Some
folk concerts.

*PRALLSVILLE MILLS
Stockton NJ (201)692-2000. Some
folk concerts.

*SINGS & STRINGS OF
 BERGEN COUNTY
29 Prospect Ave, Westwood NJ 07675.
Howard LaMell.

*BARRON ARTS CENTER
582 Rahway Ave, Woodbridge NJ (201)
634-0413. Some folk concerts.

FESTIVALS

*JUNE DAYS
Held at Eagle Rock Reservation. 127
Old Short Hills Rd, West Oragne NJ
07052 (201)731-0103. Roger Dietz.
Mid-June.

NEW JERSEY FOLK FESTIVAL
Held on Eagleton Inst Lawn.
Douglass Coll, Rutgers U, New
Brunswick NJ 08903. Concerts,
contests. Apr.

*NEW JERSEY STATE FAIR
1634 Nottingham Way, Trenton NJ
08619 (609)587-6300. Sept.

PINE BARRENS FOLK FESTIVAL
Held at Country Lakes Firehall.
120-126 Whitesbog Rd, Brown Mills
NJ 08015 (609)893-4438 (eves). Dave
& Sarah Orleans. For Conservation
Ctr. Spring.

*UNION COUNTY SUMMER ARTS FEST
Echo Lake Park, Westfield NJ (201)
352-8410. Aug. Many concerts.

*WATERLOO FOLK FESTIVAL
Waterloo Village, Stanhope NJ 07874
(201)347-0900. Bookings: John
Downey, (201)266-7900. Late Aug.

MUSEUMS

*HISTORIC GARDNER'S BASIN
N New Hampshire Ave & the Bay,
Atlantic City NJ 08401 (609)348-
2880. Maritime village.

*MUSEUM OF EARLY TRADES & CRAFTS
Main St at Green Village Rd,
Madison NJ 07940 (201)377-2982.

*HISTORIC SPEEDWELL
333 Speedwell Ave, Morristown NJ
07960 (201)540-0211. Historic
village. Occasional concerts.

*YESTERYEAR MUSEUM
20 Harriet Dr, Whippany NJ 07981
(201)386-1920. 100,000 varied
recordings.

PRINT

*NEW JERSEY
7 Dumont Pl, Morristown NJ 07960-
0120 (201)539-8230. Larry
Marschack, Ed. Glossy monthly.
Listings.

*ASBURY PARK PRESS
Press Plaza, Asbury Park NJ 07712
(201)774-7000. Greta C van
Benthuysen, Arts Ed.

*PRESS and SUNDAY PRESS
303 N Harrisburg Ave, Atlantic City
NJ 08401 (609)345-6837.

*THE RECORD
150 River St, Hackensack NJ 07602
(201)646-4000. Virginia Lambert.

*COURIER-NEWS
1201 Rte 22, Bridgewater NJ 08807
(201)722-8800.

*BURLINGTON COUNTY TIMES
Rte 130, Willingboro NJ 08046 (609)
871-8000. Lou Gaul.

*COURIER-POST
PO Box 5300, Camden NJ 08034 (609)
663-6000.

*DAILY JOURNAL
295 N Broad St, Elizabeth NJ 07207
(201)354-6000. Victor Zak, Ed.

*JERSEY JOURNAL
30 Journal Sq, Jersey City NJ 07306
(201)653-1000. Conrad Wolfson.
Listings, reviews.

*EAST COAST ROCKER
PO Box 137, 7 Oak Pl, Montclair NJ
07042. Lydia de Fretos. News,
reviews, interviews, listings.

*DAILY RECORD
55 Park Pl, Morristown NJ 07960
(201)538-2000. Jim Bohen, Music Ed.
Listings, reviews, interviews,
previews.

*CENTRAL NJ HOME NEWS
PO Box 551, New Brunswick NJ 08903
(201)246-5558. Listings.

*STAR-LEDGER
Star-Ledger Plaza, Newark NJ 07101
(201)877-4158. Michael Redmond,
Music Ed. Listings.

*HERALD-NEWS
PO Box 1019, Passaic NJ 07055 (201)
365-3100. Laurie Nikolski.

*TRENTON TIMES
500 Perry St, Trenton NJ 08605
(609)396-3232.

*TRENTONIAN
Southard at Perry St, Trenton NJ
08602 (609)989-7800. Louis Cooke.

*DISPATCH OF HUDSON COUNTY &
PATERSON NEWS
1 News Plaza, Paterson NJ 07509
(201)684-3000. Winnie Bonelli.

RADIO

*WDBK
Camden CC, Box 200, Blackwood NJ
08012 (609)227-7200 x 292. CP:
COUGAR monthly 4000.

*WFMU (91.1)
345 Prospect St, Upsala Coll, East
Orange NJ 07019 (201)266-7900. John
Downey, Terry Moore, Sonny Ochs.
Folk progs. PG: LCD, ed Ken
Freedman. CP: UPSALA GAZETTE 2x
monthly 1200.

*WDHA (105.5)
149 Rte 10, Dover NJ 07801 (201)
328-1055. Mark Chernoff.

WMCC
Middlesex CC, Woodbridge Ave,
Edison NJ 08818. CP: QUO VADIS
weekly 3000.

*WGLS (89.7)
Glassboro State Coll, Box 116,
Glassboro NJ 08028 (609)863-7336.
Dan Buskirk. CP: GLASSBORO WHIT
weekly 6000.

WWDJ
310 Commerce Ave, Hackensack NJ
07601.

*WNTI
Centenary Coll, 400 Jefferson St,
Hackettstown NJ 07840 (201)852-
1400.

*WCPR
Stevens Tech, Box 1461, Castle
Point Stn, Hoboken NJ 07030 (201)
795-4887.

*WJCS
Jersey City State Coll, 2039 Kennedy Blvd, Jersey City NJ 07305 (201)547-3556. CP: GOTHIC TIMES 2x monthly 5000.

*WVBC
Rider Coll, 2083 Lawrenceville Rd, Lawrence NJ 08646 (609)896-5211. Mitch Garrick. CP: RIDER NEWS weekly 3500.

*WBJB (90.5)
Brookdale CC, Newman Springs Rd, Lincroft NJ 07738 (201)842-1827. Ken Pauli. CP: STALL 2x monthly 5000.

WFDM
Fairleigh Dickinson U, 285 Madison Ave, Madison NJ 078940 (201)377-4700. CP: METRO weekly 3500.

*WMNJ
Drew U, 36 Madison Ave, Madison NJ 07940 (201)377-4466. J P Jones. CP: DREW ACORN weekly 4000.

*WRPR (90.3)
Ramapo Coll, PO Box 441, Mahwah NJ 07430 (201)825-7449. Dave O'Brien.

*WRSU (88.7)
Rutgers U, 350 Martin Luther King Rd, Newark NJ 07102 (201)648-5187. Cynthia Gill. CP: OBSERVER weekly 4000.

*SOLAR SANITY
63 Estella Ave, North Caldwell NJ 07006 (201)266-7900. John Downey. Radio show - energy issues. WFMU. Also folk cable show.

*WLBS
Livingston Coll, Piscataway NJ 08854.

*WLFR (91.7)
Stockton State Coll, Pomona NJ 08240 (609)652-1776. Michelle McClelland. CP: ARGO weekly 3500.

WKER
1976 Lincoln Ave, Pompton Lakes NJ 07442.

*WPRB (ABC-193.3)
Princeton U, Box 342, Princeton NJ 08540 (609)921-9284. John Weingart. Folk progs. CP: DAILY PRINCETONIAN 3200; NASSAU WEEKLY 6500.

*WCCM
CC of Morris, Rte 10 & Center Grove Rd, Randolph NJ 07801 (201)361-5000. Mike Scully. CP: YOUNGSTOWN EDITION weekly 3500.

*WFDR
Fairleigh Dickinson U, 21 Milton Ct, Rutherford NJ 07070 (201)460-5329. Peter Dragotta. CP: SPECTATOR weekly 4000.

WSOU (89.5)
Seton Hall U, 400 S Orange Ave, South Orange NJ 07079 (201)762-8950. Joe Brendan Vogel, IRISH HERITAGE. CP: SETONIAN weekly 6500.

*JOHN WEINGART
RD1, Box 240, Stockton NJ 08559 (609)452-FOLK. Programs for WPRB.

*WFDU (89.1)
795 Cedar La, Teaneck NJ 07666 (201)692-2013. Folk progs. John Stein (914)693-8247 wants to interview visiting artists. CP: GAUNTLET 2x monthly 4000.

WOCC
Ocean CC, Toms River NJ 08753 (201)255-4000. CP: VIKING NEWS weekly 4000.

*WTSR (91.3)
Trenton State Coll, Trenton NJ 08625 (609)771-2420. Janice Hill. CP: SIGNAL weekly 8000.

*WKNJ
Kean Coll, Morris Ave, Union NJ 07083 (201)289-8388. Joe Sabulka.

*WMSC (101.5)
Montclair State Coll, Student Ctr, Upper Montclair NJ 07043 (201)893-4256. Rich Rahnefeld. CP: MONTCLARION weekly 8000.

*WPSC (590AM, cable FM)
William Patterson Coll, 300 Pompton Rd, Wayne NJ 07470 (201)595-5901. CP: BEACON weekly 8000.

NEW MEXICO

*NEW MEXICO STATE LIBRARY
325 Don Gaspar St, Santa Fe NM
87503 (505)827-2033. Funding info.

VENUES

*ALBUQUERQUE CULTURAL AFFAIRS
Mayor's Office, PO Box 1293,
Albuquerque NM 87103 (505)766-7816.
Marjorie Neset.

*ALBUQUERQUE INTL FOLKDANCERS
Carlisle Gym, UNM Campus,
Albuquerque NM 87131. Gary Diggs
(505)293-5343. Sat. All levels.

*THE COOPERAGE
7220 Lomas NE, Albuquerque (505)
255-1657. Some blues.

*KIMO THEATRE
423 Central NW, Albuquerque NM
87102 (505)848-1374. Some folk
concerts.

*NM FOLKLORE SOCIETY
616 Vassar Dr NE, Albuquerque NM
87106. Frances Baughman.

*UNIV OF NEW MEXICO
Student Union, Albuquerque NM 87131
(505)277-5602. Some concerts. CP:
DAILY LOBO 14000.

*DONA ANA ARTS COUNCIL
2640 N Valley Dr, Las Cruces NM
88001 (505)523-6403.

*NEW MEXICO STATE UNIV
Box 3 SE, Pan Am Ctr, Las Cruces NM
88003 (505)646-4413. Barbara
Hubbard, Special Events Dir.

*LAS VEGAS ARTS COUNCIL
PO Box 2603, Las Vegas NM 07701
(505)454-1401.

*CLUB WEST
213 W Alameda, Santa Fe NM 87500
(505)982-0099. Music every night;
some folk, blues.

RED BARN
708 Silver Hts Blvd, Silver city NM
88061 (505)538-5666.

FESTIVALS

*MUSIC FROM ANGEL FIRE
Various sites. PO Box 502, Angel
Fire NM 87710 (505)377-6353. Mid-
Aug to early Sep. Classical, some
folk.

NEW MEXICO STATE FAIR
PO Box 8546, Albuquerque NM 87108
(505)265-1791. Sept.

MUSEUMS

*ARTESIA HISTORICAL MUSEUM
505 Richardson Ave, Artesia NM
88210 (505)748-2390. Folklore.

*MUSEUM OF INTL FOLK ART
706 Camino Lejo, Santa Fe NM 87501
(505)8277-8350.

*WHEELWRIGHT MUSEUM OF THE
    AMERICAN INDIAN
704 Camino Lejo, Santa Fe NM 87501
(505)982-4636. Musical records of
Navajo ceremonies.

*TUCUMCARI HISTORICAL RESEARCH
416 S Adamsa, Tucumcari NM 88401
(505)461-42021. Folklore, music.

PRINT

*ALBUQUERQUE JOURNAL
7777 Jefferson NE, Albuquerque NM
87109-4343 (505)823-3920. David
Steinberg.

*DAILY LOBO
Box 20, UNM, Albuquerque NM 87131
(505)277-5656. Carmella Padilla.
Mon-Fri of school year.

*ROUTE SIXTY-SIX
300 Carlisle SE, Albuquerque NM
87106 (505)265-6355. Marianne
Dickinson. 10/yr. Listngs, news,
reviews, interviews.

*NEW MEXICAN
PO Box 2048, Santa Fe NM 87501
(505)983-3303.

*NEW MEXICO
Bataan Mem Bldg, Santa Fe NM 87503
(505)827-6180. Glossy monthly.

RADIO

*KUNM
U of NM, Ornate Hall, Albuquerque
NM 87131 (505)277-4806. Folk progs.
CP: DAILY LOBO 14000.

KNMS (91.9)
NM State, Box CC, Corbet Ctr, Las
Cruces NM 88003 (505)646-4640/3505.
Raul Dorn MD. CP:ROUND-UP 3x weekly
10000.

*KRWG (91)
NM State U, Box FM91, Las Cruces NM
88003 (505)646-1327. Bruce
Bergethon. CP: ROUND-UP 3x weekly
10000.

KEDP
NM Highlands U, Las Vegas NM 87701.
CP: LA MECHA weekly 2200.

KENW (NPR-89.5)
E NM U, Portales NM 883130 (505)
562-2112. Susan Harding. CP:
EASTERN SUN-PRESS weekly 3200.

KLSK
PO Box 8580, Santa Fe NM 87504.
Rick Darby. Folk.

*KTEK (89.5)
NM Inst of Mining & Tech, Socorro
NM 87801 (505)835-5605. Mike
Palmer. CP: PAYDIRT 2x mo 1100.

*KSHI (90.9)
PO Box 339, Zuni NM 87327.

NEW YORK

*NY DIV OF TOURISM
1 Commerce Plaza, Albany NY 12245
(518)474-4116. Events listings. In
New England, E of MI and N of VA,
call (800)CALL NYS.

*NY STATE LIBRARY
Humanities Section, Empire State
Plaza, Albany NY 12230 (518)474-
7645. Funding info.

VENUES

*EIGHTH STEP COFFEEHOUSE
14 Willett St, (mail 362 State St)
Albany NY 12210 (518)434-1703. Bill
Rennie. Tues-Sat. Seats 75.

*PICK'N' & SING'N' GATHERIN'
12 Sycamore St, Albany NY 12208.

*SOC HISTORIQUE &
FOLKLORIQUE FRANCAISE
56-52 203rd St, Bayside NY 11364.
Pierre Courtines.

OFF-CAMPUS COLLEGE
SUNY, Binghamton NY 13905 (607)798-
2767. Mary Pantaleone, Ent Co-ord.
Fri noon.

*STUDIO SCHOOL & GALLERY
137 Washington St, Binghamton NY
13901. Gary Shaheen. Concerts.
Played here w/ Hap. + Art.
*ADIRONDACK LAKES CENTER
FOR THE ARTS
Box 101, Blue Mountain Lake NY
12812 (518)352-7715. Betsy Folwell,
Kim Moodie. Concerts, workshops,
films, various programs.

*LONG ISLAND FOLK & CONTRA DANC
1141 Smithtown Ave, Bohemia NY
11716 (516)589-4728. Alice
Wielunski. 2x monthly dances.

*CAPULETS
151 Montague St, Brooklyn NY 11201
(718)852-3128. Sat.

*GOOD COFFEEHOUSE
Ethical Culture Soc, 53 Prospect Pk
W, Brooklyn NY 11215 (718)768-2972.
Fri.

*PACKER COLLEGIATE INSTITUTE
160 Joralemon St, Brooklyn. Concert
series run by Elaine Sohn Prodns,
163 Joralemon St, Brooklyn NY
11201.

*BUFFALO FRIENDS OF FOLK
25 Bloomfield Ave, Buffalo NY 14220
(716)822-3881. Jim Dombrowski.

*TRALFAMADORE CAFE
100 Theater Pl, Buffalo NY 14202
(716)854-1415. Brian Dewart.

*HUBBARD HALL
25 E Main St, Cambridge NY 12816
(518)677-2495. Benjie White.
Monthly concerts.

*TRAD FMC OF CENTRAL NY
306 Mansfield Dr, Camillus NY
13031. Tom Shuman.

*PAYSON COFFEEHOUSE
St Lawrence Univ, Canton NY 13617.

*KIRKLAND ART CTR
15 Chestnut St, Clinton NY 13323
(315)798-2850. Ginger Parker.
Coffeehouse.

*TOMPKINS-CORTLAND
  COMMUNITY COLLEGE (TC3)
170 North St, Dryden NY 13053 (607)
844-8211. Dir of Activities. One
noontime event per month.

*HARD TIMES CAFE
Eagle Bay NY 13331. Scott Thompson.

*BUFFALO FRIENDS OF FOLK
9736 Transit Rd, E Amherst NY
14051.

*UNICORN COFFEEHOUSE
Union Board of Governors, SUNY
Fredonia, NY 14063. Arnold
Maggitti.

*AMERICAN MUSICAL ROOTS ASSN
101 N Bergen Pl, Freeport NY 11520
(718)343-1431. Larry Brittain. Few
concerts. Newsletter 4/yr.

*GENESEO FOLK MUSIC CLUB
SUNY, Box 82, College Union,
Geneseo NY 14454.

*OLD SONGS
PO Box 197, Guilderland NY 12084
(518)756-2815. Monthly concerts,
dances 1st & 3rd Sat. Fest June.

*TOWN CRIER CAFE
438 Beekman Rd, Hopewell Junction
NY 12533 (914)223-5555. Phil
Ciganer. Fri-Sun. Also an excellent
restaurant!

*KINGSBURY FOLK CONCERTS
RD1, Box 160, Hudson Falls NY 12839
(518)747-6221. George Wilson.

HUDSON VALLEY FOLK GUILD
1 Hillman Dr, Hyde Park NY 12538.
Kevin Becker.

*ABC CAFE
308 Stewart Ave, Ithaca NY 14850
(607)277-4770. Annie Fairchild.
Tues.

*COMMONS COFFEEHOUSE
Anabel Taylor Hall, Cornell U,
Ithaca NY 14853 (607)256-3448. Greg
King. Various nights. Seats 100.
Some concerts to 400 seats.

*CORNELL FOLK SONG CLUB
Concerts on Cornell campus. Bill
Steele, Box 782, Ithaca NY 14851
(607)273-2132.

*CORNELL UNIVERSITY
Program Board/Concert Commission,
530 W Straight Hall, Cornell U,
Ithaca NY 14853 (607)256-7132.
Dorothy Cotton, Dir of student
activities; Rene Singleton, Asst
Dir. Big concerts.

*CROSSROADS COFFEEHOUSE
Egbert Union, Ithaca Coll, Ithaca
NY 14850 (607)274-3201.

*REAL MUSIC PRODUCTIONS
1456 Mecklenburg Rd, Ithaca NY
14850 (607)272-5332. Annie
Fairchild. Some concerts.

*WILLARD STRAIGHT HALL
521 W Straigt Hall, Cornell U,
Ithaca NY 14853 (607)265-4311. Hope
Spruance. Thurs. Mostly local
players.

*JOHNSON CITY COFFEEHSE
71 Endicott Ave, Johnson City NY
13790 (607)797-1915. Bob Schofield.

*PURSUIT OF HAPPINESS CAFE
115 S Main St, Liberty NY 12754
(914)292-6760. Beverly Bark.

*ALPINE COUNTRY DANCE SOC
420 E 64th St, New York NY 10021.
Irv Kass.

*BLUEGRASS CLUB OF NEW YORK
417 E 89th St, #1B, New York NY
10028. Doug Tuchman.

*BOTTOM LINE
15 W 4th St, New York NY 10012
(212)228-6300. Alan Pepper. Most
nights. Showcase, name acts. Seats
400.

*CENTERFOLD COFFEEHOUSE
Church of St Paul & St Andrew, 263
W 86th St, New York NY 10024. Mary
Grace (212)866-4454. Fri.

*COUNTRY DANCE & SONG SOC
505 8th Ave, #2500, New York NY
10018-6505 (212)594-8833.

*EAGLE TAVERN
355 W 14th St, New York NY 10011
(212)924-0275. Varied music, Mon-
Sat. Seats 100. Mike McQuaid (212)
475-7092; Vicki Gibson (212)688-
5637, 345 E 56th St, NYC 10022.

*ETHNIC FOLK ARTS CENTER
179 Varick St, New York NY 10014
(212)675-3741. Office: 325 Spring
St, #314, New York NY 10013 (212)
691-9510. Ethel Raim, Martin
Koenig. Concerts, dances, workshops, instruction, festivals, etc.

*FOLKFONE
Listing of local events. (212)594-
6876. Run by CDS.

*HEBREW ARTS SCHOOL
Abraham Goodman Hse, 129 W 67th St,
New York NY 10023 (212)362-8060.
Concerts, music & dance workshops.
Jewish arts.

*HOSPITAL AUDIENCES INC (HAI)
1540 Broadway, New York NY 10036
(212)575-7681. Lynn Kable,
Infacility Dir. For the cultural
needs of the disabled, in
institutions and homebound. Send
audition tape of live performance.

*IRISH ARTS CENTER
553 W 51st St, New York NY 10019
(212)757-3318. Concerts, workshops,
fest, newsletter.

*NY FOLKLORE SOCIETY
116 Pinehurst Ave, New York NY.
Rivla Jennings

*NY PINEWOODS FOLK MUSIC CLUB
505 8th Ave, #2500, New York NY
10018. Don Wade (718)426-8555.
Concerts at various NYC venues.
Camps. Newsletter.

*NEW YORK REVELS
Box 556, Cathedral Stn, New York NY
10025. John Langstaff. Annual
Christmas frolics.

*PEOPLES' VOICE
Washington Sq Church Parlor, 133 W
4th St, New York NY 10012 (718)426-
2183. Sat.

*SOC FOR ASIAN MUSIC
112 E 64th St, New York NY 10021.

*SPEAKEASY MUSICIANS' CO-OP
107 MacDougal St, New York NY 10012
(212)598-9670. Every night. Varied
music. Seats 150.

TALLER LATINOAMERICANO
19 W 21st St, New York NY 10010
(212)255-7155. Workshops, concerts.
Newspaper.

*22 BELOW
155 E 22nd St, New York NY 10010
(212)674-0739. Sat.

*WORLD MUSIC INSTITUTE
155 W 72nd St, #706, New York NY
10023 (212)362-3366 or 0290. Robert
Browning. Concerts at various NYC
venues, cassettes, radio programs.

*AUTUMN CAFE
244 Main St, Oneonta NY (607)432-
6845. Thurs.

*THE MUSIC HALL
United Church, E 4th & Oneida Sts,
Oswego NY. Bookings: Cathy
Spaulding, RD1, Box 70, Martville
NY 13111 (315)564-6739. Sat, 2x
month. Seats 120.

*THE TURNING POINT
468 Piermont Ave, Piermont NY 10968
(914)359-1089. John McEvoy. Varied
music Tues-Sun. A good place.

*NYS OLDTYME FIDDLERS
RD1, Redfield NY 13437.

*OMEGA INSTITUTE
Lake Dr, RD2, Box 377, Rhinebeck NY
12572 (914)876-2058. Folk weeks.

*GOLDEN LINK FOLK SOC
1050 East Ave, Rochester NY 14607
(716)244-5830. John Stevens.

*FRIENDS OF FOLKS' MUSIC
PO Box 612, Saranac Lake NY 12983
(518)891-0878. Peter Lesser.

*CAFFE LENA
47 Phila St, Saratoga Springs NY
12866 (518)583-0022. Lena Spencer.
26 years old and still going
strong.

*LONG ISLAND TRAD MUSIC
ASSN (LITMA)
PO Box 2706, Setauket NY 11733
(516)924-0422 or 751-1339. Dances,
concerts, workshops.

*FRIENDS OF TRAD MUSIC
1459 Comstock Ave, Syracuse NY
13210 (315)476-1165. Rich Fuhrman.
Concerts, workshops, etc.

SYRACUSE BLUES SOCIETY
209 Brookles Dr, Syracuse NY 13207.

*MOTHER'S WINE EMPORIUM
Student Union, RPI, 15th & Sage,
Troy NY 12180 (518)266-8585. Dave
Parks.

CREATIVE MUSIC FOUNDATION
PO Box 671, Woodstock NY 12498.

FESTIVALS

*ADIRONDACK FOLK/GOSPEL FEST
Held at Lake Pleasant. PO Box 215,
Saratoga Springs NY 12866. Field
Horne. July.

CATSKILLS IRISH FEST
Held in E Durham. Box 467, Catskill
NY 12414 (518)943-6559. Music,
dance, food.

*CLEARWATER'S GREAT HUDSON
RIVER REVIVAL
Held at Croton Pt Park. 112 Market
St, Poughkeepsie NY 12601 (914)454-
7673. Music, dance, food, crafts.
Very varied. June.

*ETHNIC MUSIC FEST
Held at Bohemian Pk, Astoria, in
summer, Manhattan in winter. 325
Spring St, #314, NYC 10013 (212)
691-9510. Ethel Raim. Music, dance,
food. Concerts, workshops.

*FIDDLE & DANCE
RD1, Box 489, West Hurley NY 12491
(914)338-2996. Jay Ungar. Week-long
summer music and dance camps.

*INTERARTS FEST
Palenville Interarts Colony, PO Box
59, Palenville NY 12463 (518)678-
9021. End June - August.

*INTL CELTIC FESTIVAL
Bridge St, Hunter NY 12442 (518)
263-3800. August.

*IRISH TRAD FEST
Irish Arts Ctr, 553 W 51st St, New
York NY 10019 (212)757-3318. June.

*MOUNTAIN EAGLE INDIAN FEST
Bridge St, Hunter NY 12442 (518)
263-3000. August.

*NASSAU COM COLL FOLK FEST
College Union, Garden City NY
(516)222-7148. Phyllis Kurland,
Paula Ballan. April. Free. A great
mix of musics.

*NY CAJUN FESTIVAL
Held at South St Seaport. Bayou
Productions, 34-65 Amboy Rd, #3D,
Staten Island NY 10306. Matthew S
Pavis. Sept.

*NYC BLUEGRASS FESTIVAL
Held at Snug Harbor, Staten Island.
417 E 89th St, New York NY 10028.
June.

*NEW YORK STATE FAIR
State Fairgrounds, Syracuse NY
13209 (315)487-7711. Aug-Sep.

*OLD SONGS
PO Box 197, Guilderland NY 12084
(518)756-2815. Trad music and
dance. June.

*PEACEFUL VALLEY BLUEGRASS
Banker Rd, HC89, Box 56, Downsville
NY 13755 (607)363-2211. July.

*THOMAS HOMESTEAD FOLK FEST
RD1, Campbell NY 14821 (607)583-
2179. Dot Brown. July.

MUSEUMS

*EAST HAMPTON MARINE MUSEUM
Box 858, Bluff Rd, Amagansett NY
11930 (516)267-6544. FOlklore,
whaling.

*CATSKILL CULTURAL CTR benefit
Rte 28, Arkville NY 12406 (914)586-
3326. History and culture of the
Catskills.

*MUSEUM OF MIGRATING PEOPLE
750 Baychester Ave, Bronx NY 10475
(212)379-1600. Oral history.

*THE FARMERS' MUSEUM
Lake Rd, Cooperstown NY 13326 (607)
547-2593. Village museum.

*AFRICAN-AMERICAN INSTITUTE
833 United Nations Plaza, New York
NY 10017 (212)949-5666. Traditional
African crafts.

*JEWISH MUSEUM
5th Ave & 92nd St, New York NY
10028 (212)860-1888.

*MUSEUM OF AMERICAN FOLK ART
49 W 53rd St, New York NY 10019
(212)581-2475. Dennis Duke, special
events.

*SOUTH ST SEAPORT MUSEUM
207 Front St, New York NY 10038
(212)669-9400. NY maritime history.

*YESHIVA UNIV MUSEUM
2520 Amsterdam Ave, New York NY
10033 (212)960-5390. Jewish
history, art & culture.

*OLD BETHPAGE VILLAGE
Round Swamp Rd, Old Bethpage NY
11804 (516)420-5280.

PRINT

*KNICKERBOCKER NEWS
Box 15000, Albany NY 12212 (518)
454-5460. Susan Tomer.

METROLAND
1229 Central Ave, Albany NY
12295. Peter Iselin.

*TIMES-UNION
Box 15000, Albany NY 12212 (518)
454-5436. Fred LeBrun, Arts Ed.

*EVENING PRESS and SUN-BULLETIN
Vestal Pkwy E, Binghamton NY 13902
(607)798-1234.

BRONX NEWS
163 Dreiser Loop, Bronx NY 10475.

BROOKLYN DAILY BULLETIN
141 Montague St, Brooklyn NY 11201.

*THE BUFFALO NEWS
1 News Plaza, Buffalo NY 14240
(716)849-4506.

CATSKILL DAILY MAIL
30 Church St, Catskill NY 12414
(518)943-2100. Claude Haton.

CROTON CORTLANDT NEWS
PO Box 68, Croton NY 10520 (914)
271-4778. Kent Gibbons.

BONE HUNTER
PO Box 546, Elmira NY 14902.

*ELMIRA STAR-GAZETTE and
SUNDAY TELEGRAM
201 Baldwin St, Elmira NY 14902
(607)734-5151.

*VIGNETTE
Nassau Comm Coll, Garden City NY
11530 (516)222-7071. George
Mueller.

*GOOD TIMES
PO Box 268, Greenvale NY 11548
(516)294-5746. Richard Branciforte.
Events listings, reviews, etc.

*MOUNTAIN EAGLE
Bridge St, Hunter NY 12442 (518)
263-3897. Local weekly.

GRAPEVINE
114 W State St, Ithaca NY 14850.

*ITHACA TIMES
PO Box 27, Ithaca NY 14851 (607)
273-6092. Sandy List. Weekly events
listings. Previews, concert &
record reviews, etc.

LONG ISLAND JOURNAL
PO Box 697, Long Beach NY 11561.
Sally Gold.

*THE MUSIC PAPER
PO Box 304, Manhasset NY 11030
(516)883-8898. Karen Wettingfield.
News, reviews, interviews,
listings.

*NEWSDAY
235 Pinelawn Rd, Melville NY 11747
(516)454-2943.

MOUNTAIN NEWS
PO Box 910, Monticello NY 12701
(914)796-1111. Jim Jacobs.

*FRANCE-AMERIQUE
662 Main St, New Rochelle NY 10803
(914)633-0106.

*ALLIANCE
216 W 102nd St, New York NY 10025
(212)864-3101. Listings.

*ASSOCIATED PRESS (wire service)
50 Rockefeller Plaza, New York NY
10020 (212)621-1500. Services
papers worldwide.

*CITY NIGHT
19 Irving Pl, New York NY 10003.
Lydia de Fretos. Listings. weekly.

*DAILY NEWS
220 E 42nd St, New York NY 10017
(212)210-1583. Bill Zakariasen.

DOWNTOWN MANHATTAN
80 Varick St, New York NY 10013
(212)219-8629. Don Ralph. Listings,
reviews, interviews.

EAST VILLAGE EYE
611 Broadway, New York NY 10003
(212)777-6157. Celeste-Monique
Lindsey. Listings.

*FOLKFONE
Listing of local events. (212)594-
6876. Run by CDS.

*NEW YORK CITY TRIBUNE
401 Fifth Ave, New York NY 10016
(212)532-8300. Donna Selig.

*NEW YORK
755 Second Ave, New York NY 10017
(212)880-0700. Peter G Davis, Ruth
Gilbert. Weekly. Listings, reviews.

NEW YORK TALK
1133 Broadway, New York NY 10010
(212)206-1661.

*NEW YORK TIMES
229 W 43rd St, New York NY 10036
(212)556-1342. Richard Shepard
(listings); Robert Palmer, Jon
Pareles, Steven Holden.

*NEW YORKER
25 W 43rd St, New York NY 10036
(212)840-3800. Andrew Porter.
Listings "Going On About Town."

*NEWSDAY
1500 Broadway New York NY 10036
(212)730-4350. Wayne Robins,
Caroline Miller. (Also in Melville
NY).

*NOVOYE RUSSKOYE SLOVO
PO Box 748, Ansonia Stn, New York
NY 10023 (212)781-5663.

*OUR TOWN
1751 Second Ave, New York NY 10028
(212)289-8700. Listings.

*VILLAGE VOICE
842 Broadway, New York NY 10003
(212)475-2300. Doug Simmons, Bob
Christgau, RJ Smith, Geofrey
Stokes. News, reviews, interviews,
listings.

*VILLAGER
88 7th Ave S, New York NY 10014
(212)420-1660. Megan Morrow.

*WEST SIDE SPIRIT
1220 Broadway, 9th fl, New York NY
10001 (212)868-1417. Gary Stern.

*WHERE
7600 3rd Ave, New York NY 10016
(212)661-4800. Listings.

*WISDOM'S CHILD
1841 Broadway, New York NY 10023
(212)265-3270. Ruth Gilbert.
Listings.

*EVENING NEWS
PO Box 871, Newburgh NY 12550 (914)
561-3000.

*NIAGARA GAZETTE
310 Niagara St, Niagara Falls NY
14303 (716)292-2311.

*DAILY STAR
102 Chestnut St, Oneonta NY 13820
(607)432-1000. Gary Grossman. Daily
except Sun.

*POUGHKEEPSIE JOURNAL
PO Box 1231, Poughkeepsie NY 12602
(914)454-2000. Jeffrey Borak.

*ROCHESTER DEMOCRAT & CHRONICLE
and TIMES-UNION
55 Exchange St, Rochester NY 14614
(716)232-7100 x 3456.

*FOOTHILLS FOLK CALENDAR
Box 215, Saratoga Springs NY 12866
(518)885-5713. Montly calendar of
folk events.

*SARATOGIAN
20 Lake Ave, Saratoga Springs NY
12866 (518)584-4242. Jim Reilly.
Listings, reviews.

*SCHENECTADY GAZETTE
334 State St, Schenectady NY 12301
(518)374-4141.

*STATEN ISLAND ADVANCE
950 Fingerboard Rd, Staten Island
NY 10305 (718)981-1234.

*HERALD-JOURNAL and others
PO Box 4915, Syracuse NY 13221
(315)470-2263.

*TIMES-RECORD
501 Broadway, Troy NY 12181 (518)
272-2000. Doug deLisle.

*UTICA DAILY PRESS
221 Oriskany Pkwy, Utica NY 13503
(315)792-5000.

*GANNETT WESTCHESTER NEWS
(cover many towns)
1 Gannett Dr, White Plains NY 10604
(914)694-9300.

RADIO

*WAMC
318 Central Ave, Albany NY 12206
(518)465-5233. Wanda Fischer. Artie
Traum (914)679-7177 wants live
performers for show 2nd Weds 8.30-
10 pm.

WCDB (90.9)
SUNY Campus Ctr 316, 1400
Washington Ave, Albany NY 12222
(518)457-5262. Claudia Besen, MD,
Kevin Clarke. CP: ALBANY STUDENT
PRESS 2x weekly 10000.

WQBK
Box 1300, ALbany NY 12201 (518)462-
5555. Lin Bremer, Peggy Apple.

WALF
Box 548, Alfred NY 14802.

WEDT
Alfred State Coll, Alfred NY 14802
(607)871-6407.

WRUB (640AM)
SUNY, 111 Talbert Hall, Amherst NY
14260 (716)831-2479. Bob Lewis,
Stacey Plitcha.

WRHW (90.5)
SUNY, Binghamton NY 13901 (607)798-
2137. CP: PIPE DREAM 2x wkly 9000.

WKOP
Box 997, Binghamton NY 13901.

WSKG
Box 3000, Binghamton NY 13902
(607)775-0100. Tom Hill.

*WBSU (89)
SUNY, Brockport NY 14420 (716)395-
2580. Adam Wilcox, MD. CP: STYLUS
weekly 6500.

*WFUV (90.7)
Fordham U, Rosehill Campus, 3rd Ave
& E Fordham Rd, Bronx NY 10458
(212)365-8050. Mark Loponte. Varied
ethnic. CP: PAPER, RAM weekly 7000.

WHLC
Lehman Coll, Bedford Pk Blvd W,
Bronx NY 10468. CP: MERIDIAN wkly
6000.

WBCR (590AM)
Brooklyn Coll, 102A LaGuardia Hall,
Brooklyn NY 11210 (718)859-6258.
Cary Vance. CP: CALLING CARD
monthly 20K; KINGSMAN wkly 10K.

WKRB
Kingsboro CC, 2001 Oriental Ave,
Brooklyn NY 11235 (718)648-7311.
CP: SCEPTER 2x monthly 10000.

WLEX
Hunter Coll, 2845 Brighton 3rd St,
Brooklyn NY 11235. Cliff Paino.

WBNY (91.3)
Buffalo Coll, 1300 Elmwood Ave,
Buffalo NY 14222 (716)878-5104.
Dave Johnson.

WCMB
18 Agassiz Cir, Buffalo NY 14214.

WGRQ
SUNY, 1725 Millersport Hwy, Buffalo
NY 14260. CP: CURRENT wkly 18000;
SPECTRUM daily 20000.

WSLU
St Lawrence U, Payson Hall, Cnton
NY 13617 (315)379-5356. CP: HILL
NEWS weekly 2500.

WCKL
PO Box 445, Catskill NY 12414
(518)828-5006. Carmine Pizza.

WITC
Cazenovia Coll, Cazenovia NY 13035.

WHCK (88.7)
Hamilton Coll, Clinton NY 13323
(315)859-7200. Chuck Miller. CP:
SPECTATOR weekly 3500.

WSUC (90.5)
SUC, Brockway Hall, Cortland NY
13045 (607)753-4818. Tom Apostle.
CP: PRESS weekly 5500.

WCVF (89)
SUC, Fredonia NY 14063 (716)673-
3420. Eric van Rysdam, MD. CP:
LEADER weekly 5500.

WBAU (90.3)
Adelphi U, Box 365, Garden City NY
11530 (516)747-4757. Irish: Tony
Jackson; Blues: Mike Casano;
Contemporary: Ken Norian. CP:
DELPHIAN weekly 5000.

WEOS (89.7)
Coll of the Senecas, Box F-138,
Geneva NY 14456 (315)789-8970. Dave
Shane.

WCWP (88.1)
CW Post Ctr, Greenvale NY 11548
(516)299-2626. Dave Caggiano. CP:
PIONEER weekly 10000.

WRCU (90.1)
Colgate U, Dodge Hse, Hamilton NY
13345 (315)824-1212. Steve Ochs,
Mark Mularz.

WRHU (88.7)
Hofstra U, 1000 Fulton Ave,
Hempstead NY 11550 (516)489-8870.
Tony Fallon. Varied ethnic. CP: NEW
VOICE 2x monthly 12500; CHRONICLE
weekly 10000.

WQIX
Box 288, Horseheads NY 14845.

WBCG (cable)
Columbia Green CC, Box 1000, Hudson
NY 12534 (518)828-4181 x 381.

WHUC
Union Tpke, Box 123, Hudson NY
12534 (518)828-3341. Bill Winans.

*BOUND FOR GLORY
Box 843, Ithaca NY 14851 (607)844-
4535. Phil Shapiro. Sun, live from
Commons Coffeehouse. On WVBR.

WICB (91.7)
Ithaca Coll, Broadcast Ctr, Ithaca
NY 14850 (607)274-3217. Kevin
Stagg. Folk progs. CP; ITHACAN
weekly 5000.

*WVBR (93.5)
Cornell U, 227 Linden Ave, Ithaca
NY 14850 (607)273-4000. Paul
Shapiro. CP: DAILY SUN 4500.

WQMC (590AM)
Queens Coll, 1504 Jamaica Ave,
Jamaica NY 11451 (718)969-2100.
Frank Cicha. CP; NEWSBEAT, SKYLINE
weekly 10000.

WPYX
1054 Troy-Schenectady Rd, Latham NY
12110 (518)785-9800 or 9061.

WCNY (NPR-91.3)
506 Old Liverpool Rd, Liverpool NY
13088 (315)457-0400. Bill Knowlton.
Country, bluegrass, annual fest.

WVCR
Siena Coll, Loudonville NY 12211
(518)783-2366. CP: INDIAN 2x
monthly 2400.

WRNP
SUC, 13 Wurts Ave, New Paltz NY
12561. CP: ORACLE weekly 7000.

*JOE FRANKLIN radio & tv show
147 W 42nd St, New York NY 10036
(212)221-1693. Interviews.

*NATIONAL PUBLIC RADIO
801 2nd Ave, New York NY 10017
(212)490-2444. Andy Lyman.

*WBAI (PACIFICA-99.5)
505 8th Ave, New York NY 10018
(212)279-0707. Ed Haber "The Piper
in the Meadow Straying" Sun 7-9am.
Other world musics.

WBMB (560AM)
Baruch Coll, 360 Park Ave S, New
York NY 10010 (212)275-7168. Eddie
Rubinstein. CP: REPORTER, TICKER 2x
monthly (R) 5000, (T) 10000.

WCCR (640AM)
City Coll, 138th St & Convent Ave,
New York NY 10031 (212)690-8171.
CP: PAPER, CAMPUS 2x monthly 12K.

*WEVD (97.9)
770 Broadway, New York NY 10003
(212)777-7900. Joel Plavin. Ethnic
and labor.

WHBI (105.9)
80 Riverside Dr, New York NY 10024
(212)799-8000. Ethnic: 46 tongues.

*WKCR (89.9)
Columbia U, Ferris Booth Hall, New
York NY 10027 (212)280-5223. Gina
Plamsa. Varied folk/ethnic.
Listings. CP: SPECTATOR daily;
SUNDIAL weekly, 10000.

WKHK
140 W 43rd St, New York NY 10036.

*WNEW (102.7)
655 3rd Ave, New York NY 10017
(212)955-9639. Pete Fornatale
"Mixed Bag" Sunday 8-11 a.m.

*WNYC (93.9/830AM)
Municipal Bldg, 1 Centre St, New
York NY 10007 (212)566-2118. Oscar
Brand, Mike Flynn, Dave Sear.
"Prairie Home Companion."

WNYU (89.1)
New York U, 566 LaGuardia Pl, New
York NY 10012 (212)598-3036. Anne
Clark. CP: COURIER 2x monthly 10K;
WASHINGTON SQ 2x weekly 18K.

WOR TV
1481 Broadway, New York NY 10036
(212)764-7000. Myrna Pederson.
News, some music tie-in with local
appearances.

*WQXR (96.3/1560AM)
229 W 43rd St, New York NY 10036
(212)556-1144. Robert Sherman:
"Woody's Children."

WTNY
NY Inst of Tech, 1855 Broadway, New
York NY 10023 (212)757-7121. Steve
Julty. CP: SCOPE 2x monthly 1500.

WGMC
PO Box 300, North Greece NY 14575.

*WNYK
Nyack Coll, Nyack NY 10960. Also
does tape & record production.

WONY (90.9)
SUC, Alumni Hall, Oneonta NY 13820
(607)431-2712. Wendy Golden. CP:
STATE TIMES 2x weekly 4500.

WRHO
Hartwick Coll, Oneonta NY 13820
(607)432-4200.

WRVO
SUC, Lonigan Hall, Oswego NY 13126.
Folk progs. CP: OSWEGONIAN weekly
7500.

WPLT
Plattsburgh State, 65 Broad St,
Plattsburgh NY 12901 (518)564-2727.
Carson Hoag, Beth Slater.

WTSC (91.1)
Clarkson Coll of Tech, Potsdam NY
13676. Randy Humphrey. CP:
INTEGRATOR weekly 5000.

WKVR (91.3)
Vassar Coll, Box 166, Poughkeepsie
NY 12601 (914)473-5866 or 2999.
Mike Gallelli. CP: MISCELLANY
NEWS weekly 4000.

WPUR
SUNY, Purchase NY 10577. Jamie
Keyes, Saul Thaler.

WIRQ (93.3)
Irondequoit High, 260 Copper Rd,
Rochester NY 14617 (716)342-6461.
Mark Andrus.

WITR (89.7)
Rochester Inst of Tech, Box 9969,
Rochester NY 14623 (716)475-2000.
Chris Griffin. CP: REPORTER weekly
9000.

WMCC
Monroe CC, 100 E Henrietta Rd,
Rochester NY 14623 (716)424-5200.

WNYR
360 East Ave, Rochester NY 14606.

WRUR (88.5)
U of Rochester, Box 5068, River
Stn, Rochester NY 14627 (716)275-
5966. Kevin Taylor. CP: CAMPUS
TIMES 3x weekly 5000.

WXXI (NPR-91.5)
Box 21, Rochester NY 14601 (716)
325-7500. Mitzie Collins.

OUR TOWN TELEVISION
78 Church St, Saratoga Springs NY
12866 (518)587-6641. Stephen
Rosenbaum. Videos for local cable.

*WSPN (91.1)
Skidmore Coll, Saratoga Springs NY
12866 (518)584-5770. Adah Franklin,
Lena Spencer. CP: SKIDMORE NEWS
weekly 3450.

WMHT (NPR-89.1) and WMHT TV
Box 17, Schenectady NY 12301 (518)
356-1700. Stephen Honeybill.

WRUC (90.9)
Union Coll, Schenectady NY 12308
(518)370-6154. Scott Elkind. CP:
CONCORDIENSIS weekly 2700.

DAN DI NICOLA
35 Cedar Ln, Scotia NY 12302
(518)399-7938. Station: 381-4988.
TV show: interviews, records,
listings.

WPBX (91.32)
Southampton Coll, PO Box 462-S,
Southampton NY 11968 (516)283-5000.
Andy Popkin, Karen Tumelti.

WSIA (99.9)
Coll of Staten Is, 715 Ocean terr,
Staten Island NY 10301 (212)448-
9742. Robert Conroy, MD.

WUSB (90.1)
SUNY, Stony Brook NY 11794
(516)246-7901. Mike Yuhas. Varied
ethnic. CP: STONY BROOK PRESS
weekly 10000; STATESMAN.

WKWZ
Southwoods Rd, Syosset NY 11794.

WOUR
Syracuse U, University Pl, Syracuse
NY 13210. CP: DAILY ORANGE 14000;
EQUAL TIME monthly 8000.

WHCC (760AM)
Hudson Valley CC, Vandenburgh Ave,
Troy NY 12180 (518)283-1100. Megan
Carney, MD. CP: HUDSONIAN 2x
monthly 3000.

*WRPI (91.5)
Rensselaer Polytechnic Inst, Troy
NY 12182 (518)226-6248. Jackie
Alper, Sun pm. Records, listings,
interviews. CP; POLYTECHNIC weekly
9000.

WFAS
PO Box 551, White Plains NY 10602
(914)693-1900. Norman Weill.

CABLEVISION
1 Media Crossways, Woodbury NY
11797. Jean A Adams.

*WDST (100)
118 Tinker St, Woodstock NY 12498
(914)679-7266. Jan Whitman.

STORES

*MATT UMANOV GUITARS
273 Bleecker St, New York NY 10012
(212)675-2157. Sale and repair of
instruments. Accessories, books.

*SARATOGA STRING SHOP
47 Phila St, Saratoga Springs NY
12866 (518)587-4330. Daniel R Fera.
Instruments, repairs, mail order.

*COLE'S
907 19th St, Rte 7, Watervliet NY
12189 (518)273-4711. Woodwind &
brass repair.

*FOLKCRAFT INSTRUMENTS
Webatuck Craft Village, Rte 55,
Wingdale NY 12594 (914)832-6057.
Gil & Beth Anderson. Instruments,
kits, books, records, etc.

NORTH CAROLINA

NORTH CAROLINA ARTS COUNCIL
Raleigh NC 27611 (919)733-7897.
Della Coulter.

*WINSTON-SALEM FOUNDATION
229 First Utd National bank Bldg,
Winston-Salem NC 27101 (919)725-
2382. Funding info.

VENUES

*MOUNTAIN LAUREL DANCERS
48 Westover Dr, Asheville NC 28801.
Bob & Mary Thompson.

*MCDIBB'S
199 Cherry St, Black Mountain NC
28711 (704)669-2456. David Peel. 6
nights. Various music. Seats 150.

*NC FOLKLORE SOCIETY
Appalachian State, Dept of English,
Boone NC 28608 (704)262-3098. 2x/yr
journal; occasional newsletter.

*JOHN C CAMPBELL FOLK SCHOOL
Brasstown NC 28902. Weekends
throughout the year. Music, dance,
instruments, stories.

CAT'S CRADLE
113 W Franklin St, Chapel Hill NC
27514 (919)967-6666. Blues. Nwsltr.

*RHYTHM ALLEY
405-1/2 W Rosemary St, Chapel Hill
NC 27415 (919)929-8172. Judy
Hammond. Thur-Sat. Irish, blues,
bluegrass.

*CHARLOTTE FOLK MUSIC CLUB
2529 Kenmore Ave, Charlotte NC
28204 (704)375-2001. Beth Williams.

*UNIV OF NORTH CAROLINA
Charlotte NC 28223 (704)597-2256.
Douglas Orr, Jr, Vice Chancellor.
Some concerts.

WESTERN CAROLINA UNIVERSITY
Box 1989, A K Hines Ctr, Collowhee
NC 28723 (704)227-7479. Some
concerts. CP: WESTERN CAOLINIAN
weekly 6000.

DUKE UNIVERSITY
Box KM, Duke Stn, Durham NC 27706
(919)684-2911. Some concerts. CP:
CHRONICLE daily 15000.

COASTAL PLAINS FOLKLORE SOC
PO Box 2707, Greenville NC 27834

EAST CAROLINA UNIVERSITY
Mendenhall Student Union,
Greenville NC 27834 (919)757-6611.
Some concerts. CP: EAST CAROLINIAN
2x weekly 10000.

*NC STATE UNIVERSITY
Univ Student Ctr, Box 7306, Raleigh
NC 27695 (919)737-2451. Concerts.
CP: TECHNICIAN 3x wkly 15000.

*FIDDLE & BOW SOCIETY
418 Duke St, Winston-Salem NC 27103
(919)727-1038. Sonny Thomas.
Concerts, house concerts, workshops, festival.

FESTIVALS

*ASHEVILLE MOUNTAIN DANCE
  & FOLK FESTIVAL
Held at Civic Ctr Auditorium.
Chamber of Commerce, PO Box 1011,
Asheville NC 28802 (800)548-1300
(NC); (800)257-1300 (East); (704)
258-3916 (rest). Jackie Ward.
Contests. Oldtime, bluegrass. Trad,
clog dance. Founded by Bascom Lamar
Lunsford in 1927. Aug.

*BLACK MOUNTAIN FESTIVAL
Held at Black Mountain College.
Grey Eagle & Friends, PO Box 216,
Black Mountain NC 28711 (704)669-
2456. Trad music & dance. May and
Sept.

FALL FESTIVAL
Chamber of Commerce, Brasstown NC
28902 (704)837-2775. Fall.

*MOUNTAIN HERITAGE DAY
Mountain Heritage Ctr, Western
Carolina U, Collowhee NC 28723
(704)227-7234. Late Sept.

NORTH CAROLINA STATE FAIR
1025 Blue Ridge Rd, Raleigh NC
27607 (919)733-2145. Ot.

MUSEUMS

*FOLK ARTS CENTER
Milepost 382, Blue Ridge Pkwy,
Asheville NC 28815 (704)258-2850.
Demonstrations of crafts, music,
dance.

*MUSEUM OF THE CHEROKEE INDIAN
US 441, PO Box 770-A, Cherokee NC
28719 (704)497-3481. Culture &
history. Reference library.

*MOUNTAIN HERITAGE CTR
W Carolina U, Cullowhee NC 28723
(704)227-7129.

*NC DIV OF ARCHIVES
  AND HISTORY
109 E Jones St, Raleigh NC 27611
(919)733-7305. Exhibits, library.

PRINT

*ASHEVILLE CITIZEN and others
14 O'Henry Ave, Asheville NC 28801
(704)252-5611. Tony Kiss.

UNC CURRIC IN FOLKLORE NEWS
228 Grenlaw Hall, UNC, Chapel Hill
NC 27514.

*CHARLOTTE OBSERVER
PO Box 32188, Charlotte NC 28232
(704)379-6412.

*DURHAM MORNING HERALD and SUN
115-19 Market St, Durham NC 27702
(919)682-8181. Susan Broili.

MISSING LINK
PO Box 6238, Coll Stn D, Durham NC
27708. Christy Embler, Ed.

NC INDEPENDENT
PO Box 26290, 2824 Hillsborough Rd,
Durham NC 27708 (919)286-1815.
Katherine Fulton, Ed; Carol
Collier, calendar.

SOUTHERN EXPOSURE
Box 531, Durham NC 27702. Record
reviews.

*OBSERVER and TIMES
458 Whitfield St, Fayetteville NC
28306 (919)323-4848. Chris Nelson.

*GASTONIA GAZETTE
2500 E Franklin Blvd, Gastonia NC
28053 (704)864-3291. Pam Bilger.

*GREENSBORO NEWS & RECORD
PO Box 20848, 200 E Market St,
Greensboro NC 27420 (919)373-7090.
Abe D. Jones.

CHILDREN'S FOLKLORE NEWSLTR
East Carolina U, Dept of English,
Greenville NC 27834. C.W. Sullivan
III.

*HIGH POINT ENTERPRISE
PO Box 1009, High Point NC 27261
(919)885-2161. Nickie Bridgers.

*NEWS & OBSERVER
215 S McDowell St, Raleigh NC 27597
(9190829-4574. Bill Morrison.

*SOUTHERN LIFESTYLE
PO Box 10932, Raleigh NC 27605.
12/yr. Reviews.

*THE SPECTATOR
1318 Dale St, Raleigh NC 27605
(919)828-7393. Hal Crowther, Ed.

*THOMASVILLE TIMES
PO Box 549, Thomasville NC 27360
(919)475-2151.

*MORNING STAR, SUNDAY STAR-NEWS
PO Box 840, Wilmington NC 28602
(919)343-2000.

*WINSTON-SALEM JOURNAL
416-20 N Marshall, Winston-Salem NC
27102 (919)727-7360. Jim Shertzer.

RADIO

*WCQS (88.1)
1 University Hgts, Asheville NC
28804 (705_253-6875. Barbara A.
Sayer, Stn Mgr. 10 hrs folk/wk.
Live music & interviews.

*WABY
Belmont Abbey Coll, Belmont NC
28012. Bill Poole. Folk.

WASU
Appalachian State U, Wey Hall,
Boone NC 28608 (704)262-2060. CP:
APPALACHIAN 2x weekly 7000.

WUNC (NPR-91.5)
U of NC, Swain Hall 04A, Chapel
Hill NC 27514 (919)966-5454. Brett
Sutton. CP: DAILY TAR HEEL 19000;
PHOENIX weekly 10000.

WXYC
U of NC, Box 51, Carolina Union,
Chapel Hill NC 27514 (919)962-7769.
Ken Friedman.

*WFAE (NPR-90.7)
UNCC Station, Charlotte NC 28223
(704)597-2555. Fiona K Ritchie.
THISTLE & SHAMROCK (Celtic)
syndicated on APR. Folk, blues,
concerts. Interviews.

WDAV
Davidson Coll, Davidson NC 28036
(704)892-1908. Jenny Cooper. CP:
DAVIDSONIAN weekly 2000.

*WXDU (88.7)
Duke U, Box 4706, Duke Stn, Durham
NC 27706 (919)684-2957. Jim
Albright. CP: DAILY CHRONICLE
15000.

*WSOE
Elon College, 201 East Bldg,
Haggard Ave, Elon College NC 27244
(919)584-9880. Mike Wheaton.

WFSS
Fayetteville State U, Fayetteville
NC 28301. CP: VOICE mthly 2500.

*WQFS
Guilford Coll, Box 17714,
Greensboro NC 27410 (919)292-5511.
Tom Grant, Ken Goldwasser.

WUAG
U of NC, Taylor Bldg, Greensboro NC
27412 (919)379-5470. Bonnie Davis.
CP: CAROLINIAN 2x weekly 7000.

*WZMB
East Carolina Univ, Joyner Library,
Greenville NC 27834 (919)757_6656.
Spike Harward.

WKTE
Box 465, King NC 27021.

*WHST
St Andrews Coll, Box 640,
Laurenberg NC 28352 (919)276-3652.

WCPE (89.7)
4044 Wake Forest Rd, Raleigh NC
27609 (919)872-7569. Dan Keever.

*WKNC
NCSU, 3132 Univ Student Ctr,
Raleigh NC 27607 (919)737-2401.
Belea Parker. CP: TECHNICIAN 3x
weekly 15000.

WREB
Box 1050, Reidsville NC 27302.

WKTC
PO Box 100, Tarboro NC 27886.

WLOZ
U of NC, 601 S College Rd,
Wilmington NC 28403 (919)791-4330.
CP: SEA HAWK weekly 4500.

*WAKE (530AM)
Wake Forest U Union, Box 765A,
Reynolds Stn, Winston-Salem NC
27109 (919)761-5230. Noel Hunter.
CP: OLD GOLD & BLACK wkly 5000.

WFDD (NPR-88.5)
Box 7405, Reynolds Stn, Winston-
Salem NC 27109 (919)761-5257.
Howard Skillington.

WSNC
104 Comm Arts Bldg, Stadium Dr,
Winston-Salem NC 27110.

STORES

OXBOW MUSIC
Chapel Hill Rd, Durham NC 27707
(919)929-2473. Instruments etc.

*HARRY & JEANIE WEST
PO Box 17067, W Durham Stn, Durham
NC 27705 (919)383-5750. Fine
instruments, accessories. Free &
friendly advice. SASE for list.

NORTH DAKOTA

*W DAKOTA GRANTS RESOURCE CTR
Bismarck Jnr Coll Library, Bismarck
ND 58501 (701)224-5450. Funding
info.

VENUES

NORTH DAKOTA STATE UNIV
Memorial Union, Fargo ND 58105
(701)237-8459/8011. Some concerts,
CP: SPECTRUM 2x weekly 8000.

UNIV OF NORTH DAKOTA
Univ Ctr, Grand Forks ND 58201
(701)777-2644. Some concerts.

MINOT STATE COLLEGE
Student Assn, Minot ND 58701 (701)
857-3385. Some concerts. CP: RED &
GREEN weekly 2500.

FESTIVALS

NORTH DAKOTA STATE FAIR
PO Box 1796, Minot ND 58701 (701)
852-3113. July.

MUSEUM

*ND HERITAGE CENTER
Bismark ND 58505 (701)224-6666.
Exhibits, library.

PRINT

*BISMARCK TRIBUNE
Box 1498, 707 Front Ave, Bismarck
ND 58502 (701)223-2500.

*THE FORUM
Box 2020, Fargo ND 58107 (701)235-
7311. Kathy Freise.

*GRAND FORKS HERALD
114-120 N 4th St, Grand Forks ND
58201 (701)775-44211. Gail Hand.

*DAILY NEWS
301-303 4th St NE, Minot ND 58701
(701)852-23341.

RADIO

*PRAIRIE PUBLIC RADIO & TV
1814 N 15 St, Bismarck ND 58501
(701)224-1700. Donald Hoffman.

KFJM (NPR-89.3)
U of ND, Box 8116, Grand Forks ND
58202 (701)777-2577. Susan Gillies.
20 hrs folk & bluegrass. CP: DAKOTA
STUDENT 2x weekly 6500.

*KMHA (91.3)
PO Box 549, New Town ND 58763.

OHIO

*FOUNDATION CENTER
Public Library, 800 Vine St,
Cincinnati OH 45202 (513)369-6940.
Funding info.

*OHIO ARTS COUNCIL
727 E Main St, Columbus OH 43205
(614)466-2613. Tim Lloyd.

*OHIO OFFICE OF TRAVEL
    & TOURISM
PO Box 1001, Columbus OH 43216
(800)BUCKEYE. Excellent calendar of
events/festivals.

*ORACLE
30 W 15th Ave, Columbus OH 54210-
1305 (614)422-6592. Penney de Pas.
Booking consortium.

VENUES

*PIONEER AMERICA SOC
U of Akron, Dept of Geography,
Akron OH 44325 (216)375-7620. Allen
Noble.

OHIO UNIVERSITY
Baker Ctr, Athens OH 45701 (614)
594-6811. Some concerts. CP: POST
daily 12000.

*BOOKSELLERS
24031 Chagrin Rd, Beechwood OH
44122 (216)831-5035. Kathleen
Miller. Music Fri & Sat.

*CINCINNATI FOLK LIFE
210 E 8th St, Cincinnati OH 45202
(513)542-7560. Concerts, record
service. FOLKSTREAM.

*HAMMER PRODUCTIONS
2389 Wilson Ave, Concinnati OH
45231 (513)851-7683. Mark Schupp.
Concerts.

*OHIO FOLK ART ASSN
2470 Grandin Rd, Cincinnnati OH
45208. Richard Guggenheim.

*QUEEN CITY BALLADEERS
270 Calhoun St, Cincinnati OH 45221
(513)861-2700. Becky Ross (513)681-
9387. Co-op coffeehouse, concerts,
workshops, jams. Newsletter.

U OF CINCINNATI FOLKSONG SOC
539 Lowell Ave, #11, Cincinnati OH
45220. Michael Benson.

XAVIER UNIVERSITY
1401 Dana Ave, Cincinnati OH 45207
(513)745-3201. Some concerts. CP:
XAVIER NEWS weekly 12500.

*BELKIN PRODUCTIONS
2800 Chagrin Blvd, #205, Cleveland
OH 44122 (216)464-5990. Jules
Belkin. Concerts.

*CLEVELAND FOLK MUSIC SOC
1703 W 32nd St, Cleveland OH 44113.
Todd Smith.

*OHIO BLUES SOCIETY
Box 91224, Cleveland OH 44101.

*COLUMBUS ARTS CENTER
139 W Main St, Columbus OH 43215
(614)221-2000. "Music in the Air"
free concert series (150 - some
folk) in city parks.

*COLUMBUS MUSEUM OF ART
480 E Broad St, Columbus OH 433215
(614)221-6801. Sharon Kokot. Summer
afternoon garden concerts.

ENTERTAINMENT SERVICES
50 W Broad St, Columbus OH 43215
(614)228-3318. Gary Cheses.
Concerts.

*OHIO FOLKLIFE GROUP
Dept of English, Ohio State U, 164
W 17th St, Columbus OH 43210. Pat
Mullen. Concerts. MOTIF.

OHIO FOLKLORE SOCIETY
2366 Glenmawr Ave, #2, Columbus OH
43202. Elizabeth Harzaff. Journal.

*SQUARE DANCE SERIES
Olentangy Co-op Grocery, 2647 N
High St, Columbus OH (614)475-1920.
Andy Ardito.

*CANAL STREET TAVERN
308 E 1st St, Dayton OH 45402 (513)
461-9343. Mick Montgomery. Varied
music, several nights.

*CITYFOLK
PO Box 552, Dayton OH 45402
(513)223-3655. Phyllis Brzozowska.

UNIVERSITY OF DAYTON
300 Coll Park Ave, Dayton OH 45469
(513)229-4444. Some concerts. CP:
FLYER NEWS 2x weekly 5000.

*GAMBIER FOLKLORE SOC
Kenyon Coll, Gambier OH 43022 (614)
427-2244 x 2347. DIXIE BANNER.

*FLOWERS HALL DANCES
Darla Dr, Hanover OH (614)763-3680.
Chester Flowers. Every other Sat.

*GREAT BLACK SWAMP FOLK SONG
2148 Zurmehly Rd, Lima OH 45806.
Michael Wildermuth.

*OBERLIN FOLK MUSIC CLUB
Wilder Hall, Oberlin Coll, Oberlin
OH 44074 (216)775-8106. Clark
Drummond.

BIDDY MULLIGAN'S
40 S Reynolds Rd, Toledo OH 43615
(419)535-9178. 5 nights a week.

*COACH HOUSE
3141 W Central, Toledo OH 43606
(419)535-7663 (after 6pm). Michael
Singer.

*U OF TOLEDO FOLKSONG SOC
English Dept, Toledo OH 43606 (419)
537-2931. Tom Barden. Newsletter.

LIVELY ARTS OF YOUNGSTOWN
PO Box 3124, Youngstown OH 44501
(216)747-8339. Robert Varga.
Concerts.

YOUNGSTOWN STATE UNIVERSITY
Kilcawley Ctr, Youngstown OH 44555
(216)742-3575. Some concerts. CP:
JAMBAR 2x weekly 8500.

FESTIVALS

APPALACHIAN FESTIVAL
632 Vine St, #1100, Cincinnati OH
45202 (513)241-0136.

*CHALKER BLUEGRASS JAMBOREE
Held in Southington. PO Box 430,
Thornville OH 43076 (216)898-7117.
Late July.

*COLUMBUS FOLK FESTIVAL
Cultural Arts Ctr, 11-39 W Main St,
COlumbus OH 43215 (614)222-7047.
Susan Wells. Late Aug.

*DULCIMER DAYS
Held at Lake Park Pavilion, Roscoe
Village. 381 Hill St, Coshocton OH
43812 (614)622-9310. Contests,
workshops, concerts. Mid-May.

*ELK CREEK FOLK FESTIVAL
Held at Sebald Park. 1 City Ctr
Plaza, Middletown OH 45042 (513)
425-7982. Ken Schmithorst. Folk
art, music, food. Emphasis on
Appalachian traditions.

*FOLK MUSIC FESTIVAL
Held at Sharon Woods Village. 812
Dayton St, Cincinnati OH 45214
(513)721-4506. Pam Marfut. April.

*GAMBIER FOLK FESTIVAL
Held at Kenyon Coll. Box 86,
Gambier OH 43022 (614)427-2244.
Howard Sacks. Trad American music,
dance, crafts. Free. Late Oct.

*GAY NINETIES FEST
Held at Roscoe Village. 381 Hill
St, Coshocton OH 43812 (614)622-
9310. Banjo and barbershop musics.
Mid-Sept.

*INDEPENDENCE WEEKEND
  BLUEGRASS FESTIVAL
Held at Rail Fence Park, Mt Gilead.
PO Box 430, Thornville OH 43076.

*INTERNATIONAL FAIR
Held on village green. Community
Library, Sunbury OH 43074 (614)965-
3901. Rachel Edwards. Area ethnic
groups, music, food, dancing. 1st
weekend in May.

*IRISH CULTURAL FEST
Held at German Central Farm, 7863
York Rd, Parma OH. 14708 Westland
Ave, Cleveland OH 44111 (216)251-
0711. John O'Brien. Concerts,
workshops, dance. Early Aug.

*JEWISH FOLK FESTIVAL
Held in Burnet Woods Bandshell.
2615 Clifton Ave, Cincinnati OH
45220 (513)221-6728. Rabbi Abie
Ingber. Jewish music, art, food.
Free. Mid-May.

*MEXICAN-AMERICAN FESTIVAL
Held at Lucas Cnty Rec Ctr. Office:
411 Jervis St, Toledo OH 43609
(419)241-8076. Late Aug.

NORTHERN APPALACHIAN FOLKFEST
Held at Great Trail Farm. PO Box
552, Malvern OH 44644 (216)866-
2326. John Andrews. Music, dance,
contests. Early June.

OHIO FOLK FESTIVAL
Held at County Fairgrounds. 1511
Kuntz Rd, Dayton OH 45404 (513)461-
4800. Anne Matson. Music, food,
folk arts. April.

*OHIO SCOTTISH GAMES
Held on Oberlin Coll Fields. PO Box
21169, Cleveland OH 44121 (216)449-
5836. Dorothea J Kingsbury. Fair:
pipe, drum, dance competitions. 4th
Sat in June.

OHIO STATE FAIR
632 E 11th St, Columbus OH 43123
(614)294-5441. August.

*OLD WORTHINGTON FOLKLIFE
  CELEBRATION
Held on Village Green. Worthington
Arts Council, Box 612, Worthington
OH 43085 (614)431-0329. Trad music,
crafts, food. Early Aug.

*OLDE-TYME MUSIC FEST
Held at Mt Gilead State Park, SR
95, Mt. Gilead. ODNR, Fountain Sq,
Columbus OH 43224 (614)265-6549.
Concerts, jams, workshops, dances.
Free. Early June.

*SLAVIC VILLAGE HARVEST FEST
5001 Fleet St, Cleveland OH 44105
(216)271-5591. Mikelann Ward.
Music, dance, food, crafts. Free.
Early Sept.

MUSEUMS

*CENTURY VILLAGE
14653 E Park St, PO Box 153, Burton
OH 44021 (216)834-4012. Local
history, crafts. Bluegrass fest
August.

*DUNHAM TAVERN MUSEUM
6709 Euclid Ave, Cleveland OH 44103
(216)431-1060. Folklore collection.

*UKRANIAN MUSEUM
1202 Kenilworth Ave, Cleveland OH
44113 (216)781-4329. Folk arts.

*BUTLER COUNTY MUSEUM
327 N 2nd St, Hamilton OH 45011
(513)893-7111. Musical instruments.

*MILAN HISTORICAL MUSEUM
10 Edison Dr, Milan OH 44846
(419)499-2968. Folklore.

PRINT

*AKRON BEACON JOURNAL
44 East Exchange St, Akron OH 44328
(216)375-8161.

*CANTON REPOSITORY
500 Market Avenue S, Canton OH
44702 (216)454-5611.

*CINCINNATI ENQUIRER
617 Vine St, Cincinnati OH 45202
(513)369-1962.

CINCINNATI MAGAZINE
617 Vine St, Cincinnati OH 45202
(513)421-4300. Glossy monthly.

*CINCINNATI POST
125 W Court St, Cincinnati OH 45202
(513)352-2755.

CLEVELAND MAGAZINE
1621 Euclid Ave, Cleveland OH 44115
(216)771-2833. Glossy monthly.

CLEVELAND PRESS
901 Lakeside Ave, Cleveland OH
44114.

*PLAIN DEALER
1801 Superior Ave, Cleveland OH
44114 (216)344-4269.

*CITIZEN-JOURNAL and DISPATCH
34 S 3rd St, Columbus OH 43216
(614)461-8000.

COLUMBUS MONTHLY
171 E Livingston Ave, Columbus OH
43215 (614)464-4587. Glossy
monthly.

OHIO MAGAZINE
40 S 3rd St, Columbus OH 43215
(614)461-5083. Glossy monthly.

*DAYTON DAILY NEWS and
   JOURNAL-HERALD
4th & Ludlow Sts, Dayton OH 45401
(513)225-2248. Terry Lawson.

*CHRONICLE-TELEGRAM
PO Box 4010, Elyria OH 44336 (216)
329-7000.

*COURIER
701 W Sandusky St, Findlay OH 45840
(419)422-5151.

*JOURNAL-NEWS
PO Box 298, Hamilton OH 45012 (513)
863-8200. Nancy Baker.

*RECORD-COURIER
206 E Erie St, Kent OH 44240 (216)
673-3491. Margaret Garman,
Entertainment Editor.

*MANSFIELD NEWS JOURNAL
70 W 4th St, Mansfield OH 44902
(419)522-3311.

*SPRINGFIELD DAILY NEWS
202 N Limestone St, Springfield OH
45501 (513)323-3731.

*BLADE
541 Superior St, Toledo OH 43660
(419)245-6159. Tom Gearhart.

*YOUNGSTOWN VINDICATOR
Vindicator Sq, Youngstown OH 44501
(216)747-1471. Karl E. Schwab.

RADIO

WAUP (88.1)
U of Akron, 302 E Buchtel, Akron OH
44235 (216)375-7105. Clay Vause.
CP: BUCHTELITE 2x weekly 10000.

WRMU
Mt Union Coll, 1972 Clark Ave,
Alliance OH 44601 (216)821-8010.

WOUB
Ohio U, 9 S College St, Athens OH
45701 (604)594-6811. Keith Newman.

*WRCW (1060 AM)
Athens OH. Folk progs.

WBWC (88.3)
Baldwin-Wallace Coll, Berea OH
44017 (216)826-2145. John Bosalla.
CP: EXPONENT weekly 3850.

WBGU (88.1)
Bowling Green State U, 413 S Hall,
Bowling Green OH 43403 (419)372-
2826. Rich Frank. CP: BG NEWS daily
11000.

*WAIF (88.3)
2525 Victory Pkwy, Cincinnati OH
45206.

WGUC (NPR-90.9)
U of Cincinnati, 1223 Central Pkwy,
Cincinnati OH 45214 (513)475-4444.
Ann Santen. PG. CP: NEWS RECORD
3x weekly 13000.

WCLV (CMN-95.5)
Terminal Tower, Cleveland OH 44113
(216)241-0900. Robert Conrad. 2-hr
show weekly; 1-hr version on 16
stations.

*WCSB (89.3)
Cleveland State U, Rm 956, Rhodes
Tower, Cleveland OH 44115 (216)687-
3523 or 3591. Pennie Stasik.
Various folk progs, inc assorted
ethnic. CP: CAULDRON weekly 10000;
VINDICATOR 2x monthly 6000.

WRUW (91.1)
Case/West Reserve U, 11220
Bellflower, Cleveland OH 44106
(216)368-2208. Wade Talleson. CP:
OBSERVER weekly 7000.

*WBBY (104.3)
Columbus OH. Folk progs.

*WCBE (NPR-90.5)
270 E State St, Columbus OH 43215
(614)225-2750. Sharon Miller. PG.
Folk and ethnic progs.

*WMNI (920 AM)
Columbus OH. Folk progs.

WOSR (99.9)
Ohio State, 2052 Drake Union,
Columbus OH 43210 (614)422-9656.
Jeff Colon. CP: OHIO STATE LANTERN
daily 30000.

*WOSU (820AM/NPR-89.7)
2400 Olentangy River Rd, Columbus
OH 43210 (614)422-9678. Mary
Hoffman. Folk progs.

WSLN (98.7)
Ohio Wesleyan U, S Sandusky St,
Delaware OH 43015 (614)369-4431.
Carolyn Kane. CP: TRANSCRIPT
weekly 2000.

*WKCO (91.9)
Kenyon Coll, Gambier OH. Folk progs.

WKSR (730AM)
Kent State, Music & Speech Bldg,
Kent OH 44242 (216)672-2131. Shari
Wilkins. CP: DAILY KENT STATER
14000.

WKSU (NPR-89.7)
Kent State, 509 Wright Hall, Kent
OH 44242 (216)672-3411. Stephen
Silea. CP: DAILY KENT STATER
14000.

WGLE (NPR-90.2)
Lima OH 45802.

*WMAN (1400AM)
Mansfield OH. Folk progs.

*WHTH (790 AM)
Newark OH. Folk progs.

WMOA (CBS-94.3)
925 Lancaster St, PO Box 708,
Marietta OH 45705 (614)373-1490.
Vicki Vitalis.

WMRT (88.3)
Marietta Coll, Marietta OH 45705
(614)374-4800. CP: MARCOLIAN weekly
2000.

WMCO
Muskigum Coll, Stormont St, New
Concord OH 43762. CP: BLACK/MAG
weekly 12000.

*WOBC (91.5)
Oberlin Coll Student Network,
Wilder Hall, Oberlin OH 44074 (216)
775-8107. Anina Bennett. CP:
OBERLIN REVIEW 2x weekly 3500.

WMUB (NPR-88.5)
Miami U, Williams Hall, Oxford OH
45056 (513)529-5708. Janice
McLaughlin. CP: MIAMI SYUDENT 2x
weekly 10000.

WCPN
13800 Fairhill, #406, Shaker Hgts
OH 44120. Seana McDowell. 2-hr folk
show.

WKTL
111 Euclid Ave, Struthers HS,
Struthers OH 44471.

WERC (106.1)
U of Toledo, 2801 W Bancroft,
Toldeo OH 43606 (419)537-371. Karen
Bardner. CP: COLLEGIAN 2x weekly
10000.

WGTE (NPR-91.3)
415 N St Clair, Toledo OH 43604
(419)255-3330. William Engelke.

WJUC (88.7)
J Carroll U, 20700 N Park Blvd,
University Hgts OH 44118 (216)932-
7946. Jay Azzarella. CP: CARROLL
NEWS weekly 3000.

WRAC
106 Southwest St, W Union OH 45693.
Chip Kirker.

WCSU (NPR)
Central State U, Wilberforce OH
45384 (513)376-6371. Willis Parker.

WELW (AM)
36913 Stevens Bldg, Willoughby OH
44094. Ethnic, 1-hr Irish.

*WYSO (91.3)
Antioch Coll, Yellow Springs OH
45387.

WBBW
418 Knox St, Youngstown OH 44502.
Stan Vitek.

WYSU (NPR-88.5)
410 Wick Ave, Youngstown OH 44555
(216)742-3363. 2 hrs folk.

STORES

*COLUMBUS FOLK MUSIC CENTER
2194 N High St, Columbus OH (614)
291-5255. Instruments, books, etc.

OKLAHOMA

*OK TOURISM & RECREATION DEPT
500 Will Rogers Bldg, Oklahoma City
OK 73105 (405)521-2406. Events
calendar.

*TULSA CITY-COUNTY LIBRARY
400 Civic Ctr, Tulsa OK 74103 (918)
592-7944. Funding info.

VENUES

*BARTLESVILLE COMMUNITY CTR
PO Box 1027, Bartlesville OK 74005
(918)337-2787. Gary Moore. Concert
series.

*PHILLIPS UNIVERSITY
Hallie G Gantz Ctr, Box 2000,
University Stn, Enid OK 73702 (405)
237-4433. Kathy Canaday. Concert
series.

*OK BLUEGRASS CLUB
Rte 12, Box 392E, Midwest City OK
73150 (405)737-9944. Charlie
Blackwell. Ist Sat, Oct-Apr.
Newspaper.

BENCH-CARSON ATTRACTIONS
PO Box 60906, Oklahoma City OK
73146 (405)521-1444. Richard
Carson. Concerts.

*GREATER OKLAHOMA BLUEGRASS
  MUSIC SOCIETY
2737 NW 22nd St, Oklahoma City OK
73107.

*OK STATE FIDDLERS ASSN
3740 NW 20th St, Oklahoma City OK
73107. Floyd Martin.

*SECOND FRET
3009 N Classen, Oklahoma City OK
73106 (405)528-2317. Monica Falk.
Varied music, several nights.

*SOC FOR THE NORTH AMERICAN
  CULTURAL SURVEY
Dept of Geography, OK State U,
Stillwater OK 74078.

*GREEN COUNTRY BLUEGRASS ASSN
Box 6565, Tulsa OK 74156.

LITTLE WING PRODUCTIONS
423 N Main St, Tulsa OK 74103 (918)
584-2306. Scott Munz. Concerts.

*TULSA FOLK MUSIC SOCIETY
815 S Gary Pl, Tulsa OK 74104 (918)
585-5635. Bill Munger. Hosts
concerts, Guthrie fest. Networks
w/OK City & Eldorado KS.

*TULSA PERFORMING ARTS CTR
2nd & Cincinnati, Tulsa OK 74103
(918)592-7122. Paul Dixon.
Concerts.

FESTIVALS

*GRANT'S BLUEGRASS & OLDTIME
Rte 2, Hugo OK 74743 (405)326-5598.
August.

STATE FAIR OF OKLAHOMA
500 Land Rush St, Oklahoma City OK
73107 (405)942-5511.

*WOODY GUTHRIE FESTIVAL
Run by Tulsa FMS, 815 S Gary Pl,
Tulsa OK 74104 (918)585-5635. Bill
Munger.

MUSEUMS

*MUSEUM OF THE WESTERN PRAIRIE
1100 N Hightower, PO Box 574, Altus
OK 73521 (405)482-1044. Prairie
lifestyles.

*OLD TOWN & MUSEUM
Pioneer Rd & Hwy 66, PO Box 648,
Elk City OK 73648 (405)224-2207.
Music collection.

*PONCA CITY MUSEUM
1000 E Grand, Ponca City OK 74601
(405)762-6123. Recordings of native
American music.

PRINT

COLLEGIAN
Cameron U, 2800 Gore Blvd W, Lawton
OK 73505. 2x monthly 5000.

*LAWTON CONSTITUTION and
   MORNING PRESS
PO Box 2069, Lawton OK 73502 (405)
353-0620. David Everman.

*DAILY PHOENIX and TIMES-DEMO
PO Box 1968, Muskogee OK 74402
(918)682-3311. Leilani Roberts.

*TRANSCRIPT
PO Drawer 1058, Norman OK 73070
(405)321-1800. Delaine Dannelley.

*DAILY and SUNDAY OKLAHOMAN
Box 25125, Oklahoma City OK 73125
(405)231-3290.

*TULSA TRIBUNE
PO Box 1770, Tulsa OK 74102
(918)581-8464 or 8400. Ellis
Widner. Listings, some record &
concert reviews, interviews.

RADIO

*KCSC (90.1)
Central State U, 100 N University
Dr, Edmond OK 73034 (405)341-2980.
Tom Clare, Keyvan Behnis. CP: VISTA
2x weekly 5000.

KPSU
Panhandle State U, Box 430,
Goodwell OK 73939. CP: COLLEGIAN 2x
monthly 1000.

*KGOU
U of OK, 7800 Van Vleet Oval,
Norman OK 73019 (405)325-3388. CP:
OKLAHOMA DAILY 13800.

*KOSU (NPR-91.7)
OK State U, 217-1/2 S Washington,
Stillwater OK 74074 (405)624-6352.
Don Hoover. CP: DAILY O COLLEGIAN
14000.

*A MIXED BAG
815 S Gary Pl, Tulsa OK 74104 (918)
585-5635. Bill Munger. Show heard
nationally on many stations.

*CARRIE WILLIAMS COMMUNICATIONS
   FOUNDATION
PO Box 48538, Tulsa OK 74102.

KWGS (NPR-89.5)
600 S College, Tulsa OK 74104
(918)592-6000. Jeffrey Schlei.

OREGON

*LIBRARY ASSN OF PORTLAND
SW 10th Ave, Portland OR 97205
(503)223-7201. Funding info.

VENUES

JAZMIN'S
180 C St, Ashland OR 97520 (503)
488-0883. Richard.

*CORVALLIS FOLK SOCIETY
PO Box 335, Corvallis OR 97339.
John Swanson (503)753-0820; Don &
Betsy Reid (503)754-0707. Concerts
2nd Sun, dances. Newsletter.

*EASTERN EUROPEAN FOLKLIFE CTR
3150 Portland St, Eugene OR 97405
(503)344-4519. Mark Levy. Concerts,
workshops, music & dance camps.

*EUGENE FOLKLORE SOC
Box 1645, Eugene OR 97440. Nwsltr.

*OREGON FOLKLORE SOC
U of OR, Folklore & Ethnic Studies
Program, Eugene OR 97403. Bonnie
Lee.

*UNIVERSITY FOLK MUSIC CLUB
690 W 31st Ave, Eugene OR 97405.
Bob Freeman.

UNIVERSITY OF OREGON
SMU, Suite 2, Eugene OR 97403 (503)
686-4373. Some concerts. CP: DAILY
EMERALD 10000.

*OR OLDTIME FIDDLERS ASSN
8349 Booth Rd, Klamath Falls OR
97601. Lois M Tucker. THE
HOEDOWNER.

*EASTERN OREGON STATE COLLEGE
Student Activities Office, La
Grande OR 97850 (503)963-1507.
Yvonne Tagge. Some concerts.

ARTICHOKE MUSIC
6315 NE Brazee, Portland OR 97213
(503)231-4020/284-7747. Steve
Reischmann, Bill Bulick. Concerts.

EAST AVENUE TAVERN
727 E Bernside, Portland OR 97214
(503)236-6900. Barbara Luscher.
Seats 125.

KEY LARGO
Portland OR (503)224-3147.

*OR BLUEGRASS ASSN
Box 1115, Portland OR 97207.

PORTLAND COMMUNITY COLLEGE
12000 SW 49th Dr, Portland OR 97219
(503)244-6111. Some concerts. CP;
BRIDE weekly 9000.

*PORTLAND COUNTRY DANCE
  COMMUNITY
4551 NE 32nd St, Portland OR 97211.
Edith Farrar.

*PORTLAND FOLKLORE SOC
PO Box 8154, Portland OR 97207
(503)281-7475. Merle Korn. Few
concerts.

PORTLAND STATE UNIVERSITY
730 SW Mill St, Student Activities,
Portland OR 97207 (503)229-3000.
Some concerts. CP: VANGUARD 2x
weekly 10000.

FESTIVALS

BRITT BLUEGRASS/TRAD FEST
Held at Britt Gdn, Jacksonville. PO
Box 1124, Medford OR 97501 (503)
773-6077. Eli Luevano. July.

*OREGON STATE FAIR
2330 17th St NE, Salem OR 97310
(503)378-3247. Late Aug.

SCANDINAVIAN FESTIVAL
PO Box 5, Junction City OR 97448
(503)998-3300. Music, dance, food.
August.

*ZOOGRASS CELEBRATION
Held at Washington Park Zoo. 4001
SW Canyon Rd, Portland OR 97221
(503)226-1561. July.

MUSEUMS

*COLUMBIA RIVER MUSEUM
1792 Marine Dr, Astoria OR 97103
(503)325-2323. Pacific Northwest
maritime history.

*JOSEPHINE COUNTY
  KERBYVILLE MUSEUM
25195 Redwood Hwy, Box 34, Kerby OR
97531 (503)592-2076. Musical
instruments.

*PIONEER MUSEUM
2106 2nd St, Tillamook OR 97141
(503)842-4553.

PRINT

*EUGENE REGISTER-GUARD
PO Box 10188, Eugene OR 97440
(503)485-1234.

OREGON MAGAZINE
208 SW Stark, #500, Portland OR
97204 (503)223-0304. Glossy
monthly.

*OREGONIAN
1320 SW Broadway, Portland OR 97201
(503)221-8217.

*STATESMAN-JOURNAL
280 Church St NE, Salem OR 97301
(503)399-6728. Ron Cowan.

RADIO

KSOR
S OR State Coll, Ashland OR 97520
(503)482-6461. John Steffen. CP:
SISKIYOU weekly 4200.

*KMUN (Tillicum Fndn)
PO Box 269, Astoria OR 97103.
Katrin Snow. 15 hrs of folk, 6-8 of
blues weekly. Does interviews &
live shows.

*KOAB
Bend OR - see KOAP Portland.

KBVR (88.7)
OR State U, Memorial Union E,
Corvallis OR 97331 (503)754-3522.
Brandon Lieberman. CP: OSU
BAROMETER daily 15000.

*KOAC (550AM)
303 Covell Hall, Corvallis OR 97331
(503)754-4311. Frank Woodman. See
also KOAP Portland.

*KLCC (NPR-89.7)
4000 E 30th Ave, Eugene OR 97405
(503)726-2224. Michael Canning. 5
hrs folk. PG.

*KRVM (88.7)
200 N Monroe St, Eugene OR 97402
(503)687-3370. Greg Goumeniouk.

KWAX (NPR)
U of OR, Villard Hall, Eugene OR
97403. Tom Duval.

*KZEL (96.1)
Box 790128, Eugene OR 97401
(503)484-4304.

*KTEC
OR Inst of Technology, Klamath
Falls OR 97601 (503)882-6321.
Janice Bozarth.

*KEOL (91.7)
E OR State Coll, La Grande OR 97850
(503)963-1397. Mark O'Neill.

*KSLC
Linfield Coll, PO Box 365,
McMinnville OR 97128 (503)472-3851.
Kevin Baum.

*KBOO (90.7)
20 SE 8th St, Portland OR 97214
(503)231-8032. Eric Canfield.

KBPS (NPR-1450AM)
546 NE 12th Ave, Portland OR 97232
(503)234-5469. Darryl Conser.

KKSN (CMN-910AM)
Box 3910, 416 NE 158th St, Portland
OR 97208 (503)257-9106. Don Lisy.

*KLC (93.1)
Lewis & Clark Coll, Box 59,
Portland OR 97219 (503)244-6161 x
301. Dave Thomson. CP: PIONEER LOG
weekly 3000.

*KOAP (Oregon Public Radio-91.5)
2828 SW Front, Portland OR 97201-
4899 (503)295-6175. Joseph Rowe.
Folk programs, inc GLOBAL VILLAGE.
Program for KOAC-AM, KOAB-FM.

*KRRC
Reed Coll, 3203 S Woodstock Rd,
Portland OR 97202 (503)711-1112.
Fiona Martin. CP: QUEST wkly 1500.

PENNSYLVANIA

*FREE LIBRARY
Logan Sq, Philadelphia PA 19103
(215)686-5423. Funding info.

VENUES

CEDAR CREST COLLEGE
3001 W Walnut, Allentown PA 18104
(215)437-4471. Some concerts. CP:
CRESTIAD 2x monthly 9000.

*GODFREY DANIELS
7 E 4th St, Bethlehem PA 18015
(215)867-2390. David Fry. Varied
music, several nights. Seats 100.

*LEHIGH UNIVERSITY
Office of International Programs,
Univ Ctr 29, Bethlehem PA 18015
(215)861-4152. Various events, inc
arts fest with music, crafts, food
from many lands.

*THE SAURUS
109 E 3rd St, Bethlehem PA 18015
(215)691-2005. Used bookstore &
coffeehouse. Varied events, various
nights.

*BUCKS COUNTY BLUES SOCIETY
Tom Cullen (215)788-1261; Alex
Harty (215)945-6394.

*TROUBADOUR
501 Churchville La, Churchville PA
18966 (215) 860-8175. Bob
Pasquarello. Tues.

*PA FOLKLIFE SOCIETY
Box 92, Collegeville PA 19426.

*THE BARD OF THE LAKE
56 N Hamilton St, Doylestown PA
18901 (215)348-9593. Rich & Paula
Laughlin. Fri. Seats 100.

*FOLK HERITAGE INSTITUTION
Box 141, Glenville PA 18329.

*SUSQUEHANNA FOLK MUSIC SOC
3109 N 2nd St, Harrisburg PA 17110.

*SEVEN MTN BLUEGRASS ASSN
134 Hummel Ave, Lemoyne PA 17043.
Wayne Fishel.

*LOCAL MUSIC COLLECTIVE
PO Box 184, Lewisburg PA 17837.
House concerts.

*PA DUTCH FOLK CULTURE SOC
Lenhartsville PA 19534.

BALD EAGLE FOLK COLLECTIVE
PO Box 633, ock Haven PA 17745.

SCARLET D TAVERN
Chestnut St, Mifflinburg PA 17844
(717)966-1332. Bill Heim. Folk at
weekends.

*FOLK SOUP
Towpath Restaurant, 1820 W Mechanic
St, New Hope PA 18930. Bookings:
Susan White, Village 2, Smoke Rise
3B, New Hope PA 18938 (215)862-
3272. Wed. Seats 50. Trad music.

*COMHAIRLE NA GCUMANM CEILTICH
Box 647, Newtown PA 18940.

*BLUSHING ZEBRA COFFEEHSE
7167-69 Germantown Ave,
Philadelphia PA. Run by Swords into
Plowshares (below)

*BOTHY FOLK CLUB
The London, 2301 Fairmount Ave,
Philadelphia PA. Monday.

*CHERRY TREE MUSIC CO-OP
St Mary's Parish Hall, 3916 Locust
Walk, Philadelphia PA (215)386-
1640. Sun. Eclectic folk. Seats
200. Bookings: ~~Jim Lebig (609)695-
5596.~~ CatHeRiNE JacobS 215 222-3708

*HERITAGE DANCE ASSN
PO Box 42415, Philadelphia PA
19101. James T Kitch.

*INTERNATIONAL HOUSE
Folklife Ctr, 3701 Chestnut St,
Philadelphia PA 19104 (215)387-
5125. John Reynolds. Concerts.

*PAINTED BRIDE
230 Vine St, Philadelphia PA (215)
925-9914. Chris Hayes. Concerts.
Seats 250.

PENN'S LANDING
Delaware Ave @ Dock St,
Philadelphia PA 19106 (215)923-
8181. Karen Love. Concerts.

√ PERFORMING ARTS SOC OF PHILA
4944 Bingham St, Philadelphia PA
19120 (215)329-0151. Concerts.

*PHILADELPHIA CEILI GROUP
6815 Emlen St, #2, Philadelphia PA
19119 (215)849-8899. Ceilis, workshops, festival. SEANACHAI.

*PHILADELPHIA BLUES MACHINE
351 Pelham Rd, Philadelphia PA
19119 (215)849-5465. Doug Waltner.
Concerts, jams. All blues styles.

*PHILADELPHIA FOLKSONG SOCIETY
√ 7113 Emlen St, Philadelphia PA
19119 (215)247-1300. Monthly
concerts, houseconcerts, sings,
workshops, various festivals,
schools program, more. Bookings:
Stephanie Flon, house concerts
(215)247-6598; monthly concerts
Fred Kaiser (215)249-0272.

*SWORDS INTO PLOWSHARES
6626 McCallum St, Philadelphia PA
19119 (215)438-9344. Diane Tankel,
Joyce Brown. Songs of freedom &
struggle. Concerts, workshops.
Blushing Zebra coffeehouse. disconected

ALL HANDS ROUND
3441 Parkview Ave, Pittsburgh PA
15213. Dances. Newsletter.

*CALLIOPE HOUSE
1414 Pennsylvania Ave, Pittsburgh
PA 15233 (412)322-6359. George
Balderose.

*COAL COUNTY TRADITIONS
500 Sampsonia Way, Pittsburgh PA
15233 (412)321-4462. Weekly dances.
COAL COUNTY CRIER 4/yr.

*WESTERN PA BLUEGRASS
Box 5295, Pittsburgh PA 15206-5295.

YE OLD COAL HOLE
500 W Walnut, Shamokin PA 17872
(717)648-2625. Dave van Doren.
Folk, acoustic, some ethnic. Wed.

*SHEFFIELD CIVIC ASSN
PO Box 73, Sheffield PA 16347 (814)
968-3707. Ran folk arts fest in
'85, may reinstitute.

APPAL TRAIL DULCIMER/FOLK
141 Center St, Slatington PA 18080
(215)767-5257. Susan Jennings.
Monthly meetings, annual camp.

VILLANOVA UNIVERSITY
Villanova Union, Villanova PA 19085
(215)645-7280. Some concerts. CP:
VILLANOVAN weekly 8000.

*BUCKS COUNTY FOLK SONG SOC
120 Walker Rd, Washington Crossing
PA 18977. L Clikeman.

BLUE MARSH INN
RD1, Wernersville PA 19565
(215)693-6312. Steve Carvaia.

INSTITUTE OF ETHNIC STUDIES
West Chester State Coll, West
Chester PA 19380.

*APPALACHIAN FIDDLE &
  BLUEGRASS ASSN
Mountain View Park, Mountain Rd,
Wind Gap PA. Various events through
the year.

FESTIVALS

*THE GREAT ALLENTOWN FAIR
17th & Chew Sts, Allentown PA 18104
(215)433-7541. Late August.

*BETHLEHEM MUSIKFEST
Held around town. 556 Main St,
Bethlehem PA 18018 (215)861-0678.
Roland Kushner. Varied music, food,
dance, etc. Free. Mid-August.

FALL FOLK FESTIVAL
Star Route N, McConnellsburg PA
17233 (717)485-4064. Helen Overly.
Late Oct.

*HERITAGE DANCE FEST
PO Box 42415, Philadelphia PA
19101. Performances, workshops.
Varied dance styles. Late Sept.

INDIAN NECK FOLK FESTIVAL
Box 1158, Federal Sq Stn,
Harrisburg PA 17108 (717)232-6306.
Late Mar.

*IRISH MUSIC & DANCE FEST
Held at Fishers Pool, Lansdale.
6815 Emlen St, #2, Philadelphia PA
19119 (215)849-8899. Phila Ceili
Group. Sept.

*OLD-TIME COUNTRY MUSIC CONTEST
Held in Old Mill Village. PO Box
434, New Milford PA 18834 (717)465-
3448. Early Sept.

OLD MILL VILLAGE FOLK FEST
Box 434, New Milford PA 18834 (717)
465-3448. Sept.

*PHILADELPHIA FOLK FESTIVAL
Held in Schwenksville. 7113 Emlen
St, Philadelphia PA 19119 (215)247-
1300. Concerts, workshops. Camping.
Late August. *att* *Fred Kaiser*

WIND GAP BLUEGRASS FEST
Held in Mountain View Park,
Mountain Rd, Wind Gap PA. 25 Ironia
Rd, Flanders NJ 07836. Harry Grant.
Concerts, workshops, etc. June.

MUSEUMS

*OLD ECONOMY VILLAGE
14th & Church Sts, Ambridge PA
17120 (412)266-4500. 18 early
buildings. Some concerts.

*MERCER MUSEUM
Pine & Ashland Sts, Doylestown PA
18901 (215)345-0210. Folk art.

*GOSCHENHOPPEN FOLKLIFE LIBRARY
  AND MUSEUM
Rte 29, PO Box 476, Green Lane PA
18054 (215)234-8953. PA history and
folk culture. Concerts, festival.

*GRANT PARK
859 County Line Rd, Horsham PA
19044 (215)343-0965. Bob
Pasquarello. Historic site.
Scottish fest in Oct.

*PENNSYLVANIA DUTCH FOLK
  CULTURE SOCIETY
Lenhartsville PA 19534 (215)562-
4803. Folklore, folk art.

*OLD MILL VILLAGE
New Milford PA 18834.

*BALCH INST FOR ETHNIC STUDIES
18 S 7th St, Philadelphia PA 19106
(215)925-8090. Items from various
ethnic cultures. Concerts, dance.

PRINT

*THE MORNING CALL
101 N 6th St Allentown PA 18105
(215)820-6533. Paul Willistein.

*ALTOONA MIRROR
PO Box 2008, Altoona PA 16603
(814)946-7459. David Vis.

*BEAVER COUNTY TIMES
400 Fair Ave, Beaver PA 15009
(412)775-3200.

*GLOBE-TIMES
202 W 4th St, Bethlehem PA 18015
(215)867-5000. Adrienne Redd,
Charles Schenk.

*EXPRESS
PO Box 391, Easton PA 18042
(215)258-7171. Robert K Hays.
*ERIE DAILY TIMES, others
205 W 12th St, Erie PA 16534
(814)456-8531.

*HARRISBURG EVENING NEWS
and PATRIOT
812 Market St, Harrisburg PA 17105
(717)255-8251.

THE NEWS
Manoa Shpg Ctr, West Chester Pike
Havertown PA 19083. Ed Peabody.
Weekly.

*LANCASTER INTELLIGENCER JOUR
8 W King St, Lancaster PA 17603
(717)291-8700.

*BUCKS CNTY COURIER TIMES
8400 Rte 13, Levittown PA 19057.
John Fisher.

KINDRED SPIRITS JOURNAL
PO Box 542, Lewisburg PA 17837.
4/yr. Alternative loan fund. Camps,
workshops. Directory of crafts,
ecological awareness.

CITY PAPER
6381 Germantown Ave, Philadelphia
PA 19144 (215)868-7667. Chris Hill,
Ed; Mary Armstrong, listings.

CUPOLA PRODUCTIONS
966 N Randolph St, Philadelphia PA
19123. "Rocking Chair Reviews."

MUSIC ARTICLE
PO Box 12216, Philadelphia PA
19144. Morris Henken.

*PHILADELPHIA
1500 Walnut St, Philadelphia PA
19102 (215)545-3500. Glossy
monthly.

*PHILADELPHIA DAILY NEWS
400 N Broad St, Philadelphia PA
19101 (215)854-2000.

*PHILADELPHIA INQUIRER
Box 8263, Philadelphia PA 19101
(215)854-5598.

*PITTSBURGH POST-GAZETTE
50 Blvd of the Allies, Pittsburgh
PA 15222 (412)263-1577. George
Anderson.

*PITTSBURGH PRESS
34 Blvd of the Allies, Pittsburgh
PA 15230 (412)263-1514. Carl Apone.

*READING EAGLE
345 Penn St, Reading PA 19603
(215)373-4221.

*SCRANTONIAN-TRIBUNE
336 N Washington Ave, Scranton PA
18505 (717)344-7221. Pete Miller.

*SCRANTON TIMES
Box 3311, Scranton PA 18505
(717)348-9100.

*TIMES LEADER
15 N Main St, Wilkes-Barre PA 18711
(717)829-7249.

*YORK DAILY RECORD
1750 Industrial Hwy, York PA 17402
(717)757-4842.

*YORK DISPATCH
15 E Philadelphia St, York PA 17405
(717)854-1575.

RADIO

WMUH (91.7)
Muhlenberg Coll, Box 10B, Allentown
PA 18104 (215)433-5957. Randy
Cohen. CP: MUHLENBERG weekly 2000.

SING OUT RADIO
108 Stout St, Ambler PA 19002. Tor
Jonassen.

WRFT
Temple U, 105 Bright Hall, Ambler
PA 19002 (215)643-1200.

*FOLK*L POINT PRODUCTIONS
RD1, Bechtelsville PA 19505 (215)
369-0906. Margaret Cavafelli. FOLK
ALLEY, live TV show. Tues.

WLVR (91.3)
Lehigh U, Box 20A, Bethlehem PA
18015 (215)861-3913. Barbara
Schwarz. CP: BROWN & WHITE 2x
weekly 6000.

WDCV
Dickinson Coll, Holland Bldg, #640,
Carlisle PA 17013 (717)245-1555.

WDNR
Widener U, Box 1000, Chester PA
19013 (215)499-4439. CP: DOME
weekly 2500.

WCUC (91.7)
Clarion State Coll, Davis Hall,
Clarion PA 16214 (814)226-2330. CP:
CLARION'S CALL weekly 4000.

WESS (90.3)
E Stroudsburg State, Comm Ctr, E
Stroudsburg PA 18301 (717)424-3512.
Ted Ruggiero. CP: STROUD COURIER
weekly 4000.

WJRH (90.5)
Lafayette Coll, Box 4029, Easton PA
18042 (215)250-5316. Ted Nacarella.
CP: STROUD COURIER weekly 4000.

WFSE (88.9)
Edinboro State, 102 Compton Hall,
Edinboro PA 16444 (814)732-2526.
Anna Kaylor. CP: SPECTATOR weekly
4500.

WERG (89.9)
Gannon U, Box 236, Erie PA 16541
(814)459-9374. Don Dalesio. CP:
KNIGHT weekly 3500.

*WQLN (91.3)
8425 Peach St, Erie PA 16509
(814)864-3001. Christine Hilbert
hosts "Homespun Trails." Wants to
interview visiting artists.

WRKZ
PO Box 2, Hershey PA 17033. Dan
Dalion.

WIUP (90.1)
Indiana U, 8-12 Davis Hall, Indiana
PA 15705 (412)357-2490. Dean
Duvall. CP: PENN 3x weekly 10500.

WUPJ
U of Pittsburgh, Johnstown PA 15902
(814)266-9661. CP: ADVOCATE weekly
2000.

WFNM (88.7)
Franklin & Marshall Coll, Lancaster
PA 17604 (717)291-4096. Tony
DeMarco. CP: COLLEGE REPORTER
weekly 3000.

WVBU (90.5)
Bucknell U, Box 3088, Lewisburg PA
17837 (717)524-1326. Larry Gurwith.
CP: BUCKNELLIAN weekly 4200.

WARC
Allegheny Coll, Box C, Meadville PA
16335 (814)724-3376.

WDXP
LaSalle Coll, Box 698, Philadelphia
PA 19141. CP: LASALLE COLLEGIAN
weekly 3000.

*WHYY (91)
150 N 6th St, Philadelphia PA
19106. Bob Carlin. Folk programs.
Wants to interview performers.

WIDQ
Bala Cynwyd Plaza, Philadqelphia PA
(215)835-6012. Gene Shay. Folk.

WKDU (91.7)
Drexel U, 3210 Chestnut St,
Philadqelphia PA 19104 (215)895-
2580. Ginny McCracken. Folk. CP:
TRIANGLE weekly 6000.

WMMR
19th & Walnut, Philadelphia PA
19103 (215)561-0933.

WQHS
U of PA, Philadelphia PA 19104
(215)387-5405. CP: DAILY
PENNSYLVANIAN 14000.

WRTI (90.1)
Temple U, 2020 N 13th St,
Philadelphia PA 19122. Folk, blues,
ethnic. CP: TEMPLE NEWS daily 10K.

WUHY (NPR-90.9)
150 N 6th St, Philadqelphia PA
19106 (215)361-9200. Cary Smith.
Folk programs.

WXPN (88.9)
U of PA, 3905 Spruce, Philadelphia
PA 19104 (215)387-5403. Judy
Weglarski, Al Steiner, Mary
Armstrong. Folk. CP: DAILY
PENNSYLVANIAN 14000.

WDUQ (NPR-90.5)
Duquesne U, Pittsburgh PA 15219
(412)434-6030. CP: DUQUESNE
DUKE weekly 8000.

WRCT (88.3)
Carnegie-Mellon U, 5020 Forbes Ave,
Pittsburgh PA 15213 (412)621-9728.
Peter Schwartz. CP: TARTAN weekly
5900.

*WYEP (91.5)
4 Cable Pl, Pittsburgh PA 15213.
Folk programs.

*WVIA (89.9)
Public Broadcasting Ctr, Pittston
PA 18640 (717)655-2808. George
Graham.

WNOW
PO Box 2506, Pleasureville Hills PA
17405. Joyce McSherry.

WLTC and WXLV
Lehigh County CC, 2370 Main St,
Schwenksville PA 18078 (215)799-
1155.

WVMW
Marywood Coll, 2300 Adams Ave,
Scranton PA 18509 (717)348-6202.
CP: WOOD WORD monthly 2000.

WQSU (88.9)
Susquehanna U, Selingsgrove PA
17870 (717)374-9700. Sue Smith. CP:
CRUSADER weekly 2300.

WSYC (88.7)
Shippensburg SC, Cumberland Union,
Shippensburg PA 17257 (717)532-
6006. Doug Garman.

WSRN (91.5)
Swarthmore Coll, Swarthmore PA
19081 (215)447-7340. CP: PHOENIX
weekly 2200.

*WPSU (91.9)
304 Sparks, University Park PA
16802 (814)865-9191. Jerry Salem.
Folk progs.

WCSD
Box 2012, Warminster PA 18974.

WCUR
State Coll, 219 Sykes Union Bldg,
West Chester PA 19383. CP: QUAD
weekly 7000.

WCLH (90.7)
Wilkes Coll, Wilkes Barre PA 18766
(717)825-7663. CP: BEACON weekly
2500.

WRKC (88.5)
Kings Coll, 133 N Franklin, Wilkes
Barre PA 18711 (717)826-5821. CP:
CROWN weekly 2500.

WVIA
Old Boston Rd, Jenkin Township,
Wilkes Barre PA 18700 (717)826-
6144. George Graham. Folk prog of
local music, others.

STORES

*SPRING MILL MUSIC
180A Barren Hill Rd, Conshocken PA
(215)834-0860. Bill Alberts. All
kinds of instruction.

*PENNSYLVANIA DUTCH HOBBIES
208 W Main St, Kutztown PA 19530
(215)683-9060. Keith & Valerie
Brintzenhoff. Folk instruments,
PA Dutch items, crafts, etc.

RHYTHM STICK
28 N 2nd St, Lewisburg
PA 17837 (717)524-7123. Records,
tapes, books.

RHODE ISLAND

FOLK ARTS PROGRAM/
  RI ARTS COUNCIL
312 Wickenden St, Providence RI
02903 (401)277-3880. W Lambrecht,
Dir. Support and info on trad
artists, inc instrument builders.

*PROVIDENCE PUBLIC LIBRARY
150 Empire St, Providence RI 02903
(401)521-7722. Funding info.

*RHODE ISLAND TOURISM
7 Jackson Walkway, Providence RI
02903.

VENUES

*POST & BEAM COFFEEHOUSE
URI Campus, Kingston. Bookings:
Virginia Seeger, 67 Metaterrain
Ave, Wakefield RI 02879 (401)783-
8563. Friday. Seats 120.

CHANNING MUSIC SERIES
Channing Memorial Church, Newport
RI 02840 (401)847-7456. June
Doolittle.

*NEWPORT FOLKLORE SOCIETY
Box 882, Newport RI 02840 (401)245-
2984. Laura Travis. Coffeehouse at
Seamen's Institute, Sun. Seats 65.

PROVIDENCE CEILIDH CLUB
102 Melrose St, Providence RI 02907
(401)461-4764. Jimmy Devine. Held
at Blarney Stone, Pawtucket,
monthly.

*RI BLUEGRASS & TRAD MUSIC SOC
Box 2573, Providence RI 02906
(401)785-2509. Paula Gremour.
Concerts, newsletter, calendar.

*RI FOLK MUSIC SOCIETY
16 Catalpa Rd, Providence RI 02906.
Kirke McVay.

*STONE SOUP
655 Hope St, Providence. Bookings:
Jean Murphy, 10 Osborn St, Providence
RI 02908 (401)273-0261. Sat.

*WESTERLY ARTS CENTER
119 High St, Westerly RI 02891
(401)596-2854. Nancy Worthen.
Concerts, coffeehouse.

FESTIVALS

*CAJUN & BLUEGRASS MUSIC
   & DANCE FESTIVAL
Held in Escoheog. 27 Union Ave,
Providence RI 02909 (401)351-6312.
Franklin Zawacki. Concerts, free
workshops. Late August.

*NEWPORT FOLK FESTIVAL
Festival Productions, 311 W 74th
St, New York NY 10023 (212)787-
2020. George Wien, Bob Jones.

*ROCKY HILL STATE FAIR
Division St, E Greenwich RI 02818
(401)884-4114. August.

MUSEUMS

*SOUTH COUNTY MUSEUM
Quaker & Stony Lns, PO Box 182, N
Kingstown RI 02852 (401)295-0498.
Early American life.

*RI BLACK HERITAGE SOCIETY
1 Hilton St, Providence RI 02905
(401)751-3490.

*RI HISTORICAL SOCIETY
52 Power St, Providence RI 02906
(401)331-8575. Musical insts.

PRINT

*PAWTUCKET EVENING TIMES
23 Exchange St, Pawtucket RI 92760
(401)722-400. William Oziemblewski.

ANCHOR
RI Coll, Mt Pleasant, Providence RI
02908. Monthly 6000.

ISSUES
Brown U, Prospect St, Providence RI
02912. Monthly 7500.

*NEW PAPER
131 Washington St, #209, Providence
RI 02903. Jim Benson. Listings,
interviews, reviews.

*PROVIDENCE JOURNAL-BULLETIN
75 Fountain St, Providence RI 02902
(401)277-7253. Tony Lioce.

*RHODE ISLAND VOICE
4 Washington St, Warwick RI 02888.
Irwin Becker, Ed. Community issues.

*WOONSOCKET CALL
75 Main St, Woonsocket RI 02895
(401)762-3000.

RADIO

WGNG
100 John St, Cumberland RI 02864.
Sean Connor.

WRIU (90.3)
U of RI, Kingston RI 02881 (401)
789-4949. Chuck Wentworth. 5 nights
folk. CP: GOOD FIVE-CENT CIGAR
daily; GREAT SWAMP GAZETTE 2x
monthly 6000.

WBRU (95.5)
75 Waterman St, Providence RI 02901
(401)272-9550. Jim Samalia.

WDOM (91.3)
Providence Coll, Friar Box 377,
Providence RI 02918 (401)865-2460.
Bill Lane. CP: COWL weekly 3500.

WJMF (88.7)
Bryant Coll, Smithfield RI 02917
(401)232-6044. John Blowers, MD.

SOUTH CAROLINA

*CHARLESTON COUNTY LIBRARY
404 King St, Charleston SC 29401
(803)723-1645. Funding info.

SC ARTS COMMISSION
1800 Gervais St, Columbia SC 29201
(803)758-3442.

VENUES

SC FESTIVAL ASSN
PO Box 3093, Florence SC 29502
(803)669-0950.

CLEMSON UNIVERSITY
University Union, Clemson SC 29632
(803)656-2461. Some concerts. CP:
TIGER weekly 12000.

*CHARLESTON FOLK, INC.
Box 570, Sullivans Island SC 29482
(803)833-9590. Laura Katz. Concert
series Sep-Jun. Trad/bluegrass.

*PICCOLO SPOLETO CONCERTS
2525 Myrtle Ave, Sullivans Island
SC 29482 (803)883-9590. Laura Katz.
(803)577-9890. Edmund Robinson.
Concert series Sep-Apr.

FESTIVALS

PICCOLO SPOLETO TRAD FOLK FEST
Held at Charleston Museum. 2525
Myrtle Ave, Sullivans Island SC
29482 (803)883-9590. Laura Katz.
Trad, some bluegrass. Late May.

SOUTH CAROLINA STATE FAIR
PO Box 393, Columbia SC 29202 (803)
799-3387. October.

MUSEUMS

*CHARLESTON MUSEUM
360 Meeting St, Charleston SC 29403
(803)722-2996. Ethnology
collection.

*OLD SLAVE MART MUSEUM
6 Chalmers St, Charleston SC 29401
(803)722-0079. Afro-American
history and folklore.

*SC DEPT OF ARCHIVES/HISTORY
1430 Senate St, Columbia SC 29201
(803)758-5816.

*HORRY COUNTY MUSEUM
483 Main St, Conway SC 29526
(803)248-6489. Folklore collection.

*PATRIOTS POINT NAVAL &
  MARITIME MUSEUM
PO Box 264, Mt Pleasant SC 29464
(803)884-2727. Concerts.

PRINT

*INDEPENDENT and MAIL
1000 Williamston Rd, Anderson SC
29622 (803)224-4321. Karen Petit.

*EVENING POST; NEWS & COURIER
134 Columbus St, Charleston SC
29402 (803)577-7111.

*STATE
PO Box 1333, George Rogers Blvd,
Columbia SC 29202 (803)771-8498.
William W. Starr.

*GREENVILLE NEWS and PIEDMONT
PO Box 1688, Greenville SC 29602
(803)298-4320.

COLLEGIAN
SC State Coll, Orangeburg SC 29117.
2x monthly 5000

*SPARTANBURG HERALD-JOURNAL
PO Box 1657, Spartanburg SC 29304
(803)582-4511. Jill Lanford.

RADIO

WJWJ
Box 1165, Beaufort SC 29902.

*WSBF
Clemson Univ, Clemson SC 29631
(803)656-2279.

WLTR (NPR-90.9)
Drawer L, Columbia SC 29250 (803)
758-2899. John Perry.

*WUSC (90.5)
U of SC, Columbia SC 29206 (803)
777-7172. John van Citters. CP:
GAMECOCK 3x weekly 14000.

WMUU (94.5)
920 Wade Hampton Blvd, Greenville
SC 29609 (803)242-6240. Charles
Koelsch.

*WPLS
Furman Univ, Greenville SC 29613
(803)294-2757. Jerry Chapman.

*WSCI
PO Box 801, Mt Pleasant SC 29464.
Marcia Byars-Warnock.

SOUTH DAKOTA

*SD STATE LIBRARY
322 S Fort St, Pierre SD 57501
(605)773-3131. Funding info.

VENUES

*NORTHERN STATE COLLEGE
Student Activities, Aberdeen SD
57401 (605)331-6627. Some concerts.

*SOUTH DAKOTA STATE UNIV
Student Activities, PO Box 2815,
Brookings SD 57007-1599 (605)688-
6127. David Laubersheimer. Some
concerts. CP: SDSU COLLEGIAN
weekly 6800.

AUGUSTANA COLLEGE
28th & Summit, Sioux Falls SD 57197
(605)336-4419. Some concerts. CP:
AUGUSTANA MIRROR weekly 3000.

*SD FRIENDS OF OLDTIME MUSIC
PO Box 901, Sioux Falls SD 57101
(605)256-6596. Cy Rosenthal.
Newsletter.

*UNIV OF SOUTH DAKOTA
Coyote Student Ctr, Vermillion SD
57069 (605)677-8334. Patrick Gross.
CP: VOLANTE weekly 7000.

FESTIVALS

*SIOUX RIVER FOLK FESTIVAL
Held at Newton Hills Park, Canton.
Box 901, Sioux Falls SD 57101.
Music, dance, crafts. August.

SD OPEN FIDDLING CONTEST
Tourism Div, 221 S Central, Pierre
SD 57501 (800)843-1930.

*SOUTH DAKOTA STATE FAIR
PO Box 1275, Huron SD 57350 (605)
352-1431. Sept.

MUSEUMS

*SD ARCHIVES RESOURCE CTR
State Lirary, 800 N Illinois,
Pierre SD 57501 (605)773-3173.

*CTR FOR WESTERN STUDIES
Augustana Coll, 29th & S Summit,
Sioux Falls SD 57197 (605)336-4007.
Native American culture, local
history.

*SIOUXLAND HERITAGE MUSEUM
200 W 6th St, Sioux Falls SD 57102
(605)335-4210. Folk arts, oral
history, Dakota ethnology.

*SHRINE TO MUSIC
Clark & Yale Sts, USD Box 194,
Vermillion SD 57069 (605)677-5306.
Instruments, books, recordings.
Annual American Music Festival.

PRINT

*ABERDEEN AMERICAN NEWS
PO Box 4430, Aberdeen SD 57401
(605)225-4100. Don Hall, Ed.

*RAPID CITY JOURNAL
Box 450, Rapid City SD 57709
(605)342-0280. Shirle Safgren.

*ARGUS LEADER
PO Box 5034, 200 S Minnesota Ave,
Sioux Falls SD 57117 (605)331-2307.

RADIO

KESD (NPR-88.3)
SD State Coll, Pugsley Ctr, #2218B,
Brookings SD 57087 (605)688-4191.
Don Johnson.

*KILI (Lakota Communications-90.1)
PO Box 150, Pine Ridge SD 57772.

*KTEQ
SD School of Mines & Technology,
Rapid City SD 57701 (605)394-2231.
Daniel Wenzel. CP: TECH 2x monthly
1500.

*KAUR (89.1)
Augustana Coll, 28th & Summit,
Sioux Falls SD 57197 (605)335-5463.
John Cloud.

*KBHU (89.1)
Black Hills State Coll, 1200
University Ave, Spearfish SD 57783
(605)642-6737. Jim Kallas. CP: BHSC
TODAY weekly 2400.

*KSBA
U of SD, New Armory, Rm 107,
Vermillion SD 57069 (605)655-5477.
Don Zuhr.

TENNESSEE

*MEMPHIS PUBLIC LIBRARY
1850 Peabody Ave, Memphis TN 38104
(901)528-2957. Funding info.

*PUBLIC LIBRARY OF NASHVILLE
8th Ave N & Union St, Nashville TN
37203 (615)244-4700. Funding info.

*TENNESSEE ARTS COMMISSION
505 Dederick, #1700, Nashville TN
37219 (615)741-1701. Directory of
Folk Arts. Events listing.

VENUES

*APPALACHIAN MUSIC ASSN
1118 Kohn St, Bristol TN 37620.

*CHATTANOOGA AREA
   FRIENDS OF FOLK MUSIC
7 Ridgeside Rd, Chattanooga TN
37411.

AUSTIN PEAY STATE UNIV
Social Activities Board,
Clarksville TN 37040 (615)648-7838.
Some concerts. CP: ALLSTATE wkly
6000.

TENNESSEE TECHNICAL UNIV
Student Activities, Cookeville TN
38501 (615)528-3123. Some concerts.
CP: ORACLE weekly 6000.

*FOLKLIFE CENTER OF THE SMOKIES
Box 8, Hwy 32, Cosby TN 37722 (615)
487-5543. Jean & Lee Schilling.
Concerts, workshops, festival.

*DOWN HOME
300 W Main St, Johnson City TN
37601 (615)929-9822. Phil Leonard.
Varied acoustic music. Host site of
"Down Home Music" recorded-in-
performance syndicated radio
series. Seats 180.

*EAST TN STATE UNIV
Campus Activities Board, Box
23260A, Johnson City TN 37614 (615)
929-4286. Bob Plummer. Concerts.

*JUBILEE ARTS CENTER
803 S Gay St, Knoxville TN 37901
(615)522-5851. Bill Daniels.

BLUES FOUNDATION
PO Box 161272, Memphis TN 38116.
Newsletter.

*CTR FOR SOUTHERN FOLKLORE
Box 40105, Memphis TN 38104 (901)
726-4205. UPDATE. Produces records,
films. Archives.

MID-TN STATE UNIV
Box 203, Student Programs,
Murfreesboro TN 37132 (615)898-
2551. Some concerts. CP: SIDELINES
2x weekly 5000.

TENNESSEE FOLKLORE SOCIETY
Mid TN State U, PO Box 201,
Murfreesboro TN 37132. Charles
Wolfe. TSF BULLETIN 4/yr.

*12TH & PORTER
115 12th Ave N, Nashville TN. Some
folk.

*SOUTHERN FOLK CULTURAL
   REVIVAL PROJECT
339 Valerie St, Nashville TN 37210
(615)331-0602 or 834-3925. Anne
Romaine, Dir; Judith Stiles,
bookings. Organizes tours, fests,
etc. Helps with fundraising.

*STATION INN
4042 12th Ave S, Nashville TN 37203
(615)255-3307. Bluegrass Tues-Sun.

*TN PERFORMING ARTS CTR
505 Dederick St, Nashville TN 37219
(615)741-7975. Warren K Summers.

*TENNESSEE STATE UNIV
Cultural Affairs Committee, Box
632, Nashville TN 37203 (615)320-
3504. Joan C Elliott. CP: METER 2x
monthly 5000.

*VANDERBILT UNIVERSITY
402 Sarratt Ctr, West End Ave,
Nashville TN 373240 (615)322-2471.
Some concerts. CP: HUSTLER 2x
weekly 8500; VERSUS monthly 3500.

*HIGHLANDER CENTER
Rte 3, Box 170, Newmarket TN 37820
(615)933-3443. Guy Carawan, John
Egerton.

FESTIVALS

BEAN BLOSSOM BLUEGRASS FEST
3819 Dickerson Rd, Nashville TN
38000 (615)865-7491. Mid-June.

BIG RIDGE MSUIC FESTIVAL
Big Ridge State Park, Maynardsville
TN 37807 (615)992-4423. John
Howell. August.

*BLACK FOLKLIFE FESTIVAL
Fisk Univ. Oct.

DULCIMER & HARP CONVENTION
Folk Life Ctr of the Smokies, Box
8, Hwy 32, Cosby TN 37722 (615)
487-5543. Jean & Lee Schilling.
Concerts, workshops. Camping. June.

*INTERNATIONAL CHILDREN'S FEST
Cumberland Museum, 800 Ridley Blvd,
Nashville TN (615)259-6382. Dances,
folk tales, food. Oct.

INTERNATIONAL FOLKFEST
Held in various mid-TN cities.
G-106, Forest Oaks Condos,
Murfreesboro TN 37130 (615)896-
3559. Steve Cates. Music and dance
in international costume. May.

*MEMPHIS IN MAY INTL FESTIVAL
245 Wagner Pl, #220, Memphis TN
38103 (901)525-4611. Ann S Ball.
All of May.

*NATL STORYTELLING FESTIVAL
Held at Old Slemons Hse. NAPPS, PO
Box 112, Jonesborough TN 37659
(615)753-2171. Jimmy Neil Smith.
October.

ROLLEY HOLE MARBLE CHAMPIONSHIP
Standing Stone State Park,
Livingston TN 38570 (615)823-6347.
Billy Markin. Free. Music, trad
crafts. Aug.

SUMMER SAMPLER ANNUAL FAIR
Held at St. Cecilia Coll, Aquinas.
PO BOx 8222, Nashville TN (615)228-
5370. Mary V Ingram. Music, crafts,
food. Early Aug.

TN GRASSROOTS DAYS
Held at Centennial Park. 339
Valeria St, Nashville TN 37210
(615)331-0602. Anne Romaine. Free.
Musics, dance, arts, and crafts.
Late September.

UNCLE DAVE MACON DAYS
Held in the Public Square. PO Box
1333, Murfreesboro TN 37130
(615)893-2369. Gloria Wilson. Free.
Music, dance, crafts, contests.
July.

MUSEUMS

*TN RIVER FOLKLIFE MUSEUM
N B Forrest Historic Area, Eva TN
38333.

*CASEY JONES HOME &
  RAILROAD MUSEUM
Casey Jones Village, Jackson TN
38301 (901)668-1222.

*CARROLL REECE MUSEUM
E TN State U, Johnson City TN 37614
(615)929-4392. Folklore.

*TIPTON-HAYES LIVING
  HISTORICAL FARM
Erwin Hwy 91S, PO Box 225, Johnson
City TN 37601 (615)926-3631.

*COUNTRY MUSIC HALL OF FAME
4 Music Sq E, Nashville TN 37203
(615)256-1639. Huge library of
tapes, records, books. Instrument
collection.

*MUSEUM OF APPALACHIA
Box 359, Norris TN 37828 (615)494-
7680. Pioneer culture and heritage.
Concerts.

PRINT

*CHATTANOOGA NEWS-FREE PRESS
400 E 11th St, Chattanooga TN 37401
(615)756-6900. June Hatcher.

*CHATTANOOGA TIMES
PO Box 951, Chattanooga TN 37402
(615)756-1234.

*JOHNSON CITY PRESS-CHRONICLE
Box 1717, Johnson City TN 37605-
1717 (615)929-3111.

*KNOXVILLE JOURNAL
PO Box 911, Knoxville TN 37901
(615)522-4141. Matt Nauman.

*COMMERCIAL APPEAL
495 Union St, Box 334, Memphis TN
38101 (901)529-2798. Robert M
Jennings.

*THE METRO
PO Box 24486, Nashville TN 37202-
4486 (615)297-0720. Gus V Palas
III. Bi-monthly. News, reviews,
listings.

*MUSIC CITY NEWS
50 Music Sq W, #601, Nashville TN
37203 (615)329-2200. Neil Pond.
Country music news, reviews.,

*NASHVILLE
PO Box 24649, Nashville TN 37202-
4649 (615)329-1973. Susan Avery.
Glossy monthly. Listings.

*NASHVILLE BANNER
1100 Broadway, Nashville TN 37202
(615)259-8232. Michael McCall.

TENNESSEEAN
1100 Broadway, Nashville TN 37202
(615)259-8000.

RADIO

WAPX
Austin Peay SU, Trahern Bldg,
Clarksville TN 37040 (615)552-9279.
Lisa Duvall. CP: ALLSTATE weekly
6000.

WSMC (NPR-90.5)
S Missionary Coll, Collegedale TN
37315 (615)396-2320. Sam McBride.
CP: SOUTHERN ACCENT weekly 2000.

WETS (NPR-89.5)
E TN State, Box 21, 400A, Johnson
City TN 37614 (615)926-2184. Ron
Wickman. CP: E TENNESSEAN 2x
weekly 5250.

WUOT (NPR-91.9)
U of TN, 232 Comm, UEB, Knoxville
TN 37996 (615)974-5375. Glenn
Hauser. CP: CHEATSHEET monthly
16000; UT DAILY BEACON 15500.

WFMQ
Cumberland Coll, Lebanon TN 37087.

WEVL
13381 Madison Ave, Madison TN
38104. Folk and country programs.

WUTM (NPR-90.3)
U of TN, Dept of Communications,
Martin TN 38238 (901)587-7095.
Kayla Beasley. CP: PACER weekly
5000.

WKNO (NPR-91.1)
Memphis State U, Box 80000, Memphis
TN 38152 (901)458-2521. A F Willis.
CP: HELMSMAN daily 21000.

*WPLN (NPR-90.3)
222 8th Ave N, Nashville TN 37203
(615)244-4700 x 55. Suzanne Potter,
Cal Bean, Prog Mgr.

*WRVU (91.1)
Vanderbilt Univ, Nashville TN
37240 (615)322-7625. Adrien
Seybert. Bluegrass.

STORES

*FOLKLIFE CENTER OF THE SMOKIES
Box 8, Hwy 32, Cosby TN 37722 (615)
487-5543. Jean & Lee Schilling.
Instruments, records, books, gifts,
accessories.

*LANHAM'S STRINGED INSTRUMENT
  REPAIR & CUSTOM BANJO SHOP
PO Box 4781, Nashville TN 37216.
Marty Lanham.

TEXAS

*DALLAS PUBLIC LIBRARY
Grants Info Service, 1515 Young St,
Dallas TX 75201 (214)749-4100.
Funding info.

*TEXAS ARTS EXCHANGE
U of TX, FAB 2.4, Austin TX 78712-
1104 (512)471-1655. Allen Longacre.
Booking consortium.

VENUES

*ABILENE CULTURAL AFFAIRS CNCL
PO Box 2281, 341 Hickory, Abilene
TX 79604 (915)671-7241. Lynn
Barnett. Some concerts.

*AMARILLO ART CENTER
PO Box 447, Amarillo TX 79178 (806)
372-8356. Al Kochka.

*UNIVERSITY OF TEXAS
Box 19348, Student Activities,
Arlington TX 76019 (817)273-2963.
Curtis Polk Jr. Some concerts. CP:
SHORTHORN daily 18000.

*ANTONE'S
2915 Guadalupe, Austin TX (512)474-
5314. Live blues.

*AUSTIN FRIENDS OF TRAD MUSIC
PO Box 49608, Austin TX 78765 (512)
458-2623. Steve Cantry. At Soap
Creek Saloon, 2nd & 4th Suns.

*CACTUS CAFE
U of TX, Austin TX 78713 (512)471-
5651 x 228 after 4pm. Griff
Luneberg. Varied music Thur-Sat.

*CTR FOR INTERCULTURAL STUDIES
   IN FOLKLORE & ETHNOMUSICOLOGY
U of Tx, Austin TX 78712.

*FLYING CIRCUS
1025 Barton Springs, Austin TX
(512)478-4585. Live blues.

*SOAP CREEK SALON
1201 S Congress, Austin TX 78704
(512)443-1966. Ed Bennett. Folk
several nights.

*UNIVERSITY OF TEXAS
Student Activities, 200 W 21st St,
Austin TX 67612 (512)471-5319. Some
concerts. CP: DAILY TEXAN 38500.

WATERLOO ICE HOUSE
906 Congress, Austin TX 78704
(512)474-2461. Folk several nights.

*WILLOW PRODUCTIONS
500 Terrace Dr, Austin TX 78704
(512)453-3232. Ingrid Karklins.
Occasional concerts.

*POOR DAVID'S
1924 Greenville Ave, Dallas TX
75200 (214)821-9891. David Card.

*SW CELTIC MUSIC ASSN
PO Box 4474, Dallas TX 75208
(214)942-6687. Ken Fleming, Peggy
Davis. Concerts, various venues.
CEILI. Fest in March.

*N TEXAS STATE UNIV
Student Activities, Univ Union,
Denton TX 76203 (817)788-2611. Some
concerts. CP:N TX DAILY 18000.

*THE ELISSA
Galveston Historical Soc, Galveston
TX (713)488-5942. Hilary Swann,
Earl Boatman. Restored 1877 square-
rigger. Some concerts, deck or
dockside, Sat.

*ANDERSON FAIR
2007 Grant, Houston TX 77006
(713)528-8576. Tim Leatherwood.
Seats 75.

*HOUSTON FOLKLORE SOC
9700 Leawood, #415, Houston TX
77099. Chuck Thompson.

*HOUSTON PUBLIC LIBRARY
500 McKinney, Houston TX (713)224-
5441, 236-1313. Some concerts.

*INST OF INTL EDUCATION
1520 texas Ave, Houston TX 77002
(713)223-5454. Alice Pratt. Fest in
April.

*KENNEALLY'S IRISH PUB
2111 S Shepherd, Houston TX 77019
(713)630-0486. John Flowers. Wed-
Sat. A real pub.

*RICE UNIVERSITY
PO Box 1892, Houston TX 77251
(713)527-4840. Dr Ed Doughtie.

*ROCKEFELLERS
3620 Washington Ave, Houston TX
77007 (713)861-8925. Colleen
Fisher.

*SECOND SATURDAY CONCERT
5910 Fordham, Houston TX 77005
(713)660-6682. Charles Osburn. At
Community Ctr. Two bands, one
bluegrass.

*UNIV OF HOUSTON
Dept of English, University Park,
4800 Calhoun, Houston TX 77004
(713)749-3431. Dr Carl Lindahl.

*UNIV OF ST THOMAS
3812 Montrose Blvd, Houston TX
77006 (713)522-7911. Some concerts.

*WESTCREST PUB
11128 Westheimer, Houston TX 77082
(713)789-9580. Irish pub. Fri-Sat.

*SAM HOUSTON STATE UNIV
Program Council, Lowman Student
Ctr, Huntsville TX 77341 (713)295-
6211. Frank Parker. Some concerts.
CP: HOUSTONIAN 2x weekly 8200.

*TEXAS TECHNICAL UNIV
Box 4310, Student Activities,
Lubbock TX 79409 (806) 742-3621.
Mary Donahue. Some concerts. CP:
UNIVERSITY DAILY 1700.

TEXAS FOLKLORE SOCIETY
S F Austin State U, Nacogdoches TX
75962 (409)569-4407. Marlene Adams.
Newsletter, annual book.

*CARVER CULTURAL CTR
226 N Hackbery, San Antonio TX
78202 (512)229-7211. Jo Long.
Concert series.

*INST OF TEXAN CULTURES
U of Tx, 810 S Bowie St, Box 1226,
San Antonio TX 78294.

*TEXARKANA ARTS & HUMANITIES
PO Box 1171, 221 Main St, Texarkana
TX 75504 (214)792-8681. Charles R
Rogers.

FESTIVALS

GATHER OF SCOTTISH CLANS
Held at Salada. PO Box 5064, Austin
TX 78763. Mid-Nov.

*KERRVILLE FESTIVALS
Quiet Valley Ranch, PO Box 1466,
Kerrville TX 78028 (512)896-3800. Not in
service
Rod Kennedy. Folk fest May;
Goodtime Music Fest mid-Oct.

*MESQUITE FOLK FESTIVAL
Held at Eastfield Coll. 3737 Motley
Dr, Mesquite TX 75050 (214)324-
7185. Rita Gleason. Folk, gospel,
bluegrass. May.

*NACOGDOCHES SUMMER FESTIVAL
Box 907, Nacogdoches TX 75963
(409)569-6875. Bluegrass. July.

NATIONAL POLKA FESTIVAL
Held at Ennis. PO Box 5064, Austin
TX 78763. May.

*NORTH TEXAS IRISH FESTIVAL
Held at Fair Park, Dallas. PO Box
4474, Dallas TX 75208 (214)942-
6687. Regional & intl groups, music
& dance workshops, cultural
displays, arts & crafts. Early
March.

STATE FAIR OF TEXAS
PO Box 26010, Dallas TX 75226 (214)
823-9931. Oct.

*TEXAS STATE CHAMPIONSHIP
   FIDDLERS FROLICS
PO Box 46, Hallettsville TX 77964
(512)798-2311.

MUSEUMS

*NAVARRO COUNTY HISTORICAL SOC
   & PIONEER VILLAGE
912 W Park Ave, Corsicana TX 75110
(214)872-1468. Folklore.

*MEXICAN-AMERICAN CULTURAL
   HERITAGE CENTER
2940 Singleton Blvd, Dallas TX
75212 (214)630-1680. Folk arts,
crafts, dance costumes.

*HIDALGO CNTY HISTORICAL MUSEUM
121 E McIntyre, PO Box 482,
Edinburg TX 78539 (512)383-6911.
History & culture. Publishers of
"Folk Life & Folk Lore of the
Mexican Border."

*UNIVERSITY INSTITUTE OF
   TEXAS CULTURE
801 S Bowie, San Antonio TX 78205
(512)226-7651. Ethnic history and
folklore.

*YORKTOWN HISTORICAL SOCIETY
144 W Main, PO Box 884, Yorktown TX
78154 (512)564-2174. Musical
instrument collection.

PRINT

TEXAS MONTHLY
PO Box 1569, Austin TX 78767
(512)476-7085. Pepi Ploughman.

*ABILENE REPORTER-NEWS
PO Box 30, Abiene TX 79604
(915)673-4271. William Whittaker.

*AMARILLO DAILY NEWS
and GLOBE-TIMES
900 Harrison St, Amarillo TX 79166
(806)376-4488. Kay Mohr, Mus Ed.

*AMERICAN-STATESMAN
PO Box 670, Austin TX 78767 (512)
445-3500.

*AUSTIN CHRONICLE
PO Box 49066, Austin TX 78765 (512)
473-8995. Margaret Moser, Richard
Steinberg. News, reviews, listings.

*BEAUMONT ENTERPRISE
PO Box 3071, Beaumont TX 77704
(713)833-3311. Lela Davis.

*BRYAN-COLLEGE STATION EAGLE
PO Box 3000, Bryan TX 77805 (409)
779-4444. Dan Neman.

*CORPUS CHRISTI CALLER and TIMES
PO Box 91136, Corpus Christi TX
78469. Gretchen Ray.

*DALLAS TIMES HERALD
1101 Pacific Ave, Dallas TX 75202
(214)744-6223.

*MORNING NEWS
Communications Ctr, Dallas TX 75202
(214)977-8431. John Ardoin.

*EL PASO HERALD-POST
PO Box 20, El Paso TX 79999 (915)
546-6113. Michelle Martin.

*FORT WORTH STAR-TELEGRAM
400 W Severn St, Fort Worth TX
76102 (817)390-7684.

*GALVESTON DAILY NEWS
8522 Teichman Rd, Galveston TX
77553 (409)744-3611.

*HOUSTON CHRONICLE
801 Texas St, Houston TX 77002
(713)220-7171. Ann Holmes.

*HOUSTON POST
4747 Southwest Fwy, Houston TX
77001 (713)840-6713. Carl
Cunningham, Mus Ed.

*JOURNAL and NEWS
PO Box 1792, Longview TX 75601
(214)757-3311. Dolores Brown.

*AVALANCHE-JOURNAL
PO Box 491, Lubbock TX 79408 (806)
762-8844. William Kerns.

*ODESSA AMERICAN
Box 2952, Odessa TX 78760 (915)337-
4661. Eileen McClellanad, Arts Ed.

*NEWS
PO Box 789, 549 4th St, Port Arthur
TX 77640 (409)985-5541.

*SAN ANGELO STANDARD-TIMES
34 W harris, San Angelo TX 76902
(915)653-1221. Kandis Gatewood.

*SAN ANTONIO EXPRESS and
EXPRESS-NEWS (Sunday)
PO Box 2171, San Antonio TX 78297
(512)225-7411.

*LIGHT
420 Broadway, San Antonio TX 78205
(512)226-4271. John R Cochran.

*TYLER COURIER-TIMES
and TELEGRAPH
410 W Erwin St, Tyler TX 75710
(214)597-8111.

*WACO TRIBUNE-HERALD
900 Franklin Ave, Waco TX 76703
(817)753-1511. Bob Darden.

*WICHITA FALLS RECORD-NEWS
and WICHITA FALLS TIMES
1301 Lamar St, Wichita Falls TX
76307 (817)767-8341. Martha B
Steimel, Arts Ed.

RADIO

KACC
Alvin CC, 3110 Mustang Rd, Alvin TX
77511 (713)311-6111.

*KACV (89.9)
Amarillo Jnr Coll, Box 447,
Amarillo TX 79178 (806)376-7032.
Chris Albracht.

*KAZI (88.7)
3112B Manor Rd, Austin TX 78723.

*KUT (NPR-90.5)
U of TX, Ctr for Telecommunicaion
Services, Communication Bldg B,
Austin TX 78712 (512)471-6395.
Cheryl Bateman. Folk progs. Hosts
Dan Foster, Howie MacRichey, Dave
Oberman. Interviews.

KVLU (NPR-91.3)
Lamar U, 3300 Port Arthur Rd,
Beaumont TX 77710 (713)838-8164.
Scott Hanley. CP: UNIV PRESS 2x
weekly 7000.

KAMU (NPR-90.9)
Texas A & M U, College Station TX
77843 (713)845-5681. Melissa
Cotropia. CP: BATTALION daily 23K.

KETR (NPR)
E TX State U, Box BB, Commerce TX
75428 (214)886-5806. CP: EAST TEXAN
2x weekly 4500.

KKED (NPR-90.3)
PO Box 416, Corpus Christi TX 78403
(512)855-2213. David McBride.

*KNON (90.0)
4415 San Jacinto, Dallas TX 75204.

*KSMU (cable)
Southern Methodist U, Box 456,
Dallas TX 75275 (214)692-2158. John
Kuehne..

*KZEW (97.9)
Comm Ctr, Dallas TX 75202 (214)748-
9631.OJ

KTEP
U of TX, El Paso TX 79968 (915)747-
5481. CP: PROSPECTOR weekly 11000.

*KPFT (90.1)
419 Lovett Blvd, Houston TX 77006
(713)526-4000. Folk programs:
SHEPHERDS HEY host Gary Coover,
WOOD, host Michael Rex. PG. Annual
Cajun Gumbo Cookoff with music,
March.

*KTRU (91.7)
Rice Univ, PO Box 1892, Mem Ctr,
Houston TX 77001. CP: RICE THRESHER
weekly 6000.

*KTSU
Texas Southern U, 3101 Wheeler Ave,
Houston TX 77004 (713)527-7591.

KUHF
U of Houston, 4800 Calhoun, Houston
TX 77004 (713)749-1253. CP: DAILY
COUGAR 15000.

*KSHU (89.3)
Sam Houston State U, Box 2297,
Huntsville TX 77340 (713)294-1354.

KNCT
Central TX Coll, US Hwy 190W,
Killeen TX 76541.

*KWTS
W TX U, PO Box 1514, Kenyon TX
79016 (806)656-3993. Lou Vyers.

*KTXT
Texas Tech U, Journalism Bldg,
Lubbock TX 79409 (806)742-3916.
Leonard Gilliard.

KRTU (ABC-91.7)
Trinity U, 115 Stadium Dr, San
Antonio TX 78284 (512)736-8313. Ray
Mays.

*KWBU (107.1)
Baylor U, Dept of Oral Comm, Waco
TX 76706 (817)752-5015. Eric Eddy.

STORES

BEN HOGUE, LUTHIER
3291 Manchaca, Austin TX 78704
(512)441-1396. Instrument maker and
repairer.

STRAIT MUSIC
908 N Lamar, Austin TX 78703 (512)
476-6927. Instrument sale and
repair. Accessories.

UTAH

*SALT LAKE CITY PUBLIC LIBRARY
Business & Science Dept, 209 E 5th
S, Salt Lake City UT 84111 (801)
363-5733. Funding info.

UTAH FOLKLIFE CTR
617 E South Temple, Salt Lake City
UT 84102 (801)533-5760. Hal Cannon.
Helps coordinate concerts. Nwsltr.

VENUES

*CEDAR CITY MUSIC ARTS ASSN
333 S 1840 W, Cedar City UT 84720
(801)586-3888. Dianne Gubler.
Concerts.

*WEBER STATE COLLEGE
Cultural Arts Program, 316D Admin
Bldg, Ogden UT 84408 (801)626-6570.
Daniel L Martino.

*UNIVERSITY OF UTAH
Concerts, Lectures, & Special
Events, ASUU Office, Olpen Union
Bldg, Salt Lake City UT 84112
(801)581-6866. Jennifer Botte.

FESTIVALS

*UTAH ASSN OF FAIRS & SHOWS
155 N 1000 W, Salt Lake City UT
84116 (801)533-5858. Calendar of
county fairs.

*UTAH STATE FAIR
Held at State Fairgrounds. 155 N
1000 W, Salt Lake City UT 84116
(801)533-5858. Sept.

MUSEUMS

*PIONEER VILLAGE
Box N, Farmington UT 84025 (801)
292-0466.

*UTE TRIBAL MUSEUM
Hwy 40, Bottle Hollow Resort, Ft
Duchesne UT 84026 (801)722-4992.
Oral history, culture.

*DEAD HORSE POINT STATE PARK
Box 187, Moab UT 84532 (801)259-
6511. Folklore.

*MUSEUM OF PEOPLES & CULTURES
Brigham Young Univ, 710 N 100 E,
Allen Bldg, Provo UT 84602
(801)378-612.

PRINT

*OGDEN STANDARD-EXAMINER
Box 951, Ogden UT 84401 (801)394-
7711.

*DAILY HERALD
1555 N 200 W, Provo UT 84603 (801)
373-5050. Laura Jones, Arts Ed.

*DESERET NEWS
30 E 1st S, Salt Lake City UT 84111
(801)237-2147.

*SALT LAKE TRIBUNE
PO Box 867, Salt Lake City UT 84110
(801)237-2078.

RADIO

KUSU (NPR-91.2)
Utah STate Univ, 745 N 1200 S,
Logan UT 84322 (801)750-3132.
Richard .Meng. CP: STATESMAN 3x
weekly 6500.

*KPCW (91.9)
PO Box 1372, Park City UT 84060.
Beth Fratkin.

KBYU (NPR-88.9)
Brigham Young U, C-3023 HFAC, Provo
UT 84602 (801)378-3555. Walter
Rudolph. CP: DAILY UNIVERSE 19K.

*KRCL (90.9)
208 W 800 S, Salt Lake City UT
84101.

KUER (NPR-90.1)
103 Kingsbury Hall, U of UT, Salt
Lake City UT 84112 (801)581-6625.
Mike Miles. CP: UT CHRONICLE daily
16000.

VERMONT

*VERMONT COUNCIL ON THE ARTS
136 State St, Montpelier VT 05602-
9989 (802)828-3291. Janet Ressler.

*VT DEPT OF LIBRARIES
Reference Services Unit, 111 State
St, Montpelier VT 05602 (802)828-
3261. Funding info.

*VT FOLK ARTS NETWORK
PO Box 511, Waterbury VT 05676
(802)244-8620. Ann Seidenberg.
Monthly dance calendar.

VENUES

*COUNTRY DANCE SOCIETY
  OF SOUTHEAST VERMONT
RD1, Box 82D, Brattleboro VT 05301.
Tony Asch, Kathie Lovell.

*CHAMPLAIN FOLKLORE COOPERATIVE
PO Box 401, Burlington VT 05401-
0401 (802)849-6968. Concerts,
workshops. Newsletter.

*GREEN MOUNTAIN CONSORTIUM
153 Main St, Burlington VT 05401
(802)862-5121 (802)862-5121.
Anthony Miccoci. Concerts.

*GREEN MOUNTAIN FOLKLORE SOC
35 Alfgird St, Burlington VT 05401.
GREEN MT WHITTLIN'S.

*HUNT'S
101 Main St, Burlington VT 05401
(802)863-3322. Occasional folk.

*INTERFOLK CENTER
7 Burlington Sq, Burlington VT
05401 (802)658-7828.

*NORTHEAST FIDDLERS ASSN
191 Woodlawn Rd, Burlington VT
05401.

*ONION RIVER ARTS COUNCIL
32 State St, Montpelier VT 05602
(802)223-7222. Mark Greenberg.
Concerts, fest in July.

*MT SNOW EVENING CONCERTS
Box 46A, Wilmington VT 05363 (802)
464-8308. Kelly Kahler. Alt Sats.

FESTIVALS

*CHAMPLAIN VALLEY FESTIVAL
Held at Kingsland Bay State Park.
PO Box 401, Burlington VT 05401-
0401 (802)849-6968. Trad music,
dance, crafts, events. Early Aug.

*FAIRFAX FRIENDS OF OLDTIME
RD2, Box 530, Fairfax VT 05454
(802)849-6968. May.

*MIDSUMMER FESTIVAL
Vermont College, Montpelier VT
05602 (802)229-9408. Mid-Jul.

MUSEUMS

*ROKEBY (Ancestral Estate of
  Rowland Evans Robinson)
US Rte 7, Ferrisburg VT 05456 (802)
877-3406. Folklore.

*BREAD & PUPPET MUSEUM
RD1, Rte 122, Glover VT 05839 (802)
525-3031. Puppetry, masks. RECORDing

PRINT

BRATTLEBORO REFORMER
Box 802, Brattleboro VT 05301.

*BURLINGTON FREE PRESS
PO Box 10, Burlington VT 05402
(802)863-3441.

VERMONT VANGUARD PRESS
87 College St, Burlington VT 05401.
Josh Mamis. Listings, reviews.

RADIO

WRUV
U of VT, 489 Main St, Burlington VT
05405 (802)656-2249. Larry DiCapua.
CP: VERMONT CYNIC weekly 10000.

WIUV
Castleton State Coll, Castleton VT
05735 (802)468-5514. Mike O'Brien.
CP: SPARTAN TIMES weekly 2400.

WRMC
Middlebury Coll, Box 29, Middlebury
VT 05753 (802)388-6323. John Davis.
CP: CAMPUS weekly 3500.

*WNCS
Box 551, 7 Main St, Montpelier VT
05602 (802)233-2396. Jody Peterson,
MD. ON AND ON by Upstreet
Productions, Mark Greenberg.

WGDR
Goddard Coll, Plainfield VT 05667.

WHWB
PO Box 518, Rutland VT 05701.

*WRFB (101.7)
Box 26, Mountain Rd, Stowe VT 05672
(802)253-4877. Mike Levine.

WIZN
Stevens Hse, Vergennes VT 05491
(802)877-6800.

WDEV
9 Stowe St, Waterbury VT 05676
(802)244-7321. Jack Donovan.

WNHV
Box 910, White River Junction VT
05001.

*WVPR (NPR-89.5)
Box 89.5, Windsor VT 04089
(802)674-6772. Frank Hoffman.

WVPS (NPR-107.9)
Ethan Allen Ave, Winooski VT 05404
(802)655-9451. Tom Karnes, Brian
Kling.

VIRGINIA

*GRANTS RESOURCES LIBRARY
Hampton City Hall, 9th fl, Hampton
VA 23669 (804)272-6496. Funding
information.

VENUES

*BIRCHMERE
39801 Mt Vernon Ave, Alexandria VA
22305 (703)549-5919. Gary Oelze.
Acoustic music, folk, bluegrass.

CABOMA (Capital Area Bluegrass &
Oldtime Music Assn)
Lyon Park Comm Ctr, N Pershing Dr,
Arlington VA 22201 (703)691-0727.
Jams 2nd & 4th Suns.

*C & O CLUB
515 E Water St, Charlottesville VA
22901 (804)971-7044. Lany Whiting.
Varied music, various nights.

*PRISM
214 Rugby Rd, Charlottesville VA
22904 (804)97-PRISM. Bob Cox, (804)
979-9884, PO Box 157, Ivy VA 22945.
Fri & Sat. Irish, trad & other
music, dances. Seats 120.

MID ATLANTIC FOLKLIFE ASSN
George Mason U, Dept of English,
Fairfax VA 22030. Margaret Yocum.

SHENANDOAH VALL FOLKLORE SOC
James Madison U, Box 1246,
harrisonburg VA 22807.

*BLUEMONT CONCERT SERIES
Box 208, Leesburg VA 22075 (703)
777-0574. Peter Dunning, Carol
Melby. Concerts year round, open
air in Summer. Artist-in-Education
programs, community events.
BLUEMONT MUSE.

*RAMBLIN' CONRAD'S
871 N Military Hwy, Norfolk VA
23502 (804)622-8918. Bob Zentz.
Varied music, various nights.

*TIDEWATER FRIENDS OF FOLK
c/o Ramblin' Conrad's.

*A & E MUSIC
3800 Holland Rd, #104, Virginia
Beach VA 23452 (804)498-8282. John
Lawless.

*ABBY ALDRICH ROCKEFELLER
  FOLK ART CENTER
Box C, Williamsburg VA 23185.

FESTIVALS

*BLUE RIDGE FOLKLIFE FESTIVAL
*Blue Ridge Institute, Ferrum Coll,
Ferrum VA 24088. Blues, gospel,
string bands. Oct.

*BLUEGRASS FESTIVAL
Cecil Hall, Rte 5, Box 192, Stuart
VA 24171 (703)694-7009 after 6pm.
Early July.

*CARTER FAMILY MEMORIAL FEST
PO Box 111, Hiltons VA 24258 (703)
386-9480. Janette Carter. Early
August.

*GALAX OLD FIDDLERS CONVENTION
328A Kenbrook Dr, Galax VA 24333.
Oscar Hall. Early August.

*VIRGINIA STATE FAIR
PO Box 26805, Richmond VA 23261
(804)329-4437. C.L. Teachworth,
Exec VP. September.

WATERFORD HOME TOUR & FEST
Home Tour Assn, Waterford VA 22190
(703)882-3018. Music, tours. Oct.

MUSEUMS

*HUMPBACK ROCKS CENTER
Blue Ridge Pkwy, Box 481A, Afton VA
22920 (703)982-6458. Oral history,
S Appalachian rural life, folk-
tales.

*BLUE RIDGE INSTITUTE
Ferrum VA 24088 (703)365-2121 x
107. Folklore & folklife, music.
Concerts, festivals, TV & radio.

*GOOCHLAND COUNTY MUSEUM
PO Box 602, Goochland VA 23063
(804)457-4529. Folklore coll.

*HARRISONBURG-ROCKINGHAM
  HISTORICAL SOCIETY
301 S Main St, Harrisonburg VA
22801 (703)434-4762. Local folklore
collection.

*THE MARINERS MUSEUM
Museum Dr, Newport News VA 23606
(804)595-0368. Ship stuff, inc
folklore.

*COLONIAL WILLIAMSBURG
Goodwin Bldg, Williamsburg VA 23185
(804)229-1000. reconstruction of
old colony capital. Folk crafts.

PRINT

*ALEXANDRIA GAZETTE
717 N St Asaph St, Alexandria VA
22314 (703)549-0004 x 228. Mary
Jane Solomon.

NELSON COUNTY TIMES
PO Box 90, Amherst VA 24521.

*DUCKBERG TIMES
843 N Jefferson St, Arlington VA
22205. Bill Asp.

CHARLOTTESVILLE OBSERVER
310 E Market St, Charlottesville VA
22901. Kay Peaslee.

*DAILY PROGRESS
PO Box 3090, Charlottesville VA
22906. Tim Kerr.

RURAL VIRGINIAN
PO Box 278, Charlottesville VA
22903.

W ALBEMARLE CNTY BULLETIN
PO Box 278, Crozet VA 22932. Jim
Crosby.

NEWS GAZETTE
20 W Nelson St, Lexington VA 24450.

CENTRAL VIRGINIAN
PO Box 464, Louisa VA 23093.

*LYNCHBURG NEWS & DAILY ADV
PO Box 10129, Lynchburg VA 24506
(804)237-2941. Michael McGowan.

*DAILY PRESS-TIMES HERALD
7505 Warwick Blvd, Newport News VA
23607 (804)247-4794.

*VIRGINIAN-PILOT and LEDGER STAR
150 W Brambleton Ave, Norfolk VA
23501 (804)446-2338.

*PROGRESS-INDEX
15 Franklin St, Petersburg VA 23801
(703)732-3456.

*RICHMOND TIMES-DISPATCH
PO Box C-3233, Richmond VA 23293
(804)649-6362. Clarke Bustard.

*ROANOKE TIMES & WORLD NEWS
201 W Campbell Ave, Roanoke VA
24010 (7030981-3325. Sandra Kelly.

GREENE COUNTY RECORD
PO Box 90, Standardsville VA 22973.

STAUNTON NEWS-LEADER
PO Box 59, Staunton VA 24401.

NEWS-VIRGINIAN
PO Drawer 1027, Waynesboro VA
22980.

RADIO

*WETA (NPR-90.9)
5217 N 19th Rd, Alexandria VA
22207 (703)998-2790. Mary Cliff.
Folk progs. Serves DC area.

WKDE
PO Box 512, Attavista VA 24517.

WODY
Drawer 231, Bassett VA 224055.

WKEX
1501 Lark La, Blacksburg VA 24060.

*WUVT (90.7)
VA Polytechnic, 352 Squires Ctr,
Blacksburg VA 24061 (703)552-0644.
Brad Feinman. CP: COLLEGIATE TIMES
2/wk 13000.

*WTJU (91.3)
U of VA, 711 Newcomb Hall Stn,
Charlottesville VA 22901 (804)924-
3418. Cindy Swiztlowski. Folk Sun
1pm-2am. Intl, acoustic, bluegrass,
women's. Interviews. Concerts. CP:
CAVALIER 14K, JOURNAL 11K daily;
DECLARATION weekly 10K.

WKBY
Rte 2, Box 105A, Chatham VA 24531.

WQBX
PO Box 2288, Christiansburg VA
24073.

*WGMU
George Mason U, 4400 University Dr,
Fairfax VA 22153 (703)232-3590.

*WFLS
616 Amelia St, Fredericksburg VA
22401. Sonny Ludlam.

WNRG
Grundy VA 24614.

*WWHS (91.7)
Hampden-Sydney Coll, Box 606,
Hampden VA 23943 (804)223-8773.
CP: TIGER 2x monthly 1400.

WKCY
PO Box 1107, harrisonburg VA 22801.

WMRA (NPR-90.7)
James Madison U, S Main St,
Harrisonburg VA 22807 (703)433-
6221. Charles Gills. CP: BREEZE 2x
weekly 7000.

*WLUR
Washington & Lee Univ, 301 Reid
Ave, Lexington VA 24450 (703)463-
8445.

WREL
Box 902, Lexington VA 24450.

WLSA
Box 8000, Louisa VA 23093.

WWPD
Box 1390, Lynchburg VA 2430353.

WMEV
PO Box 470, Marion VA 24354.

WHRO
400 Hampton Blvd, Norfolk VA 25508.
Bob Zentz.

WNOR
700 Monticello Ave, Norfolk VA
23510.

WVRU (89.9)
Radford U, Box 5784, Radford VA
24142 (703)731-5171. Sharon
Gochenour. CP: TARTAN wkly 3800.

WRIC
Box 838, Richlands VA 24641.

*WDCE (90)
U of Richmond, Box 85, Richmond VA
23173 (804)285-6211. Eric Compton.
CP: COLLEGIAN wkly 3000.

WRXL
7100 Bethlehem Rd, Richmond VA
23228 (804)282-9731. Paul Shogrue.

WKBA
2043 10th St, NE, Roanoke VA 24012.

WEER
Box 817, Warrenton VA 22186 (703)
347-1250.

WKCW
Box 740, Warrenton VA 22186. Stu
Brooks.

*WCWM
William & Mary Coll, Williamsburg
VA 23185 (804)229-2600. Mark Davis.
CP: FLAT HAT weekly 7000.

STORE

*RAMBLIN' CONRAD'S
871 N Military Hwy, Norfolk VA
23502 (804)461-3655. Bob Zentz.
Instruments, accessories, books,
records, tuition.

WASHINGTON

*SEATTLE PUBLIC LIBRARY
1000 4th Ave, Seattle WA 98104
(206)625-4881. Funding info.

*SPOKANE PUBLIC LIBRARY
W 906 Main Ave, Spokane WA 99201
(509)838-3361. Funding info.

*SWAP NORTHWEST
2130 140th Pl SE, Bellevue WA 98005
(206)641-5356. Lynn Waring. Booking
consortium.

VENUES

ARLINGTON FOLKLORE SOCSIETY
11308 Grandview Rd, Arlington WA
98223. Lenny Silver.

*ASHFORD FRIENDS OF TRAD MUS
Box 204, Ashford WA 98304 (206)569-
2991. Paul Nerge.

*APPLEJAM
220 Union, Olympia WA (206)866-
9301.

*CENTRUM
Box 1158, Port Townsend WA 98368
(206)385-3102.

*PALOUSE FOLK MUSIC CLUB
NW 1220 Haven Circle, Pullman WA
99163 (509)332-5047. Dan Mahr.
Seats 200.

WA OLDTIME FIDDLERS ASSN
410 Skylark Dr, Remerton WA 98312.
Roberta Ponichill. Newsletter.

*BACKSTAGE
2208 NW Market, Seattle WA 98107
(206)789-6953. Bookings: Jack Burg
(206)682-3200. Varied music,
several nights. Seats 200.

*COOPERS
8065 Lake City Way, Seattle WA
(206)522-2923. Varied music,
several nights.

*MURPHY'S FOLK PUB
2110 N 45th, Seattle WA (206)634-
2210. Music 7 nights.

*NEW MELODY TAVERN
5213 Ballard Ave NW, Seattle WA
(206)782-3480. Dance & jam Monday,
music Tues-Sat: Wed jazz, Thurs
open mike.

*RAINY TOWN FOLK MUSIC CLUB
Held at Ross Hall, 262 NW 43rd,
Seattle. Run by Seattle FS, booked
by John O'Connor, (206)323-2838.
Varied acoustic music, strong
trad/ethnic bias. No sound system.
Books 3 mo in advance. Fridays.
Seats 75.

*SEATTLE FOLKLORE SOCIETY
305 Harrison St, Seattle WA 98109
(206)625-4410. Scott Nagel.

*UNCLE MYRON'S RESTAURANT
Kirkland's New Parkplace Ctr,
Central Way, Seattle WA (206)827-
4344. Acoustic music Fri-Sat.

*AHAB'S WHALE
N 1221 Stevens, Spokane WA 99201
(509)327-9778. Kent Leach. Bar,
with live music some nights. Seats
160.

*SPOKANE FOLKLORE SOCIETY
PO Box 141, Spokane WA 99210 (509)
624-5418. Catherine Brooks. One
concert/month. Various venues, up
to 300 seats.

*VICTORY MUSIC
PO Box 7518, Bonney Lake Bridge,
Sumner WA 98390 (206)863-6617.
Chris Lunn. Musicians' co-op for
folk, jazz, acoustic music. Open
mikes, kids' concerts, musician
referral, seminars. Publish VM
REVIEW (see below).

*ANTIQUE SANDWICH
5102 N Pearl, Tacoma WA (206)752-
4069. Open mike Tues, other nights.

FESTIVALS

*AMERICAN FIDDLE TUNES FEST
Held at Ft Worden State Park. PO
Box 1158, Port Townsend WA 98368
(206)385-3102. Frank Ferrel. Trad &
oldtime. Concerts, dances,
workshops. Late Jun.

*COLUMBIA RIVER BLUEGRASS FEST
PO Box 1037, Stevenson WA 98648.
Early July.

*NORTHWEST FOLKLIFE FESTIVAL
Held at Seattle Ctr. 305 Harrison
St, Seattle WA 98109 (206)625-4410.
Scott Nagel. Varied music, dance,
crafts, food. Includes Sandy
Bradley's Instrument Auction (206)
547-4456. Free. Late May.

WASHINGTON STATE FAIR
Interstate Fairgrounds, Spokane WA
99210 (509)535-1766. August.

MUSEUMS

*ANACORTES MUSEUM
1305 8th St, Anacortes WA 98221
(206)293-5198. Musical instruments.

*PACIFIC CNTY HISTORICAL SOC
PO Box P, South Bend WA 98586 (206)
875-5224. Maritime lore.

PRINT

*JOURNAL-AMERICAN
PO Box 90130, Bellevue WA 98009-
0130 (206)453-4253. Barbara Hanna.

*HERALD
PO Box 1277, 1155 State St,
Bellingeham WA 98227 (206)676-2620.

*HERALD
PO Box 930, Everett WA 98206
(206)339-3000.

*THE ROCKET
Rocket Towers, 2322 2nd Ave,
Seattle WA 98121 (206)587-4001.
Rebecca Brown, Folk Music Editor.
Monthly. Listings, interviews,
reviews.

*SEATTLE POST-INTELLIGENCER
521 Wall St, Seattle WA 98111
(206)448-8396.

*SEATTLE TIMES
PO Box 70, Seattle WA 98111 (206)
464-2583. Donna Fry, Arts Ed.

*VICTORY MUSIC REVIEW
PO Box 7518, Bonney Lake Bridge,
Sumner WA 98390 (206)863-6617.
Chris Lunn. Monthly. Jazz, folk,
acoustic music & dance. News,
reviews, listings, interviews.
Great.

*SPOKANE CHRONICLE and
   SPOKESMAN-REVIEW
W 999 Riverside, Spokane WA 99210
(509)459-5492. Tom Sowa.

*TACOMA NEWS TRIBUNE
PO Box 1100, Tacoma WA 98411 (206)
597-8673. Pat McCoid.

*COLUMBIAN
710 W 8th St, Vancouver WA 98660
(206)694-3391.

*HERALD-REPUBLIC
PO Box 9668, Yakima WA 98909
(509)248-1251.

RADIO

*KBCS (91.3)
Bellevue Community Coll, 3000
Lauderholm Circle, Bellevue WA
98007 (206)641-2329. Lindsey
Ellison. Folk, blues, bluegrass.

*KUGS (89.3)
W WA State Coll, 410 Viking Union,
516 High St, Bellingham WA 98225.
Andy Potter. Folk, blues, intl,
bluegrass, CP: WESTERN FRONT 2x
weekly 8000.

KGTS (ABC-91.3)
Walla Walla Coll, College Place WA
99324 (509)527-2991. David Bell.

*KAOS
Evergreen State Coll, CAB 305,
Olympia WA 98505 (206)866-5267.
Chris Metz, Dale Knuth. Folk 5 days
a week. CP: COOPER POINT JNL wkly
4000.

*KZUU (90.7FM, 89.1 cable)
Washington State U, Compton Union
Bldg, 3rd fl, Pullman WA 99164
(509)335-2208. Matt Yarberry. Folk
progs. PG. CP: DAILY EVERGREEN
14500.

*KEZX (99)
PO Box 31319, Seattle WA 98103.
Peyton Meys, Cyndi Bemmel. Folk.

KING (98.1)
333 Dexter Ave N, Seattle WA 98109
(206)343-3981. Dick Bailey.

KING TV (Chan 5)
333 Dexter Ave N, Seattle WA 98109
(206)343-3000. Chris Lenz.

KIRO
3rd & Broad Sts, Seattle WA 98121.
Chantelle Scott.

KOMO-TV
5th & Broad Sts, Seattle WA 98121.
Dick Foley.

*KUOW (NPR-94.9)
U of WA, 325 CMU, DS-50, Seattle WA
98195 (206)543-2710. Greg Porter.
Folk & ethnic programs. CP: DAILY
18000.

KBPX (NPR-91.1)
2319 N Monroe, Spokane WA 99205
(509)328-5729. Vernice Cohen, Jo'an
Jacobus.

*KWRS (90.3)
Whitworth Coll, Spokane WA 99251
(509)466-1000 x 575. Scott
Campbell.

*KPLU (NPR-88.5)
Pacific Lutheran U, Tacoma WA 98447
(206)535-7758. Craig Hansen. Mainly
jazz. CP: MOORING MAST weekly 3500.

KTCI
4500 Steilacoom Blvd SW, Tacoma WA
98499.

*KUPS (90.1)
U of Puget Sound, 1500 N Warner,
Tacoma WA 98416 (206)756-3277. Mark
Miller. CP: PUGET SOUND TRAIL
weekly 2500.

*KVTI (90.9)
Clover Park Voc-Tech Institute,
4500 Steilacoom Blvd SW, Tacoma WA
98499-4098. Broadcasts "Victory
Music" live from Antique Sandwich,
Tues 7-10 pm.

*KWCW
Whitman Coll, Walla Walla WA 99362
(509)527-5283.

STORES

EARLY WOODWINDS
513 Flora Vista Rd NE, Olympia WA
98506. Norman Sahl. Instruments,
accessories, etc.

*THE BANJO EMPORIUM
212 N 85th, Seattle WA 98103
(206)784-4141. Instruments,
instruction.

*GALWAY TRADERS
7518 15th Ave NW, Seattle WA 98117
(206)784-9343. Celtic records,
tapes, books.

*MONTE VISTA GUITAR SHOP
8328 S Tacoma Way, Tacoma WA 98499
(206)588-7752. Instruments,
instruction.

WEST VIRGINIA

*KANAWHA CNTY PUBLIC LIBRARY
123 Capitol St, Charleston WV 25301
(304)343-4646. Funding info.

*WV COUNCIL OF CULTURAL
    COORDINATORS
307 E Moore Hall, WVU, Morgantown
WV 26506 (304)293-4406. Cindy
Stillings, Pres. Booking
consortium.

*WV DEPT OF CULTURE & HISTORY
Arts & Humanities Div, Capitol
Complex, Charleston WV 25305
(304)348-0240. Allen B Withers.
Newsletter 4/yr listing festivals,
etc.

VENUES

*FOOTMAD - KANAWHA VALL FRIENDS
    OF OLDTIMEMUSIC & DANCE
PO Box 1684, Charleston WV 25326
(304)988-0702. Pam Curry. Concerts,
monthly square-dances, workshops,
fest, FOOTPRINT 12/yr.

*AUGUSTA HERITAGE ARTS WORKSHOP
Davis & Elkins Coll, Elkins WV
26241 (304)636-1903. Doug Hill.
Classes in folk, bluegrass, blues,
more.

*CREATIVE ARTS COUNCIL
PO Box 1878, Elkins WV 26241. Some
events.

*ELKINS COUNTRY DANCE SOC
PO Box 2436, Elkins WV 26241
(304)636-6710. Mary Ladstatter.
Occasional concerts, house
concerts, monthly square dances.
THREE FORKS OF CHEAT.

WV FOLKLORE SOCIETY
Box 446, Fairmont WV 25301.
Journal.

FESTIVALS

*AUGUSTA FESTIVAL
Davis & Elkins Coll, Elkins WV
26241 (304)636-1903. Doug Hill.
Trad folk, bluegrass, blues. Mid-
Aug.

JOHN HENRY FOLK FESTIVAL
PO Box 135, Princeton WV 24740.
Late August.

*SUMMERSVILLE BLUEGRASS COUNTRY
    MUSIC FESTIVAL
PO Box 96, Summersville WV 26651
(304)872-3145. Late June, also
early Sept.

*VANDALIA GATHERING
WV Dept of Culture & History, Arts
& Humanities Div, Capitol Complex,
Charleston WV 25305 (304)348-0240.
Allen B Withers. May.

*WV STATE FOLK FESTIVAL
200 High St, Glenville WV 26351
(304)462-7361 x 224. Diane L Bach.
June.

MUSEUM

*WV STATE MUSEUM
Capitol Complex, Charleston WV
25305 (304)348-0232. WV Folk arts,
history. Trad music festivals.

PRINT

*CHARLESTON DAILY MAIL
1001 Virginia St E, Charleston WV
25301 (304)348-4809. Kelly King.

*HERALD-DISPATACH
PO Box 2017, Huntington WV 25720
(304)536-2765.

*PARKERSBURG NEWS and SENTINEL
519 Juliana St, Parkersburg WV
26101 (304)485-1891.

*WHEELING INTELLIGENCER and
  NEWS-REGISTER
1500 Main St, Wheeling WV 26003
(304)233-0100.

RADIO

*WVBC
Bethany Coll, Bethany WV 26032
(304)829-7853.

* WVPN (NPR-88.5)
WV Public Radio, Capitol Complex,
Bldg 6, #424, Charleston WV 25305
(304)348-3239. Andy Ridenour, Larry
Gross. Produce MOUNTAIN STAGE, live
widely syndicated show. Sun 5-7pm.

WKKW
Box 2696, Clarksburg WV 26301.

*WVMR (1370AM)
Dunmore WV 24934.

WKGA
Old Rte 50, Grafton WV 26354. Dave
Elkington.

*WSYJ
WV State Coll, Box 31, Institute
WV 25112 9304)766-3648.

*WWVU (91.7)
U of WV, Mountain Lair, Morgantown
WV 26505 (304)293-3329. Tom
Koetting. CP: DAILY ATHENAEAUM
15K.

WMOV
Box 649, Ravenswood WV 26164. Ron
Osborne.

WKLC
100 Kanawha Terr, St Albans WV
25177. Neil Lasher

*WITB
Salem Coll, Salem WV 26462 (304)
782-5230. John Price.

WISCONSIN

*MARQUETTE U MEMORIAL LIBRARY
1415 W Wisconsin Ave, Milwaukee WI
53233 (414)224-1515. Funding info.

VENUES

*AMHERST HOUSE CONCERTS
6580 County K, Amherst WI 54406
(715)824-2017. Tom Pease.

*LAWRENCE COFFEEHOUSE
Lawrence U, PO Box 599, Appleton WI
54912 (414)735-6600. Charlie
Newhall. Some concerts.

*"CRAZY PAUL'S" MURRAY FOLK
Rte 1, Bruce WI 54848.

*WISCONSIN FOLKLIFE CTR
Folklore Village Farm, Rte 3,
Dodgeville WI 53533 (608)924-3725.
Philip Martin. Upper Midwest trad
folklife. Archive.

*THE JOYNT
322 Water St, Eau Claire WI 54703.
Bill Nolte. 10-12 shows a year.
Seats 100.

*NEW DELI
411 Galloway St, Eau Claire WI
54701 (715)832-6697. Bob Lowther.
Thur-Sat. Seats 110.

*GREEN APPLE FRIENDS OF FOLK
Rte 1, Box 318, Fremont WI 54940
(414)446-3906. John Wilson.

*MILL ROAD DELI
219 E Mill Rd, Galesville WI 54630
(608)582-4438. Diana Russell.

*BADGER FOLKLORE SOC
Rte 1, Box 110, Gillingham WI
54633.

*BLUE WHALE COFFEEHSE
U of WI, Good Times Prog, SS-1908,
Green Bay WI 54301 (414)465-2405.
Advisor. Every 2 wks. Seats 100.

WHEATBERRY NATURAL FOODS
407 W Milwaukee, Jonesville WI
53545 (608)755-1828. Music Fri/Sat.

*THE PUMP HOUSE
119 King St, La Crosse WI 54601
(608)785-1434. David Sailer.
Concerts 2/month. Seats 140.

*VITTERBO COLL FINE ARTS CTR
815 S 9th St, La Crosse WI 54601
(608)784-040. Also has interesting
museum.

*CLUB DE WASH
636 W Washington St, Madison WI
53703 (608)256-3302. Toni Zimar.
Comedy, some folk.

*MADISON FOLK MUSIC SOC
PO Box 665, Madison WI 53701 (608)
258-1689. Pam Mansfield. Concerts,
house concerts, singalongs 2nd Weds
@ 2416 Gregory St. MAD FOLK NEWS.
Festival in April.

*MIDWEST PEOPLE'S MUSIC NETWORK
1432 Morrison, #1, Madison WI
53703.

PICKIN' & GRINNIN' WORKSHOPS
4222 Milwaukee St, Madison WI 53714
(608)249-4889.

*WILD HOG IN THE WOODS
  COFFEEHOUSE
306 N Brooks St, Madison WI 53715
(608)835-3560. Bill Bennett. Music,
storytelling, Thur/Fri. Barn
dances.

*WI FOLKLORE & FOLKLIFE SOC
442 N Few St, Madison WI 53703.
Richard Marsh.

*GOLDEN RING HOUSE CONCERTS
1004 S 10th St, Manitowoc WI 54220
(414)684-5242. Fritz Schuler.

*ALVERNO FOLK CENTER
Alverno College, 3401 S 39th St,
Milwaukee WI 53215 (414)647-3999.
Concerts, workshops, classes,
festivals. Calendar.

*CLUB GARIBALDI
4501 S Superioer, Milwaukee WI.
Open mike every Sun.

*THE FOLK SONG CIRCLE
PO Box 9222, Milwaukee WI 53202.

*INTERNATIONAL INSTITUTE
2810 W Highland Rd, Milwaukee WI
53208 (414)933-0521. Folk fair.

*MILWAUKEE IRISH FEST WORKSHOPS
W224 S 7000 Guthrie Rd, Big Bend WI
53103 (414)662-2071. Cease
Grinwald. Puppetry & consuming for
Irish Fest. Mid-June.

*MILWAUKEE PERFORMING
  ARTS CENTER
929 N Water St, Milwaukee WI 53202
(414)273-7121. Mason Landrum.
Concerts.

*SCHLITZ AUDUBON CENTER
1111 E Brown Deer Rd, Milwaukee WI
53217 (414)352-2880. David Stokes.
Concerts 1/month. Open Tues-Sun.

*UWM FOLK CENTER
U of WI at Milwaukee, School of
Fine Arts, PO Box 413, Milwaukee WI
53201.

STUDENT CTR COFFEEHOUSE
U of WI, Platteville WI 53818
(608)342-1491. Tue-Thur. CP:
EXPONENT weekly 4100.

*BLACK HAWK FOLK SOCIETY
Rte 3, Box 109K, Wautoma WI 54982
(414)787-4544. Tim Paegelow.

FESTIVALS

*ASHLAND FOLK FEST
Northland Coll, Student Affairs
Office, Ashland WI 54806 (715)682-
4531.

DOOR COUNTY FOLK FEST
10055 GR Hwy 57, Sister Bay WIO
54234 (414)854-2986. Gerhard
Bernhard. Intl folk, dance, storytelling, workshops. Kids' events.
Late July..

*FAMILY MUSIC FESTIVAL
Held at Cave of the Mounds, Blue
Mounds. WI Folklife Ctr, Rte 3,
Folklore Village Farm, Dodgeville
WI 53533 (608)924-3725. Philip
Martin. Trad, ethnic, & oldtime
polka music. Labor Day weekend.

*GREAT NORTHERN BLUEGRASS
PO Box 625, Crandon WI 54420.

*GREAT RIVER TRAD MUSIC
  & CRAFTS FAIR
323 S 23rd St, La Crosse WI 54601.
Late Aug.

*IRISH FEST
Held on Summerfest Grounds. PO Box
599, Milwaukee WI 53201 (414)466-
6640. Ed Ward. Music, dance,
crafts, puppets, Irish sports,
theater, clan reunions, workshops.
Mid-August.

*MADISON FOLK SINGING FESTIVAL
PO Box 665, Madison WI 53701 (608)
258-1689. Pam Mansfield. Concerts,
workshops. Emphasis on audience
participation. Mid-April.

*MAKIN' JAM, ETC
Rte 1, Box 246A, Bowler WI 54416
(715)793-4709. Skip Jones.

*SHAWANO OLDTIME MUSIC
  & CRAFTS FEST
Box 213, Shawano WI 54166 (715)526-
9295. Joel Kroenke. Concerts,
workshops. Aug.

*WHITE PINE JAMBOREE
Rte 1, Box 123, Boulder Junction WI
54512 (715)385-2802. Charlie
Spencer.

MUSEUMS

*FOLKLORE VILLAGE FARM
Rte 3, Dodgeville WI 53533
(608)924-3725. Jane Farwell. Rural
folk ctr. Various festivals.
Archives. Write for list.

*OZAUKEE COUNTY HISTORICAL SOC
  PIONEER VILLAGE
W61 N619 Mequon St, Cedarburg WI
53012 (414)377-4510. Pioneer
history, folklore.

*OLD WORLD WISCONSIN
Rte 2, Box 10, Eagle WI 53119 (414)
594-2116. Folkways.

*MANITOWOC MARITIME MUSEUM
809 S 8th St, Manitowoc WI 54220
(414)684-0218. Great Lakes
shipping. Festivals.

PRINT

*APPLETON POST-COURANT
Box 59, Appleton WI 54912 (414)733-
4411. Tom Richards, Mus Ed.

WISCONSIN BLUEGRASS NEWS
PO Box 64, Eagle River WI 54521.

*GREEN BAY PRESS-GAZETTE
435 E Walnut St, Green Bay WI 54305
(414)435-4114.

*KENOSHA NEWS
715 58th St, Kenosha WI 53140 (414)
657-100. Elaine Edwards, Mus Ed.

*LA CROSSE TRIBUNE
401 N 3rd St, La Crosse WI 54601
(608)252-6482. Anita Bird.

BADGER HERALD and CARDINAL
U of WI, Madison WI 53706. BH:
weekly 15K, DC: daily 10K.

*CAPITAL TIMES
PO Box 8060, Madison WI 53706 (608)
252-6482.

*WISCONSIN STATE JOURNAL
PO Box 8058, Madison WI 53708 (608)
252-6182. Carmen Elsner, Mus Ed.

*MILWAUKEE JOURNAL
333 W State St, Milwaukee WI 53201
(414)223-5497.

*MILWAUKEE SENTINEL
918 N 4th St, Milwaukee WI 53201
(414)224-2269.

*RACINE JOURNAL-TIMES
212 4th St, Racine WI 53403 (414)
634-3322.

*WAUSAU/MERRILL DAILY HERALD
800 Scott St, Wausau WI 54401 (715)
842-2101. Jamie Orcutt.

RADIO

*WLFN
Lawrence U, 113 S Lake St, Appleton
WI 54911 (414)735-6566.

WLBL (930AM)
Auburndale WI 54412. 6 hrs folk.

WBCR (88.1)
Beloit Coll, Beloit WI 53511
(608)365-3391. Carl Balson. CP:
ROUND TABLE weekly 1800.

WHSA (89.9)
Brule WI 54820. 6 hrs folk.

WHAD (90.7)
Delafield WI 53018. 6 hrs folk.

*WUEC
U of WI, 170 Fine Arts Ctr, Eau
Claire WI 54701 (715)836-4170. Doug
Rosenberg. CP: SPECTATOR wkly 8K.

*WGBW
U of WI, Green Bay WI 54301 (414)
465-2444. Glenn Slaats. Folk.

WPNE (89.3)
Green Bay WI 54301. 6 hrs folk.

*WOJB (88.9)
Rte 2, Hayward WI 54843. Dick
Brooks, Sandy Lyon. Folk.

WHLA (90.3)
La Crosse WI 54601. 6 hrs folk.

WSLU
U of WI, 1725 State St, La Crosse
WI 54601 (608)785-8546. CP: RACQUET
weekly 5000.

*WERN (88.7)
821 University Ave, Madison WI
53706 (608)263-2243. Judy Woodward.
5 hrs folk.

*WHA - WISCONSIN PUBLIC RADIO
821 University Ave, Madison WI
53706. Tom Martin-Erickson
(608)263-2243; Judy Woodward (608)
263-8162. SIMPLY FOLK.

*WORT (89.7)
PO Box 3219, Madison WI 53704 (608)
256-2695. Danny Kahn.

WHWC (88.3)
Menomonie WI 53051. 6 hrs folk.

*WVSS
Stout U, 120 Broadway, Menomonie WI
54751 (715)232-2332.

WFMR (96.5)
711 W Capitol Dr, Milwaukee WI
53201 (414)372-8000.

*WMSE (91.7)
Milwaukee School of Engineering,
Box 644, Milwaukee WI 53201 (414)
277-7247. Richard Nitelinger FOLK
CITY Sun 8pm. Live performances,
interviews, albums, taped concerts.
CP: INGENIUM monthly 2000.

WUWM (PR-89.7)
U of WI, Box 413, Milwaukee WI
53201 (414)963-4664. Kim Grehn. CP:
POST 2x wkly, 10K; INVICTUS 2x
monthly 5K.

WYMS
PO Drawer 10K, Milwaukee WI 53201.
Ethnic programs.

*WRST (90.3)
U of WI, Oshkosh WI 54901 (414)424-
4343. Ted Nehring. CP: ADVANCE
TITAN weekly 11000.

*WSP
WI State U, 42 Pioneer Tower UW,
Platteville WI 53818 (608)342-1165.

*WXPR (91.7)
PO Box 254, Rhinelander WI 54501.

*WWSP
U of WI, CAC, Rm 101, Stevens Point
WI 54481. John Bigus.

*WSSU (91.3)
U of WI, 1800 Grand Ave, Superior
WI 54880 (715)394-8404. Brian
McDonald. CP: PROMETHEAN wkly 1800.

*WYRE
U of Washington, 1500 University
Dr, Waukesha WI 53186 (414)521-
5201. Leila Emminson.

WHRM (90.9)
Wausau WI 54401. 6 hrs folk.

WSUW
U of WI, 301 Hyer Hall, Whitewater
WI 53190 (414)472-1079. CP: ROYAL
PURPLE weekly 7000.

STORES

*SPRUCE TREE MUSIC
851 E Johnson, Madison WI 53701
(608)255-2254.

WYOMING

*LARAMIE COUNTY CC LIBRARY
1400 E College Dr, Cheyenne WY
82001 (307)634-5853. Funding info.

VENUES

*POWDER RIVER ARTS COUNCIL
PO Box 966, Gillette WY 82716. Jan
Gosse. Some concerts.

*UNIV OF WYOMING
Cultural Affairs Committee, PO Box
3943, Univ Sta, Laramie WY 82071
(307)766-6250. Patricia Tate. Some
concerts. CP: BRANDING IRON
daily 10000.

*CENTRAL WYOMING COLL
Student Activities, 2660 Peck Ave,
Riverton WY 82501 (307)856-9291.
Tonia Burnette. Some concerts.

FESTIVALS

ˣTETON COUNTY FIDDLE CONTEST
Held at Teton County Fairgrounds.
PO Box 606, Jackson WY 83001.
Bluegrass. Late July.

WYOMING STATE FAIR
Drawer 10, Douglas WY 82633
9307)358-3473. August.

MUSEUMS

*WYOMING STATE MUSEUM
Barrett Bldg, 22nd & Central Ave,
Cheyenne WY 82002 (307)777-7510.
State history & culture.

*PIONEER MUSEUM
630 Lincoln St, Lander WY 82520
(307)332-4137. Local history.

*ANNA MILLER MUSEUM
Delaware & Washington Park, PO Box
698, Newcastle WY 82701 (307)746-
4188. Folk art, archives.

PRINT

*CASPER STAR-TRIBUNE
PO Box 80, Casper WY 82602
(307)266-0585.

*WYOMING EAGLE and
STATE TRIBUNE
110 E 17th St, Cheyenne WY 82001
(307)634-3361.

RADIO

KUWR (NPR-91.9)
Box 3984, University Sta, Laramie
WY 82071 (307)766-4240. John Price.

KTAK
Box 393, Riverton WY 82501.

PUERTO RICO

*UNIV DEL SAGRADO CORAZON
M.M.T. Guevara Library, Correo
calle Loiza, Santurce PR 00914
(809)728-1515 x 343. Funding info.

VENUES

HATILLO CULTURAL CTR
Box 554, Hatillo PR 00659 (809)898-
3840. Charles Aguilar.

*FNDN ARTISTICA DE PONCE
PO Box 943, Ponce PR 00731 (809)
842-2096. Catalina Hoolland.

*UNIV OF PUERTO RICO
Cultural Activities, Box V, UPR
Sta, Rio Pedras PR 00931 (809)751-
2023. Dr. Francis Schwartz, Dir.
Some concerts.

INST DE CULTURA PR
Aptdo 4184, San Juan PR 00905
(809)723-2686. Oscar Mendoza
Riollano. Info Ctr.

PR TOURISM CO
PO Box 3072, San Juan PR 00903
(809)723-3135/722-1513. Festival.

CTR FOR PERFORMING ARTS
Aptdo 41227, Minillas Sta, Santurce
PR 00940 (809)727-7070. James
Stewart.

FESTIVALS

INTL FOLKLORIC FESTIVAL
Calla Francisco Sein 426, Hato Rey
PR 00917 (809)759-7923. Irene
McLean.

LE LO LAI FESTIVAL
PR Tourism Co, Box 3072, San Juan
PR 00903 (809)723-3135/722-1513.

MASKS FESTIVAL
Box 554, Hatillo PR 00659 (809)898-
3840. Charles Aguilar. Dec.

PUERTO RICAN MUSIC FESTIVAL
Box 4184, San Juan PR 00905
(809)723-2686. Nov-Dec.

SAN SEBASTIAN STREETFEST
Box 2053, San Juan PR 00903
(809)725-7559. Rafaela Balladares.
December.

MUSEUM

*MUSEO DE PUERTO RICO
Calle del Cristo 253, Old San Juan
PR 00901 (809)723-2320. History,
folk, Indian collections.

VIRGIN ISLANDS

*COLL OF THE VIRGIN ISLANDS
Library, St Thomas VI 00801 (809)
774-1252. Funding info.

VENUE

*REICHHOLD CTR FOR THE ARTS
Coll of the Virgin Islands, St
Thomas VI 00801 (809)774-8475.
Lawrence O Benjamin. Concerts.

MUSEUM

*CHRISTIANSTED NATL HISTORIC SITE
Church St, PO Box 160,
Christiansted, St Croix VI 00820
(404)221-6040. Danish colonial
development.

Taking Care of Business

by Heather Wood

So you've been performing for some time, and you've reached the Catch-22 point: while you're out on the road performing, you haven't the time to dig around for more gigs. "Right," you say to yourself, "What I need is a Good Agent." There is no doubt that a good agent is a performer's best friend. However, good agents are about as common as (insert favorite metaphor). And of course the good agents are already handling as many aspiring stars as they can. So you probably shouldn't waste your time and theirs by trying to persuade them to adopt you until you have, by your own efforts, reached the point at which you are making at least $200 a gig, and working four nights a week. Even then, some simple arithmetic will tell you that you're not a very attractive proposition to an agent, who is only making 10 or 15% of your income.

If you are seriously considering approaching an agent, you will need to be armed with the following: (1) A list of the places you have played, in date order, with details of audience and income. Just put the name and city for each venue. If the agent agrees to take you on, you can supply further contact information. (2) A list of contracted future dates. (3) A list of prospective future dates--people who have expressed an interest in booking you. (4) Your press-kit (see below).

It's a good idea to check out an agent by asking any of the musicians you know who already work with them, and by asking club organizers.

You should have a contract with your agent specifying the following: (1) What percentage of what you are to pay them. "Of what" because a club may pay you a fee that includes an allowance for travel. (2) What each of you will pay for in the way of phone calls, press-kit copies, postage, photos, etc. (3) How you will handle gigs you get for yourself. (4) A time limit, and details of notice required to terminate the contract. This can be very important if you become really successful, and wish to change your agent.

Your agent should supply you with business cards to give to prospective hirers. And good luck.

If you are not yet in a position to attract an agent, what can you do? The ideal interim solution is to have a dedicated person doing your booking on a part-time basis. This is often a spouse or Significant Other (which can be fatal if the relationship collapses, leaving you not knowing whether you are supposed to be in Wyoming or Alabama next week). However. Let's suppose that you are either going to do it yourself, or that you have such a sterling friend. How to start Getting Organized?

You have made a good first step by acquiring this book. Now you need: (1) A loose-leaf notebook, and a writing implement. (2) A telephone, and preferably an answering machine. If you can afford it, get one that you can call in to from the road. (3) A press-kit (see below). (4) An atlas (Rand McNally makes a good one). (5) A calculator. (6) Lots of patience.

There are certain things you need to know about any place you want to approach. If you can afford it, write this up into a form, and make many copies. The essential information includes: name, address, telephone, contact name, days open, size, average ticket price. Stuff you might need includes sound system, how often they will book a given performer (some clubs it's once a year, some it's once a month), is the booking done by one person or a committee, etc.

Pick an area where you hope to play, and a time-frame. Most clubs book several months in advance, so give yourself plenty of time. Look at your atlas, and decide on an area that makes geographical sense. Make up an idealized calendar, with all the clubs in geographical sequence, and the nights on which they run. Then make out a separate sheet for each place you plan to call. If it's somewhere you have already played, have the details of your last gig on the form (date, fee, how many people showed up, etc.). Decide how much money you need contract are: provision of accommodation and meals, sound system (needed, available, who pays for it), method of payment (it can be a problem if someone hands you a check when you were expecting cash to get you to your next gig), names and phone numbers to call on the night, directions, time of soundcheck and set(s), length and number of set(s). Your contract should include all this, plus a "no recording without permission" clause. Make three copies of the contract. Keep one, send two to the club, one to be retained, one to be signed and returned to you promptly. When the signed copy returns, copy it. Keep one copy on file, take the other on the road with you.

Cancellations. These will occur on either side, for various reasons. The general feeling at present seems to be that there's not much one can do about them.

YOUR PRESS-KIT
We went into this in some detail in our first edition, but to summarize:

Make it as professional-looking as possible. Your kit should contain a brief bio about who you are and what you play, a list of places you have performed, a photo, copies of any reviews (until you accumulate these, get letters from places you have played, on their letterhead), and a tape. Copies should be well-typed, clean, grammatically correct. Photos should be 8x10, black and white, glossy, and still viable when reduced to postage-stamp size by newspapers, club calendars, etc. Tapes should be the best quality you can afford--a live tape of your five best numbers performed in front of a good audience is ideal. Avoid hyperbolic adjectives (unless you are quoting a reviewer!).

AUDIENCE BUILDING
Let's hope that everyone who ever hears you will want to hear you again. If they are regulars at a particular club, and the club has a mailing list or newsletter, those people will learn about your next gig there. But if you want to keep them apprised of your itinerary (and, incidentally, build up a possible list of customers for your first or subsequent albums), you can collect all the names and addresses

to make in order for this tour to be viable. You should have a price in mind when you call--and be prepared to negotiate. For every call you make, note on your form the date, time (useful to know when you are likely to catch someone at home), and what is discussed. Also note any promises on your part to send material, and check it off when done.

Now comes the hard work. Making those calls can be gruelling, but will hopefully lead to some gigs. Try to be friendly and polite. Try to call at a civilized time, and ask if it is convenient before launching into your sales pitch (which you might want to write out first, and/or practice on a friend or with a tape recorder). When you reach the right person at the venue, tell them what kind of music you play, and ask if this fits in with their booking policy. If it doesn't, make a note, and pass on. You are not going to change the organizer's mind when you are completely unknown. This is the point at which you should fill out any details missing from your form. If the club holds 500, your chances of getting a gig there without a reputation are slim. If it holds 25, your chances of making money are equally slim.

If the club is responsive to your kind of music, ask how they audition performers--by tape, by word-of-mouth, by personal appearance. Note what they want, and try to supply it.

Once your material has gone out, wait a week or so, and call again. Most club organizers are pretty responsible about reviewing prospective performers, but be prepared to listen to a number of excuses. Make a date to call back (and keep it!). Keep taking notes on your form. You will find, as you talk to more and more people, that they all blur together, and only your written notes will keep you from making egregious mistakes.

If the club is interested, you must now negotiate the fee, etc. Most places will give a guarantee against a percentage. This is where the calculator comes in. You need to know the Gross Potential (number of seats X ticket price) in order to figure out your possible earnings. Other things to be discussed and included in the for your very own mailing list. A computer is obviously ideal for this, but if you can't acquire one (or the use of one), you can buy nifty labels (made by Avery, among others) from your friendly local stationery store that you can run through a photocopier. Try making your own postcards (four will fit onto an 8-1/2 X 11 sheet of thin card which most copyhouses carry). The cost of mailing one is less than for a letter. Pick a bright color which will stand out when put on someone's fridge or noticeboard. If you have a huge list you may want to look into bulk mail, but it can take a while to arrive, many people routinely ignore anything sent this way, and the Post Office will not return dead ones to you, so you will not be able to cull your list efficiently. Having a distinctive logo or type style will build what the ad boys call "product recognition."

ALTERNATIVE VENUES

As well as working the folk circuit, you might consider the possibility of performing in local hospitals, nursing homes, libraries, etc. Some areas are already organized for this (New York, for example, has Hospital Audiences, Inc.). Think seriously about whether you can handle these very different audiences--then put together a proposal letter, and send it to the relevant people (Activities Chairperson is a good title to ask for). Most of these gigs don't pay very well, but they are usually short, so you could do more than one a day. And those performers who have been playing for seniors, kids, and the institutionalized tell us that its a really rewarding experience.

© Heather Wood, 1986.

Records From Scratch

by Leslie Berman

All performers like bragging about their new records; some even like recording and promoting them. But most worry about selling enough of their first record to justify recording more of them. This is because records are seen as proof of artistic merit: as if they were awards conferred on deserving performers. But records are a consumer product-- artists who are already well-known release records by popular demand. New artists release records in hopes of creating interest in their music, and to attract fans. These two dif-

fering circumstances dictate the way records are released for different artists.

Most artists hope that a commercial company will see and hear their talents, and volunteer to enhance the artist's popularity by offering a "record deal"; very few musicians want to start their own record label. Consequently, getting a record deal--a contract for one or more albums--is seen as a substantial measurement of success. And for performers eager to make a full-time living with their music, which usually means building up a national audience via radio, it is an absolute necessity.

If you are an aspiring artist, there are many good reasons for wanting a commercial record deal. An outside company's investment of its resources in your career is a vote of confidence in your talent. You know that recording companies expect to be profit-making. Gambling that you will help them make their profit is more than a gesture on the company's part--it is the embodiment of their belief that the thousands of paid admissions you've garnered will translate to thousands of paid-for souvenirs of your performances. For many artists it's a relief to have experts exerting their skills and time to create the best possible recordings; to resolve technical problems and make and sell records professionally.

But there are good reasons too for maintaining control over the sound and look of your records, and often, a performer can only do this when s/he takes on the whole job personally. Fortunately, several innovations in the recording field have made the equipment less challenging and less costly, and numerous handbooks have been written to make it more practical for non-technicians to do just that.

In the folk field, as in other alternative music fields, having the means and ability to make records inexpensively is essential for artists who might otherwise have no recording outlet. There are many folk music recording companies listed in this directory, but not all of them solicit material from artists unknown to them. Many record only one artist. A number are performer-owned labels. Only a handful have the means to make commercial release of records viable for the many folk performers who would like to be recorded, and whose fans would like to own their records. These factors usually make it advisable for newcomers to record themselves.

You can find many detailed guides to producing and marketing your own records in your local bookstore or chainstore, and when you are actually ready to do so, I urge you to buy one. But for those of you who are intimidated by your ignorance of the process, here is a quick look at the basics:

RECORDING

You will need to start with the highest quality reel-to-reel tape recording you can afford, because some of the sound quality will be lost in the numerous transfers involved in turning your tape into a record.

Plan to record in a professional studio, where you are comfortable, and where their facilities will give you all of the following:

a) an engineer who will work with you from beginning to end of the sessions, so you can build a rapport and be assured that your ideas will be understood and transferred from your imagination to the tape, whenever possible;

b) at least eight and preferably 16 track recording capacity to capture each player separately for a clearer sound;

c) high quality recording tape included in the price;

d) mix-down from eight or sixteen tracks to a stereo master tape;

e) reference tapes of sessions in progress for at-home listening following each session;

f) use of appropriate equipment, including quality microphones, instrument amplifiers, if necessary, sound baffles or separation booths if you are using drums, etc.

THE RECORD

1) Plan ahead for your album cover, inner sleeve, and additional insert materials. Make sure you have a designer, or have yourself designed all label materials, including the round center one with or without the track xxlistings on each side of your LP. Find the highest quality printer who usually does cardboard LP jackets and paper or plastic inner-sleeves for the price you can afford. Remember that most people do judge books and records by their covers. Even your best friends will find it hard to handle your album if the package is unpleasant.

2) Take the master tape to a one-stop plating and pressing plant, or to a plater.

The interim steps in transferring sound from magnetic tape to vinyl are numerous, and some of you will be interested in learning them in detail. Your local plating or pressing plant should be willing to explain the process to you in the estimating stage.

The most important thing to stress here is that each step in the pressing process will diminish the quality of the tape you started with, and will consequently, have a great deal to do with the quality of the next step down the line, and ultimately, of the final product. So insist on the right to see and hear each of the products as they are created. Don't accept shoddy workmanship. Whenever you are unhappy with the results of some step in the process, ask for another try. You, and your audience, will suffer if you don't. Be sure you and the company agree beforehand on customer (that's you) approvals of all products, to protect your rights.

When you give your master tape to the plater, s/he will transfer its sound to etched grooves on a lacquer disc. That disc is a clean, playable, and very fragile copy of your record.
Then the lacquer is plated with a material that dips into the grooves and makes a clean reverse. The upstanding ridges of this plate will be the pattern maker for the next step known as the "mother". From the mother, another reversal will be made, forming the stamper. Two stampers (one for each side of your record) are the final parts necessary to press your records. Stampers wear out from use--if you are planning a large press run, several sets of stampers may be made from the mother, to ensure quality of stamping. In the rare cases where really large press runs are planned, several mothers may be made.
The first pressings from the stampers are known as "test pressings." You will get a test pressing to approve before actual sales copies of your record are pressed. Test pressings are intended to be of the same quality as your final sales product, so listen carefully to the test before giving your approval. This will be your last chance to ensure that your audience will be getting what it will pay for.

In addition to esthetic concerns, when you decide on a pressing plant, you should keep several financial considerations in mind. Does the plant perform all parts of the process, including pasting on the labels, placing the records in inner sleeves, placing the whole in the jackets or album covers, adding other insert materials, and covering the final package with shrink-wrapping (the disposable plastic over-cover)? Do you have to take unfinished parts and ship them elsewhere to complete the packaging? Or will you have to package your records yourself?

The most important cost question you will be asked by the pressing plant will be the state of the vinyl you want for your records. Vinyl comes to the pressing plant in pellets, or in fist-sized bisquits, that will be squeezed between the stampers to press each album individually. You can choose between black and colored vinyls, you can discuss thickness or thinness of pressing. Finally, you will usually have to choose between new or "virgin" vinyl, and used or reprocessed vinyl. Obviously, new vinyl costs more than reprocessed. Real audiophiles say they can hear the difference between new and used vinyl. Maybe you will too.
At New York's Europadisk, where I once watched the whole record-pressing process, the atmosphere is like that of a hospital lab, with green rubber mats running between each of the work areas, and a scrubbed feeling in the extra-clean manufacturing rooms. The stamping machines press fairly slowly, the vinyl oozing into place between the stampers, and around the spindles where the labels are stacked. There are many plants like them that press short runs--small quantities of records, usually with a minimum pressing requirement--at highest quality standards. Look for a pressing plant in your own area, so you can visit it, and see the way it operates, to be sure you will be satisfied with your results.

TAPE & COMPACT DISCS
Some artists make tapes available to their audiences--they feel the portability of tape makes it a better seller for impulse-buyers in concert audiences. You can choose to record tapes too, and offer your audiences a choice. Record pressing companies rarely duplicate cassette tapes, but other companies do so, and some will create a whole package for you, much the same as a record package, with labels, covers, insert materials, shrink-wrap, etc.
A few folk artists are now thinking about recording compact discs. The higher sound quality of the discs, which are played by laser, is indisputable, but the cost of producing them is very high, and there may be few compact disc player-owners among your audiences.

Think carefully about the size of your potential market before investing in your own records, tapes, or compact discs. If you do decide to release yourself, keep quality highest on your priority list, and you'll soon find your music in good company.

© 1986 LESLIE BERMAN

Enough About Me, What Do You Think of Me?

by Roger Dietz

Recently I found myself in a New York City club auditioning a singer/songwriter who wanted a gig at the coffeehouse I book. As I often do, I'd made a special effort to see the artist in concert. Rec ords and demo tapes give me some indication of a performer's ability to entertain, but booking solely from them is dangerous. Only the live audition, sans recording tricks (equalization, multi-tracks, added applause) can truly indicate what a performer might be like in front of my club's audience.

The performer in question had been around for more than ten years, but I had never heard him, and I looked forward to doing so. My luck ran out that night. I don't recall ever having been subjected to such off-key singing. It was a special kind of bad--I suspect the kind that doesn't have to be as bad as it is. This upsets me more than the other kind--the kind you can't do anything about. How was it, I wondered, that someone could make the round of clubs for a decade, yet not know that his singing was embarrassingly bad? More importantly, that his singing could be much better with some work?

The answer was supplied by a friend of the performer, who was the emcee for the evening. She confessed that he always sounded like that, but that he was such a nice guy, none of his fellow performers or friends had the heart to give him the news. Some friends! After ten years on the circuit, he was probably wondering why he wasn't a star. And his friends, who could have provided the timely advice that might have helped make him one, chickened out. If nothing else, at least I would have been spared a trip into New York to tell him what I thought of him.

Now I don't offer criticism unless the performer asks me for some (I don't like to hit anyone with a ton of bricks unless they are prepared for my opinion). I am a performer myself, and I know what it feels like. But I believe that more damage is done to an artist who is not criticized than can be done to one who is.

Criticism has unfairly come to have an unfavorable connotation. But criticism as an art form relating to the performance media, the art of evaluating or analyzing a musical performance based on knowledge and propriety, is of great value to a performer. It's hardly punishment, and therefore should not be thought of negatively. Basically, if a performer cares at all about improving, he or she should seek criticism as an essential means to advancement.

Critical analysis of a performer's merits or demerits, and judgement of the overall performance by an informed or concerned observer, is a fair and logical extension of what an audience does anyway. The difference is that when an audience applauds, remains silent, or heads for the exit, they do so based on a general impression of an act. When a critical analysis of a performance is made by a professional or a concerned observer, the reasons for gut-level reactions can often be discerned. Constructive criticism can be used by open-minded artists, to improve the quality of their performances.

And criticism can't be avoided: it comes with the territory. It's unrealistic to choose to perform, and expect not to be held accountable for one's sins. After all, the audience is doing the artist a favor by being there, not the other way around. By the rules of the game, the performer gets a chance to strut, and the audience gets its chance to respond. Every time a performer walks upon the stage, he or she is fair game for the listener. That goes for the beginner as well as the seasoned veteran.

Most performers prefer a pat on the back to any form of critical analysis, particularly at the end of a hardworked evening of singing and playing his/her heart out to a tough audience in a club or concert hall. It eases the pain. Applause and laughter during a performance are welcome, if the applause is loud and long, and the laughter is in response to one's humorous patter, not one's vocal technique. Monetary remuneration can also be a positive incentive--although this is not often the case in folk music. In the real world where it is not easy to stand up in front of people and entertain them, where fear of the spotlight is often the rule of thumb even among accomplished artists, kind words are sought, not criticism, because anything else might bruise a frail ego.

What a performer usually wants to be told is, "you're great!" And truthfully, this is what drives most musicians and singer/songwriters onward if not upoward in their careers. Onward to the next and subsequent gigs to gig and gig again. Perhaps as an opening act, or a main act in the same small clubs year, after year, with the performer presenting the same set, hoping that persistence will lead the way to the big time. Most performers either get used to this routine, or finally give up and get into the family's kitchen floor-covering business.

What performers should look and listen for is not the sycophantic "you're great" but the more valuable "you could be better, and here is what you might do to become better." Rarely is this input sought, or heeded. Many performers insulate themselves from criticism as a means of protecting themselves. In addition, self-analysis is dangerous stuff unless one has the insight to know what is helpful criticism and what is not. Not everyone has the ability to weed out irrelevant comments and take note of what applies. It helps if one's feet are firmly planted on the ground, and that one has a fair degree of objectivity.

Generally, if a performer asks, "how was I tonight" that really translates into "how good was I tonight?" Most artists don't want the gory details. They want fluff. Many are insecure and understandably so, given all the time and effort that goes into practice and career mechanics. Therefore, the typical performer shuns constructive criticism, and doesn't recognize it when confronted with it. Anything but a rave is taken personally, not professionally.

Even if the performer is secure enough to accept criticism, the point of it often misses the mark. One reason is that there is a misconception about the standards that can be applied to judge a performance. Most people think, incorrectly so, that performances come in only two varieties--the bad or the good. Usually, artists are able to categorize an effort only in these all or none terms.

This is just not the case. There is so much middle ground between a bad performance and a good one, so many kinds of bad, or good, and so many ways to be mediocre. Only by realizing this and turning one's attention to all of these factors, can one hope to substantially improve an act. To this end, an impartial observer can be of great help to an open-minded artist.

The growth of a performer, that odyssey through relative levels of bad and good, is a developmental process that can be visualized as a staircase of steps. Each subsequent higher step on the performer's staircase might be reached because of an improvement in one or another basic or higher level skill.

All of the performers I know can be placed somewhere between the upper and lower limits of that staircase. Each comes to rest at one level or another based on the absence of, or degree of development of, certain skills. Among these skills might be instrumental technique, singing ability, songwriting ability, personality, sense of humor, or ability to select interesting material. To be a successful performer one might have a great deal of talent in any one area, or a mixture of talent for this and that. There are no hard and fast rules for what works.

An artist at one step can always find some way to advance to the next by addressing some issue, improving even a small aspect of performance. Perhaps by adding some patter, telling a story, dropping or adding a song, learning a new instrumental run, or even dressing differently, that artist can become a better entertainer.

And that's the point of performing, not merely to get up on stage and sing a few tunes, not just to exhibit one skill or another (only present self-written songs, or render a Sousa march on the guitar, or sing nicely); the point of performing is to entertain an audience. That is what show biz is all about, and it is possible to be a good entertainer even when not blessed with particular virtuoso skills. Make no mistake about it, each step taken on the performer's staircase with each skill sharpened should make one a better entertainer. Therefore, the overall target of criticism should be to assess the strength of a performance, identify odd weaknesses, and make the most of what there is.

A critic, and a critical performer should ask, why is this act good? why is it not so good, how then could it be better. A successful artist does well not to ignore these questions and should do everything possible to make each upcoming performance better than the last, always working at improving, always looking for things to improve.

As for me, every time I watch a performer, I look with a critical eye, just as I do when I assess my own performance. I look for the odd secret that will make the next small step up the performer's staircase possible. They are just small steps, and there is such a long way to go, but even so, it's amazing how many other performers have passed on the way up thus far.

ROGER DIETZ is a freelance writer, and frequent contributor to the Fast Folk record/newsletter. A collection of his articles is available as The Folk Chronicles, from Rescan Assocs. (see Book Pulishers).

©Roger Dietz, 1986

Copyright Basics

If you write a song, you automatically own the copyright from the minute the song is completed. If you think it's a real winner, you will want to register your copyright. Know-it-all friends may tell you that all you have to do is send yourself a tape of the song by Registered Mail, and then not open it, or have someone witness you singing the song on a given date. While you might trust to this method, the only form of copyright registration that is unquestionably accepted as establishing the date of composition should ownership of a song ever be disputed in court is registration with the Copyright Office at the Library of Congress. They have done their best to make it extremely simple and cheap. There is a 24-hour Forms Hotline, on which you can leave a request for the forms you need. The number is (202)287-9100, and they respond amazingly fast. The forms you will most likely need are:

Circular R1 - Copyright Basics, which tells you everything you need to know.

Form PA - Registration of works of the performing arts.

With Form PA and a $10 fee, you can make a tape of a number of songs, then register them under a group title such as "Collected Works, Volume 1." Should you find that you wish thereafter to copyright one particular song from that collection, because it's being released on a record, you can do just that, with another Form PA and $10. There are other forms for copyrighting the actual recording (to prevent piracy), and the sleeve design.

The First Annual Festival of Your Dreams

by Paula Ballan

If you and your group want to produce a successful festival, start small. Many of the skills you will need to plan and run a festival are the same ones you would need to produce a single concert. Besides your good ideas and intentions, you'll need enough money, personnel, and careful organizing to keep Murphy's Law from prevailing at every turn. Just remember, "You throws the party, you gots to pay the band." If you don't have the money in the bank to throw your party, and don't know where to find some, don't throw it.

Most groups decide to hold a festival when someone bursts out with a variant of Andy Hardy saying to Judy Garland, "Hey let's put on a show." Some of the largest and most successful festivals in North America have been run for years with this same "senior show" spirit and naivete. But somewhere at the top or bottom of those organizations are a core of level-headed, highly skilled, and organized movers and shakers--the ones who get the jobs done. You will need to find or motivate a similar minigroup from among your organization's members.

BASICS

To start, you'll need to get specific about what you want to do and how you will do it. Your original inspiration might include a theme or a group of artists you'd like to get to see in your own neighborhood. Set up a small group of people who will be responsible for the research--the where, when, how much, and how many questions that must be answered before you even know how much money you'll need to throw your party.

If your core group does its homework and you are all (or most of you) still speaking to each other, you are ready to sharpen or even redefine your original concept and start seeking funds. If your group has already failed to produce "doers", table the project until you get the right people (and enough of them) for the job. Don't take it on alone; not even if your best friend swears s/he will help.

Don't book a concert hall and contract artists' and technicians' services and expect your bills and fees to be covered by a standing-room-only crowd. You might be able to sell every available seat under optimal circumstances, but no matter how popular the artists, or how well-publicized your event, you will still have to contend with the unpredictible--you never know when Hurricane Gloria will come through town, or a surprise freeze will ice your roads, turning off all but your most avid supporters.

Get all the facts first, so you know what requirements and restrictions you'll encounter. For example, if your site requires the hiring of union employees, your technician volunteers may not be able to lend you their skills. This could raise your costs. Camping may be important to your potential audience, and a major part of your planning; you might discover that in order to allow camping, you have to provide a certain number of toilets, parking spaces, gallons of fresh water, and so on, per campsite. Getting the facts in advance will help you maintain professionalism in all your dealings with artists and suppliers. This means you will spell out everything you want someone else to do, and what you will pay or give in return.

There are many ways to find the money to put on a festival; you can fundraise it from private, corporate, or foundation giving programs, you can find commercial investors or lenders who will want to make a profit on the money they lend you; there are ways to raise the money from within your own organization. Funding sources will want to see some sort of track record before they'll put money in your hands, so keep accurate financial records and promotional materials, reviews, and photos to document your before-festival events, such as a concert series. Once your series is rolling, invite reviewers, local arts council representatives, educational, institutional, and clerical contacts to see one of your productions. They might become providers of sites or money in the future if they are suitably impressed.

Don't skimp on production details because of underbudgeting. If you are lucky enough to have a strong organization, full of hard-working imaginative planners, you will still need a year to plan, raise funds, and actually create your first festival. Meanwhile, your concert series or small one-day event will give you a chance to gain and sharpen the skills (even audition some of the potential performers) necessary for the main event you have locked away in your fantasies. Be realistic: if your group doesn't succeed at presenting one evening of music, they will surely be unable to produce a multi-act or multi-day event.

Before you begin to follow the specific advice I'm going to give you or read further articles and books, contact and interview other festival promoters and organizers. Establish lines of communication with other venues on the touring circuit. Make sure your dates are not in conflict with other events in your audience-gathering radius.

PERSONNEL
Regardless of the size of your planned event, you will need to worry about: (1) the site or hall; (2) sound and lights; (3) advertising, promotion, and ticket sales; (4) artist fees, transportation, and accommodations; (5) security, ushers, stage crew and volunteers' hospitality; (6) cleanup; (7) permits and insurance.

If you are contemplating an outdoor event, add the following: (a) food and water; (b) toilets; (c) grounds maintenance, including garbage and other removal (abandoned cars, for one); (d) camping; (e) communications and medical services; (f) rain arrangements.

Carefully consider the personnel you will need to successfully produce your event. They fall into three categories, some of which overlap:
(1) The organizers arrange the budget, program, location, and hiring of paid services. (Whether organizers get paid or not will depend on your budget and philosophy). They are involved from conception until the last bills

are paid, which sometimes linger long after an unsuccessful event has passed. They must be on call for every emergency that comes up be-fore, throughout and after the event.
(2) The paid professionals provide the services that make your event work. Sometimes these services are available from some of the organizers. BEWARE! Don't substitute good intentions or friendships for professional standards. It's worth repeating: do not skimp on the best affordable sound, lights, printed materials, publicity and promotion. These are the major tools for both artistic and financial success of your event.
(3) The volunteers are the magical catalyst to the successful ambiance and flow of most folk events. Their energy and dedication can work miracles smoothing numerous aggravations. Make sure to organize them and explain exactly what you want done. Learning how to present the music is as much a part of the folk process as learning the songs. Beware of the "folk police" mentality that can turn a regular person into a folk event's version of a junior high hall monitor. And beware of over-ardent fans and groupies who tend to irritate both performers and organizers. Don't confuse someone looking for a free party with a real volunteer.

PROGRAMMING
With all of the operational elements in place, you're ready to plan the program. In this area we all suffer from champagne taste and beer budget. Very few of us will ever be able to afford the programs we fantasize. (My personal fantasy is a women's concert at Madison Square Garden with Celia Cruz, Dolly Parton, and Tina Turner.) So within the realm of what we can afford, we work with the best of what we like, what's available, and what will be saleable to our potential audience.

All the organizers and their friends will want input into the program, but one person must have final decision and negotiating power to effectively deal with artists, managers, or agents. That person should be the single source of contact between the artists and the festival, but must be the only source of contractual information. NEVER reveal the terms of any artist's contract to any other artist. The only exception to this rule is the instance where every performer will be paid the same honorarium plus travel expenses.

You must be consistent in your dealings with the professional music industry in order to gain credibility. In some areas there will be several venues vying for the appearance of the same artists. If you can't compete with higher salaries offered by other venues, you can try talking up the ambiance of your setting and accommodations, and the enthusiasm of your audience, which may bring you more "Brownie points" than one of those better paying gigs.

Make a list of who you would like to present. Check on their availability and price. You can locate their agencies through this directory; their record companies; other promoters; ethnic clubs and organizations.

Sometimes the time and location of your event will work to your advantage and an otherwise unaffordable act will become available to you. If you are in a smaller city or out-of-the-way location, you will have an advantage if you can offer your festival during the week: many acts are more available and affordable Monday to Thursday, than they are on weekends.

When you are programming a multi-act event, never commit more than 20% of your budget on support groups until you have your headliners and "ticket-sellers" in place. There have been successful events (such as the family-run, now-defunct Fox Hollow Festival in New York State) that were sold to capacity without a pre-announced program. Charm of location and long established friendships have been the magic formulae for these programs. But until and unless your site and relationships allow for this kind of success, you will have to shop and haggle with the rest of us.

A good programmer must learn how to say no. If you make no preliminary commitments to your lovers', cousins', brothers', sisters', mother's, father's, or friends' bands it will make your life much easier. You can explain that you must save your budget

to maintain a negotiable edge for the top of your bill, but that will only put off dealing with the blandishments of those nearest and dear to you. Programming can be a terrible test of friendship and tact; but in order to maintain artistic and commercial integrity for your program, you must be decisive and sometimes unpopular. Keep programming responsibilities away from personal ties remembering that even innocuous wooing, wining, dining and sudden friendliness usually means trouble.

After you have compiled your hoped-for list of artists, you should evaluate the combination. You need to provide as much variety as possible, even in a single theme event, to hold your audience's attention. To achieve this, balance the program using men and women; solos, duos, and groups; music, dance and storytelling; Anglo and other ethnic representatives, whenever possible and appropriate. Even if your event is already specific, as for example, a Celtic program, you will still be able to balance Irish, Welsh, Scottish, storytelling, music, dance, individual and group performances.

HOSPITALITY
Festivals provide hospitality services to their performers that a concert-presenting group may not have to. The more groups you hire, the more beds to find, mouths to feed, bodies and equipment to move around; so save your budget and energy, and plan to get a variety of performances from all the artists in your program. You can sometimes "create" groups for finales and workshops with the right combination of individuals who have worked together before, or whose styles, repertoire and background are complementary. NEVER plan additional work for artists, or combinations of artists, without involving them in your planning process. Expect to pay some additional sum for more than two workshops plus one concert performance per day.

How do you decide who will enjoy working at your festival, and will, because they enjoy it, give more in their performances? I frankly plan a party. Once I've decided on the first act, I imagine the after-show party, and try to anticipate who would like to get to know and jam with whom. An opportunity to meet and share music and leisure time with their peers will make your event desirable to musicians. Find an appropriate, out of the way room for this party; refreshments are a good idea.

If you're planning a generic folk festival, don't ignore the ethnic groups in your community. An unusual musical experience that educates, communicates, adds variety, and fills seats with new audiences, will do more for your program than another earnest-young-singer-songwriter. This also applies when programming a concert series which can serve as a marketing test of ethnic community interest.

In programming, remember "De gustibus non disputandum" (or there certainly ain't no arguing about taste). When you are in charge of the program, you must learn to be flexible. A successful program will often include artists whose music you frankly don't like. However, if you've done your homework, you will have included them because their presence will add variety, sell tickets, or make the appearance of some other group possible. Agents will often make the availability of an act you want contingent on the appearance of someone you don't.

Don't forget about the children in your organization and community. Well-programmed activities and performances for and by young people can often sell more tickets than the same performers can for regular programming. If you provide for this audience from the beginning, it may help to solidify your choices and will add to both the artistic and commercial success of the whole program. And there are often special cultural funds and sponsors available for children's programs that are not provided for regular concerts.

Finally, hope for the best, but prepare for the worst act of God or Murphy. Unless you're organizing a one-time fundraiser, you should not be producing the First Annual until you have the wherewithal and organization to do the Second Annual. If, after some serious thinking, you really feel that you can't do it right this time around, don't do it until you can.

PAULA BALLAN is a festival programmer currently for the Nassau Community College Folk Festival, formerly for the Philadelphia Folk Festival. She is also the project director for a Cuban traditional drumming group.

© Paula Ballan, 1986.

Collecting (Lest We Forget)

by Dr. Nancy Groce

The serious study of folklore has evolved gradually over the past two hundred years as folklorists armed at first with pen and paper and more recently with tape recorder and camera, have left the comforts of their ivory towers to study and record the traditions of individuals and their communities. Many of those "collecting" folklore have been academics, but an equal number were non-specialists who were just interested in traditional arts. Through their "fieldwork," a tremendous amount of material has already been collected, but there remains, even in our age of homogenized mass culture, a great many traditional songs, tunes, and stories that have never been recorded. If you are on the road, or are active in folk music circles, you are likely to meet scores of people who know the same versions of the same tunes, all learned from a common source or a well-known recording. But occasionally, even in the most unlikely settings, you might meet a person who knows an unusual variant of a song, or offers to introduce you to an elderly neighbor who plays "old-fashioned fiddle music" or a "strange instrument like the one you've got on stage." In case this happens to you, here are some quick tips on how to conduct a successful interview with a traditional artist, and how to get help from professional folklorists or local arts councils if you think you've met an artist who should be documented in greater depth.

SETTING UP AN INTERVIEW
This is probably the most difficult part of doing folklore fieldwork. If you know the person you will be interviewing, set up a convenient time and pick a place where you will be able to talk without a great deal of outside distractions. If you haven't met the person, a phone call or letter stating politely and concisely who you are and what you want to talk to them about is a good idea. Keep in mind that you are asking for a favor, and that a traditional artist is under no obligation to be interviewed. I've found that most people are flattered to be asked. Don't be put off by humility--"I'm really not as good as Mrs. Palmer down the road," or "You should have come a few years back when my father was still alive." But an artist does have the right to say no and mean it.

It is a good idea to set up your meeting a few days in advance, since this gives the person some time to think about the subject and perhaps recall additional information. Be very honest about how you are going to use the information. If the material is just for your own use, fine, but if you are recording someone with the idea of donating the tape to the local historical society, or playing it on the radio, you must let the performer know. To do otherwise would be extremely unethical. Also, when recording for public record, even if you are doing it for a local library or a college radio station, it is proper to have the artist sign an official release form giving you or the organization permission to use the interview for educational purposes only. (Commercial recordings are something else again which I won't deal with here.) Since this type of "official interview" is probably more formal than you have in mind, let's just assume that you've contacted the artist and set up a convenient time and place to record information for your own use.

COLLECTING
The tape recorder is by far the most useful and widely used tool in folk-lore collecting. If you are interested in interviewing I would urge you to get one. Even a moderately priced cassette recorder can give very satisfactory results, especially if used with an outside or "external" microphone. If you are using cassettes, spend a little extra and buy 60 or 90 minute chromium oxide tapes. I usually use TDK SA 60 or 90, but any mainstream brand will do. Most important is that you learn how to use your equipment before you do an interview. Few things are more upsetting to the person being interviewed--many of whom are not all that happy with recording equipment in the first place--than watching you fuss over your tape recorder while they are talking or playing. Also, be sure to bring extra tapes, batteries--in case an electrical outlet is not handy—a note pad, and if possible, a camera.

Arrive for the interview on time and find a distraction-free place where you can talk. If you are planning to record, ask the person if recording will be all right before you start to set up your equipment. I generally tell them that I failed shorthand in high school and this is the easiest way for me to remember what we will be talking about. If they are very apprehensive, offer them the option of erasing anything they feel they shouldn't have said after the interview is over. Remember you are their guest, and they have a right not to be recorded. If you are recording, however, be aggressive enough to ask that background radios or televisions be turned off, since these are often much louder on tape than they may seem at the time you are listening to them live. Air conditioners, fans, and even refrigerators can also interfere with the audibility of the tape, and it is best if you can have these turned off while you are taping.

The beginning of an interview is often uneven. Both you and the person you have come to see are probably a bit nervous, your questions will sound formal and the whole proceeding is likely to be interrupted by a child or spouse popping in to see if you would like more cream for your coffee or another cookie before you get going. Keep in mind that you are not making a radio show or an album; you're there to collect information. Don't turn your machine off for slight pauses or interruptions, and don't worry if the person you're talking to takes a while to think over your questions before answering. What seems like an eternity during an interview is usually not, and you will get better information if you don't rush the answers. Remember that the tape recorder is there merely to assist you. It shouldn't dictate the length of your interview or make it more formal. If you're using an external mike, don't wave it around like a television reporter. Just set it down where you know, because you will have already experimented with it at home, where it will pick up both your questions and the artist's answers.

It's a good idea to label the tape internally before you arrive at the artist's home. You do this by simply recording the date, the name of the artist you will be talking with, the location of the interview, and your name at the beginning of the cassette. You may think you'll always remember an artist's voice or the sound of his fiddle, but believe me, if you do many interviews, you'll be glad that you labelled the tapes.

It's best to start the interview with questions that the artist will feel comfortable answering. Starting with a person's full name, the names of their parents, and a bit of their family history, and then moving on to a chronological review of their life works well and sets up a basic structure for your conversation. If you start wtih a deeply philosophical question such as "tell me what traditional art means to you as an individual," you are likely to get a well deserved glare. How would you answer that yourself? If you are interviewing a musician, a bit of conversation before you ask them to perform often creates a more comfortable atmosphere. Good questions to ask include how did they learn to play; when did they first learn a specific piece; who taught them that song; what do they call it; do they like it, why or why not? Don't volunteer titles. If you say "isn't that so and so's reel?" they are likely to agree with you even if they know it by another title.

Also, if you hear a word, a title, a lyric, or a name which you do not understand, or a performance is in a language you do not know, make sure you ask for an explanation or translation. The singer might not know either, but often this sort of question elicits extremely interesting answers. (Having a notebook handy so you can jot down follow-up questions for later is a good idea.)

A strong word of advice for musicians: if you must take your instrument with you, leave it in the car. You are there, on someone else's time, to talk to them. If you arrive with your instrument (1) they might feel shy about playing themselves (2) feel that they should invite you to play along with or instead of them, all of which leads to (3) tune swopping. There is, of course, nothing wrong with swopping tunes, but your first interview with a folk artist is not the time to do this. If for no other reason, in several years you will be disgusted hearing yourself yet again play your version of a tune while a gifted traditional artist stands silently in the background. If you like, arrange for another time to "get together and play" but don't do it now.

Try to direct the interview so that you cover the information you want to know. Some wandering is to be expected--again you're not making a radio spot or a record--but try to avoid topics like "what's wrong with the world today" or "why I hate most of my family". As with the swopping of tunes, keep in mind that you are there to interview them, not hold a discussion. (Many first time interviewers come away with a tape filled with them doing most of the talking. Before you do an actual interview, you might want to experiment at home by interviewing someone you don't know terribly well-- like a neighbor or your teenage child.

That's about it. Successful folklore collecting contains many of the same commonsense groundrules as everyday social interactions. You've arranged to talk about a special topic with someone you probably don't know very well: be polite, listen to what they are saying, don't force issues or pry into things they'd rather not discuss. And finally, don't overstay your welcome. An hour or two of intense playing and interviewing is about all anyone can be expected to do. If need be, arrange to return at another time when both you and the artist will be fresher and better able to concentrate. After you interview someone-- who is likely to be a little nervous aobut what you thought about them and what they have told you--it's a nice idea to write and thank them for their time and let them know you appreciated talking with them.

THIS GUY'S GREAT

If you find someone whom you think is an exceptional traditional artist--for example, a man who knows a whole collection of unusual songs he learned from his grandfather, or a woman who plays regional fiddle tunes you think might never have been recorded elsewhere, or you just don't know what you have found but you think it's interesting--you might want to ask a professional folklorist for help. While there aren't a huge number of professionally-trained folklorists around, more than 30 states now have their own "state folklorists" to assist in the documentation and prservation of traditional culture. To find out if your state has one contact your state's arts council or the folk arts program, National Endowment for the Arts, 1100 Pennsylvania Avenue, NW, Washington DC 20506 (202)682-5449). The American Folklife Center of the U.S. Library of Congress, Washington DC 20540 also publishes a nice booklet called Folklife and Fieldwork: A Layman's Introduction to Field Techniques, which is available upon request.

DR. NANCY GROCE is an ethnomusicologist and a program asssociate for the New York Council on the Humanities.

© Dr. Nancy Groce, 1986

Reaching the Forgotten Audience

with definitions from Sherry Hicks Glover & introduction by Leslie Berman

The feminist women's music movement of the '70s has given a great deal to folk music--an opportunity to reappraise traditional women's roles, and the history of women's lives, as seen through the music of those times; encouragement to broaden women's opportunities in the technical and business aspects of folk music presentation and preservation. Especially valuable has been that movement's emphasis on making culture accessible to all potential audiences. The women's music presenters have shown us that non-traditional constituencies may have a great deal of enthusiasm and support for folk culture, when it is presented accessibly.

To this end, many festivals and some clubs have reached out to the disabled in their communities, to attract them as new audiences. Each group chooses its own method of outreach, but most groups make attending cultural events possible and more enjoyable by providing any or all of the following ser- over steps to concert-hall approaches; adding wheelchair-accessible toilets; preparing Braille programs and maps; and integrating the services of sign language interpreters for deaf audience members.

In the last category, there have been many advances. Interpretation of culture from any language to another requires special sensitivity to nuance and emotion. Translation from English to American Sign Language is perhaps more difficult, as hearing people use the variations of loud and soft tones, and other audible speech additions, to convey fine differences of meaning. A sign language interpreter must find other cues to present the same subtle information. Adding the interplay between music and lyrics is surely more difficult still. With encouragement from deaf audiences, many ASL interpreters have chosen to combine the visual-gestural signs of ASL and finger-spellings with movement and mime, to create a form of artistic interpretation that translates and enhances performances for deaf and hearing audiences. Some recent rock videos have employed ASL interpreters in insets onscreen. With one in 12 Americans suffering from some form of hearing impairment, this is not only laudable but necessary. Following are a few definitions and comments on artistic interpretation from a music sign language artist.

ARTISTIC INTERPRETATION is the accurate translation and expression of linguistic material in language different than the original; remaining faithful to the content, spirit, mood, and energy of the performer. The interpreter strives to preserve the artistic intent of both author and artist. This translation must make creative use of the linguistic systems of both ASL and English, to make the performance an interesting and aesthetic experience for the participants.

MUSIC SIGN LANGUAGE conveys the English flow of lyrics as the performer sings them, and adds the ASL concept when lyrics allow. In addition, instrumental music, for example drums, bells, and the sound of birds, is made visual.

INTERPRETER/PERFORMER ROLE involves the actual interpreting of the concert. The interpreter/performer should be well-prepared with lyrics and translations and be familiar with the flow of the music and the artists' style. Also, the interpreter/performer must visually convey the entire event. This includes quick decisions on how to depict artists' character through the use of facial expression, body language, intonation, and timing. Through adapting to each situation while it is happening, and making quick decisions, the interpreter facilitates communication between hearing and deaf consumers. For performing arts interpreters, this becomes a unique art form for deaf consumers' accessibility and entertainment. The active process of interpreting is uniquely exressed in a visual mode of American Sign Language (ASL) for effective communication to deaf audiences.

DEAF CONSUMERS in performing arts are the members of the audience that are hearing impaired. Through the use of the performing art interpreter accessibility of the artists' material is there for the deaf consumer's overall experience of attending a musical event.

HEARING IMPAIRED is the general ter used to describe and encompass all types of hearing defects, ranging from minute loss to profound deafness. Hearing impairment is the most prevalent chronic disability in the United States, affecting more than 13 million persons.

FINGERSPELLING is the term used for the representation of letters of the alphabet with different handshapes. Each letter has its own shape, and words are formed by spelling out letter by letter.

SPEECHREADING is watching the mout and face to read what words are being said. Research indicates that only about 3 out of every 10 words can be speechread easily.

MANUAL INTERPRETING is when the interpreter signs what the speaker says, perhaps with some mouth movement, but not mouthing every word. American Sign Language may be used.

ORAL INTERPRETING is when the inte preter mouths what the speaker says without voice, using some natural gestures and facial expressions.

Introduction by Leslie Berman, definitions from Sherry Hicks-Glover, professional CSC interpreter and music sign language artist.

Local Dance On The Upswing

by Andy Wallace

"Dance all night with a bottle in my hand, dance all night give the fiddler a dram."

Ever since some distant primal ancestor first banged two sticks together or blew into a hollow reed, people have had the urge to move their feet, and bodies, when music starts playing. Hence the world of folk dance is as broad and varied as the musics which accompany it. It ranges from elaborately costumed, highly choreographed dance troupes performing stylized versions of traditional ethnic dances in concert halls, to the Saturday night Cajun boogie in a steamy dancehall in southwestern Louisiana, or contra dance in a New England Grange Hall, with kids running around underfoot.

As with folk music, folk dance can serve a variety of functions in a culture. It can be ritual, a test of athletic prowess, or purely social. Mostly it is, or has been, the latter, a way for folks to get together, have a good time, and you bet'cha, size up prospective mates. There are as many different forms and styles and kinds and approaches to folk dancing as there are to the music. Organizations exist at every level: national, regional, state and local; devoted to folk dancing as a whole, often known as international folk dance; or to a particular national or ethnic group. Many of these organizations publish magazines or newsletters which furnish information about various activities.

In addition, many folklore societies or folk music groups sponsor dance activities or at least list them in their newsletters. In recent years there seems to be more interaction between folk music and dance enthusiasts, with more dancing to live music than was the case in the early fifties or sixties. This is particularly true of contra and square dancing which in the past fifteen years or so has reemerged as a widespread social phenomenon throughout the U.S. and, I suspect, Canada as well. Morris dancing has also blossomed into a flourishing activity in the States as has clog dancing, both southern flatfoot style and French Canadian. Many festivals now have areas devoted exclusively to participatory dancing, and hire performers who instruct festival-goers in the basics of various dance styles.

Folk dancing is a common means of preserving ethnic identity among immigrant groups and many sponsor dance troupes which meet on a regular basis, particularly in urban areas where there are large ethnic neighborhoods. A look in the phone book of any metropolitan area will unearth Polish, Ukrainian, Swedish, Slovenian, or other ethnic benevolent or protective societies. Give them a call, and chances are they can steer you towards what you're looking for.

Of course if your definition of folk dancing just means what folks are doing out there on a Saturday night, the possibilities are endless. All across the country, and I assume throughout the world, are bars, dance halls, and juke joints, featuring local bands playing the music folks like to dance to. In my area of upstate New York, the band probably plays country music standards, but usually throws in a couple of traditional "singing call" square dances. In Louisiana it may be a Cajun band (highly amplified) playing two-steps and waltzes; move over to Tulsa or Austin and it'll be a hot Western Swing band; southern Arizona may feature a Papago Indian Chicken Scratch band playing polkas; in southern California Nortena music holds sway while Chicago has numerous Polish polka bands. And that's just the tip of the iceberg.

Try the Dance section to point your feet towards some folk dance organizations, publications and activities.

ANDY WALLACE is a multi-instrumentalist and singer, performing for dances in his local region in Upstate New York. He is the President of Grass Roots Productions.

© Andy Wallace, 1986

How Far Can You Go?

by Suzette Watkins

To understand the Australian folk scene, first you have to understand that Australia is the size of the United States mainland, but has only 16 million people. That's the population of greater New York or London. Given that these few live mostly in narrow coastal strips, and congregate in seven-odd major cities, it's not too hard to see why things are very different over here.

Clubs are the major source of folk music for the majority of the people. Each city has one or more of these-- some have something happening nearly every night of the week, but that's rare. The clubs tend in the main to be tradition-oriented, and even then, the traditions drawn upon are mainly Anglo-Saxon/Celtic. Some are "listening clubs" where three or four booked artists play each night, and some are come-all-yes. Most are held in hotels, which can be very noisy.

There are several radio shows around, but only one National Folk Show. Most cities and towns of any size can boast a public radio station that will programme one to three hours each week of folk music, mostly researched, produced, and presented by volunteers. The Australian Broadcasting Corporation gives us the national show--Sunday Folk--on FM and a five-hour show that covers most of Western Australia (over 1/3 of the country) from Perth. Any coverage of folk and related music on ABC-TV or the commercial channels is purely by chance.

At present there is no Folklore Centre in Australia and very little in the way of folklore studies. This may be rectified soon, as 1985 saw the first National Folklore Conference.

The Arts Centres will take a certain amount of folk music through their doors provided that it's either free or of extremely high quality and can be guaranteed to return the money outlaid. There are several concerts run each year at other places, mostly by dedicated workers from the local clubs and other interested parties.

Each State, with the exception of Tasmania, has a State body, which to a greater or lesser degree coordinates

events, runs festivals, and keeps the public informed. Most of these have newsletters published at variable intervals. The Australian Folk Trust is the overall coordinating body.

Despite Tasmania having no State body, several private individuals run one of the best festivals in the country on the January long weekend at Longford in Tasmania. Other notable festivals (this is not a complete list) include Port Fairy Folk Festival in Victoria, the National Folk Festival (a moveable feast held each Easter at varying locations round Australia-- 1986 Melbourne, 1987 Alice Springs, 1988, Sydney). On the June long weekend, there are two festivals, one in the Top Half (either Alice Springs, Darwin, or Mt. Isa), and the other at Newcastle in New South Wales. Western Australia hosts the Toodyay Festival on the first weekend in October.

Records continue to be produced, chiefly by Larrikin Records in Sydney, Talunga Music in Adelaide, Anthology in Melbourne, Sandstock in Newcastle, and the hordes who produce their own on their own labels. There are five major importer/distributors of records, covering the retail outlets and the Festival scene.

Dance plays a fairly strong part in the Australian folk scene. The strongest, and rightly so, is the so-called Colonial dancing: the dances done up until Federation in 1901. These bear a marked resemblance to the dances of England, Ireland and Scotland. A thriving Middle Eastern and European dance scene is evident in most cities. Morris dancing is also very popular with several sides (both male and female) turning up at any festival. Not bowing to tradition, there are also three or four mixed sides.

Spoken word is a very strong tradition in Australia--poetry, storytelling and yarn spinning--with a growing number of "spruikers" showing up each year at the annual Poets dinner held in conjunction with the National Festival. New poems and stories are written and performed regularly.

Apart from the State newsletters there are also a few other publications worth a mention. Stringybark and Greenhide is a quarterly covering the national folk scene with news and reviews, letters and articles, and includes some songs and tunes. The Concertina newsletter covers the push and pull brigade with relevant information, reviews, interviews, articles, and advice.

For artists wishing to come over here and work, remember the size-to-population ratio. There just aren't enough venues and audiences to go round. If your records aren't already being sold in reasonable quantities, there's almost no hope of club organizers booking you. The clubs still prefer to book established artists who the audience knows and wants to see, rather than other artists, probably every bit as good, whom almost nobody knows. For those determined to come out willy-nilly, take note of the section on immigration etc., and remember that there's a glut of artists in the January to May period, but far fewer from August to December. All in all the Australian folk scene is fairly healthy, but relatively small. We are now being exposed to other traditions (European, Middle Eastern, and American, North and South) and these are starting to surface at festivals and on radio shows. We're growing and expanding our horizons, whilst keeping the traditions in sight. What more can we ask?

Going Legally

Any artist who wishes to work in Australia must have the correct visa. A few people have managed without, but it's getting harder to beat the system and I for one don't advise trying.

Temporary residency visas for musicians are not hard to get, provided that a few simple rules are followed: (1) You must be out here primarily to work. If there are not enough dates on the visa application to warrant the time spent here (and I've never discovered the magic number), they won't grant the visa. (2) Clearance must be sought from the Musicians' Union of Australia or Actors' and Announcers' Equity. You have to join one of these unions, even if you are a member in your home country. (3) All gigs for which you will be paid must be shown on the application form, and no deviation from this itinerary is allowed; although in practice, I've found that a simple notification of the changes to the Department of Immigration and Ethnic Affairs (provided there are only a few of them) will suffice. (4) All money to be earned must be declared on the Immigration form. If the Government finds you've understated your earnings, things can get fairly hot for you. (5) Money earned in Australia is taxable at 30 cents on the dollar from the first dollar. Tax must be paid on the gross earnings less expenses. It's best if this is done before leaving the country.

Here are a few helpful hints I've gathered over the years:

It's best if you have a Sponsor or Employer in Australia who is prepared to guarantee you. This person is responsible for your expenses (including medical), and repatriation if things go wrong, so it's a fair responsiblity that person is undertaking.

If the visa is being arranged from the Australian end, allow six to eight weeks from the beginning to visa in hand. Allow even more when filing in some cities. The people in Immigration don't always tell you everything you need to know, and things can get slowed down for weeks by missing documentation. Ask lots of questions and be sure you understand the answers.

Include an itinerary, bio or C.V., and copies of contracts between you and your employer(s) with your visa application.

Before you can enter the country, you must have joined one of the artists' unions. You should join the local branch in the first city of your tour. When deciding which union to join, apply this rule of thumb: if you mainly play an instrument, join the Musicians' Union. If more than half your act includes singing and/or jokes/patter, join the Actors' and Announcers' Equity. The unions require that an Australian artist appear on the same bill.

Pick up your completed visa from Australia House when your Sponsor/Employer is notified that it's ready. I'm not at all sure it will be sent to you automatically.

Here's a final checklist: (1) Obtain a visa application form M.1821(2-73)18, "Nomination for Temporary Entry of Overseas Entertainer(s) to Perform in Australia. (2) Include ALL relevant information--full name, address, date of birth, place of birth, dates of tour, consulate location in your home country, or wherever you will be when you will pick up the completed visa, a complete itinerary, including dates, gigs, fees, etc. (3) Return appli-cation with contracts, bio or C.V., and itinerary. (4) Join the appropriate union in Australia. (5) Wait (and wait, and wait). (6) Pick up visa from Australia House or equivalent.

SUZETTE WATKINS is a performer, promoter, agent, and record distributor (Talunga Music) in Victoria, Australia.

© Suzette Watkins, 1986.

AUSTRALIA

*ARTS COUNCIL OF AUSTRALIA
80 George St, The Rocks, Sydney NSW 2000 (02)27-2113. David Hamer.

*AUSTRALIAN FOLK TRUST
PO Box 265, Paddington QN 4064. Acts as national coordinator. Folk Directory.

*COUNTRY MUSIC AUSTRALIA SOC
Box 494, Tamworth NSW 2340 (067)65-7055. G.M. Ellis. Journal.

FOLKLORE ASSN OF AUSTRALIA
Montroy, 112 Audley St, Petersham NSW 2049. Ms. B. Spelman.

MUSEUMS

*AUSTRALIAN MUSEUM
College St, Sydney NSW 2000.

Collections of historical documents, including folklore, may be found in several libraries:

*LA STROBE LIBRARY
State Library of Victoria.

*MITCHELL LIBRARY
Sydney.

*NATIONAL LIBRARY
Canberra.

PRINT

*CONCERTINA MAGAZINE
Lot 5, Sandham Rd, Bell NSW 2785. Richard Evans. 4/yr.

*COUNTRY MUSIC AUSTRALIA
PO Box 494, Tamworth NSW 2340 (067)65-7055.

*STRINGYBARK & GREENHIDE
PO Box 424, Newcastle NSW 2300.

RADIO

*AUSTRALIAN BROADCASTING CORP
GPO Box 9994, Sydney NSW 2001 (02)339-0211.

*FEDN OF PUBLIC BROADCASTERS
PO Box 294, Milsons Point, NSW 2061

*PUBLIC BROADCASTING ASSN
80 George St, Sydney NSW 2001.

*SPECIAL BROADCASTING SERVICE
PO Box20, Sydney NSW 2001. R E Fowell, Exec Dir.

RECORD COs & DISTRIBS

*AVAN-GARDE MUSIC
134 Broadway, #2, Sydney NSW 2007
(02)211-4144. Ali Knoll.

*BATTYMAN RECORDS
PO Box 94, 101 William St, Bathurst
NSW 2795 (063)315-708. Chris Batty.

*FIDDLING FOOL PRODUCTIONS
67 King St, Glenbrook NSW 2773
(047)395-579. Gus McNeil.

*IMAGE RECORDS
137 Moray St, S Melborne VIC 3205
(03)699-9999. John McDonald.

*LARRIKIN RECORDS
PO Box 162, Paddington NSW (02)336-
567. Warren Fahey. Distrib for
Rounder (USA), Topic (UK).

FOLKWAYS MUSIC STORE
282 Oxford St, Paddington NSW 2021
(02)33-3980. Records, instruments,
books. Tuition for guitar, banjo,
mandolin, dulcimer: John Morris
(02)33-6567.

*PUB WITH NO BEER COUNTRY
    FESTIVAL & FAIR
PO Box 215, Nambucca Heads NSW 2448
(065)687-555. Doug Cole. March.

NORTHERN TERRITORIES

FOLK TOURING CIRCUIT
30 Snowdon St, Jingili NT 5792.
Jeff & Ann Carfield.

TOP HALF FOLK FEDERATION
GPO Box 883, Alice Springs NT.

*NATIONAL FOLK FESTIVAL
Easter weekend, different city each
year. 1986: PO Box 251, E Bentleigh
VIC 3165. Dennis Merlo.
1987: PO Box 1701, Alice Springs NT
5750 (089)522-536. Morag McGrath.

*TOP HALF FOLK FESTIVAL
PO Box 41551, Casuarina NT 5792
(089)277 040. Peter Bates. June.

NEW SOUTH WALES

AUSTRALIAN FOLKLORE UNIT
18 Hopetoun St, Paddington NSW.
Research, collecting, info service.

BATHURST FOLK SOCIETY
Hut G, J Oxley Village MCAE,
Bathurst NSW. S. Hilt.

ILAWARRA FOLK SOCIETY
Jnr Clubhouse, Beaton Pk Tennis
Club, Ilawarra NSW.

NSW FOLK FEDERATION
PO Box 2141, Paddington NSW 2021
(02)48-3766. Fest April.

*NEWCASTLE FOLK CLUB
Newcastle Tech Coll, Tighes Hill
NSW 2297. Fest mid-June.

*ZSER (Radio)'
Rydalmere Hos, Victoria Rd,
Rydalmere NSW 2116. Bob Schmidtman.

QUEENSLAND

QUEENSLAND FOLK FEDERATION
11 Margary St, Mt Gravatt QN 4122.

QUEENSLAND TRAD FOLK DANCE CLUB
69 Hamlet St, Annerley, Brisbane
QN 4103.

SOUTH AUSTRALIA

*CUMBIE FOLK CLUB
Cumberland Arms Hotel, Waymouth St,
Adelaide SA. Fridays.

*FOLK EDUCATION PROJECT
Education Ctr, 1st floor, 31
Flinders St, Adelaide SA (08)227-
2945. Bob Petchell, Isabel
Margrett.

*FOLK FEDERATION OF S AUSTRALIA
GPO Box 525, Adelaide SA 5001 (08)
263-1379 Paula Rawson; (08)46-4809
Ken Dell. Newsletter with listings,
reviews etc.

*PRINCE ALBERT HOTEL
Wright St, Adelaide SA. Venue for
various orgs, various nights.

*WORKERS EDUC ASSN OF S AUS
223 Angas St, Adelaide SA 5000 (08)
223-1272. Workshops, lectures.

*BROKEN HILL BUSH MUSIC CLUB
PO Box 826, Broken Hill SA 2880.

*ADELAIDE COLONIAL DANCERS
PO Box 608, N Adelaide SA 5006.

*TRAITORS GATE FOLK CLUB
Earl of Leicester Hotel, Leicester
St, Parkside SA (08)388-
2175. Derek Moule. Sat.

*5MMM-FM (Radio)
56 Magill Rd, Norwood SA. (08)42-
7911. Ron Higgins.

*5UV (Radio)
Adelaide Univ, Adelaide SA. (08)
223-3699.

*AUSTRALIAN BROADCASTING CORP
GPO Box 2451, Adelaide SA 5001. J.
Kovaricek.

*VILLAGE ALTERNATIVES STORE
120 Prospect St, Prospect SA
(08)344-7298. Books, records.

TASMANIA

*HUON FOLK CLUB
RSL Club, Cygnet. 1st Sat. Festival
in Jan.

*BROAD ARROW FOLK CLUB
Marquis of Hastings Hotel, Brisbane
St, Hobart.

*WARM SPORRAN FOLK CLUB
Launceton. 2nd Sat.

*5CAE (Radio)
GPO Box 1415P, Hobart 7001. Ben
Lee.

*TASMANIAN FOLK FESTIVAL
PO Box 298, Sandy Bay, Hobart 7005.
349250. John Bushby. January.

VICTORIA

FOLK SONG & DANCE SOC OF VICT
Box 96, Carlton VIC 3053.

*MUSICLAND RECORD DIST
Box 121, Elsternwick VIC 3158.

*PIPE IMPORTED RECORDS
37 Swanston St, Melbourne VIC 3000.

WESTERN AUSTRALIA

*WESTERN AUST FOLK FEDERATION
PO Box 198, N Perth WA 6006.

*TALUNGA MUSIC
338 Brunswick St, Fitzroy VIC 3065
(03)417-1872. Suzette Watkins.

*PORT FAIRY FOLK FESTIVAL
PO Box 269, Geelong VIC 3220
(052)780 545. March.

*YARRA JUNCTION FIDDLERS CONV
41 Comas Grove, Thornbury VIC 3077
(03)484 7981. Ken McMaster. Feb.

WESTERN AUSTRALIA

*TOUJAY FESTIVAL
Western Australia Folk Federation,
PO Box 198, N Perth WA 6006. Donna
Vaughan. October.

CANADA

NATIONAL ORGANIZATIONS

*ASSN OF NATL NON-PROFIT
ARTISTS CENTRES
217 Richmond St, Toronto Ont M5V
1W2. Publications.

*ASSN OF UNITED CANADIAN
UKRANIANS
962 Bloor St W, Toronto Ont (416)
535-1063.

*CANADIAN CTR FOR PHILANTHROPY
185 Bay St, #504, Toronto Ont M5G
1K6 (416)364-4875. Funding info.

*CANADIAN COORDINATING COUNCIL
ON DEAFNESS
55 Parkdale Ave, Ottawa Ont K1Y 1E5
(613)728-0936.

*CANADA COUNCIL
PO Box 1047, Ottawa Ont K1P 5V8
(613)237-3400. T. Porteous, Dir.

*CANADIAN FOLK ARTS COUNCIL
10 rue Notre Dame est, #200,
Montreal PQ H2Y 1B7 (514)861-0451.
Festival directory.

*CANADIAN FOLK ARTS COUNCIL
263 Adelaide St W, Toronto Ont M5H
1Y2 (416)977-8311. Fest directory.

*CANADIAN FOLK MUSIC SOCIETY
Box 4232, Stn C, Calgary Alta T2T
5N1. Annual journal, bulletin 4/yr.
FOLK FESTIVAL DIRECTORY. Mail order
service.

*CANADIAN MUSIC CENTRE
20 St Joseph St, Toronto Ont M4Y
1J9 (416)961-6601. John A. Miller,
Exec Dir.

*CANADIAN MUSIC COUNCIL
36 Elgin St, Ottawa Ont K1P 5K5
(613)238-5893. Guy Huot.

*CAPAC
1240 Bay St, Toronto Ont M5R 2C2
(416)924-4427. Performing rights
organization. Monthly mag, Richard
Flohil, editor.

*FEDN OF CANADIAN TURKISH ASSNS
Toronto Ont (416)597-2026.

*FINNISH CANADIAN CULTURAL FEDN
191 Eglinton E, Toronto Ont (416)
487-5998.

FOLKLORE STUDIES ASSN
Univ of Saskatchewan, Saskatoon
Sask S7N 0W0.

IRISH/CANADIAN ARTS &
CULTURAL SOCIETY
1650 Dupont St, Toronto Ont M6P 3T2
(416)762-2858. Henry Geraghty.

*LATIN CANADIAN CULTURAL ASSN
1653 Dufferin, Toronto Ont (416)
654-7704.

*MUSIC FOR SOCIAL CHANGE
NETWORK
20 Albert Frank Pl, Toronto Ont M5A
4B4. Topical songs info ctr.

PENNSYLVANIA GERMAN
FOLKLORE SOCIETY
U of Waterloo, Waterloo Ont.
CANADIAN-GERMAN FOLKLORE.

*SCOTTISH SOCIETIES
75 Simcoe, Toronto Ont (416)593-
4095.

AGENTS

*CAMPUS & COMMUNITY
IMPRESARIOS
McMaster Dramatic Arts, Hamilton
Ont L8S 4L9 (416)525-9410 x 4660.
Pat Young.

*CROSSTOWN ENTERTAINMENT
718 Eastlake Ave, Saskatoon Sask
S7N 1A3 (306)653-2890. Mary Watson.

*RICHARD FLOHIL & ASSOC
1240 Bay St, #805, Toronto Ont M5R
2C2 (416)925-3154. Richard Flohil.

*OAK MANAGEMENT
36 Maitland St, #G4, Toronto Ont
M4Y 1C5 (416)923-8486. Martin
Collier.

GRADUATE STUDIES

*MEMORIAL U OF NEWFOUNDLAND
St John's Nfld A1C 5S7 (709)737-
8402. BA, MA, PhD.

*UNIVERSITE LAVAL
Dept d'Histoire, Quebec PQ G1K 7P4
(418)656-7099. BA, MA, Phd.

INSTRUMENT MAKERS

A book from Mosaic Press, entitled
"The World of Musical Instrument
Makers - A Guided Tour," by William
"Grit" Laskin, lists all instrument
makers in Ontario.

*OLIVER APITIUS
14A Elizabeth St, #1, Mississauga
Ont L5G 2Y9 (416)271-0275. Luthier.
Makes guitars, mandolins. By
appointment only.

*MARK BENETEAU
St Thomas Ont (519)633-6994.
Guitars.

*WILLIAM "GRIT" LASKIN
192 Dupont St (rear), Toronto Ont
M5A 2E6 (416)923-5801. Guitars,
inlay work. By appointment only.

*PAUL MORRIS
888 Dupont St, #108, Toronto Ont
M6G 1Z8 (416)533-4875. Luthier.
Mandolins, mandolas, citterns.

NATIONAL PUBLICATIONS

*COMMUNITY NEWSPAPERS ASSN
88 University, Toronto Ont (416)
598-4277.

*DAILY NEWSPAPERS ASSN
321 Bloor St E, Toronto Ont (416)
923-3567.

*CANADIAN BLUEGRASS REVIEW
Box 143, Waterdown Ont L0R 2H0.
6/yr. Festival directory.

*CANADIAN COMPOSER -
  LE COMPOSITEUR CANADIEN
1240 Bay St, #805, Toronto Ont M5R
2A7. Richard Flohil, Editor.

CANADIAN FOLK MUSIC JOURNAL
5 Notley Pl, Toronto Ont M4B 2M7.
Edith Fowke.

*CANADIAN MUSICIAN
832 Mt Pleasant Rd, Toronto Ont M4P
2L3 (416)485-8284. Jim Norris.
Monthly.

*THE MUSIC SCENE
41 Valleybrook Dr, Don Mills Ont
M3B 2S6 (416)445-8700. Jeff
Bateman, Editor.

*THE RECORD
Box 201, Sta M, Toronto Ont M6S 4T3
(416)533-9417. Weekly music
industry paper. Radio play info,
charts, reviews, news.

RECORD COs & DISTRIBS

*CANADIAN INDEPENDENT RECORD
  PRODUCTION ASSOCIATION
144 Front St W, #330, Toronto Ont
M5J 2L7 (416)593-4545. Earl Rosen.
Also FACTOR - Fndn to Assist
Canadian Talent on Records.

*CANADIAN RECORDING INDUSTRY
  ASSOCIATION
89 Bloor St E, Toronto Ont M4W 1A9
(416)967-7272. Brian Robertson.

*ATTIC RECORDS
624 King St W, Toronto Ont M6S 2G3
(416)862-0352.

*AURAL TRADITION RECORDS
3271 Main St, Vancouver BC V5V 3M6.

*BOOT RECORDS
1343 Matheson Blvd E, Mississauga
Ont L4W 1R1 (416)625-2676. Distrib.

*CANADISC
PO Box 142, Saulnierville NS B0W
2Z0. Paul E. Comeau. Indie distrib.

*CELTIC PRODUCTIONS
15016 62nd St, Edmonton Alta T5A
2B5 (403)478-6417. Jim & Janet
McLaughlin. Importers, esp British,
Celtic.

*FESTIVAL RECORDS
3271 Main St, Vancouver BC V5V 3M6
(604)879-2931. Gary Cristall.
Producers and distributors.

*FOGARTY'S COVE & COLE HARBOR
  MUSIC
23 Hillside Ave S, Dundee Ont L9H 4H7
(416)627-9808. Ariel Rogers.

*HOLBORNE RECORDS
PO Box 309, Mt Albert Ont L0G 1M0
(416)284-3085.

*SEFEL RECORDS
150 Simcoe St, Toronto Ont M5H 3G4
(416)979-9740.

*STONY PLAIN RECORDS
PO Box 861, Edmonton Alta T5J 2L8
(403)477-6844. Holger Petersen.

TURTLE RECORDS
Box 131, Stn A, Winnipeg Man R3K
1Z9.

*VALERIE ENTERPRISES
RR1, Hannon Ont L0R 1P0 (416)692-
4020. Valerie Rogers.

LISTINGS BY PROVINCE

ALBERTA

*TRAVEL ALBERTA
Capitol Sq, 14th fl, 10065 Jasper
Ave, Edmonton Alta T5J 0H4 (403)427-
4321.

VENUES

*BANFF CTR THEATRE COMPLEX
PO Box 1020, Banff Alta T0L 0C0
(403)762-6365. Kurt Bagnell.
Concerts.

CALGARY FOLK CLUB
71 Stratton Cres SW, Calgary Alta
T3H 1T7 (403)246-0546. Annie
Davies. Every other Friday.

*NICKELODEON
924 33rd St NW, Calgary Alta T2N
2W8 (403)283-3099. Bob de Wolff.
Concerts various nights, at
Crescent Hgts Community Hall, 1101
2nd St, Calgary. Seats 200.

ROCKY MOUNTAIN FOLK CLUB
3319 Bar Rd NW, Calgary Alta T2L
1M7 (403)282-3683. Daphne
Rackstraw. Every other Friday.

SATURDAY NITE SPECIAL
87 Malibu Rd SW, Calgary Alta.
(403)253-2507. Chuck Frank. Sat.

*SILVER LINING PRODUCTIONS
2205 2nd Ave NW, Calgary Alta T2N
0H1 (403)283-0488. Julie Walker.

SOUNDS OF THE WORLD
150 58th Ave SW, Calgary Alta T2H
0A2 (403)253-8227. Concerts.

*ALBERTA COLLEGE
10041 101st St, Edmonton Alta T5J
0S3 (403)428-1851. Some concerts.

*CELTIC PRODUCTIONS
15016 62nd St, Edmonton Alta T5A
2B5 (403)478-6417. Jim McLaughlin.

*EDMONTON FOLK FEST CONCERTS
PO Box 4130, Edmonton Alta T6E 4T2
(403)429-1899. Holger Petersen.
Concert series.

PROVINCIAL MUSEUM & ARCHIVES
12845 102nd Ave, Edmonton Alta T5N
0M6. Folklore archives.

FESTIVALS

There are almost 200 festivals
across Canada which present folk
music in some form. These are
covered in the Canadian Folk
Festival Directory, published by
DFMS, PO Box 4232, Sta C, Calgary
Alta T2T 5N1. We have listed those
returning questionnaires, or known
to us personally.

*DIR OF HERITAGE ARTS FESTS
Canadian Folk Arts Council - see
National Organizations for address.

*EDMONTON FOLK MUSIC FESTIVAL
PO Box 4130, Edmonton Alta T6E 4T2
(403)429-1899. Holger Petersen.
August.

*JASPER HERITAGE FOLK FEST
PO Box 1704, Jasper Alta T0E 1E0.
Sherrill Meropoulis. August.

PRINT

*CALGARY HERALD
PO Box 2400, Calgary Alta T2P 7W9
(403)235-7580.

*CALGARY SUN
2615 12th St NE, Calgary Alta T2E
7W9 (403)250-4200.

*EDMONTON JOURNAL
Box 2421, Edmonton Alta T5J 2S6
(403)429-6345. Jim McNulty.

*EDMONTON SUN
9405 50th St, Edmonton Alta T6B 2T4
(403)468-6111.

RADIO

CBC
1724 Westmont Blvd, Calgary Alta
T2P 2M7 (403)283-8361. Les
Siemieniuk. Various folk programs.

*CSJW
U of Calgary, Macewan Hall, Rm 118,
Calgary Alta T2N 1N4. PG: VOX
monthly. Chris Glynn, Editor.

*CJSR (88.5)
U of Alberta, Rm 224, S.U.B.,
Edmonton Alta T6G 2J7 (403)432-
5244. Michelle Dawson, MD; Don
Buchanan. Folk 9-11 am weekdays.
PG: AIRTIGHT has reviews, columns,
interviews.

*CKUL (560AM)
U of Lethbridge, 4401 University
Dr, Lethbridge Alta T1K 3M4. Sheri
Rhodes. Some folk.

BRITISH COLUMBIA

*BC TOURING COUNCIL FOR THE
  PERFORMING ARTS
518 Beatty St, Vancouver BC V6B 2L3
(604)669-2800. Virginia Cleary.

*TOURISM BRITISH COLUMBIA
1117 Wharf St, Vancouver BC V8W 2Z2
(604)387-6417.

VENUES

*SIMON FRASER UNIVERSITY
Ctr for the Arts, Burnaby BC V5A
1S6 (604)291-3363. Some concerts.
CP: THE PEAK Jeff Buttle.

*COMMUNITY CTR THEATRE
Penticon BC (604)493-4171. Paul
Johnson. Concerts.

VANCOUVER EAST CULTURAL CTR
1895 Venables St, Vancouver BC V5L
2H6 (604)254-6679. Murray Farr.

*VANCOUVER FESTIVAL CONCERTS
3271 Main St, Vancouver BC V5V 3M6
(604)879-2931. Gary Cristall.
Concert series.

VANCOUVER FOLKSONG SOCIETY
333 Carroll St, Rm 101, Vancouver
BC V6B 2J4.

*CLUB HACIENDA
560 Johnson St, Victoria BC
(604)384-1514.

*HARPO'S
15 Bastion Sq, Victoria BC (604)
385-5333. Gary. Pop folk acts.

VICTORIA FOLK MUSIC SOCIETY
539 Pandora Ave, Victoria BC V8W
1N5. Newsletter.

FESTIVALS

*VANCOUVER FOLK FESTIVAL
3721 Main St, Vancouver BC V5V 3M6
(604)879-2931. Gary Cristall. July.

PRINT

*VANCOUVER PROVINCE and SUN
2250 Granville St, Vancouver BC V6H
3G2 (604)732-2222.

*RANDOM THOUGHT
PO Box 5341, Stn B, Victoria BC
V8R 6S4 (604)386-5037. Matthew
Mallon, Editor. Weekly.

*TIMES-COURANT
PO Box 300, 2621 Douglas St,
Victoria BC V8W 2N4 (604)382-7211.

RADIO

*CFRO (102.7)
Vancouver Co-op Radio, 337 Carrall St, Vancouver BC V6B 2J4 (604)684-8494. Folk, ethnic.

*CITR
6138 Student Union Bldg, Vancouver BC V6T 2A5. PG: DISCORDER 10/yr.

*CFUV (105.1)
U of Victoria, Student Union Bldg, PO Box 1700, Victoria BC V8W 2Y2 (604)721-8607. Mary Ackerman, folk; Mike Corcoran, bluegrass. 15 hrs folk per week.

STORES

*BLACK SWAN RECORDS
2930 W 4th, Vancouver BC.

*HIGHLIFE RECORDS
1317 Commercial, Vancouver BC.

*RUFUS' GUITAR SHOP
2586 Alma, Vancouver BC. (604)734-5125. Guitars, books, accessories.

LABRADOR

LABRADOR HERITAGE SOCIETY
PO Box 719, Stn B, Happy Valley, Goose Bay Lab A0P 1E0 (709)896-3764.

MANITOBA

TRAVEL MANITOBA
Dept 5055, Winnipeg Man R3C 3H8 (800)665-0040.

VENUES

*THE PAS FRIENDSHIP CTR
Box 2638, The Pas Man R9A 1M3 (204)623-6459. Dawna Pritchard. Concert series, school workshops.

FOLK ARTS COUNCIL
Box 229, 375 York Ave, Winnipeg Man R3C 3J3 (204)944-9793. Heather Johnson.

*STAR-KOMMAND PRODUCTIONS
PO Box 127, Winnipeg Man R3C 2G1 (204)947-9216. Gary M. Stratychuk. Concerts.

*WINNIPEG FOLK FEST CONCERTS
8-222 Osborne St, Winnipeg Man R3L 1Z3 (204)284-9840. Rosalie Goldstein. Concert series.

FESTIVALS

*THOMPSON FOLK FESTIVAL
Box 766, Thompson Man R8N 1N6.

*WINNIPEG FOLK FESTIVAL
8-222 Osborne St, Winnipeg Man R3L 1Z3 (204)284-9840. Rosalie Goldstein. July.

PRINT

*WINNIPEG FREE PRESS
300 Carlton St, Winnipeg Man R3C 3C1 (204)943-9331.

WINNIPEG SUN
1700 Church Ave, Winnipeg Man R2X 3A2 (204)957-0710. Maureen Scurfield.

RADIO

CBC
PO Box 160, Winnipeg Man R3C 2H1 (204)774-9733.
CFRW
1445 Pembina Hwy, Winnipeg Man R3C 5C2 (204)477-5120. Brenlee Carrington.

CHMM
930 Portage Ave, Winnipeg Man R3G 0P8 (204)786-6884. Dolores Hagarty.

CKND
603 St Mary's Rd, Box 60, Winnipeg Man R2M 4A5 (204)233-3304. Bea Broda.

*WINNIPEG TODAY (cable TV show)
964 Manitoba Ave, Winnipeg Man R2X 0K3 (204)586-7919. Christopher Guly, Producer-host.

STORES

*HOME-MADE MUSIC
218 Osborne St S, Winnipeg Man R3L 1Z3 (204)284-5150.

*IMPULSE RECORDS
259 Lilac St, Winnipeg Man R3M 2G3.

*PRAIRIE STRINGED INSTRUMENTS
869 Westminster Ave, Winnipeg Man
(204)774-0262. Daryl Perry,
luthier. New, used, vintage.
Repairs, accessories.

NEW BRUNSWICK

*DEPT OF TOURISM
PO Box 12345, Fredericton NB E3B
5C3 (800)561-01023.

ARCHIVES ACADIENNES
L'Universite de Moncton, Moncton
NB. Folklore archives.

*UNIV OF NEW BRUNSWICK
Creative Arts Committee, PO Box
4400, Fredericton NB E3B 5A3
(506)453-4762.

*MOUNT ALLISON UNIV
Performing Arts Series, Sackville
NB E0A 3C0 (506)536-2040. Some
concerts.

PRINT

*TELEGRAPH-JOURNAL and
  EVENING TIMES-GLOBE
Box 2350, St John NB E2L 3V8
(506)632-8888. Helmer Biermann.

NEWFOUNDLAND

*DEPT OF TOURISM
PO Box 2016, St John's Nfld A1C 5R8
(800)563-NFLD.

*ARTS & CULTURE CTR
PO Box 1854, St John's Nfld A1C 5P9
(709)576-3650. Richard Stoker.

*MEMORIAL U OF NEWFOUNDLAND
St John's Nfld A1C 5S7 (709)737-
7487. Dept of Folklore - graduate
studies program, journal. Some
concerts.

PRINT

*EVENING TELEGRAPH
PO Box 5970, St John's Nfld A1C 5X7
(709)364-6300.

NOVA SCOTIA

*DEPT OF TOURISM
Box 456, Halifax NS B3J 2R5.

*BROOKES DIAMOND
PO Box 3130, Halifax NS B3J 3H4
(902)422-9663. Concerts.

*DALHOUSIE UNIVERSITY
Arts Ctr, 6101 University Ave,
Halifax NS B3H 3J5 (902)424-2267.
John Wilkes, Dir.

*PRIVATEERS WAREHOUSE
Historic Properties, Waterfront,
Halifax NS B3J 1S9 (902)422-1289.
Robyn Quinn. Pub, 5 nights a week.

BEATON INSTITUTE
Sydney NS. Folklore archives.

*ACADIA UNIVERSITY
Performing Arts Series, Wolfville
NS B0P 1XD (902)542-2201. Owen
Stephens, Chairman.

PRINT

*CHRONICLE-HERALD and MAIL-STAR
1650 Argyle St, Halifax NS B3J 2T2
(902)426-2626. Basil Deakin, Arts
Editor.

RADIO

*CKDU
Dalhousie Univ, SU Bldg, Halifax NS
B3H 4J2. Steve Kay. AGENDA.

N.W. TERRITORIES

*TRAVEL ARCTIC
Box 1320, Yellowknife NWT X1A 2L9
(403)873-7200. Festivals.

*FOLK ON THE ROCKS
Box 326, Yellowknife NWT X1A 2N3
(403)920-2058. Folk, Inuit and Dene
music, dance, crafts. June.

ONTARIO

*ONTARIO ARTS COUNCIL
151 Bloor St W, #500, Toronto Ont
M5S 1T6 (416)961-1660.

*ONTARIO TRAVEL
Queen's Park, Toronto Ont M7A 2E5.

VENUES

*BRANTFORD FOLK CLUB
73 Ashgrove Ave, Brantford Ont N3R
6E6 (519)759-7676. Don McGeoch. Alt
Fridays. Seats 120.

*DESERT ROSE CAFE
42 Mill St W, Elora Ont N0B 1S0
(519)846-0433. Resa Lent.

*TIMERS
80 MacDonnell St, Guelph Ont
(519)837-0170. Nori Tanaka. Seats
50.

*GOWN & GAVEL
24 Hess St S, Hamilton Ont. Charlie
Bald. Tues.

*HAMILTON FOLK ARTS HERITAGE
PO Box 2040, Hamilton Ont L8N 3T4
(416)526-0092. Concerts, fest.

*GOLDEN VALLEY CAFE
Gen Dlvy, Hwy 6, Mar Ont N0H 1X0
(519)354-1039. Bill & Colleen
Johnson.

*OSHAWA FOLK ARTS COUNCIL
Box 342, Oshawa Ont L1H 7L3
9416)725-1624. Concerts, festival.

*BARRYMORE'S IMPERIAL THEATRE
323 Bank St, Ottawa Ont K2P 1X9
(613)238-5842. Gordon Rhodes.
Several nights. Seats 300.

CTR FOR FOLK CULTURE STUDIES
Museum of Man, Ottawa Ont. Folklore
archives.

*GREAT CANADIAN THEATRE CO
910 Gladstone Ave, Ottawa Ont K1R
6Y4 (613)236-5192. Kathy Miller.
Concert series "Acoustic Waves."

*NATIONAL ARTS CTR
PO Box 1534, Stn B, Ottawa Ont K1P
5W1 (613)996-5051. Yvan Saintonge.

*OLD SOD SOCIETY
285 Spencer St, Ottawa Ont K1Y 2R1
(613)722-0482. Ian Robb. Concerts,
house concerts.

*GEORGIAN BAY FOLK SOCIETY
Box 521, Owen Sound Ont N4K 5R1
(519)371-2995. Debbie Barker, Pres.
Concerts, festival.

*GREY-BRUCE ARTS COUNCIL
Box 184, Owen Sound Ont N4K 5P3.
Co-founder of Owen Sound Festival.

*CLUB BOREAL
Box 1236, Stn B, Sudbury Ont P3E
4S7 (705)674-5512. Stewart Cameron,
(705)560-3008. Festival, SPECTRA
schools program. Concerts 1/mo held
at 100 Ramsey Lake Rd. Seats 300.
Booking: Sandra Marsh.

FOLKLORE INSTITUTE
U of Sudbury, Ramsey Lake Rd,
Sudbury Ont. Folklore archive.

*1001 FRIDAY NIGHTS OF
    STORYTELLING
Toronto School of Art, 225
Brunswick Ave, Toronto Ont M5S 2M6.

A C T COFFEEHOUSE
370 Queen St E, Toronto Ont (416)
362-0354. Friday.

BALKAN MUSIC CAFE
Esperides, 125 Danforth Ave,
Toronto Ont (416)461-1839. Thurs.

*BRUNSWICK
481 Bloor St, Toronto Ont M5S 1X9
(416)924-3884. Derek Andrews.

*CELTIC MUSIC SOCIETY
113 Spadina Rd, Toronto Ont M5R 2T1
(4176)925-1102. Dan Meaney.
Festival.

*COMHALTAS CEOLTOIRI EIREANN
1650 Dupont St, Toronto Ont. Irish
concerts, dances.

*CONCERT PRODNS INTL
39 Spadina Rd, Toronto Ont M5R 2S9
(416)968-2550.

*DEVELOPMENT EDUCATION COUNCIL
427 Bloor St W, Toronto Ont (416)
964-6560. Some concerts.

*FAT ALBERT'S COFFEEHOUSE
300 Bloor St W, Toronto Ont. Weds.

*FIDDLER'S GREEN
199 Erskine Ave, Toronto Ont M4P
1Z5 (416)489-3001. Tam Kearny.
Sun, plus occasional concerts.

*FINKELSTEIN MANAGEMENT
92 Queen St E, Toronto Ont M5C 1S6
(416)364-6040. Concerts.

*RICHARD FLOHIL & ASSOC
1240 Bay St, #805, Toronto Ont M5R
2C2 (416)925-3154. Richard Flohil.
Concerts, promotion, publicity.

*FLYING CLOUD
Held at Tir Na nOg, 50 Portland St,
Toronto. Bookings: Dan Meaney, 113
Spadina Rd, Toronto Ont M5R 2T1
(416)925-1022. Traditional music of
various styles. Fridays. Seats 100.

*FREE TIMES CAFE
320 College St, Toronto Ont (416)
967-1078. Varied music Mon-Sat.
Open stage Monday.

*GROANING BOARD
131 Jarvis St, Toronto Ont (416)
363-0265. Restaurant with music.

HARBOURFRONT EVENTS
235 Queens Quay W, Toronto Ont
(416)364-5665. Concerts.

*HOTEL ISABELLA
556 Sherborne St, Toronto Ont M4X
1L3 (416)921-4167/5450. Joe Fried.
Many nights, varied music.

JAILHOUSE CAFE
97 Main St, Toronto Ont (416)691-
1113.

*MARIPOSA FESTIVAL CONCERTS
525 Adelaide St E, Toronto Ont M5A
3W4 (416)363-4009. Rick Bauer.
Concerts, fests, Mariposa in the
Woods.

*NATIVE CANADIAN CENTRE
16 Spadina Rd, Toronto Ont M5R 2S7
(416)964-9087. Some concerts, craft
store.

NEW TROJAN HORSE CAFE
179 Danforth Ave, Toronto Ont (416)
923-6641.

OAKUM HOUSE
63 Gould St, Toronto Ont (416)769-
3638. Ed Shuster. Thur/Fri.
ONTARIO FOLK DANCE ASSN
43 Cynthia, Toronto Ont M6N 2P8.
Newsletter ONTARIO FOLKDANCER.

*TIR NA NOG
50 Portland St, Toronto Ont (416)
598-5673. Concerts mostly Sat,
FLying Cloud Club Fri.

UNICORN
175 Eglinton Ave, Toronto Ont (416)
487-0020. Mon.

FESTIVALS

*HOME COUNTY FESTIVAL
33 Beaconsfield Ave, London Ont N6C
1B6 (519)432-5800. Rob Dean. July.

*MARIPOSA FOLK FESTIVAL
525 Adelaide St E, Toronto Ont
(416)363-4009. Rick Bauer. July.

*NORTHERN LIGHTS -
FESTIVAL BOREAL
PO Box 1236, Sta B, Sudbury Ont P3E
4S7 (705)674-5512. Weekend after
Dominion Day.

*OWEN SOUND SUMMERFOLK
PO Box 521, Owen Sound Ont N4K 5R1
(519)371-2995. Neil Glenn. Mid-
August. Varied music, crafts. One
of the best.

PRINT

*SPECTATOR
44 Frid St, Hamilton Ont L8N 3G3
(416)526-3333.

*KITCHENER-WATERLOO RECORD
225 Fairway Rd, Kitchener Ont N2G
4E5 (519)894-2231. Don McCurdy.

*LONDON FREE PRESS
PO BOX 2280, TERMINAL A, London Ont
N6A 4G1 (519)438-0230.

*LE DROIT (French)
375 Rideau, Ottawa Ont K1N 5Y7
(613)560-2711. Jean-Jacques von
Vlasselaer.

*OTTAWA CITIZEN
1101 Baxter Rd, Ottawa Ont K2C 3M4
(613)596-3730.

*ST CATHERINES STANDARD
17 Queen St, St Catherines Ont L2R
5G5 (416)684-7251. Alide Le Page,
Entertainment Editor.

*SUDBURY STAR
33 McKenzie St, Sudbury Ont P3C
4Y1 (705)674-5271.

*GLOBE & MAIL
444 Front St W, Toronto Ont M5V 2S9
(416)585-5000. Liam Lacey.

*TORONTO STAR
1 Yonge St, Toronto Ont M5E 1E6
(416)367-2000. Greg Quill, Pete
Goddard.

*TORONTO SUN
333 King St E, Toronto Ont M5A 3X5
(416)947-2278. Wilder Penfield.

*WINDSOR STAR
167 Ferry St, Windsor Ont N9A 4M5
(519)256-5533. John Laycock.

RADIO

*CFNY
83 Kennedy Rd S, Brampton Ont L6W
3P3.

*CKPC
571 West St, Brantford Ont N3T 5P8
(519)759-1000. Jan van der Horst.
Folk programs, interviews.

*CING (108)
Burlington Ont. Norman B.

CFRU
U of Guelph, Univ Ctr, #210, Guelph
Ont N1G 2W1. PG: CROOKED BEAT
SHEET MONTHLY.

*CFMU
Hamilton McMaster University, S301,
Hamilton Ont L8Z 4K1. Bruce Mowat.

*CFRC
Queens U, Kingston Ont K7L 3N6.
Arthur Zimmerman.

*CHRW (94.7)
U of W Ont, Community Ctr #42,
London Ont N6A 3K7.

*CIXX (106.9)
Fanshawe Coll, London Ont. Alistair
Brown. 9-11am Sun.

CHEZ
126 York St, #509, Ottawa Ont K1N
5T5 (613)563-1919.

*CKCU
Carleton Univ, Rm 517, Unicentre,
Col Bay Dr, Ottawa Ont K1S 5B6. PG:
TRANS-FM monthly. John Tobin, Ed.

*CBC
PO Box 520, Stn A, Toronto Ont M5W
2J4. RADIO GUIDE.

*CJRT (91.4)
297 Victoria St, Toronto Ont (416)
595-0404. Joe Lewis. Listings.

CJUT
Univ. of Toronto, Toronto Ont M5S
1A1. Paul Trafford.

*CKLN (88.1)
380 Victoria St, Toronto Ont M5B
1W7 (416)595-1477. THE LONG NOTE,
Mike Casey, Colm O'Brien; ACOUSTIC
ESPIONAGE, Tim Harrison.

*CJAM (91.5)
U of Windsor, Windsor Ont N9B 3P4.
Andrew Altmann. Blues, ethnic. PG:
SELECTOR.

*CKNX (920AM, 102FM)
315 Carling Terr, Wingham Ont N0G
2W0 (519)357-1310. Jerry Chomyn,
PD. Folk progs. Interviews etc.

STORES

*LONDON GUITAR SHOPPE
364 Richmond St, London Ont N6A 3C3
(519)439-2000. Instruments,
accessories.

*THE MUSIC SHOP
748 2nd Ave E, Owen Sound Ont
(519)376-6464. Keyboards.

*FRANK EDGLEY
2346 Meldrum Rd, Windsor Ont N8W
4E4 (519)948-9149. Great Lakes
Concertina Society. Concertina
repairs.

PR. EDWARD ISL.

*DEPT OF TOURISM
Box 940, Charlottetown PEI G0A 7M5
(902)892-2457.

QUEBEC

*TOURISME QUEBEC
CP 20.000, Quebec PQ G1K 7X2
(514)873-2016.

VENUES

*GOLEM COFFEEHOUSE
3460 Stanley St, Montreal PQ H3A
1R8 (514)845-9171. Mike Regenstreif
(514)935-5066. Various nights,
varied music.

YELLOW DOOR
3625 Aylmer St, Montreal PQ
(514)845-8818. Laurie Silver.

CELAT
Univ Laval, Cite Universitaire,
Quebec PQ G1K 7P4. Folklore
archive.

OLDTIME COUNTRY MUSIC
1421 Gohier Ave, St Laurent PQ H4L
1X1 (514)272-1401.

FESTIVALS

*FESTIVAL D'ETE DE QUEBEC
26 rue St-Pierre, Quebec PQ G1K 7A1
(418)692-4540. Music, dance,
theatre. July.

PRINT

*DIMANCHE-MATIN (French)
5701 Christophe-Colomb, Montreal PQ
H2S 2E9 (514)274-2501. Manon
Peclet, Music Editor.

*GAZETTE
250 St Antoine St W, Montreal PQ
H2Y 3R7 (514)288-2222.

*LE DEVOIR (French)
211 rue du St-Sacrement, Montreal
PQ H2Y 1X1 (514)844-3361.

*LE JOURNAL DE MONTREAL (French)
155 Port Royal W, Montreal PQ H3L
2B1 (514)382-8800.

*LA PRESSE (French)
7 St Jacques St, Montreal PQ H2Y
1K9 (514)285-7070.

*LE SOLEIL (French)
390 rue St-Vallier E, Quebec PQ G1K
7J6 (418)647-3400. Marc Samson,
Music Editor.

*LA TRIBUNE (French)
1950 Roy St, Sherbrooke PQ J1K 2X8
(819-9569-9201. Pierrette Roy.

*SHERBROOKE RECORD
2850 DeLorme St, Sherbrooke PQ
J1K 1A1 (819)569-6345.

*LE NOUVELLISTE
500 St Georges, Trois-Rivieres PQ
G9A 5J6 (819)376-2501. Andre
Gaudreault, Music Editor.

RADIO

CBC
14 Blvd Dorchester E, Montreal PQ
H2L 2M2. David Ryan.
CHOM
1355 Greene Ave, Benoit du Fresne,
Montreal PQ H3Z 2A5 (514)935-2425.
Mike Williams.

*CRSG
Concordia Univ, 1455 de Maisonneuve
W, Montreal PQ H3G 1M8 (514)879-
4598.

*CKRL
Universite Laval, P 0447 Pav de
Koninck, Quebec PQ G1K 7P4. Pierre
Mathieu.

SASKATCHEWAN

*SASKATCHEWAN TOURISM
2103 11th Ave, Regina, Sask S4P 3V7
(306)787-2952. Travel & fest info.

*SASKATCHEWAN CULTURAL EXCH
1850 Broad St, Regina Sask (306)
757-8330. John Dufont.

VENUES

*REGINA GUILD OF FOLK ARTS
PO Box 1203, Regina Sask S4P 3B4.
Concerts, festival, workshops.
GUILD GAZETTE.

*UNIV OF REGINA
Regina Sask (306)352-5801.
Concerts.

*SASKATCHEWAN CTR OF THE ARTS
200 Lakeshore Dr, Regina Sask S4S
0B3 (306)584-5050. George C Haynes,
Exec Dir. Some concerts.

*CAFE DOMINGO
Saskatoon Sask (306)664-2137. Steve
Cashion.

CROSSTOWN ENTERTAINMENT
718 Eastlake Ave, Saskatoon Sask
S7N 1A3 (306)665-2430. Concerts.

MAD MARY'S
8th St @ Louise Ave, Saskatoon Sask
(306)955-2565.

*SASKATOON FOLK MUSIC ASSN
Box 8591, Saskatoon Sask (306)374-
4727. Harold Pexa. Sundays.

FESTIVALS

*REGINA FOLK FESTIVAL
Held in Victoria Park. Box 1203,
Regina Sask S4P 3B4 (306)337-FOLK.
Gord Fisch. All kinds of music,
dance, crafts, kids' events, food.
Free. Mid-June.

PRINT

*LEADER-POST
1964 Park St, Regina Sask S4P 3G4
(306)565-8278. Ed Schroeter, Ents
Editor.

*STAR-PHOENIX
204 5th Ave N, Saskatoon Sask S7K
2P1 (306)652-9200.

YUKON

*TOURISM YUKON
Box 2703, Whitehorse Yuk Y1A 2C6
(403)667-5340.

UNITED KINGDOM

The English Folk Dance & Song Society is headquartered at Cecil Sharp House, 2 Regents Park Rd, London NW1 7AY. It is the centre of a large nationwide organisation which supports folk music in many ways.

Facilities at Cecil Sharp House include the Vaughan Williams Memorial Library (which may be used by non-members on payment of a nominal fee). The collection includes books, tapes, films, records, photograhps, wax cylinders, and manuscripts.

The Folk Shop sells books, records, instruments and gifts on the premises or by mail order.

The annual Folk Directory is extremely comprehensive, and covers the UK. We have decided not to print it in its entirety!

Because the EFDSS has been experiencing financial difficulties, some of the services listed above may not be available. We suggest calling 01-485 2206 to check.

FESTIVALS

Please be sure to contact festivals and verify dates, venues and so forth, to avoid disappointment.

Festivals are listed in the *FOLKWEAVE FESTIVAL GUIDE, 1 Heron's Lea, Sheldon Ave, London N6 01-404-4293. Lynda Morrison.

For the purposes of this Directory, the UK has been divided into areas (see map). Listings are arranged by category in each area. National organisations, press, etc., are listed separately.

Area 1
London

Area 2
Kent
Surrey
Sussex

Area 3
Dorset
Hampshire
Wiltshire

Area 4
Avon
Cornwall
Devon
Gloucestershire
Somerset

Area 5
Bedfordshire
Berkshire
Buckinghamshire
Hertfordshire
Oxfordshire

Area 6
Derbyshire
Herefordshire
Northamptonshire
Shropshire
Staffordshire
Warwickshire
West Midlands

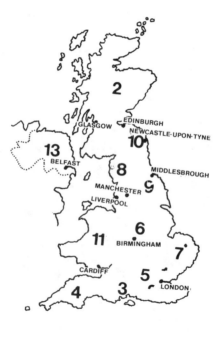

Isle of Man

Channel Islands

Area 7
Cambridgeshire
Essex
Lincolnshire
Norfolk
Suffolk

Area 8
Cheshire
Cumbria
Lancashire
Leicestershire
Gtr Manchester
Merseyside

Area 9
Humberside
Nottinghamshire
Yorkshire

Area 10
Cleveland
Co Durham
Northumberland
Tyne & Wear

Area 11
Wales

Area 12
Scotland

Area 13
N Ireland

NATIONAL ORGANIZATIONS

*ARTS COUNCIL OF GREAT BRITAIN
105 Picadilly, London W1V 0AU. 01-629 9495.

*BRITISH ACADEMY OF SONGWRITERS,
COMPOSERS, AND AUTHORS
148 Charing Cross Rd, London WC2H
0LB. 01-240-2823.

*BRITISH GOSPEL MUSIC ASSN
Meredale, The Dell, Reach Lane, nr
Leighton Buzzard, Beds. 052 523-7700. Paul Davis.

*CTR FOR ENGLISH CULTURAL
TRADITION AND LANGUAGE
U of Sheffield, Sheffield, W Yorks
S10 2TN. 0742-78555. Derek
Schofield. LORE & LANGUAGE;
FOLKLORE RESEARCH REGISTER 1/yr.

*COMMONWEALTH INSTITUTE
Kensington High St, London W8 6NQ.
01-603 4535. Info centre on the
Commonwealth. Arts centre, art
galleries. Library/bookshop.

*ENGLISH FOLK DANCE
& SONG SOCIETY
Cecil Sharp Hse, 2 Regents Park Rd,
London NW1 7AY. 01-485-2206.
National folk HQ. Concerts, dances,
workshops. Library of books and
recordings. Journal, magazine.
Records.

*ENGLISH TOURIST BOARD
Thames Tower, Blacks Rd, London W6
9EL. 01-846 9000.

*FESTIVAL WELFARE SERVICES
347A Upper St, London N1 0PD.
Coordinating committee.

*FOLK CAMP SOCIETY
27 Peter St, Taunton, Devon TA2
7BY. 0823-86517. Camps at various
sites, various times. Crafts,
dance, singing, music workshops.

*THE FOLKLORE SOCIETY
University College, Gower St,
London WC1E 6BT. 01-387 5894.
Founded 1878. First org in the
world devoted to the study of trad
culture. Derek Froome, Hon
Publicity Officer. Journal FOLKLORE
2/yr. Lectures. Library/archive.
Katharine Briggs Folklore Award:
annual book prize. Research Grants
& Essay Prizes. Mistletoe Books.

*MECHANICAL COPYRIGHT
PROTECTION SOC (MCPS)
41 Streatham High Rd, London SW16
1ER. 01-769 4400.

*OCARINA SOCIETY
68 St Mary's Rd, Kettering,
Northants NN15 7BW. 0536-81547.
OCARINA 2/yr.

*PERFORMING RIGHT SOC (PRS)
29033 Berners St, London W1P 4AA.
01-580 5544.

*SHANTYMAN
6 Brafferton Rd, Croydon, Surrey
CR0 1AD. 01-688 3580. Chris Roche.
Intl org for shanty devotees.

*SPORTS COUNCIL
16 Upper Woburn Pl, London WC1H
0QP. 01-388 1277. Covers folk
dance.

NATIONAL PUBLICATIONS

*BLUES & RHYTHM
18 Maxwelton Close, Mill Hill,
London NW7 3NA. Blues, vintage
soul, gospel. 10/yr.

*BLUES & SOUL
153 Praed St, London W2. 01-402
6869. Bob Kilbourn.

*BLUES UNLIMITED
36 Belmont Pk, Lewisham, London
SE13 5DB.

*ENGLISH DANCE & SONG
Fern Cottage, Debden, Saffron
Walden, Essex CR11 3NB. 0799-41299.
Dave Arthur, Ed. 3/yr. EFDSS.

*FIRST HEARING
63 Little Moss, Scholar Green,
Cheshire. Simon Jones.

*FOLK DIRECTORY
EFDSS, 2 Regents Park Rd, London
NW1 7AY. 01-435 2206. Annual.
Extremely comprehensive listing of
clubs, organisations, festivals,
publications, etc.

FOLK REVIVAL COMPENDIUM
New Ways, 19 The Gardens, Monmouth,
Gwent NP5 3HF. 0600-2221. Owen
Jones. List of all folk performers,
records, etc.

*FOLK ROOTS
PO Box 73, Farnham, Surrey GU9 7UN.
0252-824638. Ian A. Anderson.
Monthly. News, reviews, interviews,
features.

FOLK SONG RESEARCH
6 South St, Totnes, Devon. Sam
Richards and Tish Stubbs. 4/yr.

*GUITAR INTERNATIONAL
Guitar Hse, Bimport, Shaftesbury,
Dorset. 0747-3427. George Clinton.

*GUITARIST
1 Milton Rd, Cambridge CB4 1UY.
0223-313722. Geoff Twigg.

*INSTEP
15 Wolverleigh Terr, Newcastle-
upon-Tyne NE3 1UP. 091-284 1259.
Chris Metherell. Clog and step-
dancing. 3/yr.

*MUSEUMS & GALLERIES
Windsor Ct, E Grinstead Hse, E
Grinstead, W Sussex RH19 1XA. 0342-
26972. Annual directory.

*MUSIC WEEK DIRECTORY
Greater London Hse, Hampstead Rd,
London NW1 7QZ. David Dalton.
Annual guide to the UK music
business. Lists record cos, orgs,
radio, etc.

*MUSICAL TRADITIONS
98 Ashingdon Rd, Rochford, Essex
SS4 1RE. 0702-548876. 3/yr. Various
ethnic and trad musics.

*OLD TIME MUSIC
22 Upper Tollington Pk, London N4
3EL. Tony Russell. Trad American,
country, and folk. 4/yr.

*STRIKE A LITE
6 Brafferton Rd, Croydon, Surrey
CR0 1AD. 01-688 3580. Chris Roche.
Sea songs, shanties, history. Free
for SAE. Occasional.

*SWING 51
41 Bushey Rd, Sutton, Surrey SH1
1QR. Ken Hunt. 2/yr.

RADIO

*BRITISH FORCES BROADCASTING
Bridge Hse, North Wharf Rd, London
W2 1LA. 01-724-1234.

*BBC LOCAL RADIO HQ
The Langham, Portland Pl, London
W1A 1AA. 01-580 4468.

*BBC RADIO TWO
2 Broadcasting Ctr, Pebble Mill Rd,
Birmingham B5 7QQ. 021-472 5353.
"Folk On Two," producer Geoffrey
Hewitt; presenter Jim Lloyd. Only
national folk programme.

*BBC WORLD SERVICE
Bush Hse, London W2. 01-240 3456.

*INDEPENDENT BROADCASTING
  AUTHORITY
70 Brompton Rd, London SW3 1EY. 01-
584 7011.

AGENTS

*ACORN ENTERTAINMENTS
Winterfold Hse, 46 Woodfield Rd,
Kings Heath, Birmingham B13 9UJ.
021-444 7258.

*ASGARD
155-157 Oxford St, London W1. 01-
734 3426. Paul Charles.

*CIRCUIT ARTISTS
1 Holly Terr, York YO1 4DS. 0709-
585977.

*FOLK MUSIC SERVICES
2 Eastdale, East St, Farnham,
Surrey GU9 7TB. 0252-724638.

*GREENWICH VILLAGE
104 Charlton La, London SE7. 01-
858-0366.

*CHRIS JOHNSON AGENCY
12 Front St, Sherburn Village,
Durham DH6 1HA. 0385-720803.

*MAYMORN FOLK AGENCY
9 Cressy Ct, Fort Pitt Hill,
Chatham, Kent ME4 6TW. 0634-815490.

*ALAN ROBINSON MGMT
1 St Albans Rd, Kingston, Surrey.
01-965 0155.

*STAGE 1
c/o Wimbledon Theatre, Broadway,
London SW19. 01-543 3751. Johnny
Jones.

*THE TWO JAYS
34 Woodhouse Rd, Broseley, Salop.
0952-882316. Jenny Hannon & Jenny
Speller.

RECORD COs & DISTRIBs

New releases are listed in Music
Week, provided that they get the
information. So if you release a
record in the UK, send details to
Tony Adler, Music Week, Greater
London Hse, Hampstead Rd, London
NW1 7QZ.

*ACE RECORDS
48-50 Steele Rd, London NW10 7AS.
01-453-1311.

*AWARENESS RECORDS
6 Vernon Ave, Raynes Park, London
SW20. 01-543-1537. Andy Ware. SAE
for lists. Has Roy Harper, others.

*BLACKTHORNE RECORDS
35 Stanley Ave, Beckenham, Kent BR3
2PU. Ewan MacColl & Peggy Seeger.

*C M DISTRIBUTION
4 High St, Starbeck, Harrogate, N
Yorks. 0423-888979. Records & books
by mail order.

*CELTIC MUSIC
4 High St, Starbeck, Harrogate N
Yorks. 0423-888979. Licenses many
labels inc. Folk Freak, Larrikin.

*CHRISTABEL RECORDS
PO Box 232, Harrow, Middx HA1 2NN.
01-907 1905.

*CONIFER RECORDS
PO Box 27, Saffron Walden, Essex
C11 3NB. 0279-850145.

*DAMBUSTER RECORDS
12D Stortford Rd, Gt Dunmow, Essex.
0371-5965.

*DEMON RECORDS
Western Hse, 928 Great West Rd,
Brentford, Middx TW8 9EW. Labels:
Edsel, Hi, Zippo.

*EARTHWROKS RECORDS
71 Collier St, London N1. 01-833
3952. Jumbo Van Rienen.

*EFDSS RECORDS
Cecil Sharp Hse, 2 Regents Park Rd,
London NW1 7AY.

*FAMILIAR RECORDS
7B Farnaby Rd, Bromley, Kent BR1
4BL. 01-460 8103.

*FELLSIDE RECORDINGS
15 Banklands, Workington, Cumbria
CA14 3EW 0900-61556.

*FOLKSOUND MAIL ORDER
250 Earlsdon Ave N, Coventry.
0203-711935.

*FOLKTRACKS CASSETTES
16 Brunswick Sq, Gloucester GL1
1UG. 0452-415110. Peter Kennedy.

*FUSE RECORDS
28 Park Chase, Wembley Park, Middx
HA9 8EH. 01-902 0655. Leon
Rosselson.

*GLOBESTYLE - see ACE

*GO! DISCS
8 Wendell Rd, London W12. 01-743
3845 or 3919. Andy MacDonald. Has
Billy Bragg, others.

*GOAT BAG RECORDS
7 Nesbit Close, London SE3 0XB. 01-
318 7389.

*GREENWICH VILLAGE RECORDINGS
41 Sowerby New Rd, Sowerby Bridge,
W Yorks HX6 1DY. 0422-832 6333. Jim
Couza.

*HANNIBAL RECORDS
36 Berwick St, London W1V 3RF. 01-
439-0808. Joe Boyd.

*J S P RECORDS
112 Sunny Gardens Rd, London NW4.
01-203 1324. Blues, Cajun. Free
catalogue. John Steadman.

*JEWISH MUSIC
PO Box 232, Harrow, Middx HA1 2NN.
01-907 1905.

*JIGSAW RECORDS
115 Old Lodge La, Purley, Surrey.
01-668-3457.

*LAPWING RECORDS
82 Sunnyside Rd, Aberdeen, Scotland
AB2 3LR. 0224-43696.

*LISMOR RECORDS
42 Kilmarnock Rd, Glasgow G41 3NH.
041-632 9269. Ronnie Simpson.

*LOGO RECORDS
52 Red Lion St, London WC1. 01-242
8397. Label: Transatlantic.

*MIKE'S COUNTRY MUSIC ROOM
18 Hilton Ave, Aberdeen, Scotland.
Distrib for many US labels. Have
rare bluegrass.

*MILL RECORDS
Drumclog, Strathaven Scotland ML10
6RG. 035-74 250.

*MRS ACKROYD RECORDS
62 Cotton Hill, Manchester M20 9XR.
061-432-6898. Records and books.

*NOSUCH
3 St Hilary Dr, Wallasey, Merseyside L45 3NB. Gill Burns.

PLANT LIFE RECORDS
Spirella Bldg, Letchworth, Herts.
04626-6901.

*POKE RECORDS
74 Ashley Rd, Walton-on-Thames,
Surrey KT12 1HR.

*PROJECTION RECORDS
74 High St, Old Town, Leigh-on-Sea,
Essex. Records & books by mail
order. Catalogue, newsletter 4/yr.

*PUKKA RECORDS
13 Longport, Canterbury, Kent.
0227-456172.

*RECORDIAU AR LOG
17 Heal Conwy, Portcanna, Cardiff,
Glam. 0222-397318. Welsh
specialists.

*RED SKY RECORDS
57 Essex St, Oxford OX4 3AW. 0865-
724408.

*REL RECORDS
40 Sciennes, Edinburgh EH9 1NH.
031-668 3366.

*ROGUE RECORDS
2 Eastdale, East St, Farnham,
Surrey GU9-7TB.

*SAIN RECORDS
Llandwrog, Caernarfon, Gwynnedd,
Wales LL54 5TG. 0286-831 111. Free
catalogue. Welsh folk specialists.

*SAYDISC RECORDS
The Barton, Inglestone Common,
Badminton, Glos GL9 1BX. 045424-266

*STICK RECORDS
129 Westcott St, Hull, E Yorks HU8
8NB. 0482-703261. Jim Eldon.

*STOPTIME RECORDS
10 Hugo Rd, Tufnell Park, London N19
5EU. 01-607 9999.

*T RECORDS
PO Box 25, Pudsey, W Yorks LS28
5SU.

*TEMPLE RECORDS
Shillinghill, Temple, Midlothian,
Scotland EH23 4SH. 087 530-328.
Robin Morton.

*TOPIC RECORDS
50 Stroud Green Rd, London N4 3EF.
01-263 6403. Tony Engel. Distrib
for Rounder in U.K.

*TOUCH RECORDS
PO Box 139, London SW18 2ES. 01-
874-9018. Mike Harding.

*WATERFRONT MUSIC
74 High St, Old Town, Leigh-on-Sea,
Essex. 0702-72281.

*WOMAD FOUNDATION
85 Park St, Bristol BS1 5JN. Send
SAE for catalogue.

*WOODWORM RECORDS
PO Box 37, Banbury Oxon OX15 4BH.
Primarily Fairport Convention and
related aggregates.

INSTRUMENT MAKERS

*ALBION MUSIC STRINGS
S&J Music Services, 37 New Horse
Rd, Cheslyn Hay, Walsall,
W Midlands WS6 7BH. 05438-71049.

ANDY'S GUITAR WORKSHOP
27 Denmark St, London WC2. 01-836
0899. A.J. Preston. Guitar maker
and repairer.

JAMES ARMITAGE
14 Fieldgate Mansions, Murdle St,
Whitechapel, London E1. Woodwinds.

ASHWORTH PICKUPS
Le Nevek, Greenwith Hill,
Pettonwell Stn, nr Truro, Cornwall.
0872-863912. Transducer pickups.

BARLEYCORN CONCERTINAS
13 St Chad's Rd, Tunstall, Stoke-
on-Trent, Staffs ST6 6EL. 0782-
816504. Chris Alger.

*RICHARD BARTRAM
2 Welfare Cottages, Hale Fen,
Littleport, Ely Cambs CB6 1EJ.
0353-862043. Guitars, banjos, etc.

*BELL MUSIC
Hallatrow Rd, Paulton, Nr. Midsomer
Norton, Avon. 0761-413123. Branches
in Edinburgh, Aycliffe, Surbiton,
Bournemouth. New & used accordions,
repairs, instruction, etc.

*CALTON CASES
6 Grove Rd, Ash, Aldershot, Hants
GU12 5BD. 0252-314300.

*COLLET'S RECORD SHOP
129-131 Charing Cross Rd, London
WC2 0EQ. 01-734 0782. Gill Cook.
Great selection of records and
books. Mail order. Secondhand too.

CONCERTINA REPAIR
The Grange, Grange Ave, Manchester
M19 2EY. 061-224-5104. Dave Praties,
Steve Moss. Restoration and repair,
all makes.

*TREVOR COUVELLE
74 Church Rd, Wootton, Isle of
Wight. 0983-882782. Make & repair
dulcimers, guitars, kanteles, etc.

*COLIN DIPPER
West End Hse, Heytesbury, Wilts
BA12 0EA. 0985-40516. Concertina
restoration and repair.

DOBELL'S FOLK RECORD SHOP
21 Tower St, London WC2. 01-240
1354. Les Fancourt. Good selection
of records, books, secondhand too.

CHRIS EATON HURDY-GURDYS
38 Hamtun Cres, Totton,
Southampton, Hants 0703-861639.

*FINGERBONE GUITARS
Windsor Pl, Jarvis Brook,
Crowborough, Sussex TA1 2HU. 089
26-4266. Make & repair guitars,
also new & used equipment.

*ROGER FROOD
Dover Workshops, Barton Rd,
Butleigh, Glastonbury, Somerset.
0458-50682. Hammered dulcimers.

*A GREAT WESTERN MUSIC SERVICE
131 St Georges Rd, Bristol BS1 5UW.
Bristol 293939. New & used
instruments, repairs, accessories.

*GREAT NORTHERN CONCERTINA CO
39 Totties Hall, Holmfirth,
Huddersfield HD7 1UW. 0484-685664.

HANDMADE MUSIC
41a Ilfracombe Gdns, Whitley Bay,
Tyne & Wear NE26 3NA. Whitley Bay
527490. Sale and repair of stringed
instruments.

CHRIS HARRIS
11 The Square, Upper Cwmbran,
Gwent. Cwmbran 60858. Hammered
dulcimer.

HIGHLY STRUNG
153 Vale Rd, Ash, Aldershot, Hants
0252-313352. Instruments, strings.
Renovation and repair.

*HOBGOBLIN MUSIC
17 Northgate Parade, Crawley, W
Sussex RH10 2DT. 0293-515858. All
kinds of instruments, new & used.
Repairs, accessories, etc.

*M. HOHNER LTD
39-45 Coldharbour La, London SE5
9NR. Harmonicas.

*HOWARD WHISTLES
Enterprise Works, Nursery St,
Sheffield S3 8GG.

*ROBERT LANGSTAFF
Orchard View, Appleton Rd,
Longworth, Abingdon, Oxon OX13 5EF.
0865-820206. Folk and early
instruments.

*DAVE MALLINSON MUSIC
3 East View, Moorside, Cleckheaton,
W Yorks BD19 6LD 0274-879768.
Melodedons: sale, repairs,
instruction.

*MANSON GUITARS
Wyndham Hse, Bondleigh, N Tawton
Devon EX20 2AN. Andy Manson.

*MARCUS MUSIC
Tredegar Hse, Country Pk, Newport,
Gwent. 0633-54353. Make bodhrans,
concertinas, tabors. Buy, sell and
repair traditional instruments.

*OAKWOOD INSTRUMENTS
8 Ladywood Rd, Leeds LS8 2QF. 0532-
658585. Hammer dulcimers, mandolas,
mandolins, citterns, harps.

*OCARINA WORKSHOP
68 St Mary's Rd, Kettering,
Northants NN15 7BW. 0536-81547.

*OLD FATHER ABRAHAM
  BOOKSELLERS
12 Market St, Hatherleigh, Devon.
0837-810413. Books, records,
instruments.

*TOM PALEY
8 Angel Hse, London N1. 01-837
6857. Fiddles, accessories.

*GRAHAM PARISH
62 Market St, Hoyland, Barnsley,
S Yorks S74 0ET. 0226-744462.
Dulcimers.

*I G PICKARD
3 Calvert Rd, Hastings, Sussex
0424-716127. Hand built guitars and
other fretted instruments.

*REDWING MUSIC
Walcot, Mount Hill, Ewhurst, Surrey
GU6 7PX. Strings.

*RHYTHM RECORDS
281 Camden High St, London NW1. 01-
267 0123. New and secondhand.

*ARTHUR ROBB
79 Gloucester Rd, Malmesbury,
Wilts. Malmesbury 2945. Makes and
repairs guitars, lutes, hammered
& Appalachian dulcimers, Aeolian
harps.

COLIN ROSS
5 Denebank, Whitley Bay, Tyne &
Wear NE25 9AE. Smallpipes.

*DAVE SHAW
2 Shafto Cottage, Craghead,
Stanley, Co Durham DH9 6DW 0207-
231474. Makes and repairs
smallpipes.

*STEFAN SOBELL
The Old School, Whitley Chapel,
Hexham, Tyne & Wear NE47 0HP. 043-
473567. Fine guitars, citterns,
mandolas.

*STENTOR MUSIC COMPANY
Reigate, Surrey RH2 7EZ. 07372-
40226. Banjos, mandolins, guitars.
"Ozark" range.

THORNBORY GUITARS ETC - see
  HIGHLY STRUNG

*M J VANDEN
Hellesdon, 4 Barford Rd, Bloxham,
Nr Banbury, Oxon. 0295-720562.
Guitars, inc flat top, arch top
jazz.

*C. WHEATSTONE & COMPANY
2 Redhouse Yards, Thornham Magna,
Gislingham Rd, Nr Eye, Suffolk IP23
8HH. 0379-8367. Concertinas. Send
SAE for catalogue.

XYLO WOODEN PERCUSSION INSTS
Anderson Bldg, St John St,
Bedminster, Bristol BS3 4JF.0272-
66954. SAE catalogue.

LISTINGS BY REGION

AREA 1 LONDON

VENUES

For weekly listing of folk events,
get CITY LIMITS or TIME OUT,
available at most newsstands.

*BATTEREA FOLK CLUB
At The Plough, St John's Hill,
Clapham, London SW11. Booking:
Clare McDonnell, 148A Merton Rd,
London SW18. 01-874 6637. Thurs.

*BUNJIE'S
27 Litchfield St, London WC2. 01-
240 1976. A Diaz. Every evening.
One of the longest-running clubs
around.

*THE CARLTON
33 Carlton Vale, London NW6. Free
country blues on Sat.

*THE CELLAR UPSTAIRS
At Black Horse, 313 Royal College
St, London NW1. Booking: Sheila
Miller, 01-272 8273. Sat.

*THE CENTRAL CLUB
At Sols Arms, Hampstead Rd, London.
Booking: C F Gonge, 31a Aylmer
Parade, London N2 0PH. Tues.

*CHESTNUTS FOLK CLUB
At Chestnut Tree, Lea Bridge Rd,
Walthamstow. Booking: Alan bearman,
71 Somerset Rd, London N18 1HH. 01-
803 1757. Sunday.

*CRYPT FOLK CLUB
St Martin-in-the-Fields, Trafalgar
Sq, London WC2. 01-930 0889.
Booking: Owen, 01-346-6605.

*EALING FOLK CLUB
94 St Mary's Rd, London W5. Thurs.

*FLOUNDER & FIRKIN
50 Holloway Rd, London N7. 01-609
9574. Fri.

*FOX & HOUNDS
492 Hornsey Rd, London N19. 01-263
8688. Irish band sessions.

*FUDDLING FOLK
At Rose & Crown, 61 High St,
Hampton Wick. Booking: Miles &
Sylvia Couchman, 43 Oak Ave,
Hampton Wick, London. 01-979 2375.
Saturday.

*THE GRAPES
Borough High St, London SE1. 01-231
9284. Sat.

*HALF MOON
93 Lower Richmond Rd, Putney. 01-
788 2387. Music every night; folk,
rock, country.

*HERGA FOLK CLUB
At Royal Oak, Peel Rd, Wealdstone,
Middx. Bookings: John Heydon,
Aylesbury, Bucks. 0296-85995. Mon.

*MAID OF ALE
At Trusott Arms, Shirland Rd,
London W9.

*MANOR FOLK CLUB
At Eton Manor Rugby Cluib, Sidmouth
Rd, Leyton.

*OLD BULL ARTS CENTRE
68 High St, Barnet, Herts. 01-
449 5189. Various nights.

*SINGERS CLUB
At Marquis of Cornwallis, Coram St,
London WC1. Ewan McColl & Peggy
Seeger. Sat.

*WHITE HORSE
176 Church Rd, London NW10.

FESTIVALS

*CAPITOL RADIO FOLK EVENTS
Euston Tower, London NW1 3DR. 01-
388 1288. Several summer events.

*CHESTNUTS FOLK FESTIVAL
At Chestnut Tree, Lea Bridge Rd,
Walthamstow. Booking: Alan Bearman,
71 Somerset Rd, London N18 1HH. 01-
803 1757.

SOUTH BANK SUMMERFOLK
Events Office, Royal Festival Hall,
South Bank, London. August.

MUSEUM

*GEFFRYE MUSEUM
Kingsland Rd, London E2 8EA. 01-739
8368 or 9893. Period rooms from
1600. Library, exhibitions.

*HORNIMAN MUSEUM
London Rd, Forest Hill, London SE23
3PQ. 01-699 1872. Musical
instruments through the ages.

PRINT

*FOLK LONDON
4A Kenilworth Rd, Petts Wood,
Orpington, Kent. Orpington 25263.
6/yr. News, reviews, etc.

STORES

*KAY'S IRISH MUSIC
161 Arlington Rd, London NW1. 01-
485-4880. Records, instruments.

*RAY'S JAZZ SHOP
180 Shaftesbury Ave, London WC2H
8JS. 01-240 3969. Records, esp
jazz/blues.

AREA 2

VENUES

*MARLBOROUGH SINGERS CLUB
At Marlborough Hotel, Princes St,
Brighton. Booking: Sat - Indrani
Shough, 28 Loder Rd, Brighton BN
1 6RJ, 0273-558849; Wed - Ian
Fyvie, 180 Brentwood Rd, #4,
Brighton BN1 7ES.

*CHAMPION MUSIC CLUB
At George Hotel, Cranbrook, Kent.
Booking: Chris Rose, 35 Bower St,
Maidstone, Kent. 0622-61186. 3rd
Friday.
*2-4-5 CLUB
At The Bar, Bewbush Leisure Ctr,
Breezehurst Dr, Bewbush. Booking:
Joan Gifford, 9 Moat Walk, Pound
HJil, Crawley, W Sussex RH10 4ED.
0293-882079. 2nd & 4th Sat.

*COACH HOUSE
At Pied Bull, Farningham, Kent.
0322-71712. Guests Fri, come-all-ye
Sunday. Residents: Skinner's Rats.

*THE MINSTREL FOLK CLUB
Minstrel Wine Bar, Knightrider St,
Maidastone, Kent. 0622-55655.
Thurs.

*COPPERSONGS FOLK CLUB
Central Club, 232 South Coast Rd,
Peacehaven, E Sussex. 079 14-5439.
Bob & John Copper. 1st Thurs.

FESTIVALS

*BOGNOR REGIS FOLK FESTIVAL
15 Milton Rd, Pound Hill, Crawley,
W Sussex RH10 3AX. 0293-29892.
Richard Gough. July.

*BUTLINS SPRING FESTIVAL
Butlins Holiday Ctr, Bognor Regis,
W Sussex PO21 1JJ. Roger
Billington. April.

MUSEUMS

*MUSEUM OF KENT RURAL LIFE
Lock Ln, Sandling, Kent. 0622-
63936.

MUSEUM OF SUSSEX FOLKLORE
Parsonage Row, High St, Worthing, W
Sussex. 0903-36385. Traditional
beliefs, pastimes, and customs.

PRINT

*KASEBOOK
55 Broom Hill Rd, Strood,
Rochester, Kent ME2 3LF. 0634-
717943. Sue Duff. 6/yr.

*SUSSEX FOLK DIARY
3 Chester Terr, Brighton BN1 2YA.
0273-606383. Jim Marshall & Vic
Smith. 6/yr.

AREA 3

*SOUTHERN COUNTIES FOLK
  FEDERATION (SCOFF)
115 Wilton Cres, Shirley,
Southampton, Hants. 0703-775019.

VENUES

*BRADFORD-ON-AVON FOLK
  MUSIC CLUB
At Riverside Bar, St Margaret's St,
Bradford-on-Avon, Wilts. Booking:
Rosie Upton, 13 Bearfeld Bldgs,
Bradford-on-Avon, Wilts. 022 16-
5107. Tuesdays.

*CROYDON FOLK CLUB
At Arnhem Gallery, Fairfield Halls,
Park Ln, Croydon. Booking: Sue
Rule, St Clare Cottage, Mill Hill,
Edenbridge, Kent TN8 5DQ. 0732-
832760. Info: Rita Cherriman, 6
Brafferton Rd, Croydon, Surrey CR0
1AD. 01-688-3580. Monday.

*FOX & HOUNDS FOLK CLUB
At Fox & Hounds, Crookham Rd,
Fleet, Hants. Booking: Pete & Pam
Edwards, 22 Durnsford Ave,, Fleet,
Hants GU13 9TB. 02514-20289.

*PARCEL OF ROGUES FOLK CLUB
Godalming Town Football Club, Wey
Ct, Meadow Rd, Godalming, Surrey.
048 68-21867. Alan Bridger. Sunday.
*YETTIES MUSIC CLUB
Booking: Pete Shutler, Maybank,
Marston Rd, Sherborne, Dorset DT9
4BJ. 0935-814667.

*FO'C'SLE FOLK CLUB
At Joiner's Arms, St Mary St,
Southampton. Booking: Terry
Gregory, 36 Ampthill Rd,
Southampton, Hants SO1 3LL. 0703-
229515. Friday.

FESTIVALS

*CHIPPENHAM FOLK FESTIVAL
The Bridge Ctr, Chipppenham, Wilts
SN15 2AA. 0249-657190. Dick
Stanger. May.

*FOLK UNDER ARIES
At Salisbury Arts Ctr, Bedwin St.
Booking: Gary Nunn, 2 Bourne
Villas, College St, Salisbury,
Wilts. 0722-335654. April.

MUSEUMS

*PORTLAND MUSEUM
217 Wakeham, Portland, Dorset.
Local life, inc quarrying.

*GREAT BARN MUSEUM
Avebury, Wilts. 067 23-555. Folk
life and crafts of Wiltshire.

PRINT

*FOLK ON TAP
5 Penshurst Way, Boyatt Wood,
Eastleigh, Hants. 0703-641872.
Richard Dean. 4/yr.

AREA 4

VENUES

*BODMIN FOLK CLUB
At Garland Ox, Bodmin. Booking:
Jeannie Blayney, 1 Barossa Pl,
Torpoint, Cornwall PL11 2BT. 0752-
812895. Friday.

*EXETER FOLK CLUB
At The Mill on the Exe, Bonhay Rd,
Exeter. Booking: Gordon Kane, 1
Waverley Ave, Exeter, Devon EX4
4NL. 0392-31791. Tues.

*FOLK IN THE BATH
At Bath Arms, Cheddar. Booking:
Jane Hill, Littlecot, East
Horrington, Wells, Somerset. Sun.

*SMITH'S FOLK CLUB
At Smith's Assembly Rooms, Westgate
Bldgs, Bath, Avon. 0225-313551.
Simon Lane. Friday.

*YESTERDAYS FOLK SONG CLUB
At Yesterdays, 14 King St, Bristol.
Booking: Tony Slinger, 25
Beaconsfield Rd, Clifton, Bristol
BS8 2TS. 0272-734899. Monday.

FESTIVALS

*CORNWALL FOLK FESTIVAL
145 Hillside Pk, Bodmin, Cornwall
PL 31 2NQ. 0208-4783. Sue
Millington. August.

*SIDMOUTH INTL FOLKLORE FEST
Festival Office, 11 The Knowle,
Sidmouth, Devon EX10 8HL. John
Dowell. August.

MUSEUMS

*GLOUCESTER FOLK MUSEUM
99-103 Westgate St, Gloucester GL1
2PG. 0452-26467. Area social
history, folk lore, crafts and
industry housed in 3 restored
mediaeval buildings.

*HELSTON FOLK MUSEUM
Old Butter Market, Helston,
Cornwall. Folk life in the Lizard
Peninsula.

*WAYSIDE MUSEUM
Old Millhouse, Zennor, Cornwall.
Domestic, farm, and mining
exhibits.

PRINT

*FOLKNEWS KERNOW
Trenillocs, St Columb, Cornwall TR9
6JN. 0637-880394. Christopher
Ridley. 6/yr.

*SWAGBAG
31 Victoria St, Staple Hill,
Bristol. Bristol 570323 or 570427.
Tony & Jean Slinger, Sue & Keith
Davis.

STORES

*OLD FATHER ABRAHAM
  BOOKSELLERS
12 Market St, Hatherleigh, Devon.
0837-810413. Books, records,
instruments.

AREA 5

VENUES

*HANDSOME MOULDIWARP FOLK CLU
At South Hill Park Arts Ctr,
Bracknell, Berks. Booking: Don
Morgan, 10 Ringwood Rd, Blackwater,
Camberley, Surrey. 0252-874461.
Saturday.

*LUTON FOLK CLUB
At Chiltern Room, Red Lion Hotel,
Castle St, Luton. Booking: Ann
Mullings, 4 Bank Close, Luton, Beds
LU4 9NX. 0582-599316. Sunday.

*MAIDENHEAD FOLK CLUB
At Stag & Hounds, Pinkneys Green.
Booking: John Parkinson, 73A St
Mark's Rd, Maidenhead, Berks SL6
3DT. 0628-38359. Thursday.

*HODDESDON FOLK MUSIC CLUB
At The Crown, Hoddesdon Rd, St
Margarets, nr Ware. Booking: Lynne
Morgan, 29 Cappell Ln, Stanstead
Abbotts, nr Ware, Herts. 0920-
870558. Friday.

*EAST OXFORD FOLK CLUB
E Oxford Community Ctr, Princes St,
Oxford. 0865-65849. Colin & Helen.
Sunday.

FESTIVALS

*FAIRPORT CONVENTION REUNION
At Cropredy. Wormwood Records, PO
Box 37, Banbury, Oxon OX15 4BH.
0869-38286. Dave Pegg. August.

*TOWERSEY VILLAGE FESTIVAL
"Glorishears," Thame, Oxon OX9 3LP.
084 421-2231. August.

MUSEUMS

*MUSEUM OF ENGLISH RURAL LIFE
U of Reading, Whiteknights,
Reading, Berks. 0734-875123 x 475.
National collection.

PRINT

*SHIRE FOLK
1 Pound Cottage, Thame Rd,
Blackthorn, Bicester, Oxon OX6 0TE.
0869-241971. Jon Eastmond & Sue
Rose. 3/yr. free.

*UNICORN
6 Dudley St, Luton, Beds LU2 0NT.
0582-33113. Alan Creamer. 4/yr.

AREA 6

*WEST MIDLANDS FOLK FEDN
26 The Oaklands, Kidderminster, W
Midlands. 0562-741023. Kim
Sinclair.

VENUES

*RED LION CLUB
At Red Lion, Vicarage Rd, Kings
Heath, Birmingham. Booking: Jim
McPhee, 46 Woodfield Rd, Kings
Heath, B'ham B13 9UJ. 021-444 7258.
Sat.

*SHREWSBURY FOLK CLUB
At Seven Stars, Coleham, Shrewsbury,
Salop. Booking: Pat Sheard, 3
Severn Bank, Castlefields,
Shrewsbury. 0743-246835. Tuesday.

*FOLK AT THE PACKHORSE
Newcastle & Potteries Folk Song
Club, at Packhorse Inn, Station St,
Longport, Stoke-on-Trent. Booking:
Jason Hill, 54 Price St, Burslem,
Stoke-on-Trent, Staffs ST6 4EN.
0782-813401. Friday.

FESTIVALS

*NATIONAL FOLK MUSIC FESTIVAL
At School of Agriculture, Sutton
Bonington, nr Loughborough, Leics.
Booking: John Heydon, 5 Church St,
Aylesbury, Bucks HP20 2QP. April.

*WARWICK FOLK FESTIVAL
13 Styvechale Ave, Earlsdon,
Coventry CV5 6DW. 0203-78738.
Frances Dixon. August.

MUSEUMS

*BASS MUSEUM OF BREWING HIST
Horninglow St, Burton-upon-Trent,
Staffs. 0283-42031. J Brian Curzon.
Displays of beer drinking, trad pub
games, Shire horses. Folk sing-
arounds, Morris Days, Harvest Ale
Fest in Oct.

*RUTLAND COUNTY MUSEUM
Catmos St, Oakham, Rutland,
Leicestershire LE15 6HW. 0572-3654.
Museum of Rutland rural life.

PRINT

*SINGABOUT
Woodland View, Kirkham Ln,
Fritchley, Derbs. 077-385 3428.
Mick Peat. Monthly.

*MIDLANDS FOLK DIARY
121 Morris Ave, Coventry, W
Midlands CV2 5GS. 0203-444405. Joe
Smith. Monthly.

AREA 7

VENUES

*CAMBRIDGE FOLK CLUB
At Golden Hind, Milton Rd,
Cambridge. Booking: Dill Davies, 8
Rutland Green, Hilton, Huntingdon,
Cambs. 0480-830721. Friday.

*COLCHESTER FOLK CLUB
Arts Ctr, Church St, Colchester,
Essex CO1 1NF. 0206-577301. Monday.

*IPSWICH FOLK MUSIC CLUB
At Rose & Crown, Norwich Rd,
Ipswich. Booking: Alan Walters, 16
Goodwood Close, Ipswich, Suffolk.
0473-49636. Thursday.

FESTIVALS

*CAMBRIDGE FOLK FESTIVAL
Festival Office, Amenities &
Rereation Dept, Kent Hse, Station
Rd, Cambridge CB1 2JX. Ken
Woollard. August.

MUSEUMS

*CAMBRIDGE FOLK MUSEUM
2-3 Castle St, Cambridge. 0223-
355159. Domestic and farming
bygones.

*NORFOLK RURAL LIFE MUSEUM
Beech Hse, Gressenhall, Dereham,
Norfolk. 0362-860563.

*BYGONES AT HOLKHAM
Holkham Pk, Wells-next-theSea,
Norfolk. 0328-710806.

PRINT

*ESSEX FOLK NEWS
7 Ferndale Rd, Rayleigh, Essex SS6
9NN. 0268-779721. Ron Cowell. 4/yr.

AREA 8

*NW FEDN OF FOLK CLUBS
62 Sydney Ave, hesketh Bank, nr
Preston, Lancs. 077-4773 3267. Ian
Wells.

VENUES

*CARLISLE FOLK CLUB
At Micks Club, 6 Fisher St,
Carlisle. Booking: Alison Morrison,
80 Richardson St, Carlise, Cimbria.
0228-368865. 1st, 3rd & 5th Thurs.

*SING OUT FOLK CLUB
At Sydney Arms, Sydney Rd, Sydney.
Booking: Alan Casey, 15 Park Rd,
Haslington, Crewe, Cheshire CW2
8AR. 0270-581198.

*JACQUI & BRIDIE'S
  COACH HOUSE FOLK CLUB
At Penny Lane Wine Bar, Liverpool.
Booking: Bridie O'Donnell, 221
Allerton Rd, Liverpool 18. 051-724
2038. Monday.

FESTIVALS

*FYLDE FOLK FESTIVAL
55 The Strand, Fleetwood, Lancs FY7
8NPO. 03917-2317. Alan Bell.
August.

MUSEUMS

*MILLOM FOLK MUSEUM
St Georges Rd, Millon, Cumbria.
0657-20328. Miner's cottagae,
smithy, and iron ore drift mine.

*WIGAN PIER
Wigan, Lands WN3 4EU. 0942-323666.
Canalside heritage centre.

PRINT

*BUZZ
62 Ridge Cres, Hawk Green, Marple,
Stockport, Cheshire SK6 7JA. 061-
427 4430. Milly Chadband. 4/yr.
Covers Gtr Manchester/Cheshire.

AREA 9

*S YORKS & DISTRICT FOLK ASSN
20 Howarth Rd, Brinsworth,
Rotherham, S Yorks S60 5JS. 0709-
64155. Christine Hewitson.

*TYKES' ASSN OF FOLK CLUBS
24 Sunny Mount, Braithwaite,
Keighley, W Yorks BD22 6PU. 0535-
605310. Jenny Scott.

VENUES

*ROBIN HOOD FOLK CLUB
Beech Tree Lodge, Middle St,
Beeston, Notts. Booking: Dave & Ruth
Cooper, 61 Blake Rd, Stapleford,
Notts NG9 7HP. 0602-399730. Sat.

*THE TOPIC FOLK CLUB
At Star Hotel, Westgate, Bradford,
W Yorks. Booking: Ronnie Wharton,
132 Upper Woodlands Rd, Bradford, W
Yorks. 0274-493572. Friday.

*BACCA PIPES FOLK CLUB
At The Globe, Park Lane, Keighley.
Booking: Jenny Scott, 24 Sunny
Mount, Braithwaite, Keighley, W
Yorks BD22 6PU. 0535-605310. Fri.

*BAYFOLK
At Bay Hotel, The Dock, Robin
Hood's Bay. Booking: Brian Krengel,
Boggle Hole Youth Hostel, Mill
Beck, Fylingthorpe, Whitby, N Yorks
YO22 4UQ. 0947-880352. Friday.

*SCARBOROUGH FOLK CLUB
At Hole in the Wall, Vernon Rd,
Scarborough. Booking: Mac
MacKenzie, 20 Chatsworth Gdns,
Scarborough, N Yorks YO12 7NQ.
0723-372287. Monday.

*WHITBY FOLK SONG CLUB
At The Plough, Baxtergate, Whitby.
Booking: John & Angie Barker, 6
Falcon Terr, Whitby, N Yorks YO21
1EH. 0947-605304. Weds.

FESTIVALS

*BEVERLY FOLK FESTIVAL
Variuos venues in Beverley. 2 Star
Row, N Dalton, Driffield, N
Humberside YUO25 9UR. 037781-662.
Chris Wade. Varied music and dance.
Late June.

*CLEETHORPES FOLK FESTIVAL
At the Winter Gardens. 66 Poplar
Rd, Cleethorpes, S Humberside DN35
8BQ. 0472-698750. Kath Compton.
May.

*STAINSBY FOLK FESTIVAL
67 Stretton Ln, Higham, Derbs DE5
6EJ. 0773-834421. Brenda Whitmore.
August.

*WHITBY FOLK WEEK
26 Marine Ave, North Ferriby, E
Yorks HU14 3DR. Malcolm Storey.
Late Aug.

MUSEUMS

*RYEDALE FOLK MUSEUM
Hutton-le-Hole, N yorks. 075 15-
367.Folk park houses smithy and
Elizabethan glass furnace.

*SWALEDALE FOLK MUSEUUM
Reeth, nr Richmond, N Yorks. 0748-
84373.

*BISHOP'S HOUSE
Meersbrook Pk, Sheffield, W Yorks.
0742-557701. Tudor house, local and
social history.

*W YORKS FOLK MUSEUM
Shibden Hall, Shibden Park,
Halifax, W Yorks. 0422-52246. Folk
life and crafts.

PRINT

*STIRRINGS
92 High Storrs Rd, Sheffield S11
7EL. 0742-663569. Laura Jane
McCafferey. 4/yr.

*TYKES' NEWS
11 THomas Pk, Shipley, Bradford,
Yorks. 4/yr.

AREA 10

VENUES

*BIG JUG MUSIC CLUB
At Castle Chase Arts Ctr, Durham.
Booking: Chris Johnson, 12 Front
St, Sherburn Village, Durham OH6
1HA. 0385-720803. Sunday.

*DURHAM CITY FOLK CLUB
At Bridge Hotel, North Rd, Durham.
Booking: Ian McCuloch, 8 Cedar
Close, Gilesgate Moor, Durham.
0385-65754. Thurs.

*HARTLEPOOL FOLK SONG CLUB
At Nursery Inn, Hart Ln,
Hartlepool. Booking: John & Sue
Barnett, 2 Whitfifeld Dr,
Hartlepool, Cleveland TS25 5BH.
0429-62808. Sunday.

*CUTTY WREN FOLK SONG CLUB
At Zetland Hotel, Marske, nr
Redcar. Booking: John Taylor, Fren
Cottage, Dalehouse, nr Staithes,
Whitby, N Yorks. 0947-840928. Fri.

*FOLKSONG & BALLAD
At Bridge Hotel, Castle Garth,
Newacstle-upon-Tyne. Booking:
Harvey Young, 27 Aln Ave, Grange
Estate, Gosforth, Newcastle-upon-
Tyne NE3 2LS. 0632-843693. Thurs.

*BELFORD HOUSE FOLK CLUB
At Belford Hse Sports Club, Belford
Rd, Sunderland. Booking: Ian
Storey, 9 Romford St, Pallion, Tyne
& Wear SR6 6LX. 0783-652848. Thurs.

*SOUTH TYNE MUSIC CLUB
At Douglas Vaults, Barrington St,
South Shields. Booking: John
Grover, 171 S Frederick St, South
Shields, Tyne & Wear. 0632-540269.
Friday.

FESTIVALS

*CLEVELAND INTER-TIE
PO Box 41, Middlesbrough, Cleveland
TS1 2HE. 0642-246601. Alan
Kitching, Chmn. Cleveland's international Eisteddfod, to promote
understanding & goodwill. Contests
in music and dance.

*DURHAM CITY FOLK FESTIVAL
8 Cedar Close, Gilesgate Moor,
Durham. 0385-65754. Ian McCulloch.
August.

*KENDAL FOLK FESTIVAL
Brewery Arts Ctr, Highgate,
Kendall, Cumbria LA9 4HE. 0539-
25133. Bill Lloyd. August.

*REDCAR FOLK FESTIVAL
Fern Cottage, Dale hse, Staithes,
Saltburn, Cleveland TS13 5DT. 0947-
830928. July.

MUSEUMS

*THE BAGPIPE MUSEUM
The Black Gate, St Nicholas St,
Newcastle-upon-Tyne. Comprehensive
collection of pipes.

PRINT

*FOLK ROUNDABOUT
201 Darlington Ln, Stockton-on-
Tees, Cleveland TS19 0NW-E. 0642-
617009. Harry Lockey. 4/yr.

*NORTHUMBRIANA
Westgate Hse, Dogger Bank, Morpeth,
Northumberland NE61 1RF. 0670-
513308. Roland Bibby. 4/yr.

AREA 11 WALES

VENUES

*WELSH FOLK DANCE SOCIETY
Dolawenydd, Betws, Ammanford, Dyfed
SA18 2HE. 0269-2837. Jean Huw Jones.
*WELSH FOLK SONG SOCIETY
Hafan, Criccieth, Gwynedd, N Wales.
Criccieth 2096. B Lloyd Roberts.
*ABERGAVENNY FOLK CLUB
At Farmer's Arms. Bookings: Tom
Cribb, 1 Oxford St, Abergavenny.
0873-78457. Sunday.

*ABERYSTWTH FOLK CLUB
At Cooper's Arms. Bookings: Alan
Smith, Ceredigian Hall, Marine
Terr, Aberystwth, Dyfed SY23 2BY.

*STARFOLK
Star Ctr, Splott, Cardiff, S Glam.
Alan Jones. Friday.

*GWENT TRAD MUSIC CLUB
At Usk Memorial Hall. Bookings: Les
Chitteburgh, 43 Forest Close, Coed
Eva, Cwmbran, Gwent NP44 4TE. 022-
33131. Odd Sats.

*HA'PENNY FOLK CLUB
At the Greyhound, Oldwalls,
Llanrmidian, Gower. Sunday.

*VALLEY FOLK CLUB
At Ivybush Hotel, Brecon Rd.
Bookings: Gwyn Jones, 32 Rhyd-y-
Coed, Birchgrove, Swansea, W Glam
SA7 9PE. 0792-813131. Friday.

*AFAN VALLEY FOLK CLUB
Forge Tavern, Forge Rd, Port
Talbot, W Glam. Bob WIlliams, 14
Church St, Pontardawe, Swansea
Valley SA8 4JW. 0792-865057.
Mondays.

*SWANSEA FOLK CLUB
At Coach Hse, West St. Bookings:
Dave Robinson, Baglan Lodge E, #3,
Thorney Rd, Baglan, Port Talbot, W
Glam SA12 8LW. 0639-814696. Tues.

*HORSESHOE FOLKCLUB
Arddleen, nr Welshpool, Powys. Alex
White, 093 875-318 2nd Wed.

FESTIVALS

*ISLWYN FOLK FESTIVAL
17 The Grove, Pontllanfraith,
Blackwood, Gwent NP2 2EQ. 0495-
222173, 244168, 200281. Music,
dance, camping, crafts, kids
events. Late May.

*LLANTRISANT FOLK FESTIVAL
1 Ty Clwyta Cottages, Cross Inn,
Llantrisant, Mid Glam 0443-226892.
Mick Tems. April.

*PONTARDAWE FOLK FESTIVAL
10 Rhyd y Gwin, Craig Cefn Oark,
Swansea, W Glam SA6 5TQ. 0792-
844824. Cas Smith. August.

MUSEUMS

*WELSH FOLK MUSEUM
St Fagans Castle, St Fagans, nr
Cardiff, S Glam. 0222-569441. Great
collection of restored houses etc.
Library by appointment.

*GWENT RURAL LIFE MUSEUM
The Malt Banr, New Market St, Usk,
Gwent. 063 349-315. Agriculture,
crafts. Open all year.

PRINT

*TAPLAS
182 Broadway, Roath, Cardiff CF2
1QJ. 0222-499759. Keith Hudson.
News, reviews, listings etc. 4/yr.

RADIO

*RADIO WALES (340m/882kHz)
Broadcasting Hse, Llandaff, Cardiff
CF5 2YQ. 0222-564888. Geoff Cripps.
Folk on Monday.

STORE

*MARCUS MUSIC
Tredegar Hse, Newport, Gwent. 0633-
54353. Instruments, repairs.

AREA 12 SCOTLAND

*AN COMUNN GAIDHEALACH
Abertarff Hse, Church St,
Inverness. 0463-231226. Promotes
Gaelic language and culture.
Festivals.

*SCHOOL OF SCOTTISH STUDIES
Edinburgh U, 27 George Sq,
Edinburgh EH8 9LD. 031-667 1011 x
6676. Hamish Henderson. Archive,
library, research and recording
projects. TOCHER 2/yr.

AGENTS

*BECHHOFER AGENCY
51 Barnton Park View, Edinburgh EH4
6HH. 031-339 4083.

*M.A.S.S.
123 Nicholson St, Edinburgh. 031-
667 8662, 0875-812474.

VENUES

*ABERDEEN FOLK CLUB
At the Three Poceros, John St.
Bookings: Alison Mackinnon,
Viewfield, 2 Ashgrove Cottages,
Rattray, Blairgowrie, Perthshire
PH10 7EX. 0250-5539. Monday.

*EDINBURGH FOLK CLUB
Scottish Ctr, Princess St.
Bookings: Hilda Scott, 15 Mertoun
Pl, Edinburgh EH11 1JU. 031-229
6583. Weds.

*THIRD EYE CTR FOLK CLUB
Third Eye Ctr, 350 Sauchihall St,
Glasgow. 041-332 7521. M A
McDiarmid. Occasional.

*INVERNESS FOLK SONG CLUB
At Beaufort Hotel, Culduthel Rd.
Bookings: Jackie Sinclair, 13 Union
Rd, Inverness IV2 3JY. 0463-238565.
Sunday.

LINLITHGOW FOLK CLUB
At Star & Garter Hotel, High St.
Bookings: Nora Devine, Hillside,
Back Stn Rd, Linlithgow, W Lothian
EH49 6AD. 050 684-4733. Monday.

FESTIVALS

*EDINBURGH FOLK FESTIVAL
Shillinghill, Temple, Midlothian
EH23 4SH. 087 530-298 or 328. Robin
Morton. Late March.

*GIRVAN TRAD FOLK FESTIVAL
16 Annandale Gdns, Crosshouse,
Kilmarnock. 0563-29902. Pete
Heywood. May.

*INVERNESS FOLK FESTIVAL
13 Union Rd, Inverness IV2 3JY.
0463-238565. Jackie Sinclair.
March.

*ORKNEY FOLK FESTIVAL
12 Guardhouse Park, Stromness,
Orkney. 0856-85-773. Johnny Mowat.
May.

MUSEUMS

*MUSEUM OF SCOTTISH TARTANS
Comrie, Perthshire PH6 2DW. 0764-
70779.

*WEST HIGHLAND MUSEUM
Cameron Sq, Fort William,
Invernessshire. 0397-2169. Folk
life, '45 Rising.

*ANGUS FOLK MUSEUM
Kirkwynd Cottages, Glamis, Angus.
030784-72646.

*HIGHLAND FOLK MUSEUM
Kingussie. 054 02-307.

*BORDER COUNTRY LIFE MUSEUM
Thirlestane Castle, Lauder,
Berwickshire. 05782-254. Rural and
natural history.

*SHETLAND MUSEUM
Lower Hillhead, Lerwick, Shetland
ZE1 0EL. 0595-5057. Folk life.

PRINT

*THE BROADSHEET
35 Graham Ave, Hamilton, Lanarks
ML3 8AB. 0698-421762. Jack Foley.
News, reviews, etc. Fortnightly.

*FOLK'S ON
4 Merchiston Bank Ave, Edinburgh
EH10 5ED. 031-447 7544. Lynn
Cooper. News, reviews, etc. 10/yr.

SCOTTISH FOLK DIRECTORY
12 Mansfield Rd, Scone, Perth.
Scone 51500. Sheila Douglas. Lists
performers, festivals, clubs, etc.

RADIO

*BBC RADIO SCOTLAND (370m/810 kHz)
5 Queen St, Edinburgh EH2 1JF. 031-
225 3131. Archie Fisher.

*RADIO CLYDE (261m/1152 kHz)
Clydebank Business Park, Clydebank,
Glasgow G81 2RX. 041-941 1111.
Gordon Hotchkiss.

STORES

DISCOUNT FOLK RECORDS
3 Morven St, Edinburgh 031-3394567.
Ian D Green. Catalogue available.

OTHER RECORD SHOP
46 High St, Edinburgh. 031-556
0478. Large record stock.

AREA 13 N. IRELAND

*ARTS COUNCIL
181A Stranmills Rd, Belfast BT9
5DU.

*N IRELAND TOURIST BOARD
48 High St, Belfast. 0232-231221.
Maria Newell. Info on events.
Produces "What's On" posters which
can include folk information.

*SPORTS COUNCIL
House of Sport, Upper Malone Rd,
Belfast NT9 5LA. 0232-661222.

VENUES

Many pubs have informal ceilidhs
and sessions at odd times.

ARMAGH FOLK CLUB
15 Woodford Dr, Armagh, Co Armagh.
Paul McAvinchey. Last Thurs in mo.

ARMAGH PIPERS CLUB
40 Newry Rd, Armagh, Co Armagh.
Brian Vellely.

DOWN COAST FOLK SOC
At Windsor Bar, Bangor, Co Down.
Booking: Trevor Killen, 90
Greystown Ave, Belfast. Weds.

DOWNPATRICK FOLK CLUB
Pillarwell Ln, Downpatrick, Co
Down. Noel Traynor. Various nights.

PURER DROP FOLK CLUB
At Sarsfield's Gaelic Athletic
Club, Belfast. Booking: Danny
O'Neill, 41 Bingnian Dr, Belfast
BT11 8JA. Sunday.

*SUNFLOWER FOLK CLUB
At Sunflower Bar, Corporation St,
Belfast. Booking: Geoff Harden, 22
Glandore Gdns, Belfast BT15 3FF.
0232-773153. Trad and contemp. Fri,
Oct-May.

FESTIVALS

*BELFAST FOLK FESTIVAL
Various venues inc Ulster Hall and
Forum Hotel. Office: 22 Glandore
Gdns, Belfast BT15 3FF. 0232-
773153. Geoff Harden. Irish & intl
concerts, some workshops, dance,
theatre. Trad and contemporary.
Mid-Sept.

MUSEUMS

*ULSTER-AMERICAN FOLK PARK
Camphill, Omagh, Co Tyrone. Story
of Irish migration to the U.S.

*ULSTER FOLK MUSEUM
Cultra Manor, Holywood, Co Down
BT18 0EU. Exhibits and archives.

PRINT

*IRISH NEWS
113 Donegall St, Belfast BT1. 0232-
42614. Barbara Boyd.

*ULSTER FOLK NEWS
22 Glandore Gdns, Belfast BT15 3FF.
0232-773153. Geoff Harden. News,
reviews, etc. 6/yr.

RADIO

*BBC NORTHERN IRELAND
Broadcasting Hse, Ormeau Ave,
Belfast BT2 8HQ. 0232-44400.

*DOWNTOWN RADIO
PO Box 96, Newtonards BT23 4ES.
0247-747570.

CHANNEL ISLANDS

*JERSEY FOLK CLUB
The Priory, Devil's Hole, St. Mary.
Pat Clarke: 8 le Jardin de la
Fontaine, St Martin, Jersey. 0534-
54602. Thurs.

FESTIVALS

*GUERNSEY FOLK FESTIVAL
Nick Naftel 0481-20662. Aug.

*JERSEY FOLK FESTIVAL
8 le Jardin de la Fontaine, St
Martin, Jersey. 0534-54602. Pat
Clarke. September.

RADIO

*BBC RADIO GUERNSEY
Commerce Hse, Les Banques, St Peter
Port, Guernsey. 0481-28977.

*BBC RADIO JERSEY
Broadasting Hse, Rouge Bouillon, St
Helier, Jersey. 0534-70000.

ISLE OF MAN

*PERREE BANE
Crosby Church Hall, Peel. Gregory
Joughin: Ballachrink Farm,
Poortown. 0624-834 3318. Trad song
& dance. Sunday.

*MANX FOLK DANCE SOCIETY
22 Malvern Rd, Douglas. Ms M
Holgate.

FESTIVALS

*YN CHRUINNAGHT (Interceltic
  Fest of dance, music, song)
Scacarfel, Lezayre Rd, Ramsey.
July.

MUSEUMS

*MANX MUSEUM & NATIONAL TRUST
Douglas. 0624-75522. Founded 1886.
National Reference Library. Museum
of folk life, history, art, etc.,
open all year. Administers other
museums (below), which open late
Apr-late Sept.

*CREGNEASH OPEN-AIR FOLK MUSEUM
Cregneash, nr Port St Mary. 0624-
75522. Traditional Manx cottages,
crafts.

*GROVE RURAL LIFE MUSEUM
Andreas Rd, Ramsey. 0624-75522.
Victorian house, early agricultural
equipment.

*NAUTICAL MUSEUM
Castletown. 0624-75522. Includes
C18 Manx yacht, Quayle room, Cabin
room.

RADIO

*MANX RADIO
Broadcasting Hse, Douglas Head,
Douglas 0624-3277. John Kaneen.

EUROPE

*EUROPEAN ASSN OF MUSIC FESTS
Villa Moynier, rue de Lausanne 122,
CH-1202 Geneva SWITZERLAND. (022)
32-28-03. Dr Tassilo Nikola, Pres.

AUSTRIA

INTL COUNCIL OF FOLK ART
Hauptstr 38, A-2340 Moedling.
Alexander Veigl. List of festivals
& conferences.

*COUNTRY MUSIC INFORMATION
Erlaufstr 13/3, A-2344 Suedstadt
(022 36)87-152. Peter Anderl, DJ.
Information service.

FESTIVALS

*VIENNA FOLK FESTIVAL
Alserstr 37/18, A-1080 Vienna
(0222)43-13-45. Milica Theessink-
Djokic. Excellent, eclectic fest.

PRESS

BLUES LIFE (German)
PO Box 33, A-1035 Vienna. 4/yr.

RADIO

*AUSTRIAN RADIO/TV (ORF)
Wuerzburggasse 30, A-1136 Vienna.
Tel: 65950.

RECORD COS

*BELLAPHON
Grunsteingasse 5, A-1160 Vienna
(0222)43-61-22.

*EXTRAPLATTE
Alserstr 37/18, A-1080 Vienna
(0222)43-13-45.

BELGIUM

*see STICHTING VOLKMUSIEK under
The Netherlands for directory of
Benelux resources.

*COMMISSARIAAT-GENERAAL voor de
   INTL CULTURELE SAMENWERKING
Trierstraat 100-104, B-1040
Brussels.

CLUBS

PILORI MORRIS MEN
Vieux Chemin de Nivelles 31, B-3440
Braine-le-Chateau. Jean Delmee.

MAINS-UNIES FOLK CAMPS
383 rue Vanderkindere, B-1180
Brussels. 344-46-53. Eric Limet.
Family camps, also Swing Partners
Dance Society.

FESTIVALS

*BOERKE NAAS
Sint Jansstraat, B-2700 Sint
Niklaas. Dance, flags.

COUNTRY FOLK & BLUEGRASS
Gemeentelijke Feestzaal, Schoten.
August.

*DRANOUTER FESTIVAL
Zwartemolenstraat 10, B-8951
Dranouter-Heuvelland (057)444-890.
Alfred den Ouden, Programme.
Eclectic intl acts. Concerts, work-
shops, camping, parking, free kids'
garden, photo contest. 1st full
weekend Aug.

FESTIVAL BROSELLA-FOLK
Rue St-Catherine 11, B-1000 Belgium
(02)511-15-05. Mid-July.

*INTL FOLK-DANCE FESTIVAL
Oudstrijderslaan 7, B-2120 Schoten
(031)58-55-12. Early July.

*INTL FOLKLORE FESTIVAL
Postbus 106, B-2800 Mechelen (015)
20-04-74. August.

*RHYTHM 'N BLUES FESTIVAL
Rozenlaan 16, Peer (011)73-70-07.
Misjel Daniels. Late Jul.

SAVOOIEFESTEN
Savooiplein, Ninove (054)33-06-86.
Mid-August.

PRESS

LE CANARD FOLK (French)
4 Sq Robert Allein, B-1090
Brussels. Marc Bauduin.

GANDALF (Flemish)
Halsbeekse Steenweg 170, B-3200
Kessel (02)759-59-25. Raf Venken.
News, reviews, listings.

RADIO

*BRT/RTBF BELGIAN RADIO & TV
August Reyerslaan 52, B-1040
Brussels (02)737-21-11.

RECORD COS

*NEW MUSIC CORP
30 rue St Christophe, B-1000
Brussels (02)512-9375.

INSTRUMENTS

*ANDREAS GLATT
Kerselareveldstraat 14, B-1743 St
Martens-Bodegem. Recorders.

BULGARIA

*CTR FOR AMATEUR ART
8 Bul Rouski, Sofia. Tel: 870720.
Runs various festivals.

*COMMITTEE FOR CULTURE
17-A Stomboliisky Blvd, Sofia 1000.
Tel: 861-11. State music assn; Ctr
for Amateur Arts.

*INSTITUTE OF FOLKLORE
Bulgarian Academy of Sciences,
Sofia. Folklore studies, archives,
libraries.

Folk music is studied in: The State
Conservatory, Sofia; Higher Musical
Pedagogy Inst, Plovdiv; High
Schools of Music in Sofia, Plovdiv,
Varna, Bourgas, Pleven, Rousse;
State Choreography School, Sofia;,
specialized music schools in Kotel
and Shiroja Luka.

Our thanks to the Embassy of the
People's Republic of Bulgaria,
Washington, DC, for their help.

FESTIVALS
*BOURGAS FOLKLORE FESTIVAL
Theatres & Music, Alabin St 56,
Sofia. Biennial - odd years. Held
at Slantchev Bryag. Aug.
*NATL AUTHENTIC FOLKLORE FEST
Koprivshtitza. Every 5 yrs. Aug
'86.

PRESS

*BULGARSKA MUSICA
Ivan Vasov Str 2, Sofia. Dimiter
Zenginov, Ed.

RADIO

*COMMITTEE FOR RADIO
T. Strashimirov Str 2, Sofia. Boyan
Traykov, pres. Sofia Radio has 3
folk progs.

*COMMITTEE FOR TELEVISION
Dragan Zankov Str 4, Sofia. Ivan
Slavkov, Dir gen. 2 folk progs.

RECORD CO

*BALKANTON
6 Haydouchka Polyana St, 1612
Sofia. Tel: 52-54-61.

CYPRUS

*CYPRUS TOURISM
Zena Bldg, PO Box 4535, Nicosia
(021)43374.

*FOLKLORE SOC OF PAPHOS
Paphos (061)32867. Runs Folk Art
Festival, early August.

CZECHOSLOVAKIA

*MUSIC INFORMATION CENTERS OF
THE CZECH MUSIC FUND
(1) Besedni 3, 11800 Prague 1.
Tel: 5305 46. (2) Smetanova 14, 600
00 Bmo. Tel: 516 09.

*PRAGOKONCERT
Maltezske nam 1, 118-13 Prague 1.
Tel: 533-441. Exclusive agency for
international artists.

*SLOVAK MUSIC FUND
Fucikova 29, 811 02 Bratislava.
Tel: 33-67-62.

FESTIVALS
*FOLKLORE FEST OF STRAZNICE
Ustav Lidoveho umeni, 696 62
Straznice. Tel: 942587. June.

*PRAGOKONCERT
Maltezske nam 1, 118-13 Prague 1.
Tel: 533-441. Fests in April, May.

PRESS

*MUSIC NEWS FROM PRAGUE
Music Info Ctr, Besedni 3, 118 00
Prague 1.

RADIO

*CZECH RADIO, PRAGUE
VINOHRADSKA c 12, 120 99 Prague 2,
Tel: 2115.

*CZECH RADIO, SLOVAKIA
Mytna 1, 811 03 Bratislava. Tel:
48-305. Igor Dybak.

RECORD COS

*ARTIA
Ve Smeckach 30, 11127 Prague 1.
Tel: 24-60-41.

*PANTON
Ricni 12, 118-39 Prague 1. Tel: 53-
81-51.

*SLOVART
Gotwaldova nam 6, 817 64
Bratislava. Tel: 488-41.

*SUPRAPHON
Palackeho 1, 112 99 Prague.
Tel: 26-25-62.

DENMARK

*DANISH MUSIC COUNCIL
Nybrogade 2, DK-1203 Copenhagen
(01)13-93-01.

*DANISH MUSIC INFORMATION CTR
Skoubrogade 2, DK-1158 Copenhagen K
(01)11-20-66.

CLUBS

*OLDTIME, BLUEGRASS & COUNTRY
Fuglevadesvej 50-B, DK-2800 Lyngby
(02)888-766. Info ctr. Monthly
jams. Music & dance workshops.

FESTIVALS

*ROSKILDE FESTIVAL
Parkvej 5, DK-4000 Roskilde (03)36-
66-13. June.

*TONDER FOLK-OG JAZZ FEST
Sondergade 2, DK-6270 Tonder.
August.

PRESS

*LYDHULLET
(formerly Broken Strings)
Fuglevadesvej 50-B, DK-2800 Lyngby
(02)888-766. Margot Gunzenhauser,
Ed.

RADIO

*DANISH RADIO & TV
Radiohuset, DK-1999 Fredriksberg CV.

RECORD COS

*INDEPENDENT MUSIC DISTRIBUTORS
OF SCANDINAVIA
Jersie Strandvej 5, Box 49, DK-2680
Solrod Strand (03)14-66-44.

*SONET/DANSK GRAMMOFON
St Kongensgade 40-G, DK-1264
Copenhagen K (01)13-42-11.

INSTRUMENTS

*TURE BERGESTROM
Hastrupvej 2, DK-4720 Praesto.
Reeds, recorders, early
instruments. ·

FINLAND

*FINNISH BLUES SOCIETY
Telekkakatu 2, SF-00150 Helsinki
15. Tel: 639-143. Pertti Nurmi.

*FINNISH MUSIC INFORMATION CTR
Runeberginkatu 15 A1, SF-00100
Helsinki 10 (90)409-134. Pekka
Kalio, Pres.

*FOLK & COUNTRY MUSIC SOC
PO Box 181, SF-00531 Helsinki 53.
Jyrki Heiskonen, Chairman. FOLK &
COUNTRY.

NORDIC INST OF FOLKLORE
Henrikinkatu 3, SF-20500 Turku 50.

FESTIVALS
*FINLAND FESTIVALS
Simonkatu 12-B, SF-00100 Helsinki
10 (90)694-3972. Runs several
festivals of assorted musics.

*KAUSTINEN FOLK MUSIC FEST
Pelimannitalo, SF-69600 Kaustinen.
Tel: 968-611-252. Kauppi Virkkala.
3rd week July.

*KOTKA SHANTY & SEA SONG FEST
PO Box 205, SF-48110 Kotka 10. Tel:
12220. Sakari Puuras, Mgr. August.

*PISPALAN SOTTIISI
Raummantic 1-B, SF 00356 Helsinki.
Early June.

*TURKU MUSIC FESTIVAL
Sibeliusenkatu 2-B, SF-20110 Turku.
August.

PRESS

*BN (BLUES NEWS) (Finnish)
PL 257, SF-00531 Helsinki 53. Tel:
760-755. Pertti Nurmi, Ed. Mag.

KANSANMUSLIKKI (Finnish)
Folkmusic Institute, SF-69600
Kaustinen.

SALENE MUSIC (English/Finnish)
PL66, SF-08101 Lohja 10. 6/yr.
Covers Scandinavian music scene.

RADIO

*FINNISH RADIO (OY YLEISRADIO)
PO Box 10, SF-00241 Helsinki 24.

RECORD COS

*DIGELIUS MUSIC OY
Laivurinrinne 2, SF-00120, Helsinki

*OY MUSIC CO
Tommolankatu 18-K, SF-18130 Heinola
13. P. Hallman.

INSTRUMENTS

*ASSN OF MUSICAL INSTRUMENT MFRS
Kauppiaankatu 7, SF-00160 Helsinki
16 (358-0)170-322. Ragnar Lindberg,
Pres.

FRANCE

AACP MEL'USINE
12 rue de St-Geours, F-40140
Soustons (58)41-58-12.

ATELIERS DE LA FONTAINE
rue Borien, F-12200 Villefranche-
de-Rouergue (65)29-02-22.

CTR NATL D'ACTION MUSICALE
51 rue Vivienne, F-75002 Paris.
Tel: 233-28-24. Info ctr. Lists of
musicians, clubs, resources.

CHANSON 358 ASSN
Ctr Culturel des Mazades, F-31200
Toulouse (61)47-53-51. Coordinates
Midi-Pyrenees region.

*FNAMU: FEDERATION NATL DES
  ACTIVITIES MUSICALES
41 bis, quai de la Loire, F-75019
Paris (01)201-95-98.

*INTERNATIONAL MUSIC COUNCIL
%UNESCO, 1 rue Miollis, F-75015
Paris (01)577-16-10.

L'ESCARGOT
43 rue Leon Frot, F-75011 Paris.
Tel: 370-43-33. Nicholas Cayla.

UVPCA
Reysset, St-Avit Senieur, F-24440
Braumont (53)22-41-75.

FESTIVALS

*BLUES FESTIVAL DE CANNES
CFR/OMACC, La Malmaison, 47 La
Croisette, F-06400 Cannes. Aug.

BREST FESTIVAL
Le Pontois, La Roche Maurice,
F-29220 Landerneau (98)20-46-69.

*FEST DE CONFOLENS
BP 14, F-16500 Confolens (45)84-00-
77. August.

*FESTIVAL DE CORNOUAILLE
1 bis, rue de Pont-l'Abbe, BP 77,
F-29103 Quimper Cedex (98)90-09-33.
A. Vergos. Last Sun July +
preceding week. Arts & traditions
of Brittany. Town-wide events:
films, concerts, parades, contests,
workshops, lectures, tours, more.

FESTIVAL DE FOLKLORE
4 Av de la Republique, F-03800
Gannat (70)90-12-67. July.

FEST DE KERTALG EN BRETAGNE
Maelen-sur-Mer (98)39-67-07.
July.

*FEST DE MUSIQUE ANCIENNE
Mairie d'Etampes, F-91150 Etampes.
Late May-early June.

*FEST DES ARTS TRADITIONELS
Msn de la Culture, 1 rue St Helier,
F-35008 Rennes Cedex (99)79-26-26.
March-June.

*FESTIVAL FOLKLORIQUE
Syndicate d'Initiative, F-17100
Saintes (46)74-23-82.

*FESTIVAL INTERCELTIQUE DE
   CORNEMUSES
Mairie, F-56321 Lorient Cedex
(97)21-20-51. August.

MUSIC OF MARTINIQUE
%Eds Celini, rue Stoelcher, F-97100
Pointe-a-Pitre. July.

RENCONTRES D'ETE
La Chartreuse, F-30400 Villeneuve-
lez-Avignon (90)25-05-46. Jul-Aug.

*TOULOUSE BLUEGRASS FEST
31 rue des Marchands, F-31000
Toulouse. Tel: 6125-1959.

*TRADITIONAL SAIL FESTIVAL
BP 159, F-29171 Douamenez Cedex.
Shanty sessions, concerts. August.

INSTRUMENTS

MORRIS GUITARS
Gamme, 17 rue Laperouse, F-93400
Pantin. Tel: 844-53-83.

PRESS

*ANCHE LIBRE (French)
3 le Parc de Petit Bourg, F-91000
Evry. For free reed enthusiasts.
6/yr.

*BACKUP (French)
31 rue des Marchands, F-31000
Toulouse. Tel: 6125-1959. Bluegrass
magazine.

*NEUMUSIK
2 Ave de la Paix, F-67000
Strasbourg. David Elliott.
ROCK & FOLK (French)
9 rue Chaptal, F-75009 Paris. Tel:
285-10-20. Philippe Paringaux.
Monthly mag. News, reviews,
interviews, listings.
RADIO

*SOC NATL DE RADIODIFFUSION
116 Av du president Kennedy,
F-75016 Paris (01)45-24-24-24.
RECORD COS

*EDWARDS RECORDS
58 rue du Docteur Calmette, F-59320
Sequedin (20)07-57-01.

KELTIA-MUSIQUE RECORDS
1 Place au Beurre, F-29000 Quimper.

*META RECORDS
85 rue Foch, F-54130 St Max.

*SCOP DU CHASSE-MARIE
Abri du Marin, F-29100 Douarnenez.

*SHANDAR
rue Magazine 40, Paris. Chantal
d'Arcy.

*SIRENES MUSIQUE
4 rue Bonnier d'Alco, F-34000
Montpelier.

*VOGUE PIP
82 rue Maurice Grandcoing, F-94340
Velletaneuse. Tel: 821-25-00.

*WAVE DISTRIBUTION
13 rue Bergeret, F-33000 Bordeaux.

GERMANY (E)

*INTERNATIONAL MUSIC COUNCIL
Leipzigerstr 26, DDR-1008. Tel:
229-2772.

FESTIVAL

*BERLINER FESTTAGE
Scharrenstr 17, DDR-1002 Berlin.
Tel: 212-73-01. October. Various
arts; seminars, children's shows.

RADIO

*RUNDFUNK DER DDR
Nalepastr 18-50, DDR-1199 Berlin-
Adlershof. Tel: 6310.

RECORD CO

*DEUTSCHE SCHALLPLATTEN
Reichstagufe 4-5, DDR-1008 Berlin
(0311)220-9201.

GERMANY (W)

*DEUTSCHER MUSIKRAT
Am Michaeshof 4-a, D-5300 Bonn.2
(0228)36-40-85. Dr. Richard Jacoby.
*MUSA E.V.
Boeweg 3, D-3400 Goettingen
(0551)300-355. Info ctr, club Tues,
workshops, annual free fest, etc.
MUSIKBLATT 6/yr. Wieland Ulrichs.

CHRIS FLANGER GUITAR STUDIO
Bahnhofstr 15, D-7130 Muehlacker
(07041)43388. Workshops, tuition.

*COUNTRY MUSIC ASSN
Friedenstr 44, D-7530 Pforzheim
(07231)2-44-60. Juergen Kramar.
BRITISH FORCES FOLK FEDERATION
Burg Morenhaven, D-5357 Swisttal
(02226)3951. Mary J Wilkinson.

FESTIVALS
BONN FESTIVAL
Hartsteinstr 2, D-5300 Bonn (228)
21-02-54. Bernhard Honnecken.
*BREMEN FOLK FESTIVAL
Jurgen Schmitz. 0421-411069.

FREIBURGER FESTIVAL
Eisenbahnstr 64, D-7800 Freiburg im
Breisgau (0761)22422. Dieter Ott.

*INTERFOLK TAGE
Haus der Jugend, Innenstadt,
Osnabrueck (0541)3234178. Celtic
music. March.
MUSIKTAGEA
Staedtisches Verkehrsamt, D-3524
Amoenenberg. Folklore, folk dress,
village bands. Late June.
WESTDEUTSCHER RUNDFUNK FOLK
Appellhofplatz 1, D-5000 Cologne
(0221)22-04-68. Dr Werner Fuhn.
Held in Domplatz. Free. Late July.

PRESS

*BLUEGRASS BUHNE
Eberhardstr 14/1, D-7900 Ulm (0731)
28642. Eberhard Finke.

BLUES FORUM (German)
Glogauerstr 22, D-1000 Berlin 36.
Articles, reviews, etc.

BAYERISCHE VOLKSMUSIK (German)
Kolpingstr 2, D-8938 Buchloe/
Allgaeu. Josef Rietzler, Ed. 12/yr.

*FOLKBRIEF, FOLK RECORD REGIST
Folkshop Edition, Burgstr 9, D-4405
Nottuln 1 (02502)6151. Essays,
events, record lists.

GERMAN BLUES CIRCLE (German)
GBC-Info, Postfach 180212, D-6000
Frankfurt 10. Monthly newsletter.

*MICHEL VOLKZEITUNG
Rheinaustr 221, D-5400 Bonn 3
(0228)47-43-87. Mike Kamp, Pub.
Quarterly.

MUSIKBLATT (German)
Boieweg r, D-3400 Gottingen
(0551)300355. Wieland Ulrich.
Monthly. Folk etc.

RADIO

*SUDWESTFUNK
Moitkestr 5, D-7570 Baden Baden.
Otto Thornik, Mus Dir.

*RADIO BREMEN
Heinrich Herzstr 13, D-2800 Bremen
33 (0421)42-71. Hans Otte.

*JURGEN SCHMITZ
Prangenstr 34, D-2800 Bremen 1.
Broadcasts on Radio Bremen and
Radio Cologne.

*BRITISH FORCES BROADCASTING
Parkstr 61, D-5000 Cologne 51.

*WESTDEUTSCHER RUNDFUNK
Appellhofplatz 1, D-5000 Cologne.
Karl O Koch.

*HESSISCHER RUNDFUNK
Bertramstr 8, D-6000 Frankfurt.
Hans Wilhelm Kulenkampf.

*NORDDEUTSCHER RUNDFUNK
Rothenbaum-Chaussee 132-134, D-2000
Hamburg. Herbert Sielmann.

*SUEDFUNK
Kriegstr 168, D-7500 Karlsruhe. Udo
Seiwert-Fauti hosts folk program.

*BAYERISCHER RUNDFUNK
Rundfunkplatz 1, D-8000 Munich.
Siegfried Goslich.

*SUDDEUTSCHER RUNDFUNK
Neckarstr 145, D-7000 Stuttgart.
Willy Gaessler.

RECORD COS

*AUTOGRAM & FOLK RECORDS
Burgstr 9, D-4405 Nottuln (Kreis
Munster) (02502)61-51.

*FOLK-FREAK RECORDS
Bergstr 28, D-3401 Ebergoetzen.
(0557)846.

*FOLKVARIETY RECORDS
Postfach 110142, D-2800 Bremen
(0421)7-49-10. Juergen Fuess.

*THOROFON
Am Sande 7, D-3002 Wedemark 1
(051130)41-76. Helga & Helmut
Koenig.

INSTRUMENTS/STORES

*DAS BURO
Furstenwall 64, D-4000 Dusseldorf.

*FOLKSHOP
Burgstr 9, D-4405 Nottuln 1. Vast
range of records. Newsletter.

*BERNHARD KURZKE MUSIC CTR
Talstr 70, D-2000 Hamburg 4
(040)31600. Pro & vintage guitars.

*MOECK VERLAG
Postfach 2143, D-3100 Celle. Early
music instruments.

*HERBERT PAETZOLD
  BLOCKFLOETENBAU
D-8939 Schnerzhofen 17. Recorders.

*RIP OFF RECORDS
Feldstr 48, D-2000 Hamburg 6.

GREECE

*INTERNATIONAL MUSIC COUNCIL
38 Mitropoleos St, Athens. Tel:
3223-302.

*INTL ORG OF FOLK ART
24 Ypczeldon St, GR-10558 Athens.
Tel: 3231-671.

*NATIONAL TOURIST ORGANIZATION
2 Amerikis St, Athens 133. Tel:
3223-111.
TRADITIONAL DANCE CTR
12 Massalias St, Athens 1444. Tel:
360-9037.
FESTIVALS

*CORFU DANCE FEST
Natl Tourist Org, Kerkyra
(0661)30520. Corfu Ballet performs
traditional dances. May-Sept.
*DORA STRATOU DANCE
Dora Stratou Theater, Philopappou
Hill, Athens. Tel: 3224-861. May-
September.

*FESTIVAL OF DEMETRIA
8 Aristotelous Sq, Thessaloniki
(031)225-770. October.

*OLYMPUS FESTIVAL
Estia Pieridon Mouson, Place de la
Liberte, Katerini, Macedonia (0351)
20681. Greek & intl performers.
Jul-Aug.

*RHODES FOLK DANCE THEATER
Old City Theater, Rhodes (0241)20-
157. Nelly Dimoglou, Dir. Jun-Oct.

RADIO & TV

*GREEK RADIO/TV 1
432 Messoghion St, Athens. Tel:
659-5970.

*GREEK RADIO/TV 2
136 Messoghian St, Athens. Tel:
770-1911.

STORES

*NAKAS & CO
Panepistimiou 44, Athens.
Instruments, accessories.

HUNGARY

*INTERCONCERT
Vorosmarty ter 1, H-1368 Budapest V
(361)176-222.

*INSTITUTE FOR MUSICOLOGY
Hungarian Academy of Sciences, PO
Box 28, H-1250 Budapest 1. Tel:
161-522. Prof Zoltan Falvy, Dir.
Museum of History of Music.

FESTIVALS

*DANUBE FEST OF FOLKLORE
Bacsmegyei Muvelodesi Kozpont,
Kecskemet. Dance, music, exhibits,
folklore conference. Every 3 yrs,
July.

*SZEGED INTL FOLK DANCE FEST
Csongradmegyei Szakszervezetek
Megyei Tanacsa, Szeged, Eszperanto
utca 5-7. July, odd-numbered years.

*OFFICE OF MUSIC COMPETITIONS
  & FESTIVALS
PO Box 80, H-1366 Budapest V
(361)179-910.
PRESS
*OKL. VILLAMOSMERNOK
Parkany U 22 IX 55, H-1138
Budapest. Rudolf Radnai, Ed. Arts
magazine.

RADIO

*HUNGARIAN RADIO
Brody Sandor Utca 5-7, H-1800
Budapest. Tibor Erkel, Mus Dir.

RECORD COS

*HUNGAROTON
Vorosmarty ter 1, H-1368 Budapest V
(361)176-222. Also record store.

*KULTURA
PO Box 149, H-1389 Budapest 62.
Tel: 388-511.

ICELAND

*ICELAND MUSIC INFORMATION CTR
PO Box 978, Freyjugata 1,
Reykjavik. Tel: 42037.

RADIO

*ICELAND STATE RADIO
Skulagata 4, Reykjavik. Tel: 22260.

RECORD COS

*ICELANDIC RECORDINGS
Laugavegi 33, 101 Reykjavik (91)
29554.

IRELAND

*ARTS COUNCIL
70 Merrion Sq, Dublin 2 (01)764-
685. C. O'Briain, Dir.

*ASSN OF IRISH TRAD MUSICIANS
6 Harcourt St, Dublin 2.
*CELTIC LEAGUE
9 Bothar Chnoc Sion, Drumcondra,
Dublin 9. CARN.

*FOLKLORE OF IRELAND SOC
University College, Dublin 4.
BEALOIDEAS.
*COMHALTAS CEOLTOIRI EIREANN
32 Belgrave Sq, Monkstown, CO
Dublin. Tel: 800-295. About 300
branches throughout the country.
Info service, workshops, festivals,
etc. Newsletter COGAR.

DEPT OF IRISH FOLKLORE
University Coll, Earlsfort Terr,
Dublin 2 (01)752-116.

CLUBS

Many pubs around the country have
weekly (and sometimes nightly)
music sessions and jams.

*FOLK FIANNE
8 Bunting Rd, Walkinstown, Dublin
12 (01)517-259. League of Irish
folk clubs.

*FOLK MUSIC SOCIETY
15 Henrietta St, Dublin 1 (01)744-
447. Nicholas Carolan.

*MERRIMAN TAVERN
Scariff, Co Clare (0619)21011.
Aidan O'Beirne. Concerts in bar &
beer garden, jam sessions.

FESTIVALS

*CORK INTERNATIONAL CHORAL
    & FOLK DANCE FEST
38 McCurtain St, Cork. May.

*DUBLIN ARTS FESTIVAL
Dublin Tourism, 51 Dawson St,
Dublin 2 (01)747-733. March.

*FLEADH NUA
Held in Ennis, Co Clare. Comhaltas
Ceoltoiri Eireann, Belgrave Sq,
Monkstown, Co Dublin (01)807844.
May-June.

*LETTERKENNY INTL FOLK FEST
Letterkenny, Co Donegal.
Letterkenny 429. Late Aug.

LISDOONVARNA FOLK FESTIVAL
111 Greenlea Rd, Dublin 6 (01)96-
19-22. Gerry Harford.

WILLY CLANCY WEEK
Community Hall, Miltown Malbay.
(065)84365. Tom Munnelly. Summer
school, workshops, lectures.
Piping, whistles, etc. Early Jul.

MUSEUM

*NATIONAL MUSEUM OF IRELAND
Kildare St, Dublin (01)608533.
Folklife collection.

*MONAGHAN COUNTY MUSEUM
The Hill, Monaghan (047)82928.
Local history, folklife, crafts.

PRESS

*IRISH PRESS
Burgh Quay, Dublin 1 (01)741871.

*IRISH TIMES
11-15 D'Olier St, Dublin 2.
(01)722022.

*IRISH MUSIC SCENE
Bunbeg, Letterkenny, Co Donegal
(075)31176. Donal K O'Boyle.

RADIO

*RAIDIO NA GAELTACHA
Casla, Conamara, Co Galway.
(091)62161. Gaelic folk programs.

*RADIO TELEFIS EIREANN (RTE)
Donnybrook, Dublin 4 (01)693-111.
John Kinsella, Music Head.

*DOWNTOWN RADIO
Kiltonga Radio Ctr, PO Box 293,
Newtownards, Co Down (0247)815555.
Folk programs.

RECORD COS ETC.

*CLADDAGH RECORDS
Dame Ho, Dame St, Dublin 2 (01)788-
034. Garech Browne.

*GAEL-LINN
26-27 Merrion Sq, Dublin 2 (01)767-
283.

*HOMESPUN RECORDS
13-A Conyngham Rd, Dublin 8
(01)714-688. Also Praise, Glen,
A.R.A. Records.

*TARA RECORDS
5 Tara St, Dublin 2 (01)776-921.
John Cook, Man Dir.

INSTRUMENTS ETC.

*MUSICAL INSTRUMENT MAKERS
85 Idrone Pk, Templeogue, Dublin 16
(01)941-868. John Fry. Info
service.

*NA PIOBAIRI UILLEAN
15 Henrietta St, Dublin 1 (01)744-
447. Breandan Breathnach. Uillean
pipers. Info service, classes.

STORES

*FM TRACKS
Ballast Hse, Westmoreland St,
Dublin 2 (01)775-2000. Records,
cassettes, concert tickets.

ITALY

*CLUB AMICIDELL' OCARINA BUDRIO
Sede Sociale Via Golinelli 5, 40054
Burdio (Bologna). International
ocarina club.

FESTIVALS

*ASSISI FESTIVAL
Via Villa Maggiorani 20, Rome. Jul-
Aug.

*FESTIVAL DELLA ZAMPOGNA
Acquafondata. Italian bagpipe fest,
January.

*INTL FOLKLORE FESTIVAL
Azienda Autonoma de Soggiorno e
Turismo, Piazza V. Emanuele, 92100
Agrigento, Sicily. February. Dance
contest.

PRESS

*FOLK GIORNALE
Via D. Chiesa 31, San Daniele del
Friuli (UD). Andrea Del Favero.

*HI FOLKS
Res Sagittario, 133 Milano 2, 20090
Segrate (02)215-40-12. Pierangelo
Valenti. Mag & record label.

IL BLUES
Piazza Grandi 12, I-20135 Milan.
Blues magazine.

L'ULTIMO BUSCADERO (Italian)
Via Pastore 20, I-21010 Verghera de
Samarate (Ve). Tel: 86-81-71. Aldo
Pedron. Monthly, rock/folk.

RADIO

*RADIOTELEVISIONE ITALIA (RAI)
Viale Mazzini 14, I-00195 Rome.

RECORD COS

FLIPPERMUSIC RECORDS
Via A Riboty 22, I-00195 Rome
(06)315-615.

*FONIT-CETRA
Via G. Meda 45, I-20121 Milan
(02)843-2551.

LUXEMBOURG

*see STICHTING VOLKMUSIEK under
Netherlands for directory of
Benelux resources.

*RADIO-TELE LUXEMBOURG
BP 1002, Villa Louvigny.

MONACO

*RADIO MONTE-CARLO
16 Blvd Princess Charlotte, Monte
Carlo. Tel: 50-52-52.

NETHERLANDS

AMSTERDAM ARTS COUNCIL
Kloveniersburgwal 47, NL-1011
Amsterdam JX (020)264315.

*DONEMUS (DOCUMENTATION OF
NETHERLANDS MUSIC)
Paulus Potterstr 14, Amsterdam
(020)76-44-36.

*MUSIEK INFORMATIE BEURS
Box 1525, NL-1000 BM Amsterdam
(020)16-32-42.

VOLKSDANSVERENIGING
De Wieken 45, NL-1622 Hoorn GM.
Peter Den Dunnen. Mostly Brit folk
dancing.

*PARADOX AGENCY
PO Box 155, NL-2300 AD Leiden
(071)219479. Bernard Kleikamp.
Folk, blues, jazz.

RAINBOW MUSIC AGENCY
Postbus 2151, NL-5001 Tilburg CD.
(013)634200.

*SOC FOR DUTCH MUSIC HISTORY
Drift 21, NL-3512 BR Utrecht (030)
31-68-41.

*STICHTING VOLKMUSIEK NEDERLAND
Postbus 331, NL-3500 AH Utrecht.
Tel: 1130-002. Hans Peters, Paul
Noordermeer. National org:
workshops, courses. Publishes:
FOLKADRESSENGIDS - directory for
Benelux; JANVIOOL 6/yr; DIATONISCH
NIEUWSBLAD 4/vr. about melodeons.

FESTIVALS

VLAARDINGEN FESTIVAL
Jupiterlaan 14, NL-3235 Rockanje
TB. Jan van Rij.

ROTTERDAM FOLK FESTIVAL
Kruisstraat 2, NL-3012 Rotterdam
CT (01)1411-29-11. Huub van Dael,
Leny Baartmans.

MUSEUMS

*GEMEENTEMUSEUM
41 Stadhouderslaan, The Hague.
Musical instrument collection.

*NOORDBRABANTS MUSEUM
4 Bethaniestraat, s'Hertogenbosch.
Folklore & crafts collections.

*RIJKSMUSEUM VOOR VOLKENKUNDE
1 Steenstraat, Leiden. First
scientific ethnological museum in
Europe.

PRESS

BLOCK (Dutch)
Postbus 244, NL-7600 Almelo AH.
Rien & Marion Wisse. Blues mag.

*PIBROCH (Dutch)
Dubbelstr 50, NL-4611 GL Bergen-Op-
Zoom. Philippe von Wersch. Bi-
monthly magazine.

*DIATONISCH NIEUWSBLAD (Dutch)
Uigeverij 11 & 30, Postbus 331, NL-
3500 AH Utrecht. Paul Noordermeer.
Melodeons and such. 4/yr

JANVIOOL
Postbus 331.3500, NL-3500 Utrecht
AH (30)885011. Liesbeth Puts.
6/yr.

*STRICTLY COUNTRY
Molenkampwenweg 5, Harpel, NL-9541
TK Vlagtwedde. Rienck Jannsen. Mag
& record label (mainly bluegrass).

RADIO

*NOS (NED OMROEP STICHTING)
Box 10, Hilversum (035)77-91-11.

RECORD COS ETC

*BOSSHECK
Box 53, NL-2110 AB Aerdenhout.

*PAN MUSIEKDOCUMENTATIE
PO Box 84440, NL-2508 AK
Gravenhage. Imp/export, mail order.

*PARALLAX
PO Box 155, NL-2300 AD Leiden
(071)219479. Bernard Kleikamp.
Music publishing.

INSTRUMENTS

*FRED LINDEMAN
344 Uiterwaardenstraat, DK-1079 DC
Amsterdam. Violins.

NORWAY

*RADET FOR FOLKMUSIC OG
   FOLKEDANS
Sekretariat, N-7055 Dragvoll.

CLUB 7
Munkedamsveien 15, Oslo (02)42-30-
60. Ole Rolstad, Attila Horvath.

*NORWEGIAN MUSIC INFO CTR
Tordenskioldsgate 6-B, Oslo 1 (02)
41-72-90. Lisbeth Risnes.

PRELATEN
Storgaten 71, N-9000 Tromso.
(083)82-085. Finn Steffen Johansen.

FESTIVALS

*BERGEN INTL FESTIVAL
PO Box 183, N-5001 Bergen (05)23-
00-10. Daniel Bohr. May-Jun.

*FESTSPILLENE I NORD-NORGE
Storgaten 4, PO Box 901, N-9401
Harstad (082)64 680. June.

PRESS

*AGITASJON
Lastad/Falsenvei 63, N-5032 Minde.
Jarl Hugo.

*NORSK MUSIKERBLAD
Norsk Musikerforbund, Youngsgt 11,
N-0181 Oslo 1. 10/yr.

RADIO

*NORSK RIKSKRINGSKASTING
Bjornsterne Bjornsons plass 1,
N-0340 Oslo 3.

RECORD COS

*UNITON
Slemsdalsveien 77, Oslo 3. Tormod
Opedal.

POLAND

*POLISH MUSIC COUNCIL
Rynek Starego Miatsa 27, 00-272
Warsaw. Tel: 31-06-07.

*POLONIA
ul Krakowskie Przedmiescie 64, 00-
322 Warsaw. Art society, sponsors
events, offers study programs,
grants. Festival every three years.

FESTIVALS

*FESTIVAL OF POLISH SONG
Radio Station, Piatowska 20, 45-081
Opole. Late June.

RADIO

*POLISH COMMITTEE FOR RADIO & TV
Woronicza 17, 02-625 Warsaw. 43-85-
01.

STORES

*PIATKOWSKI
Ul Komarowa 8, 62-051 Poznan-Wiry.
Dioni Piatkowski also does radio.

PORTUGAL

*INTERNATIONAL MUSIC COUNCIL
Instituto de Alte Cultura, Prace do
Principe Real 14, Lisbon.

*MIN DO COMERCIO E TURISMO
Av A.A. Aguiar 86, Apdo 1929, 1004
Lisbon Codex.

Ethnography and folklore are
studied in:

*INST NOVAS PROFISSOES
Av Duque de Loule 47-10, 1000
Lisbon.

*INST SUPEREIO DE LINGUAS
   E ADMINISTRACAO
Escola Superior de Turismo, Rua das
Pracas 47, 1200 Lisbon.

FESTIVALS

*BRITEIROS FOLKLORE FEST
Rancho Folclorico da Casa do Povo,
Briteiros, Guimaraes, Braga. Aug.

FOLKLORE FESTIVAL
Rua Ataide Oliviera 100, Faro. Tel:
25-404, 24-067. August.

*GOUVEIA FESTIVAL OF FOLKLORE
Grupoi Folclorico de Gouveia,
Gouveia, Viseu. Tel: 42215. Aug.

*GUARDA NATIONAL FESTIVAL
Rnacho Folclorico da Guarda,
Guarda. Summer.

*GULPIHARES FESTIVAL
Rua Joao Ovarense, Guipihares,
Vila Nova de Gaia, Porto. Tel:
9622188. July.

*MAIORGA FESTIVAL
Casa do Povo de Maiorga, Figueira
da Foz, Coimbra. Sept.

*MEADELA INTL FESTIVAL
Comissao de Festas da Meadela,
Meadela, Viana do Castelo. Aug.

*MONSANTO FESTIVAL
Rancho Folclorico, Monsanto,
Castelo Branco. Sept.

*PORTOZELO INTL FOLKLORE FEST
Comissao de Festas de Santa Marta
de Portozelo, Viano do Castelo.
Aug. Float procession + festival.

RADIO & TV

*RADIODIFUSAO PORTUEGUESA
Direccao de Programas, Rua do
Quelhas 2, 1200 Lisbon.

*RADIOTELEVISAO PORTUGUESA
Direccao de Programas, Av 5 de
Outobre 197, 1000 Lisbon.

RECORD COS

*POLYGRAM
Rua Professor Reinaldo dos Santos
12, 1500 Lisbon.

*VALENTIM DE CARVALHO
Rua Nova do Almada 95, 1200 Lisbon.

ROMANIA

*CULTURE & EDUCATION COUNCIL
Casa Scinteii, Pieta Scinteii 1,
71341 Bucharest 1. Tel: 17-60-10.

FESTIVALS

*FEST OF WINTER TRADITIONS
County Tourist Office, 4 Cuza Voda
St, Botosani. End Dec.

*"HERCULES" FOLKLORE FEST
County Tourist Office, 64 Traian
St, Drobeta-Turnu Severin. Aug.

MARIE TANASE FOLK MUSIC
    FESTIVAL & CONTEST
Craiova.

RADIO

*RADIO-TELEVISION ROMAIN
Str Nuferilor 62-64, Bucharest.
Tel: 16-20-80. Iosif Conta.

RECORD COS

*ELECTRECORD
Str Emil Budnaras 94, 78702
Bucharest. Tel: 78-60-78.

SPAIN

SOC FOR TRADITIONAL MUSIC
Alcon 32, 40 Izq, Ponferrada, Leon.
Xesus Lopez Temex. Info ctr, books,
records, etc.

*INTERNATIONAL MUSIC COUNCIL
Martin de los Heros 56, Madrid 8.
Tel: 241-5841.

LOCALES
Tablada 25, Madrid. Gathering
place.
*MINISTERIO DE LA CULTURA
Po de la Castellana 109, Madrid.

FESTIVALS
*FEST INTL DE SANTANDER
PO Box 258, Santander. June.

PRESS

*REVISTA DE FOLKLORE
Fuente Dorada 6-7, 474001
Valladolid (983)351200. Joaquin
Diaz. Oral culture, ethnology.

RADIO

*RADIO NACIONAL DE ESPANA
Casa de la Radio, Prado del Rey,
Madrid. (91)218-29-18. Fernando
Delgado, Dir.

*CARLOS VIGON
Perez de Ayala 12-3 Izda, 33007
Oviedo. Hosts LA CONEXION, on 3 FM
stations 6 nights a week.

RECORD COS

*COMPANIA FONOGRAFICA ESPANOLA
Augusto Figueroa 39, Madrid 4 (91)
222-7474.

SWEDEN

*SCANDINAVIAN BLUES ASSN
Tallkrogsvaegen 8, S-122 83 Enskede
(08)59-54-43. Joergen Sandin, Pres.

*FOLKMUSIKKAFEET
Allegarden, Sodra Alleg 4,
Goteborg. (31)13-02-67. Fri.
*SVENSKA UMDOMSRINGEN FUR
  BYGDEKULTUR
Bastugrand 4, S-824 00 Hudiksvall
(0650)93227. Rolf Leander.

*FOLKMUSIKCAFE
The Big Bang, Agatan 28, Linkoping.

*CAFE STRAVINSKY
Surbrunnsg 25, Stockholm.

*CTR FOR FOLK SONG & FOLK
  MUSIC RESEARCH
Hagagatan 23-A, S-113 47 Stockholm.
Tel: 46-834-0935.

*FOLKLORE CENTRUM
Box 15015, Gotgatan 26, S-104 65
Stockholm (08)43 46 27. Israel
Young. Instruments, etc. Concerts,
workshops, classes. Newsletter with
many listings.

*INTERNATIONAL MUSIC COUNCIL
c/o Royal Academy of Music,
Blasieholmstorg 8, S-111 48
Stockholm (08)11-57-20.

*SWEDISH MUSIC INFORMATION CTR
Box 5091, S-102 42 Stockholm 5.

*SWEDISH TOURIST BOARD
Box 7475, S-103 92 Stockholm. Lists
of events & festivals.

*COUNTRY MUSIC ASSN
Box 6015, S-183 06 Taeby-Stockholm
(0762)1-02-00.

*SWEDISH CONCERTINA SOCIETY
Saves vag 13, S-752-63 Uppsala.
Goram Rahm.

FESTIVALS

*FALUN FOLK MUSIC FEST
Tourist Bureau, Falun. (023)836-37.
Workshops etc. July.

*JARNAFESTIVALEN
Vansbro Kommunbibliotek, S-780 50
Vansbro (0281)111-00. Peter
Ejewall. Late June.

*TORSAKER BLUEGRASS AND
  OLDTIME FESTIVAL
Gastrikland. Leif Sunnebrandt
(0290)910-47. May.

*VASTERVIK FESTIVAL
Karl XI Gatan 13, S-222 20 Lund
(046)13-97-68. Hansi Schwarz. Jul.

VAXHOLM FESTIVAL
Kungsgatan 9, Vaxholm (0764)30027.
Git Magnusson.

PRESS

*WORLD MUSIC
Farstorp, S-280 20 Bjarnum.

SCHLAGER MUSIC PAPER (Swedish)
Stockholm. Entertainment guide.

RADIO

*SVERIGES RIKSRADIO
S-105 10 Stockholm. (08)34-89-25.

RECORD COS

*AMIGO MUSIK
Box 6058, Norrbackgatan 47, S-10231
Stockholm (08)34-89-25.

MANIFEST RECORDS
Hermelinsgatan 21, S-951 31 Lulea.

*SKIVAN
Box 3036, S-55003 Jonkoping.

*SONET GRAMMOFON
Box 1205, Atlasvaegen 1, S-181 23
Lidingoe (08)767-0150.

SWITZERLAND

FOLKFESTIVAL GURTEN
Lombachweg 389, CH-3006 Bern
(031)43-40-40. Claudia Contieri,
Chita Fricker.

INTERNATIONAL JAZZ FEST
Tourism Dept, Grand rue 42, CH-1820
Montreux (021)63-12-12. July.

PALEO FOLK FESTIVAL
Case Postale 177, CH-1260 Nyon
(022)61-01-01. Andre Crousaz. July.

RADIO

*DEUTSCHE & RAETOROMANISCHE
   SCHWEIZ
Frensehstr 1-4, CH-8052 Zurich-
Oerlikon (01)305-66-11.

*RADIO SUISSE ROMANDE-ESPACE 2
CP 233, CH-1211 Geneva 8. Tel: 29-
23-33. Pierre-Yves Tribolet, Radio
Music Manager.

*RADIOTELEVISIONE DELLA
   SVIZZERA ITALIANA
Casella Postale, CH-6903 Lugano-
Besso (091)58-16-61.

TURKEY

*TOURISM & INFORMATION
Mesrutiyet Cad No 57-B, Galata-
saray, Istanbul. Tel: 145-68-75.

*ISTANBUL FNDN FOR CULTURE
   & THE ARTS
Yildiz Kultur ve Sanat Merkezi,
Yildiz Sarayi, Besiktas, Istanbul.
Tel: 160-45-33. Fest Jun-Jul.

FESTIVALS

*FEST OF CULTURE & ARTS BODRUM
Turizm ve Tanitma Bakanligi,
Ankara. Aug. Music, dancing in
medieval castle.

*FEST OF MUSIC, FOLKLORE,
   & WATER-SPORTS
Foca. Late July.

*INTL FOLK DANCE FEST
Samsun. July.

RADIO

*TRT (TURKISH RADIO & TV)
Genel Mudurluk Binasi, Ankara.

USSR

CULTURE & ARTS INFO CTR
Pr Kalinia 3, Moscow. 202-83-12.
Irina Bagrova, Gen Mgr.

*INTERNATIONAL MUSIC COUNCIL
% Union of Composers of the USSR,
Ul Nyezhdanovi 8, Moscow K-9.

FESTIVALS

*LENINGRAD MUSIC SPRING
%VAAP, Vladimirsky per 2,
Leningrad. April.

MOSCOW STARS
Mosconcert, Ul Kalantchovskaya 15,
Moscow. Music, dance. Apr-May.

RUSSIAN WINTER
Gosconcert, Neglinnaya 15, Moscow.
Sergei Lapin. Dec-Jan.

RADIO

*TZENTRAINOE TELEVIDENIE &
   VSESOYUZNOYE RADIO
Ul Koroliova 12, Ostankino, Moscow
1-427.

*USSR STATE COMMITTEE FOR TV
   & BROADCASTING
Ul Piatnitskaya 25, Moscow. Sergei
Lapin, Chairman.

RECORD COS

*MELODIYA
24 Tverskoi Blvd, Moscow K-9. Tel:
229-9248.

*MEZHDUNARODNAYA KNIGA
32-34 Smolenskaya-Sennaya Pl,
Moscow 121200. Tel: 244-1022.

YUGOSLAVIA

*INTL FNDN OF FESTIVAL ORGANISERS
PO Box 370, 58000 Split (058)5141-
014. Augusto Alguero, Pres.

*INTERNATIONAL MUSIC COUNCIL
Misarska 12-14, Belgrade (011) 334-
7711.

*KONCERTNA AGENCIJA JUGOSLAVIJE
Terazje 41, 11000 Belgrade. Concert
agency.

FESTIVALS

*FEST OF KAJKAVIAN MUSIC
Nova Ves 33, 41000 Zagreb. Held at
Krapina, mid-Sept.

*ILIDZA
Radio-TV Sarajevo, Muzicka
Produkcija, Marsala Tita 24/11,
71000 Sarajevo. Mid-June.

*MOKRANJCEVI DANI (Mokranjac Days)
Dositejeva 2, 19300 Negotin. Late
Sep-early Oct.

*MUSIC OF ISTRIA & QUARNERO
Koncertni Ulred, Zrtava Fasizma 18,
51000Rijeka. Jun. 2 week traveling
music & folklore fest.

*PESMA LETA (Song of the Summer
Music Caravan
%Redakcija Lista, "Politika
Ekspres," Makedonska 29. Jul. Held
in Belgrade & all large towns.

*SUSRETU DRUGARSHVA
%Republicki Odbor Sindkata Radnika
Industrije I Rudarshva Srbje,
Mose Pijade 14, 11000 Belgrade.
Fall.

RADIO

*JUGOSLOVENSKA RADIODIFUZIJA R
Udruzenje Radio Stanica SFRJ,
Borisa Kidrica 70, 11000 Belgrade
(011)433-693.

RECORD COS

*JUGOTON
Niska bb, 41040 Zagreb (041)251-
155.

ABU DHABI

*DOWNSTAIRS FOLK CLUB
Intercontinental Hotel, Abu Dhabi.
Chris Simpson & Linda Taylor. Sun-Fri.

ARGENTINA

*TRIBUNA MUSICAL (Publication)
Av del Libertador 3576, 1425 Buenos
Aires. Tel: 773-5450.

*RADIO NACIONAL
Ayacucho 1556, 1112 Buenos Aires.
84-2021.

BERMUDA

*BERMUDA SOCIETY OF ARTS
PO Box 1202, Hamilton 5. (809)292-3824. Vivian Elkins, Pres.

*BERMUDA FOLK CLUB
PO Box WK158, Warwick. (809)298-8393. Bob Bradbury, Pres. Concerts
and Singers' Nights. Newsletter.

*BERMUDA FESTIVALS
PO Box 297, Hamilton 5 (809)295-1291. W.W. Lockwood, Jr.

*BERMUDA BROADCASTING CO
PO Box 452. Hamilton 5. Tel: 5-2828. Michael Tindell, Gen Mgr.

BOLIVIA

MIN DE EDUCACION & CULTURA
La Paz.

BRAZIL

TOURISM INFO CENTER
Rua Barata, Ribiero 272, Rio de
Janeiro. (0320)255-0150.

*INSTITUTO NACIONAL DO
  FOLCLORE/FUNARTE
Rua Do Catete 179, 22220 Rio de
Janeiro. Amalia Lucy Geisel, Dir.

*MIN DE EDUC & CULTURA
Rua da Imprensa 16, 20030 Rio de
Janeiro. 220-2139. Villa-Lobos
Museum.

*RADIO MEC
Praca da Republica 141A, Rio de
Janeiro.

CHILE

FESTIVAL DE MUSICA CHILENA
Univ de Chile, Faculdad des Artes,
Cas 2100, Santiago.

*REVISTA MUSICAL CHILENA (Journal)
Cas 2100, Santiago. Tel: 65767.
Samuel Claro Valdes, Dir. 4/yr.

*RADIO UNIVERSIDAD DE SANTIAGO
Ecuador s/n, Santiago. Tel: 97668.

CHINA (PR)

MINISTRY OF CULTURE
Arts Education Dept, Beijing. Huang
Chen.

*PEOPLE'S MUSIC (Journal)
Beijing. Chang Hsuan, Ed.

*ARS MUSICAE (Journal)
Shanghai Conservatory of Music, 20
Fen-Yang Rd, Shanghai 200031.

*CENTRAL RADIO STATION
Beijing. Tel: 868581.

COLUMBIA

*INST COLOMBIANO DE CULTURA
Carrera 3, No 18-24,
Bogota. GACETA DE COLCULTURA.

*MUSEO DE ARTE Y
  TRADICIONES POPULARES
Carrera 8 No 7-21, Bogota.
Traditional handicrafts.

*CUMBIA FESTIVAL
Calle 3, No 3-37, El Banco,
Magdalena. June. Folk dance.

*RADIOFUSORA NACIONAL
Centro Administrativo Nacional,
Bogota.

COSTA RICA

*MIN DE CULTURA JUVENTUD
   Y DEPORTES
Apdo 10227, San Jose. Dra Marta
Eugenia Picado. Festival August.

ECUADOR

*CASA DE LA CULTURA ECUATORIANA
Apdo 67, Quito. Dr Galo Rene
Perez, Natl Dir.

*AGUILAR DISCOS (Record Co)
Apdo 933, Velez 409, #203,
Guyaquil. Tel: 515-727.

EGYPT

*FESTIVAL OF THE NILE
3 Medan El Sheik Yousef, Garden
City, Cairo. Spring.

EL SALVADOR

INST DE TURISMO
Calle Ruben Dario 619, San
Salvador. 22-8000.

GHANA

*ORG OF MUSEUMS, MONUMENTS
 & SITES OF AFRICA
PO Box 3343, Accra, Ghana.
K.A. Myles, Sec gen.

GUADELOUPE

*MUSIC OF MARTINIQUE &
 GUADELOUPE
Eds. Celini, Rue Schoelcher, 97100
Pointe-A-Pitre. Festival Jul-Nov.

GUATAMALA

DIR GENERAL DE CULTURA
3a Ave 7-40, Zona 1, Guatemala
City. Norma Padilla, Dir.

*REVISTA MUSICA (Journal)
16 Calle 11/84, Zona 1, Guatemala
City.

*RADIODIFUSION NACIONAL
5a Ave 13-18, Zona 1, Guatemala
City. 25045.

HONG KONG

HONG KONG FOLK SOCIETY
1C Broadwood Rd, Happy Valley. Iris
Benzie.

*HONG KONG TOURIST ASSN
PO Box 2597. Tel: 5-244191. Chinese
New Year Fest, Feb.

URBAN COUNCIL CULTURAL DEPT
City Hall, 6/F, High Block.
(5)233800. Oswald Lim, Mgr.

*GUITAR JOURNAL
PO Box K-96256, Central PO,
Kowloon. (3)389339.

*RADIO HONG KONG
20 Broadcast Dr, Kowloon.
(3)370211.

*SHUN CHEONG RECORD CO
Bank Ctr, #1208, 636 Nathan Rd,
Kowloon (3)853007.

INDIA

*INDIAN MUSICOLOGICAL SOCIETY
Jumbu Bet, Dandia bazar, Baroda.
Journal.

*MADRAS MUSICAL ASSN
PO Box 1412, 53 Sir Thyagara Rd, T
Nagar, Madras. Tel: 60017.

*NATIONAL CENTER FOR THE
   PERFORMING ARTS
Rabindra Bhavan, Ferozeshah Rd, New
Delhi 1. Journal.

*FESTIVAL ASSN
88 Janpath, Delhi. Tel: 320005.
Various fests at various sites, inc
PONGOL SANKRANTI, Karnataka (music
& drums); SPRING FEST, Kashmir;
REPUBLIC DAY, Delhi, late Jan.

INDONESIA

*DIRECTORATE GENERAL OF TOURISM
Jalan Kramat Raya 81, Jakarta. Tel:
43150.

REGIONAL TOURIST OFFICES:

*DIPARDA BALI
Jalan Kemuning 1, Denpasar, Bali.
Various festivals.

*DIPARDA JAWA TENGAH
Jalan Pahlawan 10, Semarang,
Central Java. Various festivals.

*BAPPARDA JAWA TIMUR
Jalan Yos Sudarso 3, Surabaya, East
Java. Various festivals.

*DIPARDA JAWA BARAT
Jalan Asia Afrika 67, Bandung, West
Java. Various festivals.

*DIPARDA D I YOGYAKARTA
Jalan Kepatihan Danurjan,
Yogyakarta, Java. Various
festivals.

*BAPPARDA MALUKU
Kantor Gubernur KDH Maluku, Ambon,
Moluccas. Various festivals.

*DIPARDA SULAWESI SELATAN
Kantor Gubernur kdh Sulawesi
Selatan, Ujung Pandang, Celebes.
Various festivals.

*DIPARDA SUMATERA UTARA
Jalan Palang Merah 66, Medan, N
Sumatra. Various festivals.

ISRAEL

HAIFA MUSIC MUSEUM
23 Ariosoroff St, Haifa. Music
library & archives.

*INTERNATIONAL MUSIC COUNCIL
PO Box 176, Jerusalem.

ISRAEL FOLKLORE SOCIETY
10 Vitkin St, PO Box 413, Tel Aviv.
YEDA-AM.

*ISRAEL MUSIC INSTITUTE &
 MUSIC INFORMATION CTR
PO Box 11523, 6 Chen Blvd, Tel Aviv
(03)28-95-14. Also records.

*ISRAEL MUSICOLOGICAL SOCIETY
PO Box 503, Jerusalem. Journal.

*JEWISH MUSIC RESEARCH CTR
Hebrew Univ, Box 503, Jerusalem.
(02)30211 x 682. YUVAL.

*MINISTRY OF EDUCATION & CULTURE
15 Schocken St, Tel Aviv
(03)831121. Ben-Zion Orgad,

*NATL COUNCIL FOR CULTURE & ART
3 Tel-Hay St, Tel Aviv (03)281236.
Avner Shalev.

*TEL AVIV UNIVERSITY
Musicological Dept, Tel Aviv
(03)420111. ORBIS MUSICAE.

*ISRAEL BROADCASTING AUTHORITY
PO Box 1082, Jerusalem 91010. Uri
Porat, Director-General.

*HATAKLIT (Record Co)
3 Yoel St, Haifa (04)64-55-21.

IVORY COAST

*SOC IVOIRIENNE DU DISQUE
10 BP 503, Abidjan 10. Tel: 36-10-
25.

JAPAN

*COUNCIL OF MUSIC EDUCATION
 & RESEARCH
c/o Kyoiku Shuppan 2-10, Jimbo-cho,
Kanda, Chiyoda-ku, Tokyo 101
903)261-0191. Tomojitro Ikeuchi, Pres.
*COUNCIL OF UNIV MUSIC DEPTS
%Musashino Univ of Music, 1-13
Hazawa, Nerima-ku, Tokyo 176
(03)992-1121.
JAPAN PERFORMING ARTS FNDN
5-1-20 Yoguma Meguro-ku, Tokyo
152(03)723-2356. Tagatsugu Sasaki.

*JAPANESE FOLKLORE ASSN
1-11-6 Akasaka, Minato-ku, Tokyo
107. Kozaburo Okasima.
*PASUTERU MUSIC LAB
3-18-8 Nakazato, Kitaku Tokyo.
(03)915-6312. Yuji Saito.
*TOKYO FOLKLORE CENTER ROOM
1-5-15 Chitose, Sumida-ku, Tokyo
130 (03)631-8273. Kiyohide
Kunizaki. Concerts. Newsletter.

*NATIONAL ARTS FESTIVAL
Education Ministry, Tokyo 100. Oct.

*PREFECTURAL MUSEUM OF TRAD
 PRODUCTS & CRAFTS
Ishikawa.

*HIDA FOLKLORE VILLAGE and
    HIDA CRAFTS HALL
Near Takayama. Village has 30 old
farmhouses, craft demos.

*KUSAKABE FOLK CRAFTS HALL
Takayama. Traditional carpentry and
furniture.

JUKE (Magazine)
37-5 Nishikamata, 7-chome, Ohta-ku,
Tokyo. Blues.

*MODERN GUITAR (Magazine)
2-12 Ikebukuro, Toshima-ku, Tokyo
171 (03)784-5601. Monthly.
*MOONSHINER (Magazine)
6-5-18 Kawamo, Takarazuka-Hyogo
665. Sab Watanabe.

*NHK JAPAN BROADCASTING CROP
2-2-1 Jinan, Shibuya-ku, Tokyo 15D.
(03)465-1111.
*BLUEGRASS ENTS (Record Co)
Kasai Bldg, 6-15-1 Honkomagome,
Bunkyo-ku, Tokyo 113 (03)946-4663.

*BLUES INTERACTIONS (Record Co)
Sun-East Bldg 402, 3-24-9 Higashi,
Shibuya-ku, Tokyo 150 (03)400-1688.

*B O M SERVICE (Record Distrib)
6-5-18 Kawamo, Takarazaku, Hyogo
605 (0797)87-0561. Distrib for
Rounder, Flying Fish. Records and
books.
*COSDEL (Record Co)
8-1 Yuraku-cho, 1-chome, 、 」 」da-
ku, Tokyo 100.

*DISK HOUSE TAKAHARA (Record Co)
8-5 1-chome, Kamisugi, Sendai/
Miyagi.

*EASTERN WORKS DISTRIBS
2-A Hasegowa 1-37-4, Yoyogi Shib,
Tokyo 151.
*KING RECORD CO
12-13 Otowa 2-chome, Bunkyo-ku,
Tokyo 112.
YAMAHA INSTRUMENTS
10-1 Nakazawa-cho, Hamamatsu,
Shizuoka 430 (053)465-1111.

KENYA

*A I T RECORDS
PO Box 41152, Nairobi. Tel: 24725.

KOREA

*MINISTRY OF CULTURE & INFO
Seoul. National Folklore & Arts
Festival.

*FEDERATION OF ARTISTIC &
    CULTURAL ORGS
110 Insa-dong, Chongo-gu, Seoul.
722-9073.

*KOREAN CULTURE & ARTS FNDN
1-110, Dongsoong-dong, Chongro-
ku, Seoul. 762-5231. Han-Mo Chung,
Pres.

KOREAN GUITAR ASSN
362-4 Daehyun-dong, Seoul. Tel:
363-1407. Eung-Ju Lee, Dir.

*RECORD EUMAK (Magazine)
300-14, 2-ga, Sungsu-Dong, Seoul.
Quarterly.

*KBS KOREAN BROADCASTING SYSTE
1 Yeoido, Seoul. 7803-1.

MEXICO

*BIBLIOTECA BEN FRANKLIN
Londres 16, Mexico City 6, DF
(525)591-0244. Funding info.

*CASA DE LA CULTURA
Puebla, Puebla. Festival.

*CONSEJO NACIONAL DE TURISMO
Mariano Escobedo 726, Maeixo City
DF 5. (905)533-0540.

*OFFICE DE TURISMO
Palacio Municipal, Cuautla,
Morelos. Intl Folk Fest, mid-Aug.

*OFFICE DE TURISMO
Emiliano Zapata No 27 Pte, Tepic,
Nayarit State. Tel: 2-02-74.
*OFFICE DE TURISMO
Palacio de Gobierno, Toluca, State
of Mexico. Tel: 5-21-87.

*OFFICE DE TURISMO
Esq Av Independencia y Garcia
Vigil, Palacio Municipal, Oaxaca.
Tel: 6-38-10.
*OFFICE DE TURISMO
Palacio Municipal, Tuxpan,
Veracruz. Tel: 4-01-77.

MOROCCO

*FESTIVAL OF FOLKLORE
Tourist Office, Place Abdelmoumen
Ben Ali, Marrakesh. Tel: 302-58.
May. Intl music & dance.

NEW ZEALAND

*NATIONAL MUSIC COUNCIL
PO Box 6425, 96 Tory St, Wellington.
856-798. Betty Aikman.

*BALKAN FOLKLORIC ENSEMBLE
68 McLean Ave, Papatoetoe,
Auckland. B. Holden.

*DEVONPORT FOLK MUSIC CLUB
Box 32010, Devonport, Auckland. R.
Bostock.

*TITIRANGI FOLK MUSIC CLUB
61 Bollard Ave, Avondale, Auckland.
J. Watkins.

*NEW EDINBURGH FOLK CLUB
PO Box 6093, Dunedin. Fri at 6
Carroll St, Dunedin.

*GISBORNE FOLK MUSIC CLUB
Box 594, Gisborne. Mrs. J. Gray.

*NELSON FOLK MUSIC CLUB
4 Sutton St, Nelson. Alison Giles.

*NEW PLYMOUTH FOLK MUSIC CLUB
50 Hobson St, New Plymouth. Mrs.
Spence.

*TAURANGA FOLK MUSIC CLUB
Box 52, Tauranga. Chris Ingram.

*PEMBROKE FOLK CLUB
Cardrona, RD1, Wanaka. Martin
Curtis.

*WELLINGTON FOLK CENTRE
10 Holland St, PO Box 27-191,
Wellington. 850-617. Vanessa
Lenton. Concerts, festival.

*WHARE FLAT FOLK FESTIVAL
PO Box 6093, Dunedin. Sue Harkness.
End Dec.

*RADIO NEW ZEALAND
PO Box 2092, Wellington. 721-7777.

*ODE RECORDS
PO Box 1535, Auckland (64)790-007.

PARAGUAY

*RADIO NACIONAL
Edificio MOPC, 6th fl,Oliva
c/Alberdi, Asuncion. 46-409.

PERU

*DIR GEN DE TURISMO
San Isidro, Lima. Dance fest mid-
August.

*CASA DE LA CULTURA DEL PERU
Casilla 5247, Lima. CULTURA &
PUEBLO.

*INST NACIONAL DE CULTURA
Casilla 5247, Ancash 390, Lima.
Tel: 287990.

*FESTIDANZA (Festival)
Concejo Provincial de Arequipa-
Peru, Portal de la Municipalidad
110, Arequipa. Tel: 26160. Aug.

PHILIPINES

*CULTURAL CENTER
Roxas Blvd, Manila. Tel: 832-1125.
Runs Natl Music Competitions, Nov.

*CULTURAL FOUNDATION
San Luis Terr, Rm 502, Kalaw St,
Ermita, Manila. Tel: 571311.

*FOLK ARTS THEATRE
Manila. Tel: 589-621.

*NATIONAL MUSEUM OF THE
PHILIPPINES
Manila 2801.

SINGAPORE

*CULTURAL AFFAIRS DIVISION
Ministry of Community Development,
City Hall, 4th fl, Singapore 0617.
ARTS DIARY 12/yr.

*SINGAPORE BROADCASTING CORP
Caldecott Hill, Singapore 1129.

SOUTH AFRICA

The editors of this Directory are supporting the United Nations Cultural Boycott of South Africa, in protest against its Apartheid policies. We havea not included any South African listings, and we encourage performers to reject engagements there, as appearances by artists from abroad have been used as propaganda by the South African regime. We sympathize with residents of South Africa who are working against Apartheid, and hope that they will understand our support, even though it cuts them off from the music.

SRI LANKA

CULTURAL COUNCIL
135 Dharmapala Mawatha, Colombo 7. Tel: 26125.

MINISTRY OF CULTURAL AFFAIRS
212 Bauddalaka Mawatha, Colombo 7. Tel: 85888.

*TOURIST BOARD
25 Galle Face Ctr Rd, Colombo 2. Tel: 321-78.

*SRI LANKA BROADCASTING CORP
Torrington Place, Colombo 7. 92281. RADIO TIMES.

SURINAM

*DIDI RECORDS
Box 183, 2420 Paramaribo. Tel: 76398.

THAILAND

*FINE ARTS DEPT
Thanon Na Phrathat, Bangkok 10200. Info center.

TUNISIA

*MIN DES AFFAIRES CULTURELLES
Tunis. Tel: 260-088.

*NATIONAL TOURISM OFFICE
51 Ave de la Liberto, Tunis. Tel: 286-844.

URUGUAY

*CENTRO CULTURAL DE MUSICA
Apdo 5, Av 18 de Julio 1006, 6th fl, Montevideo. Jorge Calvetti.

*INDEF-INST INTERAMERICANO DE ETNOMUSICOLOGIA & FOLKLORE
Urb Colinas de Charallavito, Calle Miranda, Qta San Jose, Caracas 1080. 771110. Isabel Aretz, Dir.

*INST NACIONAL DE FOLKLORE
Urb Cumbres de Curumo, Av Salto Caroni, Qta El Descanso, Caracas 1080. 774661. Manuel Ortiz, Dir.

*NATIONAL FEST OF FOLKLORE
Casa Municipal de Cultura, Piriz y Batlle-Durazno, Dept de Durazno. Tel: Durazno 111. January.

*DIRECCION DE RADIODIFUSION
Calle Mercedes 823, Montevideo.

VENZUELA

CONSEJO NACIONAL DE LA CULTURA
Urb Chuao, Ed Los Roques, Av Princ, Caracas. Tel: 911580.

*INSTITUTO NATIONAL DE FOLKLORE
Av Salto Caroni, Apdo Postal 81015, Urb Colinas de Charallavito, Calle Miranda, Caracas. Tel: 77-11-10. REVISTA INIDEF.

*RADIO NACIONAL
Av Final de la Av Las Marias, Detras del Country Club, Urb El Pedregal, Chapellin. 74-66-66.

WEST INDIES

*MIN OF COMMUNITY DEVELOPMENT
1 La Fantasie Rd, St Anns, Trinidad. Best Village Folk Festival. November.

*NATL BROADCASTING SERVICE
17 Abercromby St, Port of Spain, Trinidad.

SURVEY QUESTIONNAIRE:

If you would be interested in further information about the proposed folk music trade organization mentioned in "Still Crazy After All This Year" (Page 3), please return this form. It doesn't commit you to anything: we are simply polling the industry for first reactions.

NOTE BEFORE STARTING: Much of the information requested is also requested on the Listings Form (next page). You may prefer simply to fill out that form and simply mark here if interested in the trade organization:

_____ Yes, I'm interested. Put me on the mailing list for information.

NAME OF ORGANIZATION:

STREET:

CITY:

STATE/ZIP CODE:

COUNTRY:

TELEPHONE:

CONTACT NAME:

CATEGORY (CLUB, SOCIETY, STORE, PUBLICATION, ETC):

What areas that a trade organization might cover are of interest to you?

ANY ADDITIONAL COMMENTS OR SUGGESTIONS?

Please return this form (or send the information on a separate sheet) to:

GRASS ROOTS PRODUCTIONS
444 West 54th Street, New York NY 10019, USA

LISTING FOR THE NEXT EDITION

Note: if your organization appears in the Second Edition, you will have been sent a copy of that listing, with a request for changes. Use this form for new listings, or to make changes after you've sent in that listing.

INFORMATION TO BE PUBLISHED:

NAME OF ORGANIZATION:

STREET:

CITY:

STATE/ZIP CODE:

COUNTRY:

TELEPHONE:

CONTACT NAME:

DAYS OF MEETINGS, ETC:

CATEGORY (CLUB, SOCIETY, STORE, PUBLICATION, ETC):

DATE & SITE (FOR FESTIVALS):

INFORMATION:

(NOT FOR PUBLICATION):

NAME OF CONTACT FOR FURTHER INFORMATION:

ADDRESS/TELEPHONE:

ANY ADDITIONAL COMMENTS OR SUGGESTIONS?

Please return this form (or send the information on a separate sheet) to:

GRASS ROOTS PRODUCTIONS
444 West 54th Street, New York NY 10019, USA